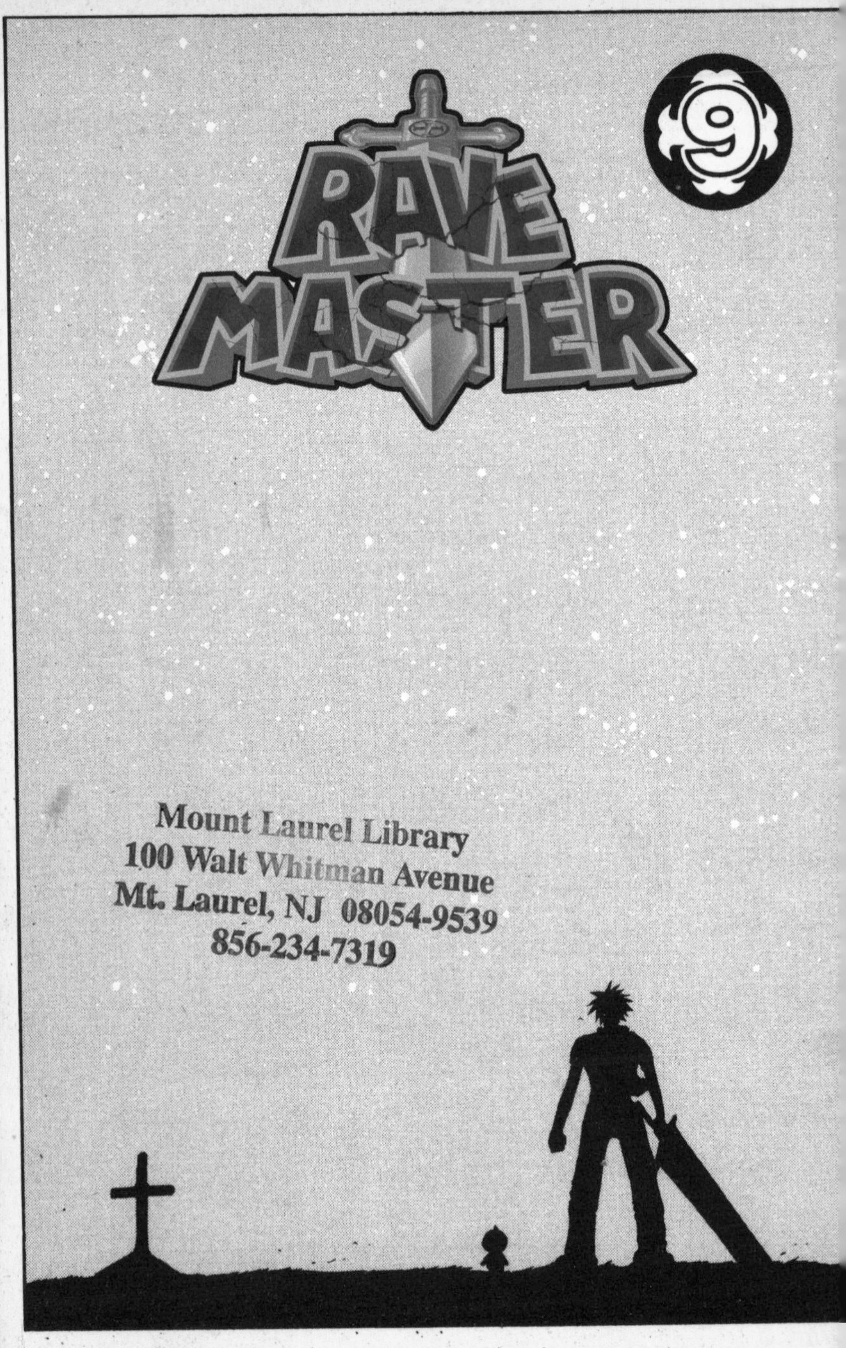
RAVE MASTER
9

Translator - Brian Dunn
Retouch and Lettering - Marnie Echols
Cover Layout - Raymond Makowski
Graphic Designer - James Lee

Editor - Jake Forbes
Digital Imaging Manager - Chris Buford
Pre-Press Manager - Antonio DePietro
Production Managers - Jennifer Miller, Mutsumi Miyazaki
Art Director - Matt Alford
Managing Editor - Jill Freshney
VP of Production - Ron Klamert
President & C.O.O. - John Parker
Publisher & C.E.O. - Stuart Levy

E-mail: info@TOKYOPOP.com
Come visit us online at www.TOKYOPOP.com

A 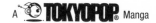 Manga

TOKYOPOP Inc.
5900 Wilshire Blvd. Suite 2000
Los Angeles, CA 90036

Rave Master Vol. 9

ISBN: 1-59182-519-9

First TOKYOPOP printing: June 2004

10 9 8 7 6 5 4 3 2 1

Printed in the USA

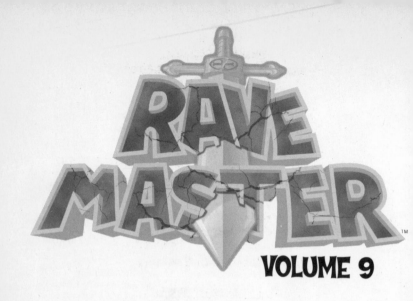

VOLUME 9

Story and Art by
HIRO MASHIMA

TOKYOPOP®

Los Angeles · Tokyo · London · Hamburg

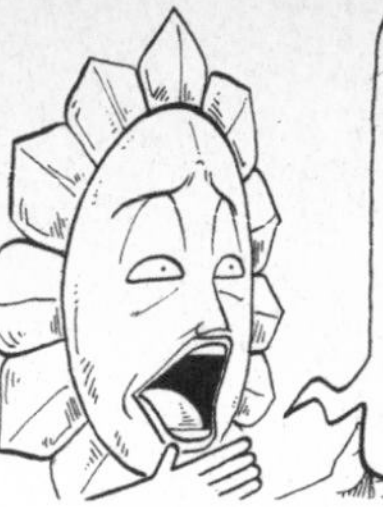

Haru's search for the Rave of Combat led him to the embattled city of Rabarrier. When Haru learned that the one leading the attacking Demonoid forces was named Gale—the same name as his dad—he had to go investigate. Gale Glory was indeed at the Demoid base, the Tower of Din, but he wasn't leading them—he was fighting against them. The Gale in charge was none other than Demon Card leader Gale Raregroove, a.k.a. King. The reunited father and son enter the tower in order to stop King's "Enclaim," a process for creating new Dark Bring. With the help of Musica and the others, they defeated King's elite Palace Guardians, but when they reached the top of the tower, they found King waiting for them with a Dark Bring more powerful than they had ever imagined possible.

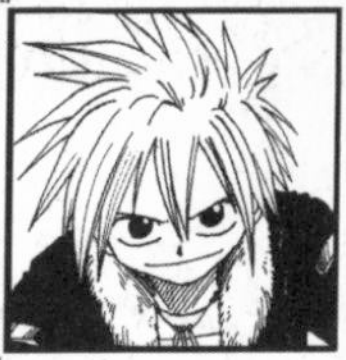

HARU GLORY: The Rave Master. Haru is the heir to Rave, the only one capable of wielding it and destroying Dark Bring. Impulsive and headstrong, he's not afraid to put himself in danger to do what is right. His father disappeared in search of Rave when he was very young.

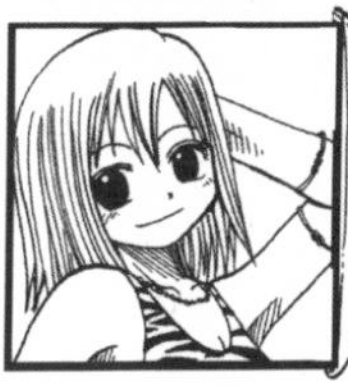

ELIE: A girl with no past. Elie travels the world in search of the key to her forgotten memories. Outwardly cheerful, she hides a great sadness from her past. She's hot-headed, so when she pulls out her explosive Tonfa Blasters, bad guys watch out!

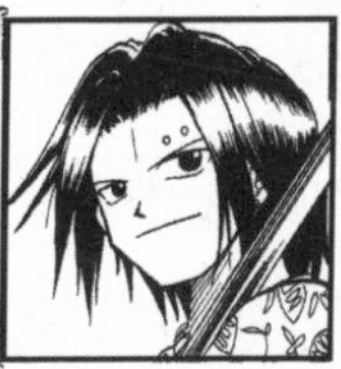

MUSICA: Leader of the Silver Rhythm Gang. An orphan whose family was slaughtered when he was a baby, Musica became a street-fighting petty thief, but he has a good heart.

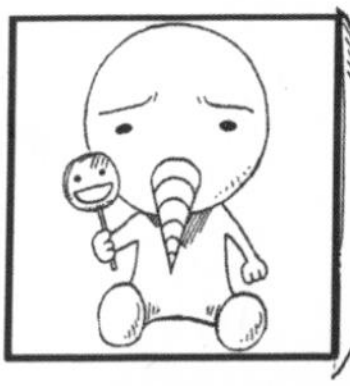

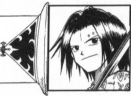

PLUE: The Rave Bearer. Plue is supposed to be Haru's guide in finding the Rave Stones, but so far he's just gotten him in and out of trouble. No one knows exactly what Plue is, but he seems to have healing abilities and is smarter than your average...whatever he is.

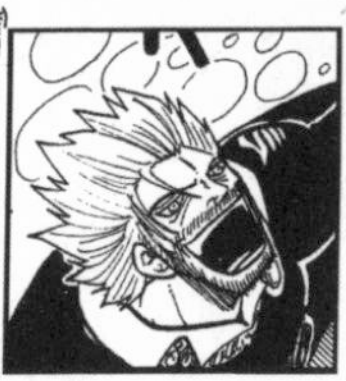

KING: Supreme leader and co-founder of Demon Card. He fights with the Decalogue Sword, a Dark Bring that mimics the abilities of the Ten Powers. His real name is Gale Raregroove, and he used to be friends with Gale Glory.

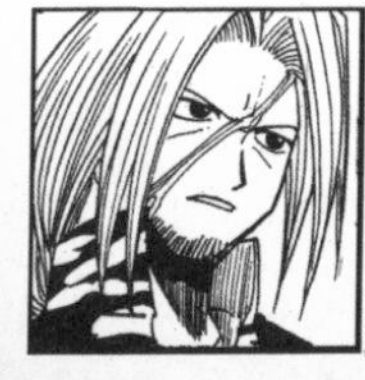

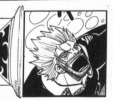

GALE GLORY: Haru's father, he left home in search of the Raves fifteen years ago and hasn't seen his family since. Gale Glory and Gale Raregroove (a.k.a. King) seem to have known each other for a long time, but how?!

RAVE MASTER 9
CONTENTS

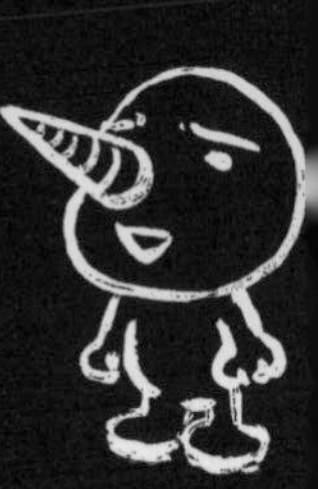

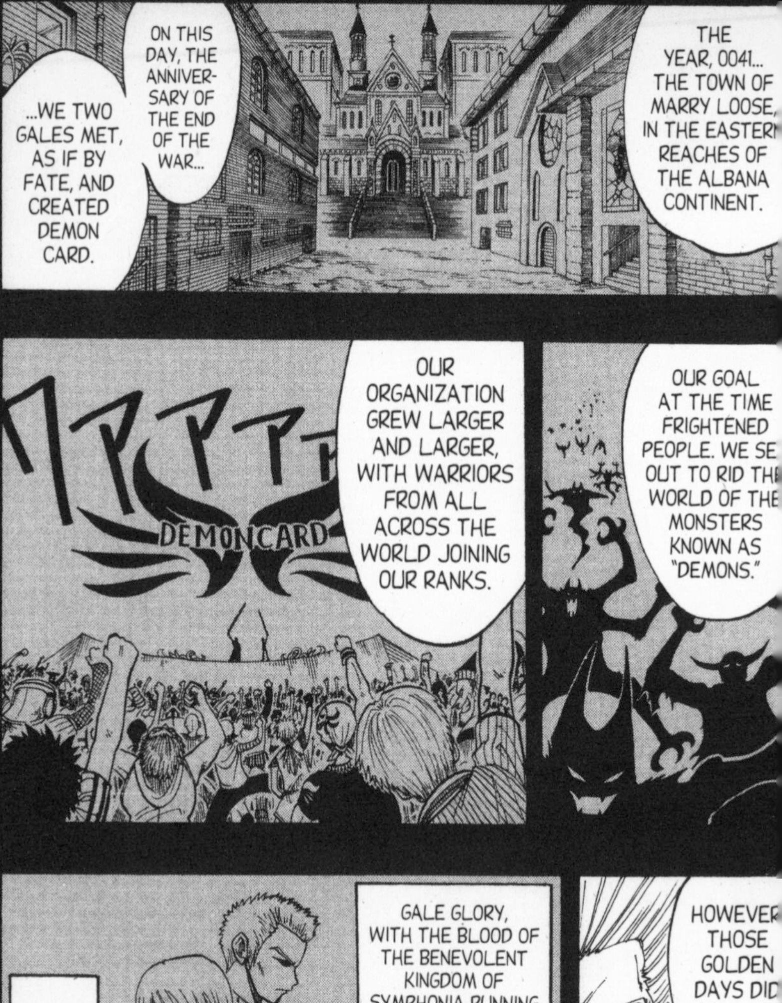
THE YEAR, 0041... THE TOWN OF MARRY LOOSE, IN THE EASTER REACHES OF THE ALBANA CONTINENT.
ON THIS DAY, THE ANNIVER-SARY OF THE END OF THE WAR...
...WE TWO GALES MET, AS IF BY FATE, AND CREATED DEMON CARD.
OUR GOAL AT THE TIME FRIGHTENED PEOPLE. WE SE OUT TO RID TH WORLD OF THE MONSTERS KNOWN AS "DEMONS."
OUR ORGANIZATION GREW LARGER AND LARGER, WITH WARRIORS FROM ALL ACROSS THE WORLD JOINING OUR RANKS.
DEMONCARD
HOWEVE THOSE GOLDEN DAYS DI NOT LAS LONG...
GALE GLORY, WITH THE BLOOD OF THE BENEVOLENT KINGDOM OF SYMPHONIA RUNNING THROUGH HIS VEINS, AND I, KING (GALE RAREGROOVE), WITH THE BLOOD OF DEMONS RUNNING THROUGH MINE...
PERHAPS THIS FEUD WAS PREOR-DAINED BY OUR BLOOD.

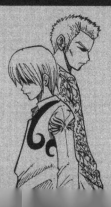

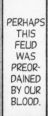

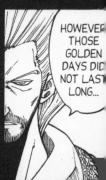

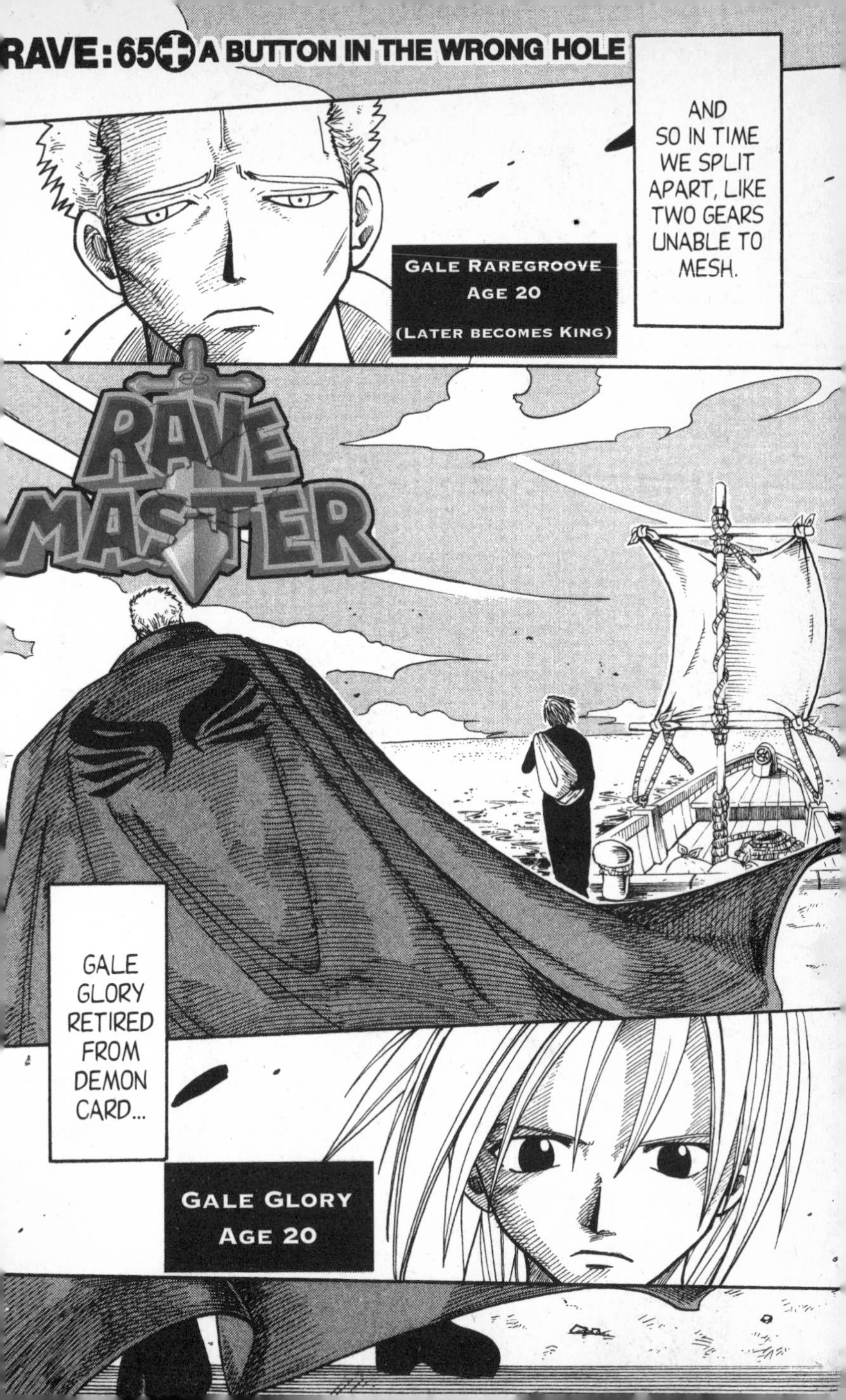
RAVE: 65 A BUTTON IN THE WRONG HOLE
AND SO IN TIME WE SPLIT APART, LIKE TWO GEARS UNABLE TO MESH.
GALE RAREGROOVE AGE 20 (LATER BECOMES KING)
RAVE MASTER
GALE GLORY RETIRED FROM DEMON CARD...
GALE GLORY AGE 20

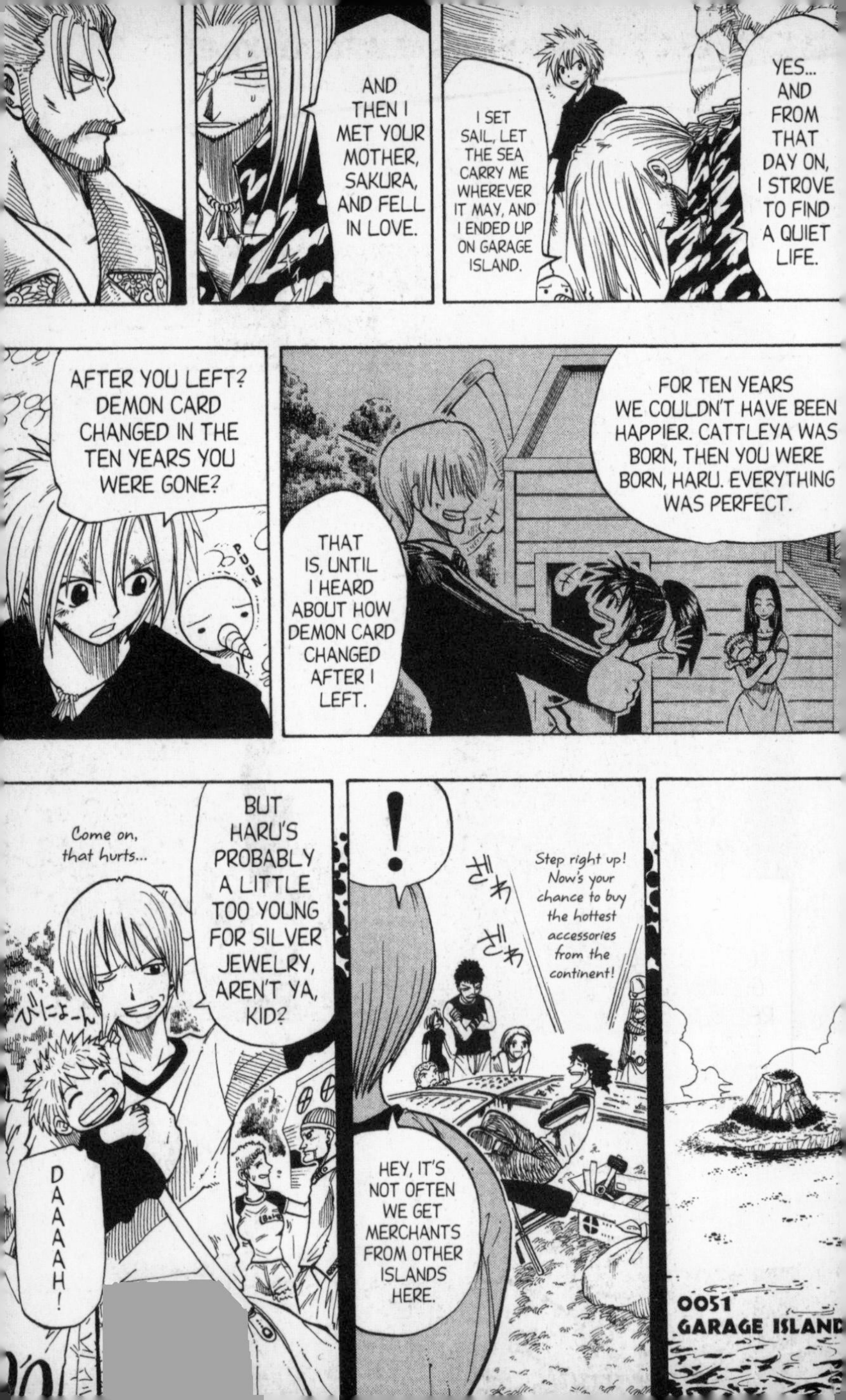
YES... AND FROM THAT DAY ON, I STROVE TO FIND A QUIET LIFE.
I SET SAIL, LET THE SEA CARRY ME WHEREVER IT MAY, AND I ENDED UP ON GARAGE ISLAND.
AND THEN I MET YOUR MOTHER, SAKURA, AND FELL IN LOVE.
FOR TEN YEARS WE COULDN'T HAVE BEEN HAPPIER. CATTLEYA WAS BORN, THEN YOU WERE BORN, HARU. EVERYTHING WAS PERFECT.
THAT IS, UNTIL I HEARD ABOUT HOW DEMON CARD CHANGED AFTER I LEFT.
AFTER YOU LEFT? DEMON CARD CHANGED IN THE TEN YEARS YOU WERE GONE?
PUUN
0051
GARAGE ISLAND
!
Step right up! Now's your chance to buy the hottest accessories from the continent!
ざわ
ざわ
HEY, IT'S NOT OFTEN WE GET MERCHANTS FROM OTHER ISLANDS HERE.
BUT HARU'S PROBABLY A LITTLE TOO YOUNG FOR SILVER JEWELRY, AREN'T YA, KID?
Come on, that hurts...
びにょ-ん
DAAAAAH!

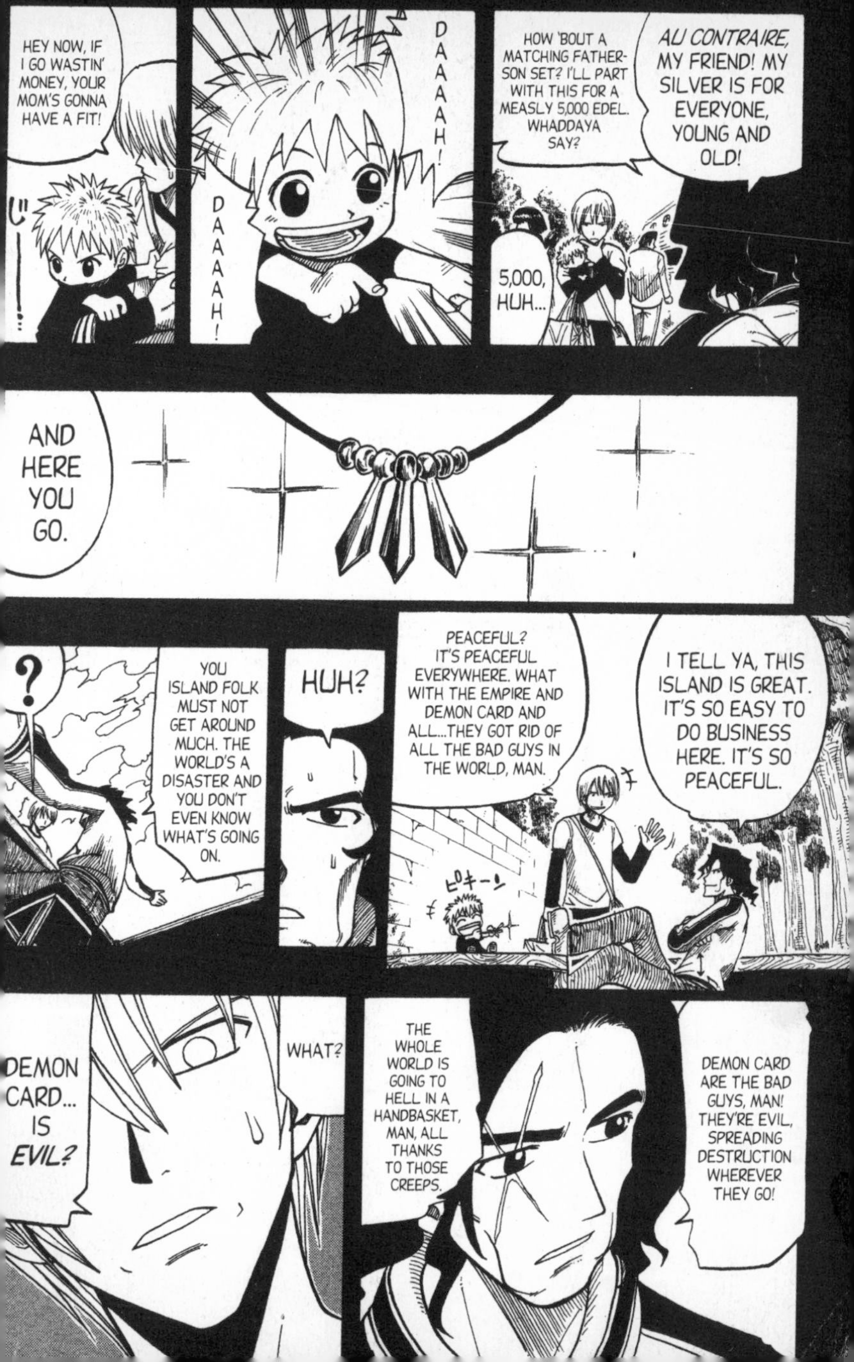
AU CONTRAIRE, MY FRIEND! MY SILVER IS FOR EVERYONE, YOUNG AND OLD!
HOW 'BOUT A MATCHING FATHER-SON SET? I'LL PART WITH THIS FOR A MEASLY 5,000 EDEL. WHADDAYA SAY?
5,000, HUH...
DAAAAAH!
DAAAAAH!
HEY NOW, IF I GO WASTIN' MONEY, YOUR MOM'S GONNA HAVE A FIT!
AND HERE YOU GO.
I TELL YA, THIS ISLAND IS GREAT. IT'S SO EASY TO DO BUSINESS HERE. IT'S SO PEACEFUL.
PEACEFUL? IT'S PEACEFUL EVERYWHERE. WHAT WITH THE EMPIRE AND DEMON CARD AND ALL...THEY GOT RID OF ALL THE BAD GUYS IN THE WORLD, MAN.
HUH?
YOU ISLAND FOLK MUST NOT GET AROUND MUCH. THE WORLD'S A DISASTER AND YOU DON'T EVEN KNOW WHAT'S GOING ON.
?
DEMON CARD ARE THE BAD GUYS, MAN! THEY'RE EVIL, SPREADING DESTRUCTION WHEREVER THEY GO!
THE WHOLE WORLD IS GOING TO HELL IN A HANDBASKET, MAN, ALL THANKS TO THOSE CREEPS.
WHAT?
DEMON CARD... IS *EVIL?*

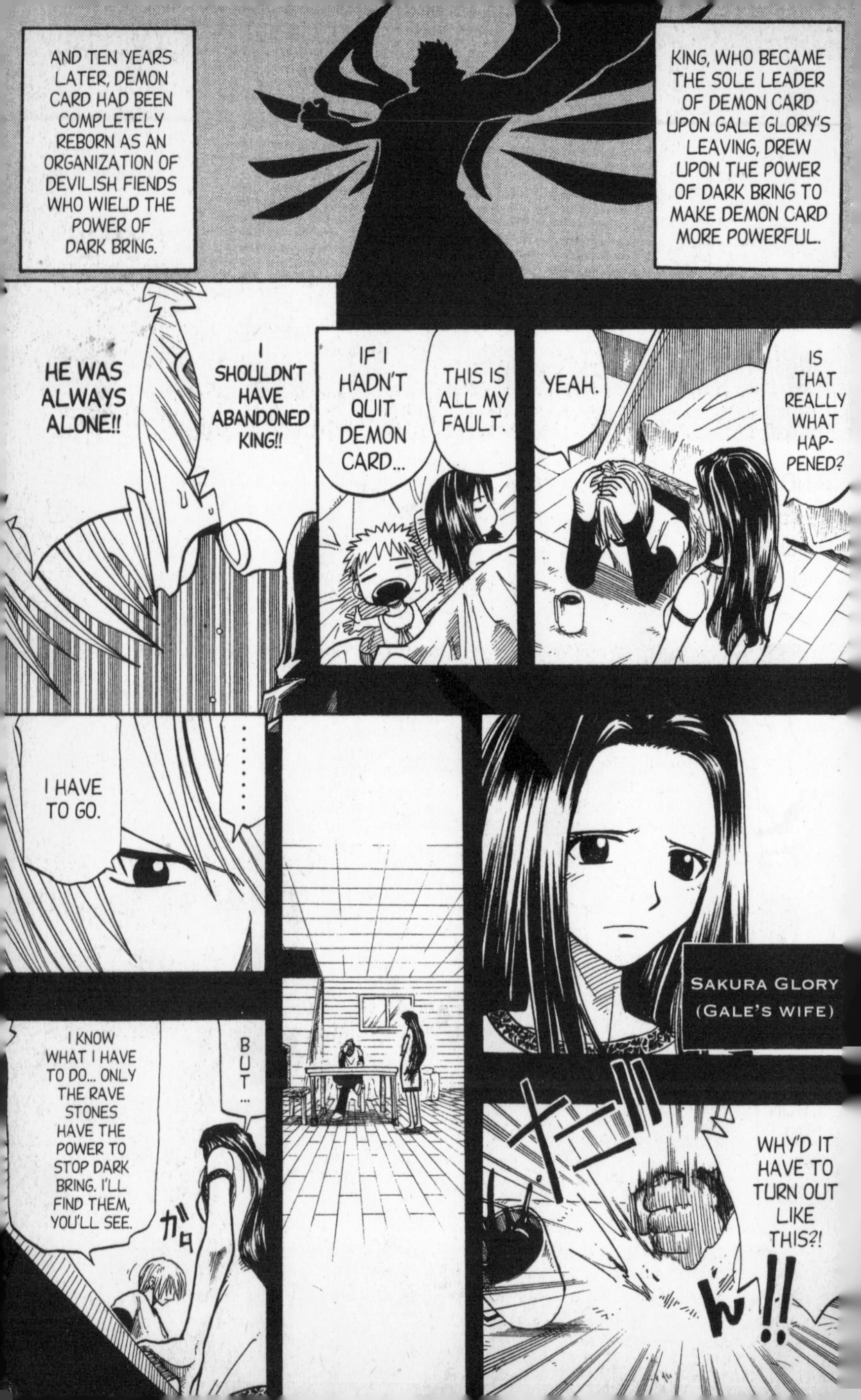
KING, WHO BECAME THE SOLE LEADER OF DEMON CARD UPON GALE GLORY'S LEAVING, DREW UPON THE POWER OF DARK BRING TO MAKE DEMON CARD MORE POWERFUL.
AND TEN YEARS LATER, DEMON CARD HAD BEEN COMPLETELY REBORN AS AN ORGANIZATION OF DEVILISH FIENDS WHO WIELD THE POWER OF DARK BRING.
IS THAT REALLY WHAT HAP-PENED?
YEAH.
THIS IS ALL MY FAULT.
IF I HADN'T QUIT DEMON CARD...
I SHOULDN'T HAVE ABANDONED KING!!
HE WAS ALWAYS ALONE!!
SAKURA GLORY (GALE'S WIFE)
WHY'D IT HAVE TO TURN OUT LIKE THIS?!
......
I HAVE TO GO.
BUT...
I KNOW WHAT I HAVE TO DO... ONLY THE RAVE STONES HAVE THE POWER TO STOP DARK BRING. I'LL FIND THEM, YOU'LL SEE.
ガタ

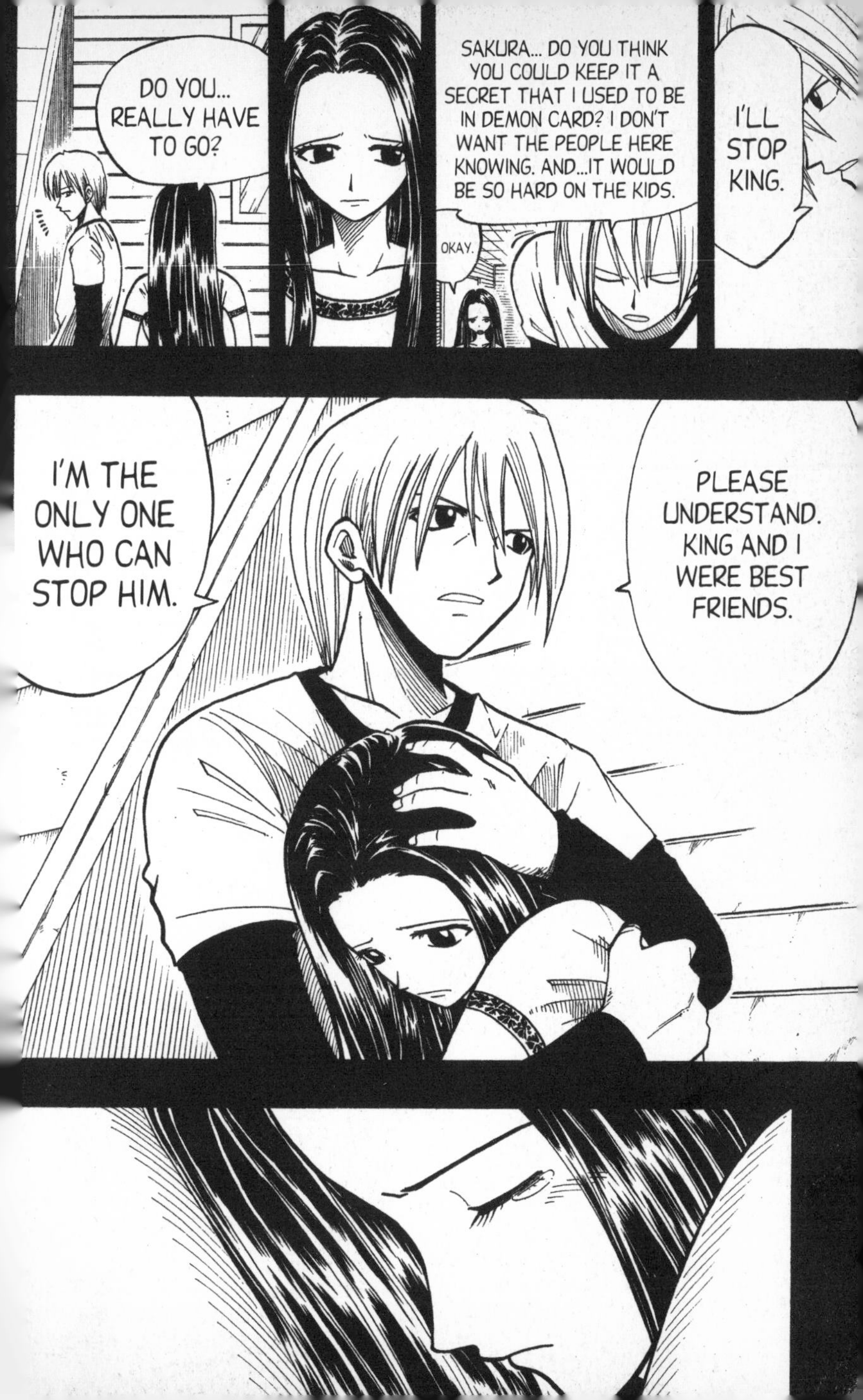
I'LL STOP KING.
SAKURA... DO YOU THINK YOU COULD KEEP IT A SECRET THAT I USED TO BE IN DEMON CARD? I DON'T WANT THE PEOPLE HERE KNOWING. AND...IT WOULD BE SO HARD ON THE KIDS.
OKAY.
DO YOU... REALLY HAVE TO GO?
PLEASE UNDERSTAND. KING AND I WERE BEST FRIENDS.
I'M THE ONLY ONE WHO CAN STOP HIM.

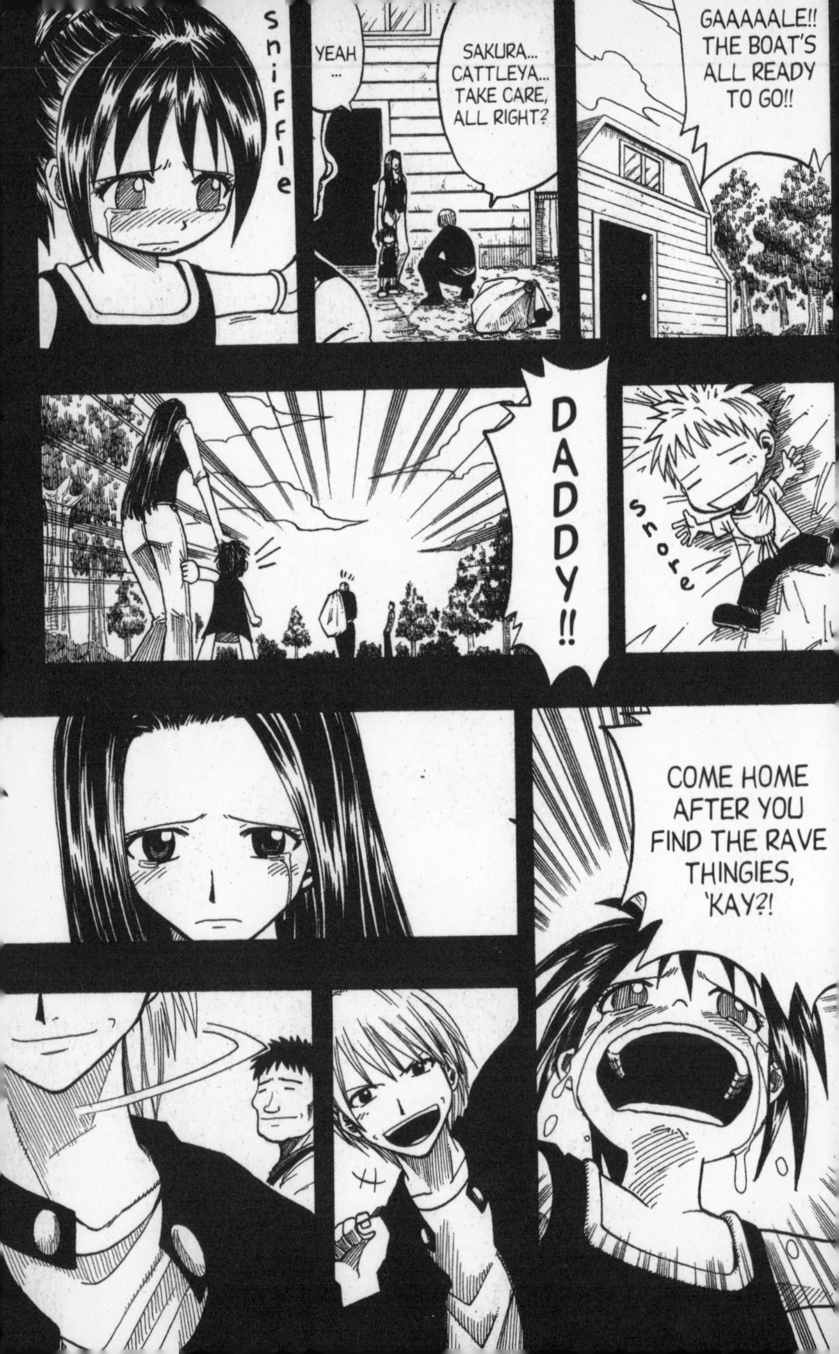
GAAAAALE!! THE BOAT'S ALL READY TO GO!!
SAKURA... CATTLEYA... TAKE CARE, ALL RIGHT?
YEAH ...
sniffle
snore
DADDY!!
COME HOME AFTER YOU FIND THE RAVE THINGIES, 'KAY?!

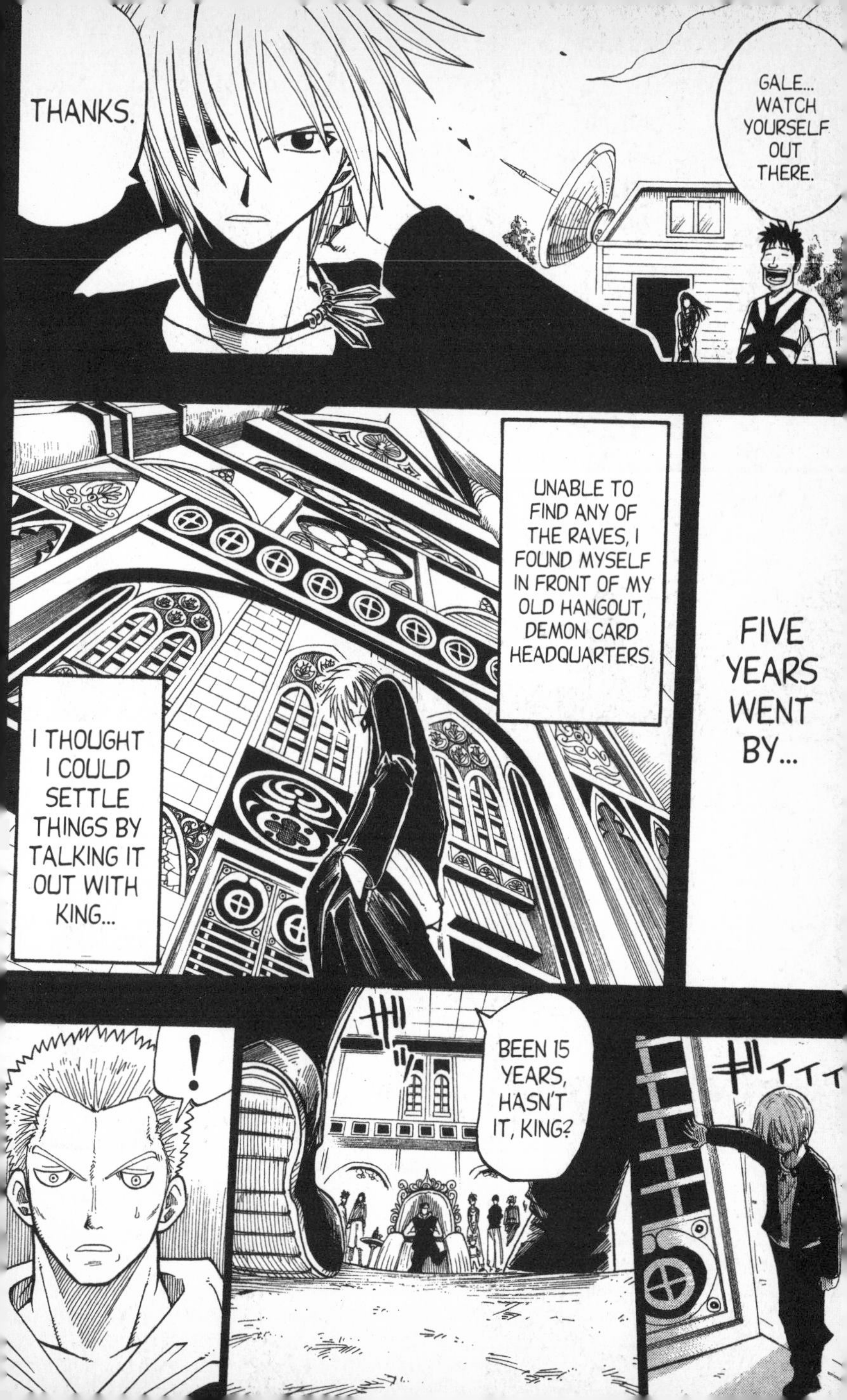
GALE... WATCH YOURSELF OUT THERE.
THANKS.
FIVE YEARS WENT BY...
UNABLE TO FIND ANY OF THE RAVES, I FOUND MYSELF IN FRONT OF MY OLD HANGOUT, DEMON CARD HEADQUARTERS.
I THOUGHT I COULD SETTLE THINGS BY TALKING IT OUT WITH KING...
BEEN 15 YEARS, HASN'T IT, KING?
!

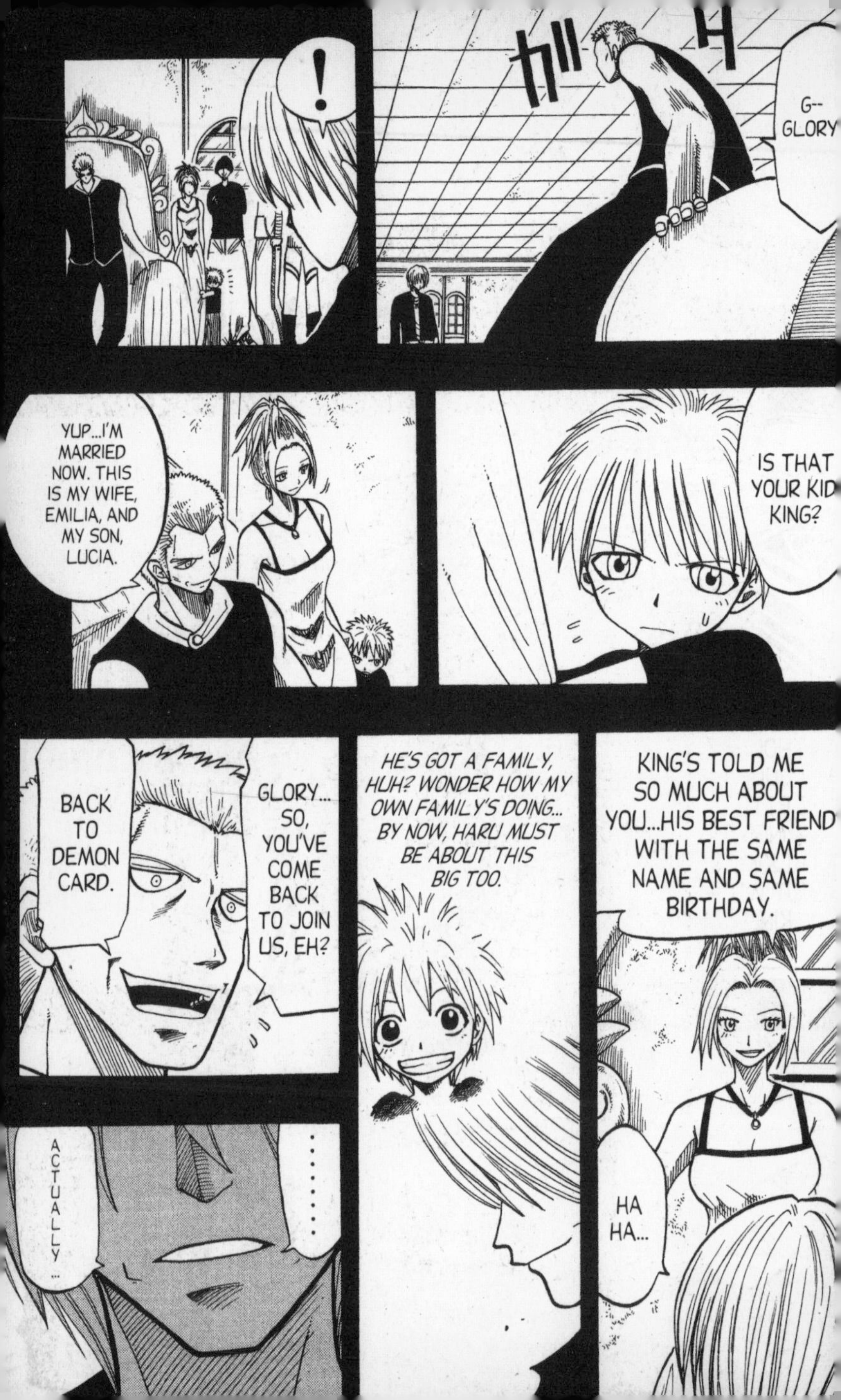
G-- GLORY
!
IS THAT YOUR KID KING?
YUP...I'M MARRIED NOW. THIS IS MY WIFE, EMILIA, AND MY SON, LUCIA.
KING'S TOLD ME SO MUCH ABOUT YOU...HIS BEST FRIEND WITH THE SAME NAME AND SAME BIRTHDAY.
HA HA...
HE'S GOT A FAMILY, HUH? WONDER HOW MY OWN FAMILY'S DOING... BY NOW, HARU MUST BE ABOUT THIS BIG TOO.
GLORY... SO, YOU'VE COME BACK TO JOIN US, EH?
BACK TO DEMON CARD.
......
ACTUALLY...

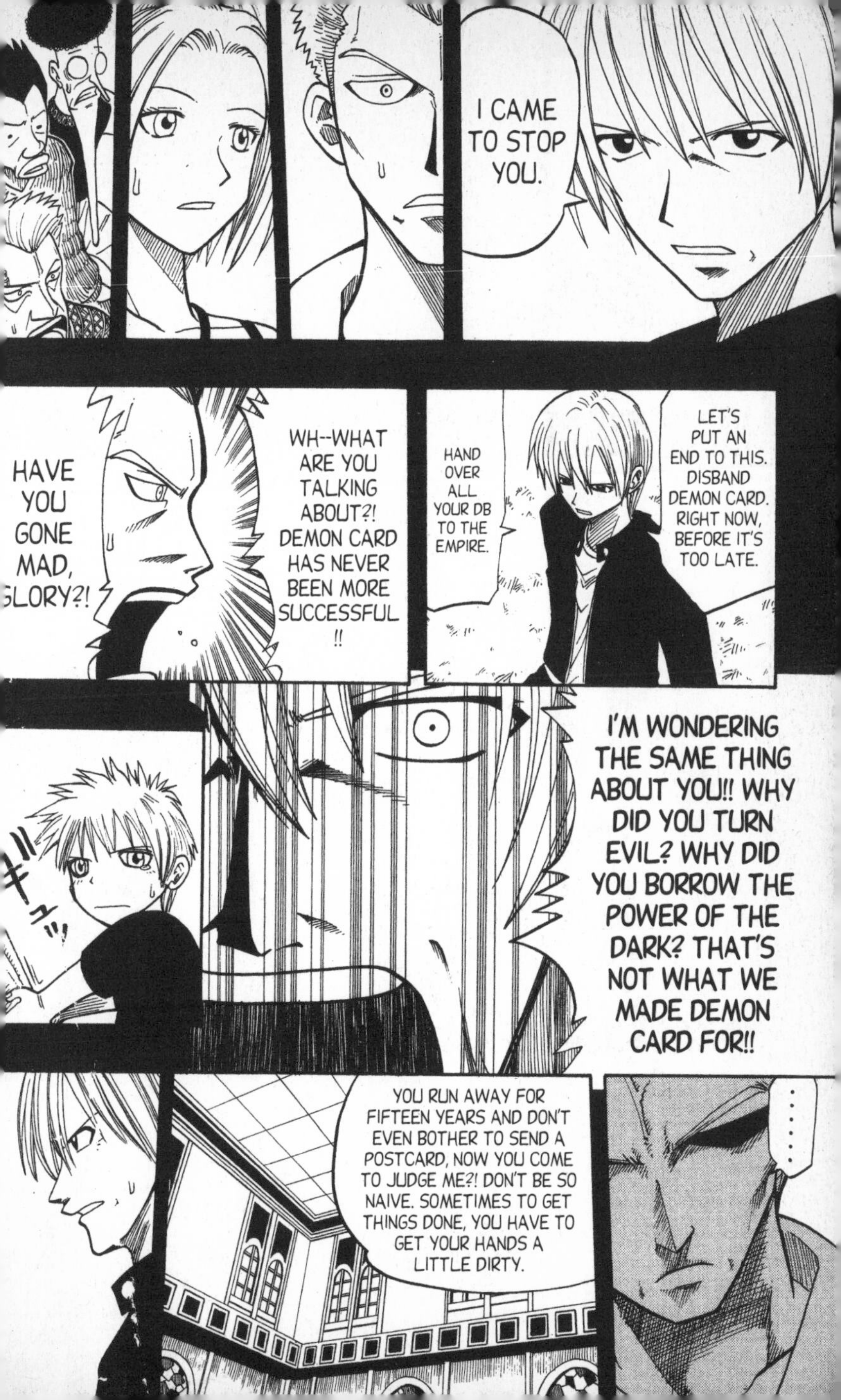

I CAME TO STOP YOU.
LET'S PUT AN END TO THIS. DISBAND DEMON CARD. RIGHT NOW, BEFORE IT'S TOO LATE.
HAND OVER ALL YOUR DB TO THE EMPIRE.
WH--WHAT ARE YOU TALKING ABOUT?! DEMON CARD HAS NEVER BEEN MORE SUCCESSFUL!!
HAVE YOU GONE MAD, GLORY?!
I'M WONDERING THE SAME THING ABOUT YOU!! WHY DID YOU TURN EVIL? WHY DID YOU BORROW THE POWER OF THE DARK? THAT'S NOT WHAT WE MADE DEMON CARD FOR!!
......
YOU RUN AWAY FOR FIFTEEN YEARS AND DON'T EVEN BOTHER TO SEND A POSTCARD, NOW YOU COME TO JUDGE ME?! DON'T BE SO NAIVE. SOMETIMES TO GET THINGS DONE, YOU HAVE TO GET YOUR HANDS A LITTLE DIRTY.

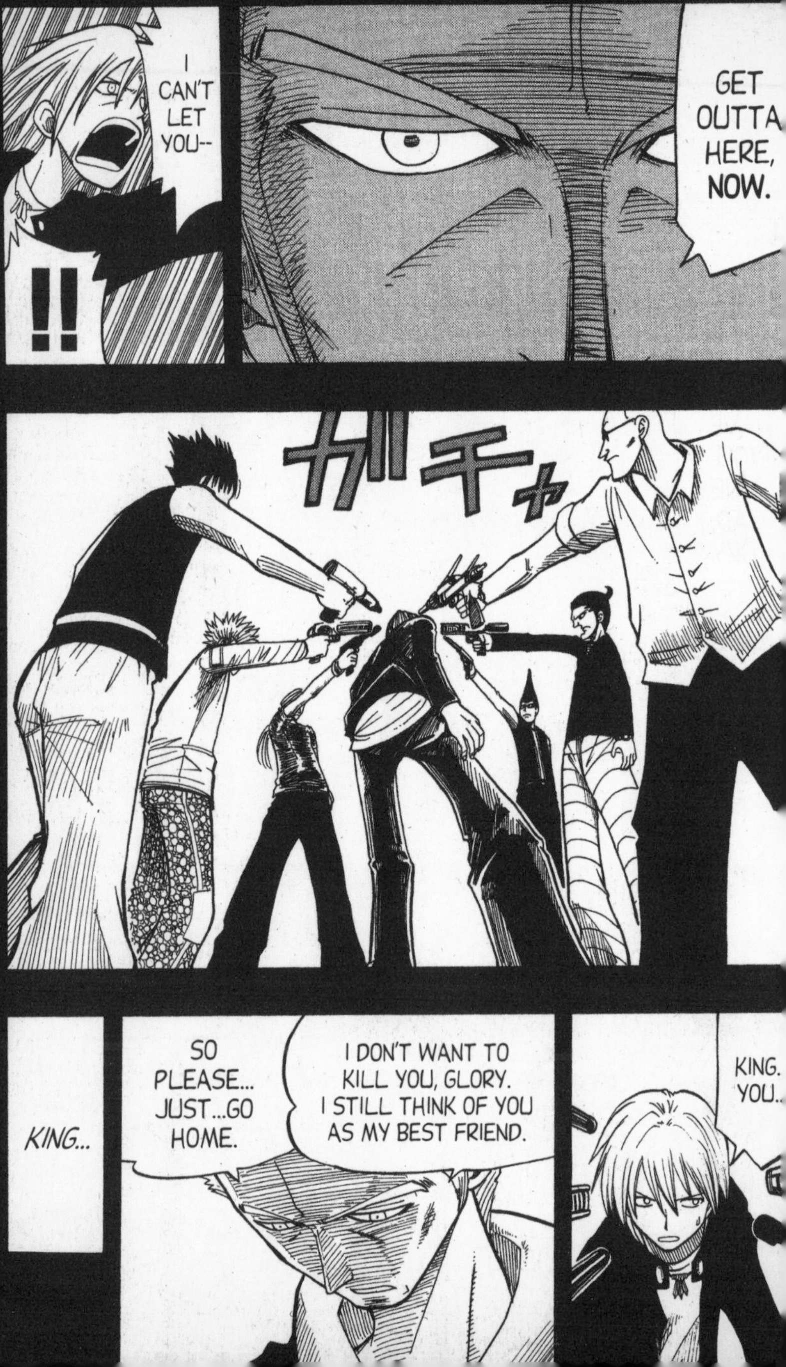
GET OUTTA HERE, NOW.
I CAN'T LET YOU--
!!
ガチャ
KING. YOU..
I DON'T WANT TO KILL YOU, GLORY. I STILL THINK OF YOU AS MY BEST FRIEND.
SO PLEASE... JUST...GO HOME.
KING...

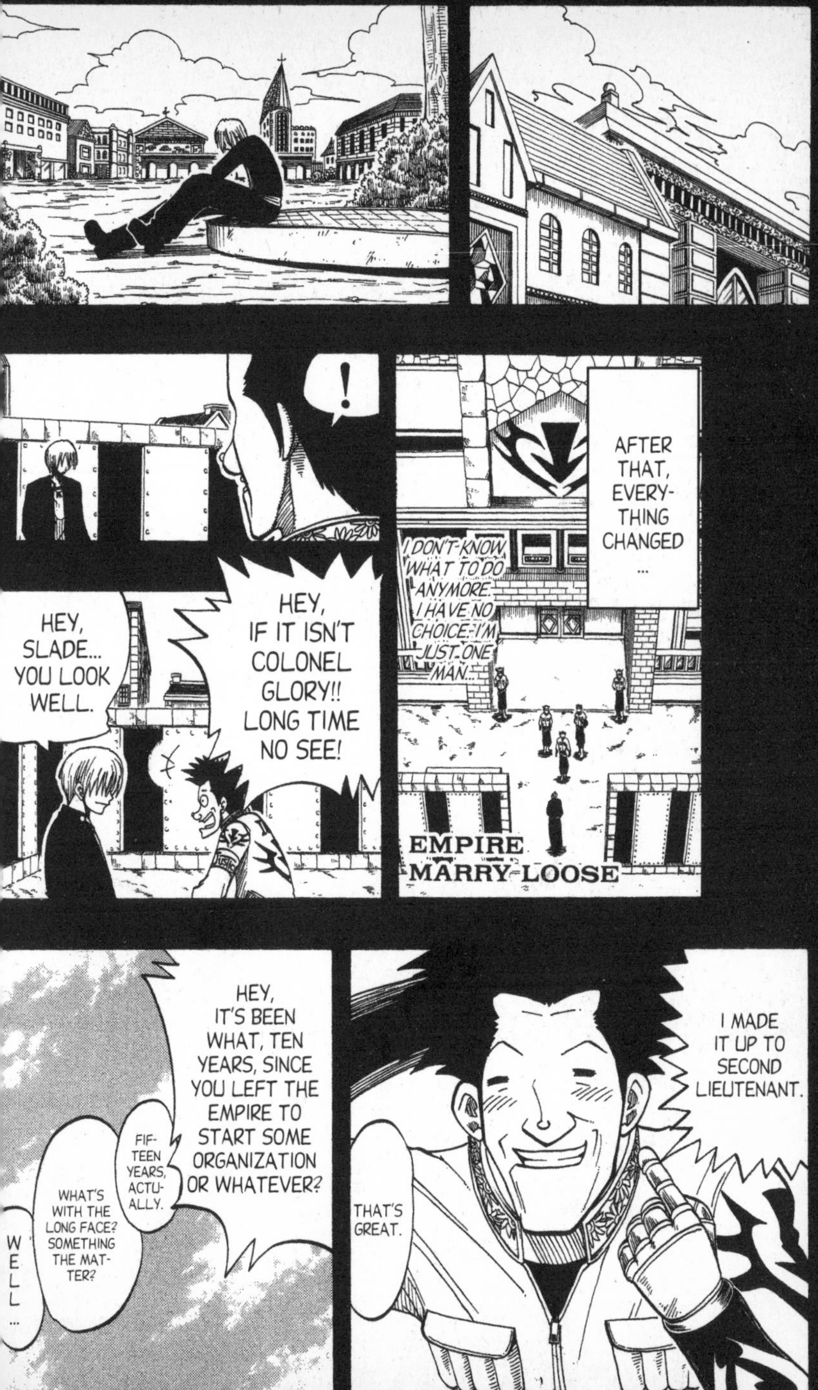
AFTER THAT, EVERYTHING CHANGED ...
I DON'T KNOW WHAT TO DO ANYMORE. I HAVE NO CHOICE. I'M JUST ONE MAN...
EMPIRE MARRY-LOOSE
!
HEY, IF IT ISN'T COLONEL GLORY!! LONG TIME NO SEE!
HEY, SLADE... YOU LOOK WELL.
I MADE IT UP TO SECOND LIEUTENANT.
THAT'S GREAT.
HEY, IT'S BEEN WHAT, TEN YEARS, SINCE YOU LEFT THE EMPIRE TO START SOME ORGANIZATION OR WHATEVER?
FIFTEEN YEARS, ACTUALLY.
WHAT'S WITH THE LONG FACE? SOMETHING THE MATTER?
WELL ...

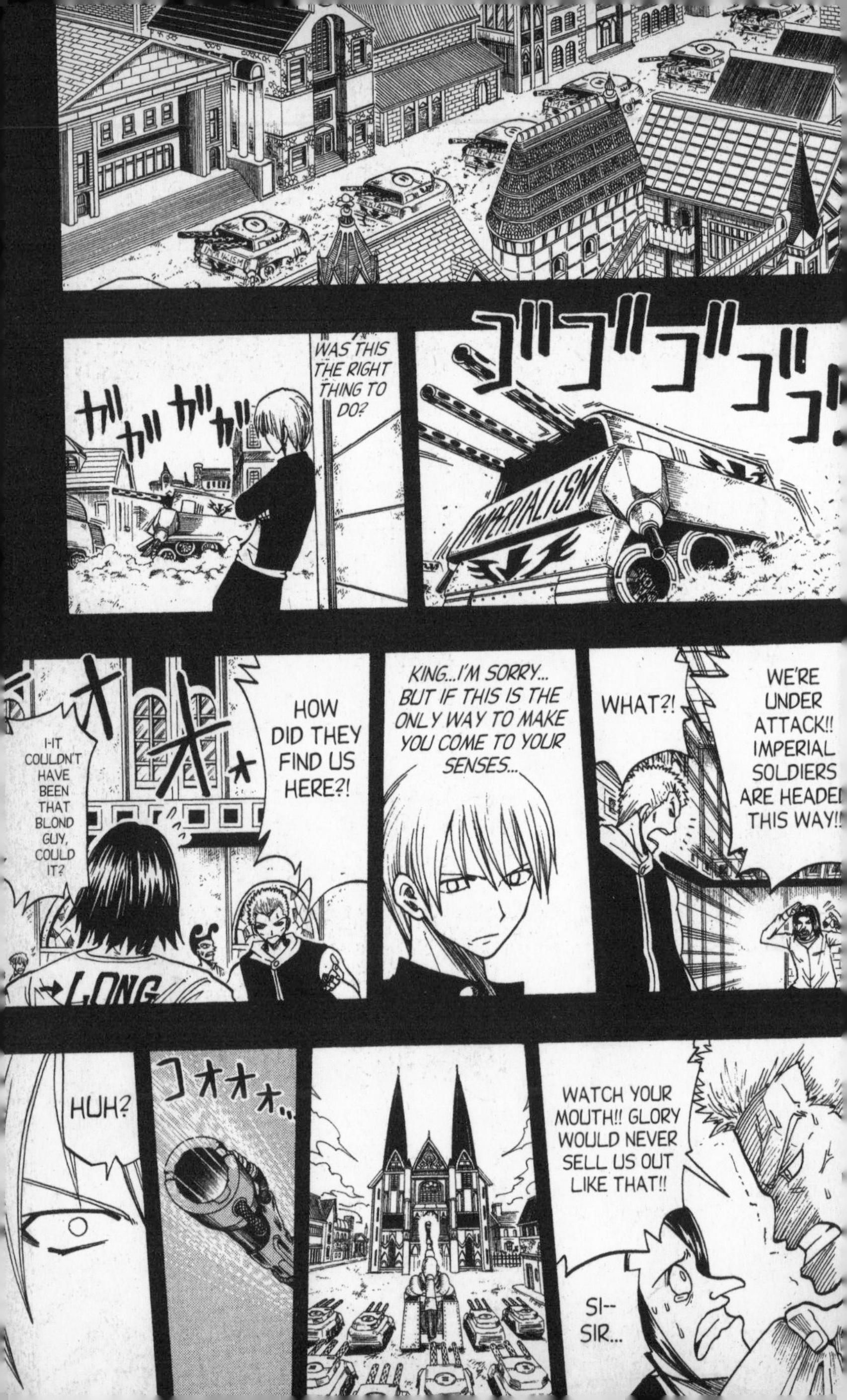
ゴゴゴゴ
WAS THIS THE RIGHT THING TO DO?
ガガガガ
WE'RE UNDER ATTACK!! IMPERIAL SOLDIERS ARE HEADED THIS WAY!!
WHAT?!
KING...I'M SORRY... BUT IF THIS IS THE ONLY WAY TO MAKE YOU COME TO YOUR SENSES...
HOW DID THEY FIND US HERE?!
I-IT COULDN'T HAVE BEEN THAT BLOND GUY, COULD IT?
LONG
WATCH YOUR MOUTH!! GLORY WOULD NEVER SELL US OUT LIKE THAT!!
SI-- SIR...
コオオオ...
HUH?

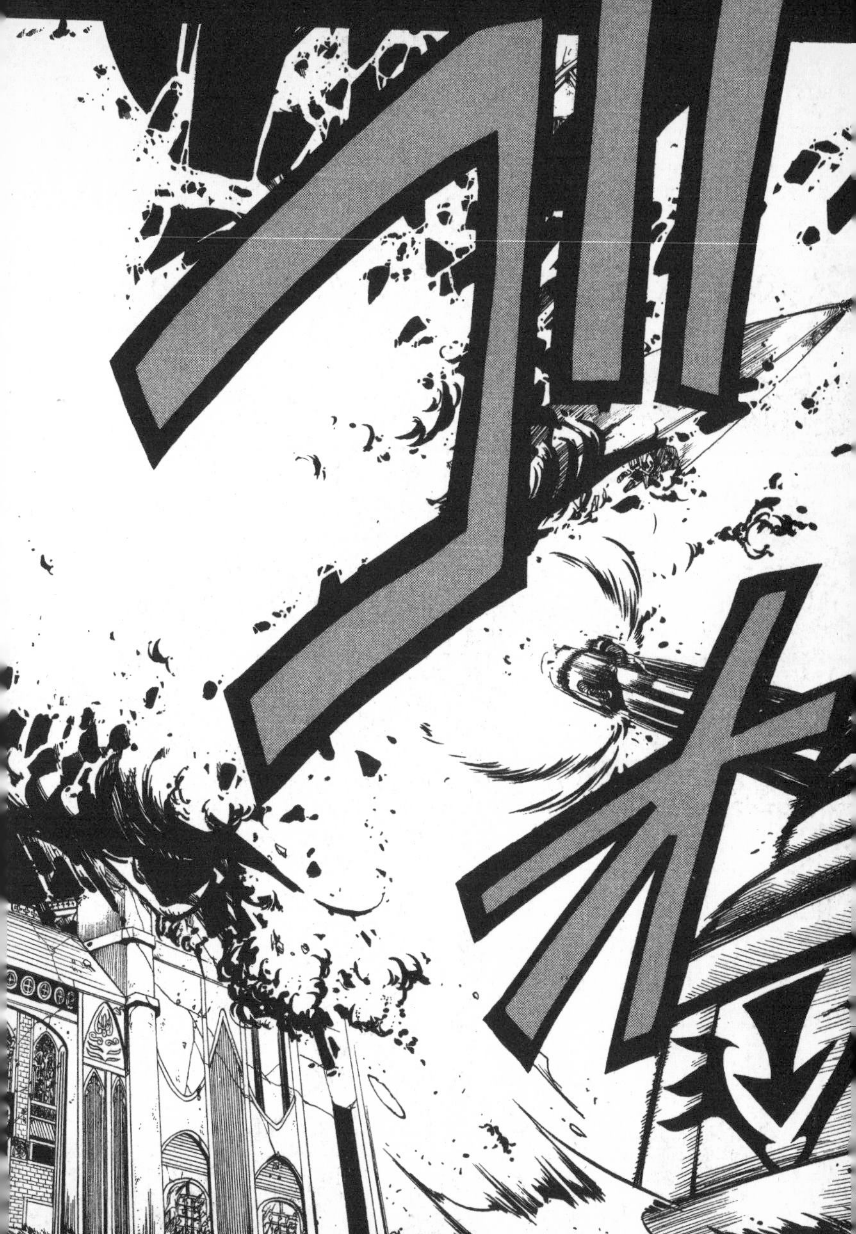

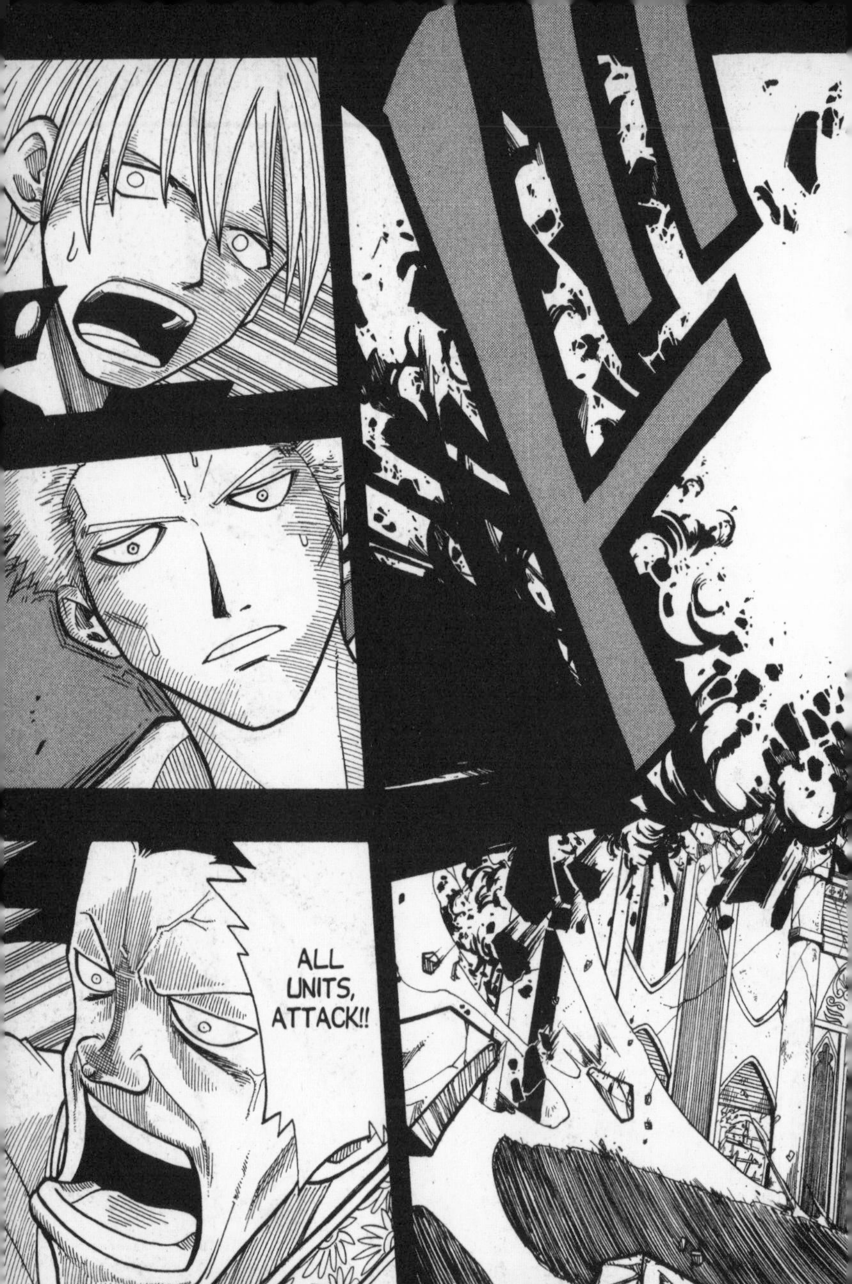
ALL UNITS, ATTACK!!

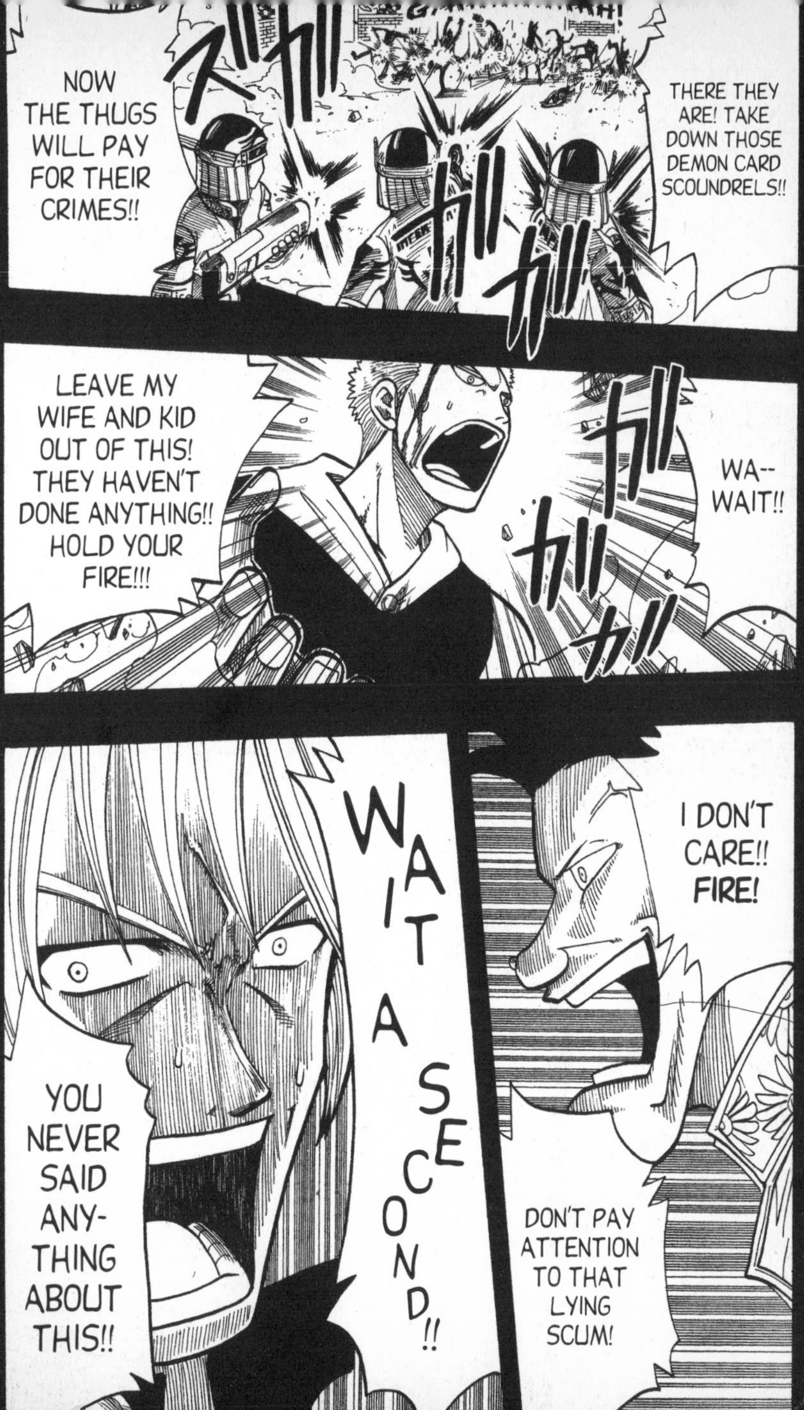
THERE THEY ARE! TAKE DOWN THOSE DEMON CARD SCOUNDRELS!!
NOW THE THUGS WILL PAY FOR THEIR CRIMES!!
WA-- WAIT!!
LEAVE MY WIFE AND KID OUT OF THIS! THEY HAVEN'T DONE ANYTHING!! HOLD YOUR FIRE!!!
I DON'T CARE!! FIRE!
DON'T PAY ATTENTION TO THAT LYING SCUM!
WAIT A SECOND!!
YOU NEVER SAID ANY-THING ABOUT THIS!!

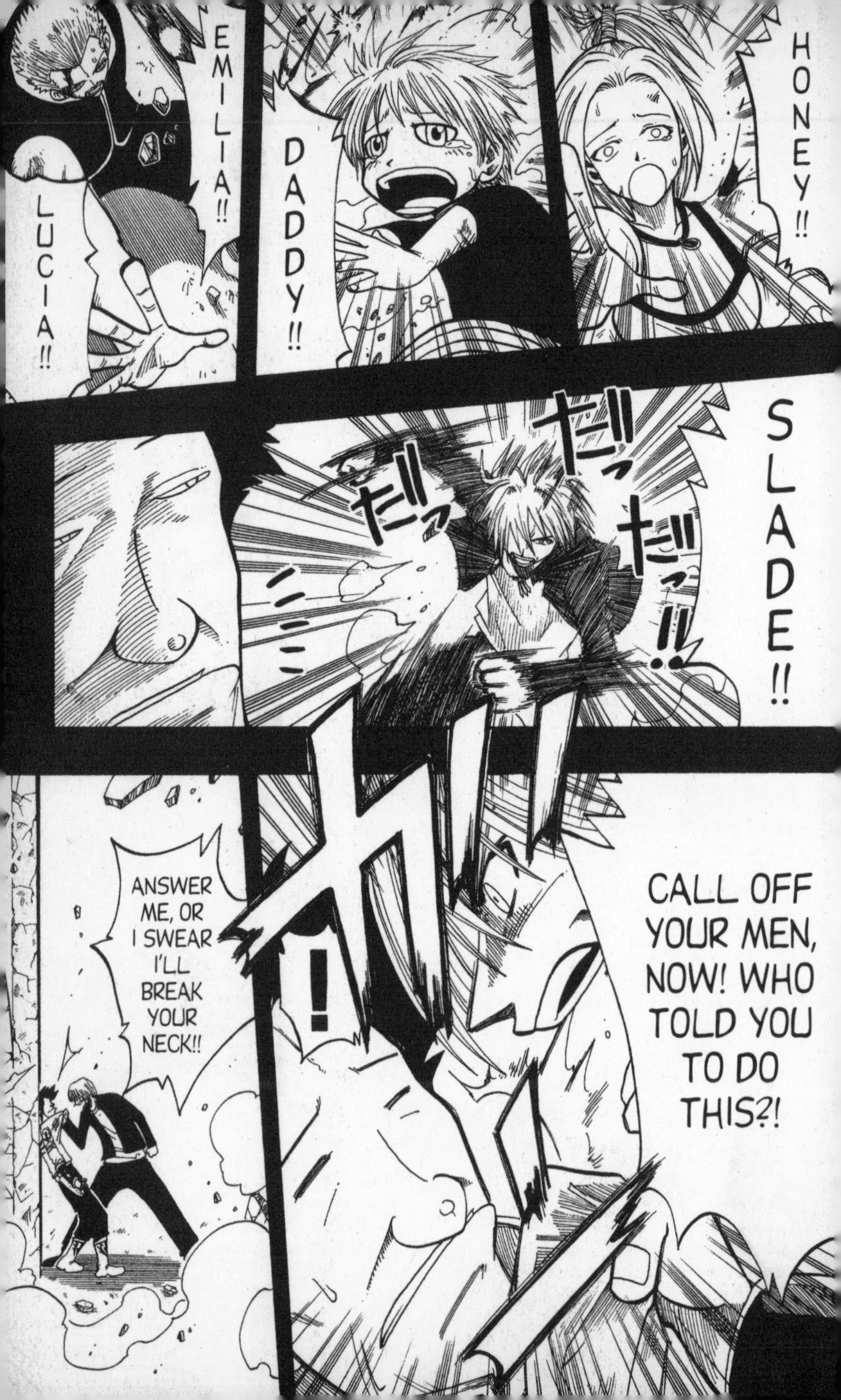
HONEY!!
DADDY!!
EMILIA!!
LUCIA!!
SLADE!!
だっ
だっ
だっ!!
CALL OFF YOUR MEN, NOW! WHO TOLD YOU TO DO THIS?!
!
ANSWER ME, OR I SWEAR I'LL BREAK YOUR NECK!!

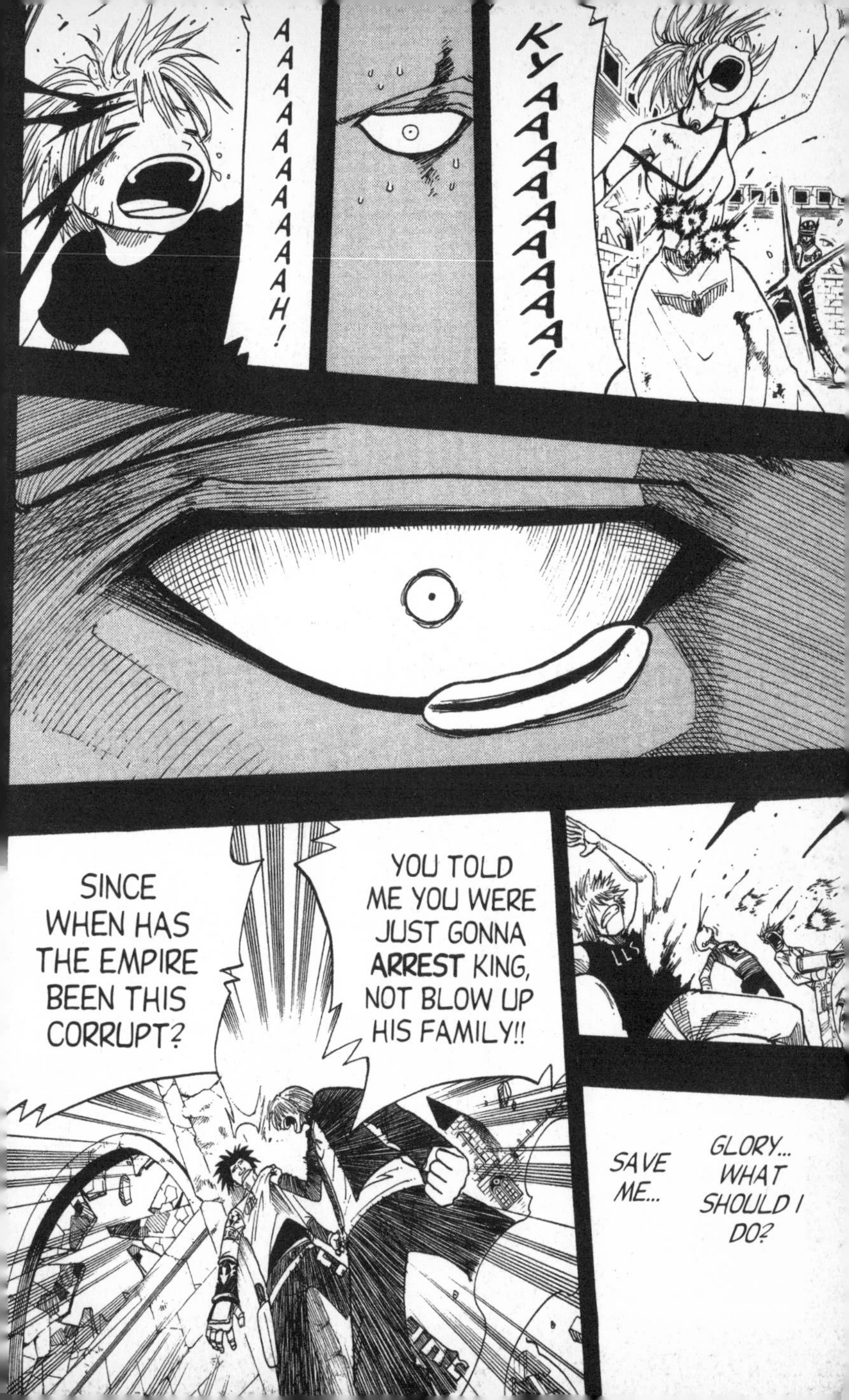

KYAAAAAAAAAA!
AAAAAAAAAH!
GLORY... WHAT SHOULD I DO?
SAVE ME...
YOU TOLD ME YOU WERE JUST GONNA **ARREST** KING, NOT BLOW UP HIS FAMILY!!
SINCE WHEN HAS THE EMPIRE BEEN THIS CORRUPT?

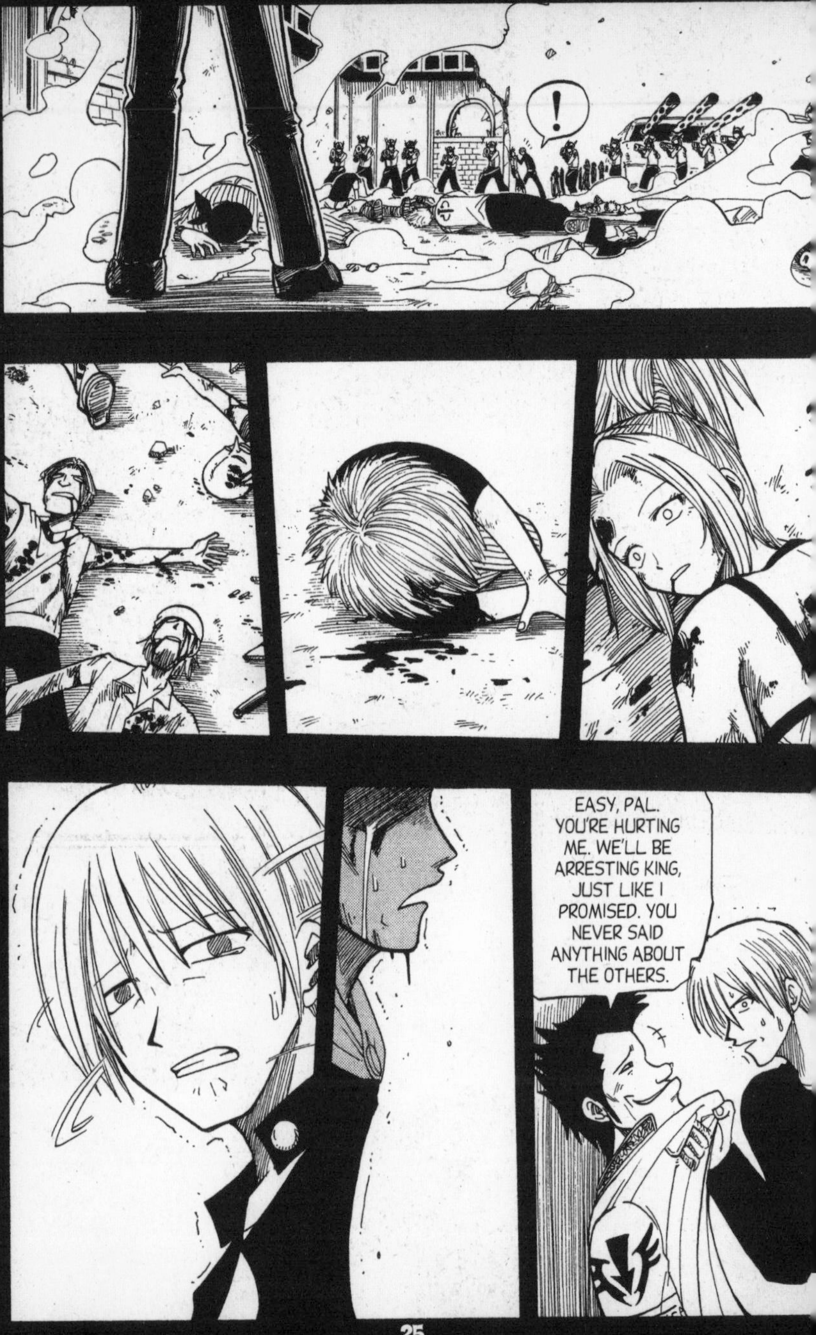
!
EASY, PAL. YOU'RE HURTING ME. WE'LL BE ARRESTING KING, JUST LIKE I PROMISED. YOU NEVER SAID ANYTHING ABOUT THE OTHERS.

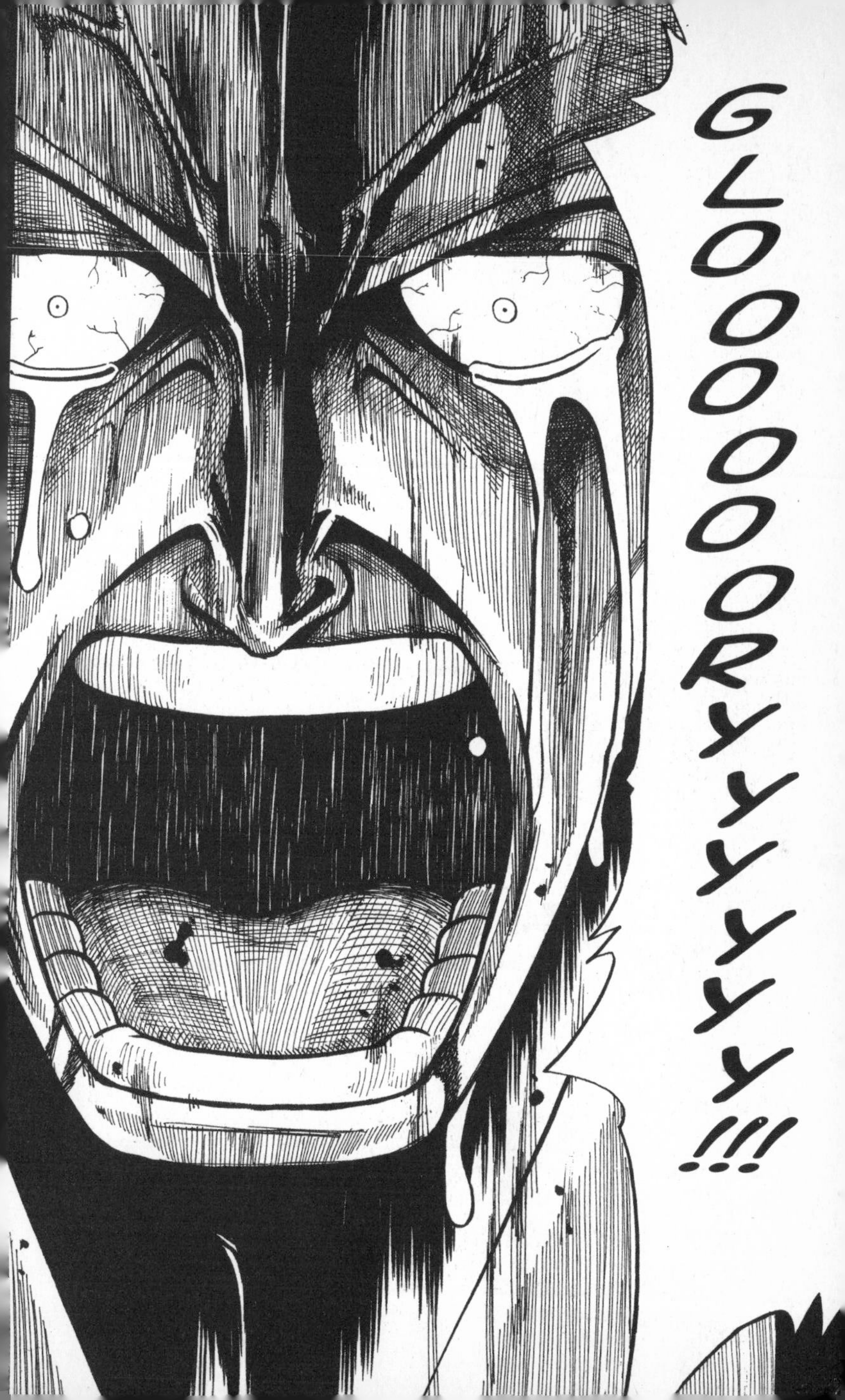
GLOOOOOORYYYYYY!!!

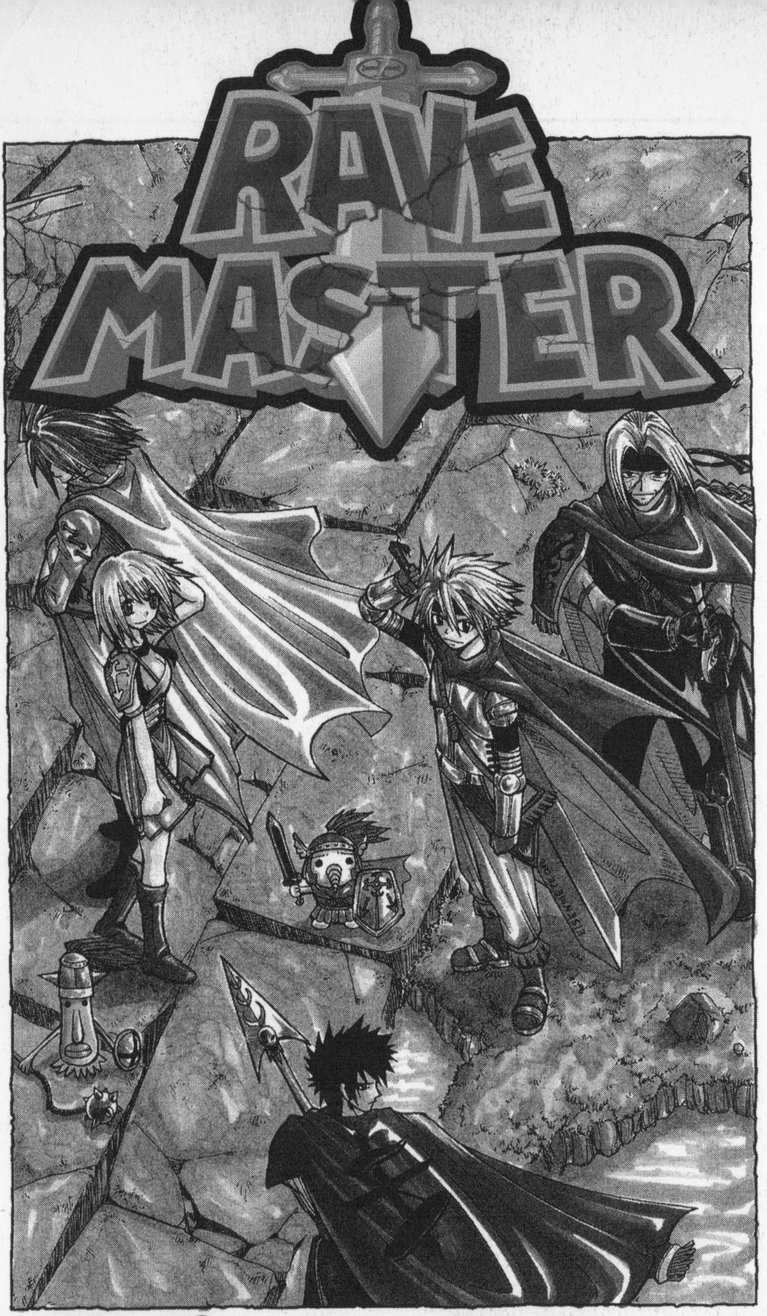
RAVE MASTER

RAVE:66 ✚ AT THE EDGE OF HATE

The results are in for the first character popularity ranking! (Japanese readers)

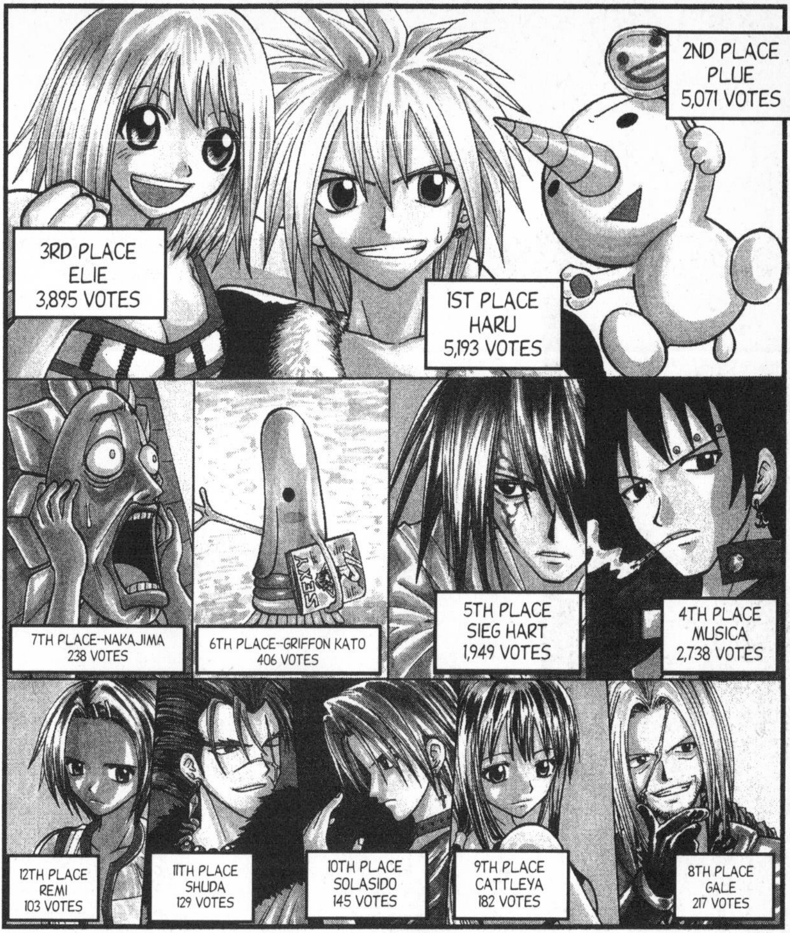
2ND PLACE
PLUE
5,071 VOTES
1ST PLACE
HARU
5,193 VOTES
3RD PLACE
ELIE
3,895 VOTES
4TH PLACE
MUSICA
2,738 VOTES
5TH PLACE
SIEG HART
1,949 VOTES
6TH PLACE--GRIFFON KATO
406 VOTES
7TH PLACE--NAKAJIMA
238 VOTES
8TH PLACE
GALE
217 VOTES
9TH PLACE
CATTLEYA
182 VOTES
10TH PLACE
SOLASIDO
145 VOTES
11TH PLACE
SHUDA
129 VOTES
12TH PLACE
REMI
103 VOTES

And to all those characters who didn't make it, there's always next time!

22 -- ROSA
23 -- JIGGLE BUTT GANG
24 -- GENMA
25 -- SHIGE
26 -- DR. SCHNEIDER
27 -- DEERHOUND
28 -- NUMBERMAN 5
29 -- MIKAN
30 -- RIZE

13 -- TANCHIMO
14 -- REINA
15 -- KOMEKICHI
16 -- MELODIA
17 -- HIRO MASHIMA
18 -- GO
19 -- JEGAN
20 -- SHIBA
21 -- FUA

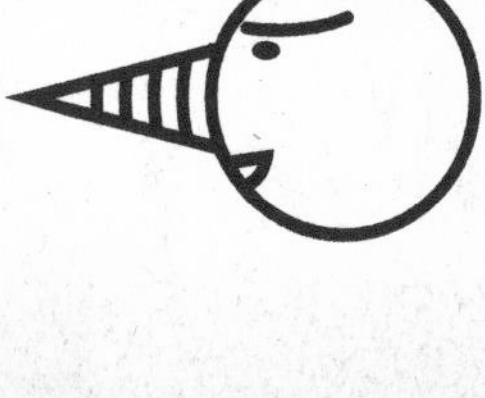

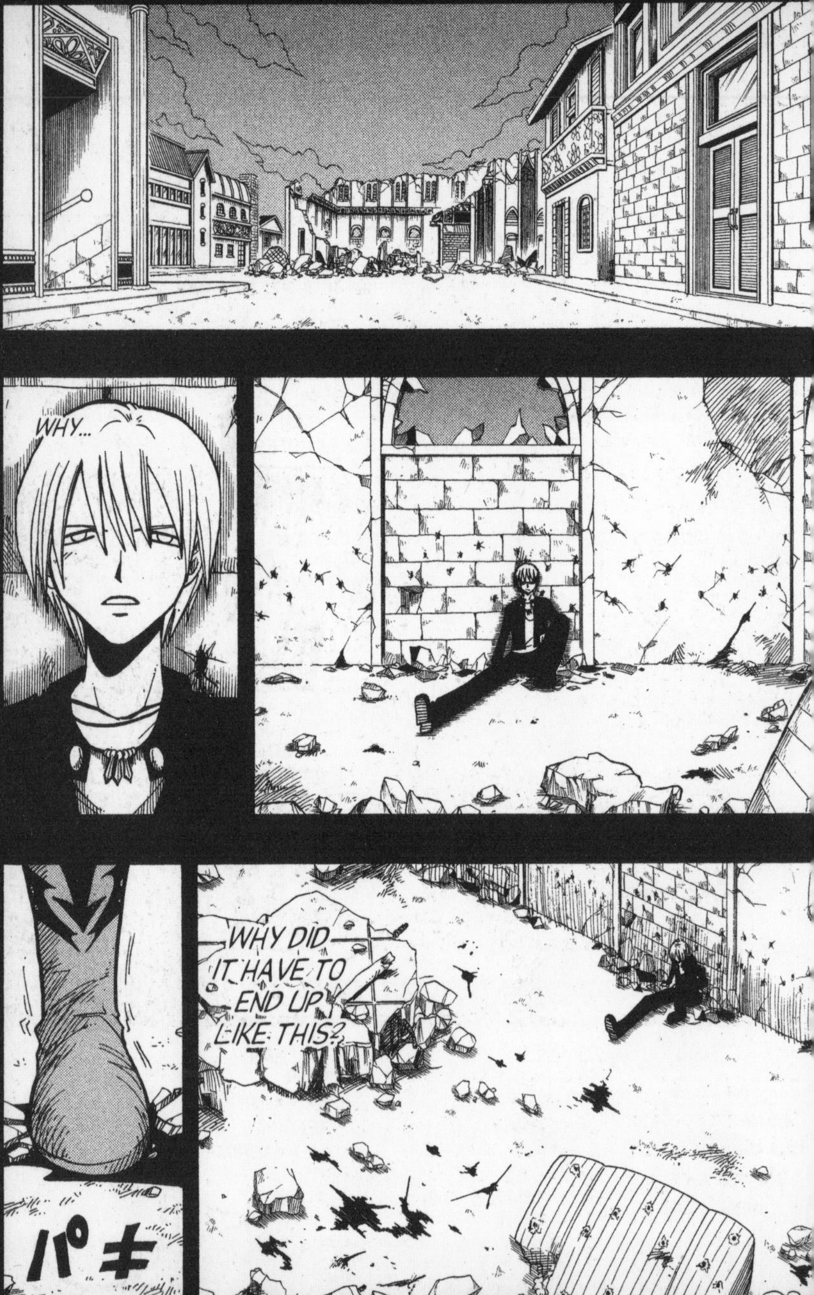

WHY...
WHY DID IT HAVE TO END UP LIKE THIS?
パキ

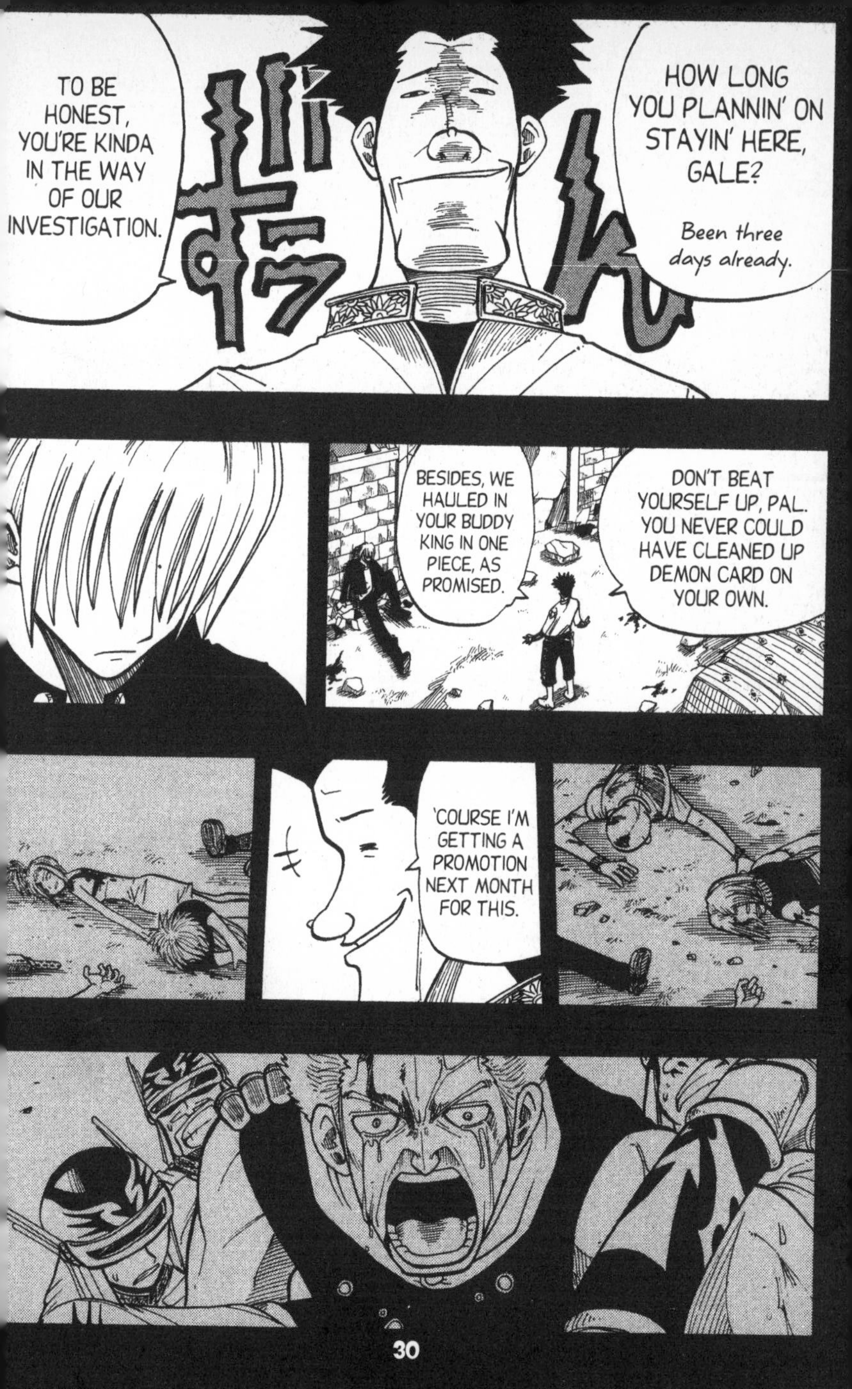
HOW LONG YOU PLANNIN' ON STAYIN' HERE, GALE?
Been three days already.
TO BE HONEST, YOU'RE KINDA IN THE WAY OF OUR INVESTIGATION.
DON'T BEAT YOURSELF UP, PAL. YOU NEVER COULD HAVE CLEANED UP DEMON CARD ON YOUR OWN.
BESIDES, WE HAULED IN YOUR BUDDY KING IN ONE PIECE, AS PROMISED.
'COURSE I'M GETTING A PROMOTION NEXT MONTH FOR THIS.

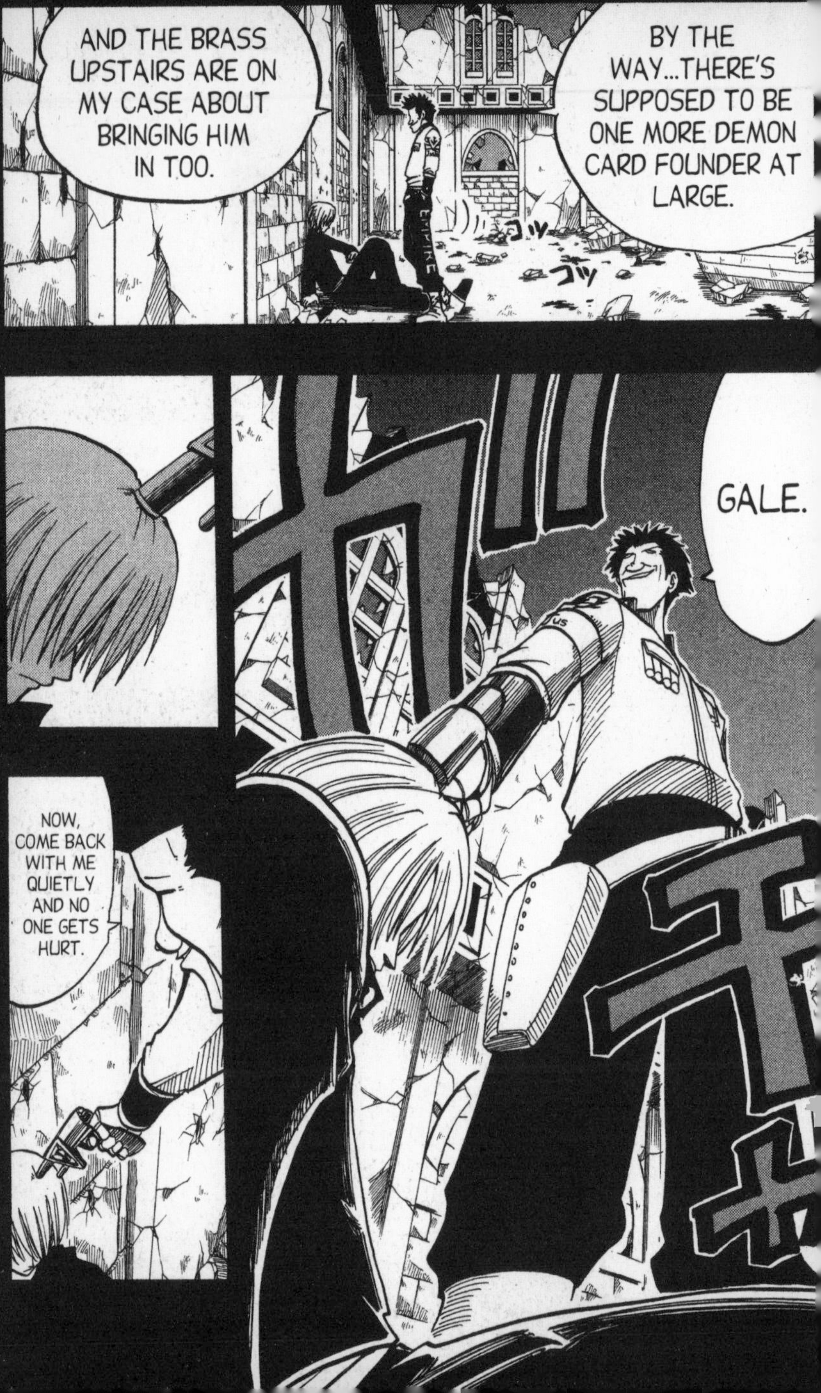
BY THE WAY...THERE'S SUPPOSED TO BE ONE MORE DEMON CARD FOUNDER AT LARGE.
AND THE BRASS UPSTAIRS ARE ON MY CASE ABOUT BRINGING HIM IN TOO.
ゴッ
ゴッ
GALE.
NOW, COME BACK WITH ME QUIETLY AND NO ONE GETS HURT.

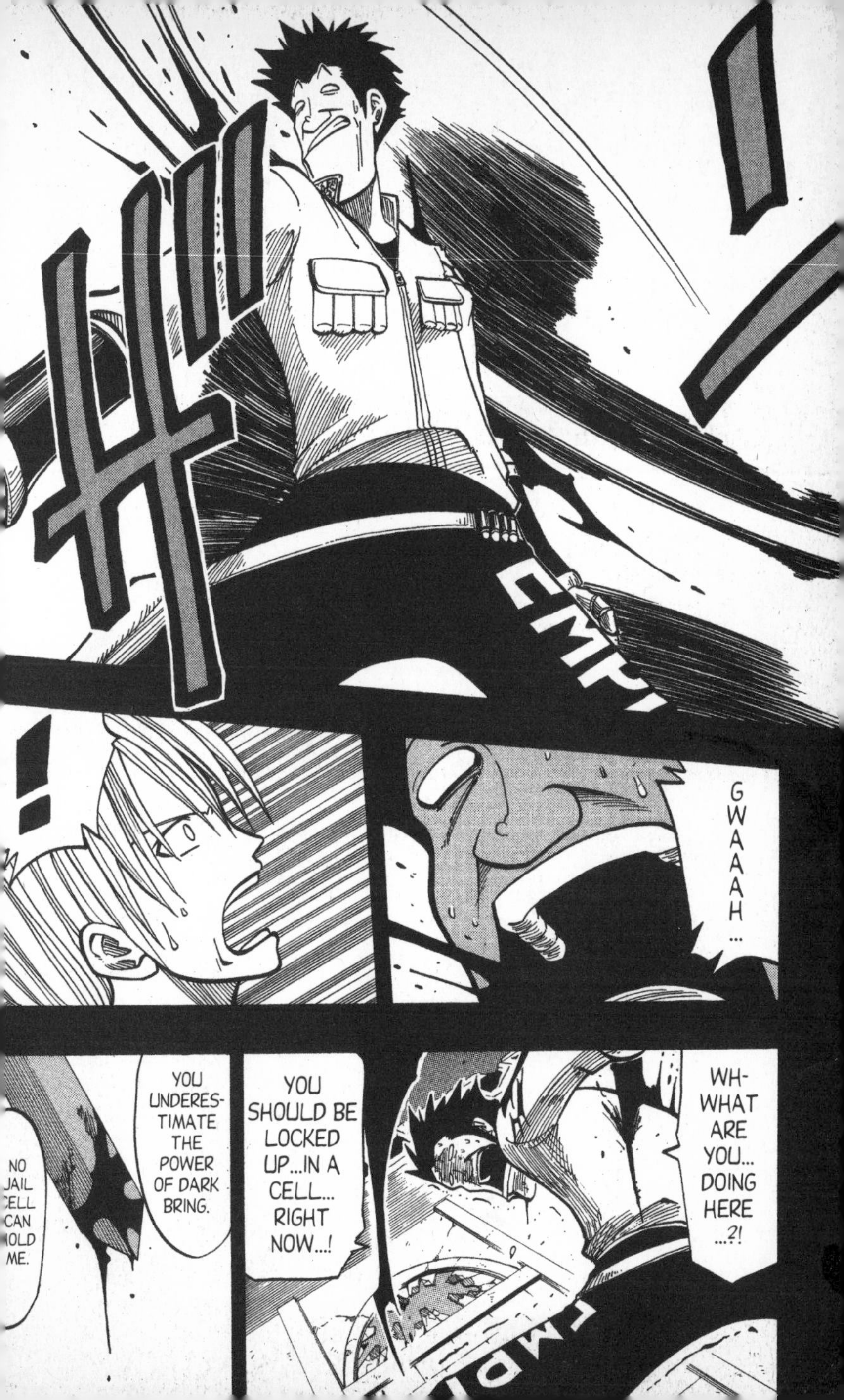
GWAAAAH...
!
WH-WHAT ARE YOU... DOING HERE ...?!
YOU SHOULD BE LOCKED UP...IN A CELL... RIGHT NOW...!
YOU UNDERES-TIMATE THE POWER OF DARK BRING.
NO JAIL CELL CAN HOLD ME.

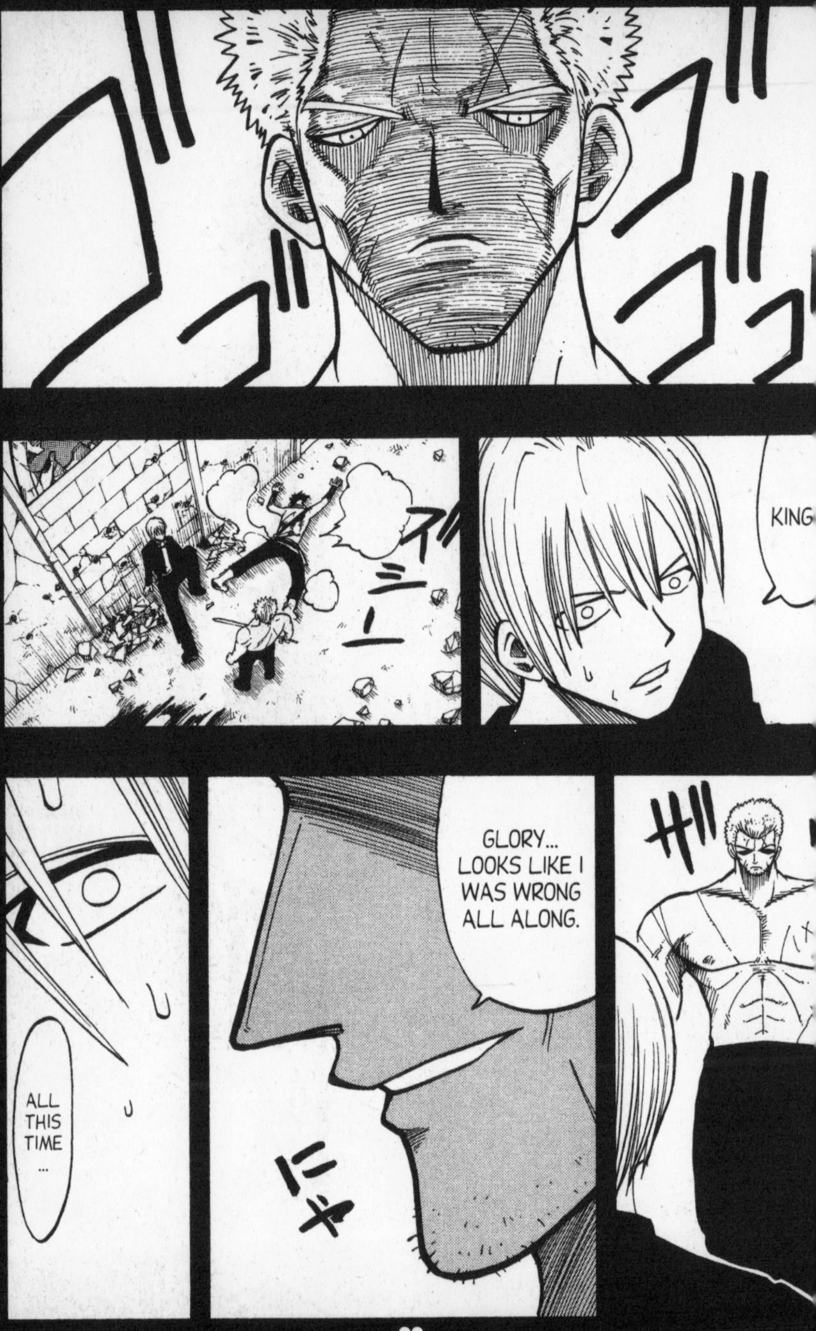
ゴゴゴ
KING
ズシーン
ザッ
GLORY... LOOKS LIKE I WAS WRONG ALL ALONG.
ニヤ
ALL THIS TIME ...

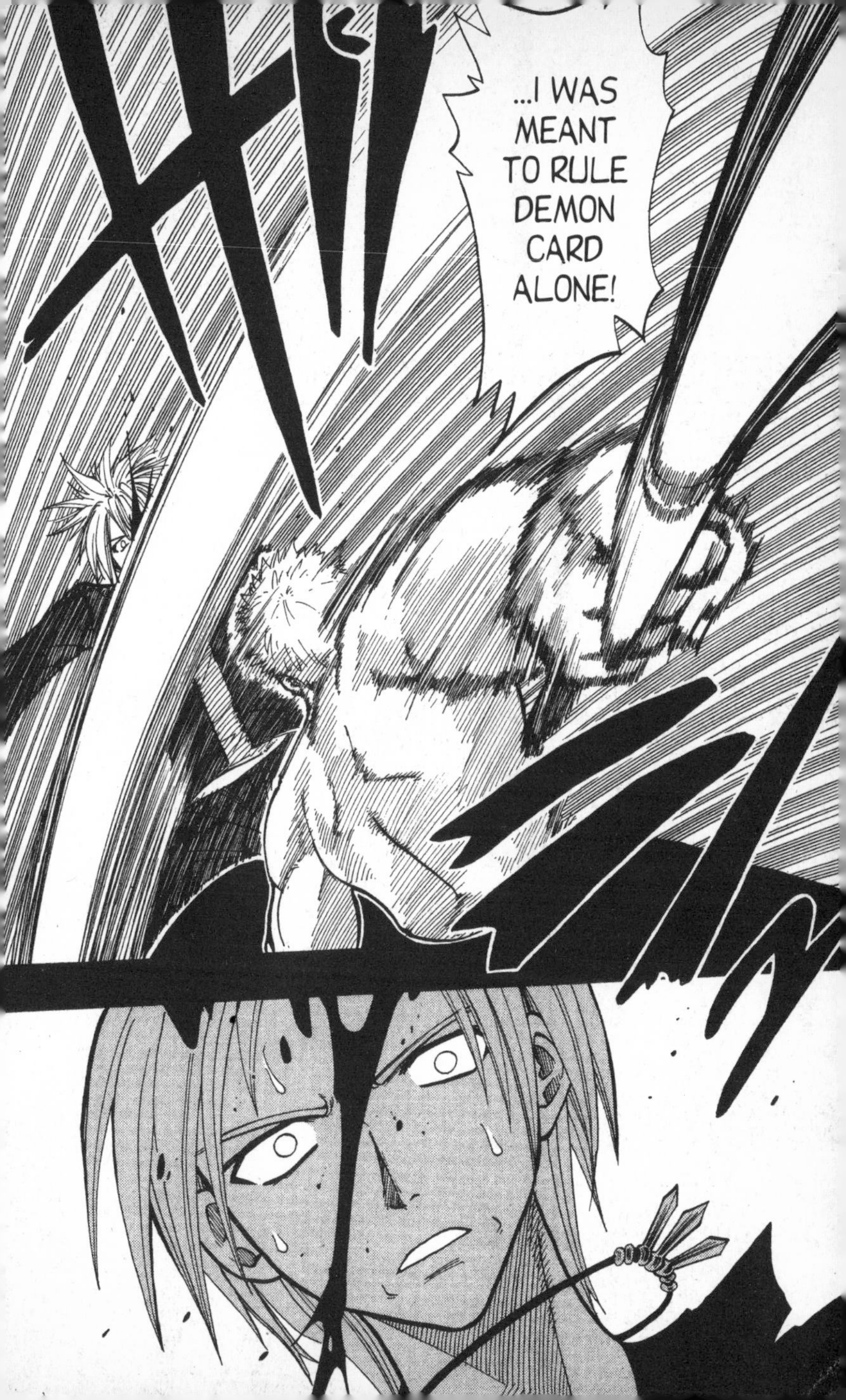
...I WAS MEANT TO RULE DEMON CARD ALONE!

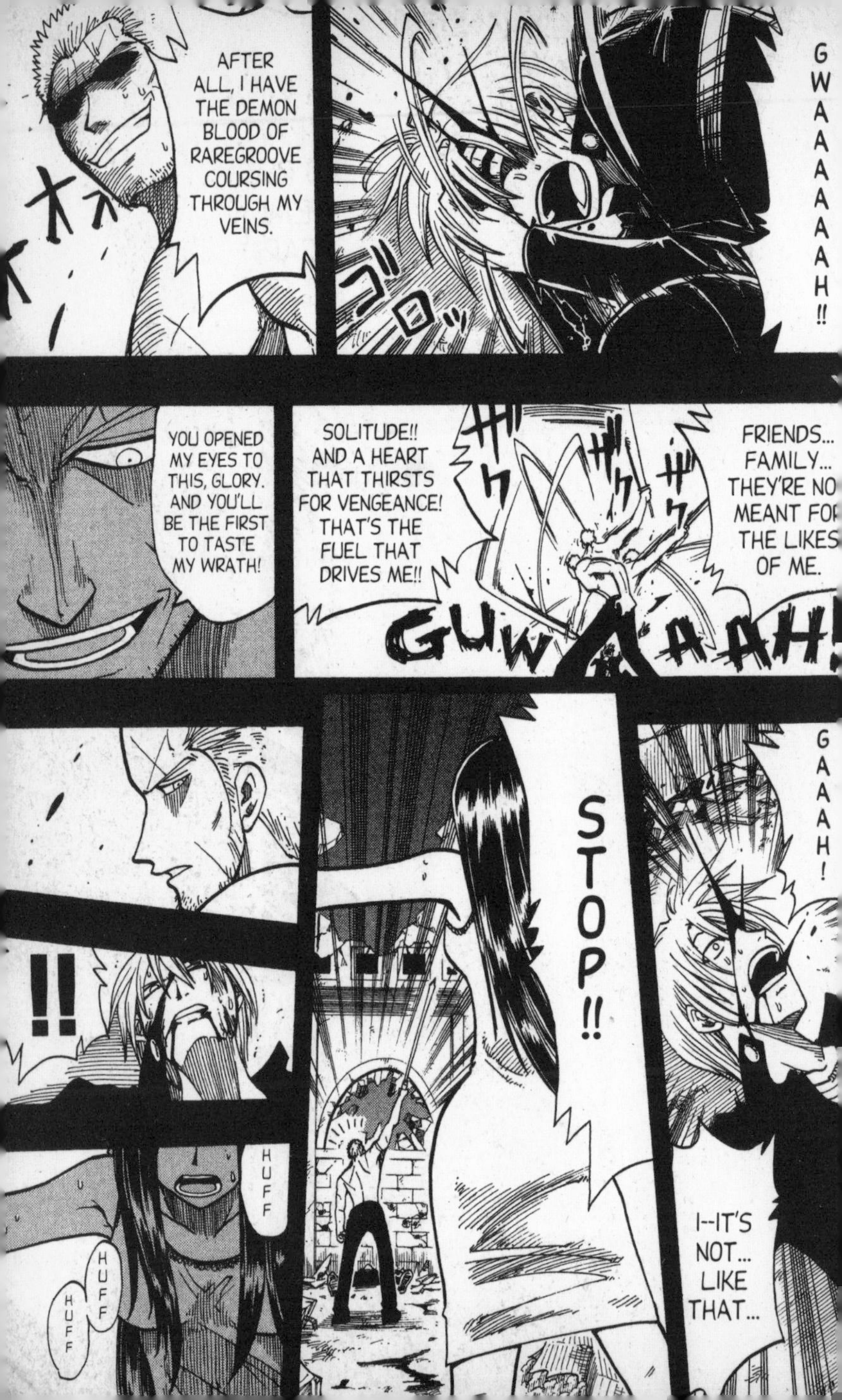
GWAAAAAAAH!!
AFTER ALL, I HAVE THE DEMON BLOOD OF RAREGROOVE COURSING THROUGH MY VEINS.
FRIENDS... FAMILY... THEY'RE NOT MEANT FOR THE LIKES OF ME.
SOLITUDE!! AND A HEART THAT THIRSTS FOR VENGEANCE! THAT'S THE FUEL THAT DRIVES ME!!
GUWAAAH!
YOU OPENED MY EYES TO THIS, GLORY. AND YOU'LL BE THE FIRST TO TASTE MY WRATH!
GAAAH!
I--IT'S NOT... LIKE THAT...
STOP!!
!!
HUFF
HUFF
HUFF

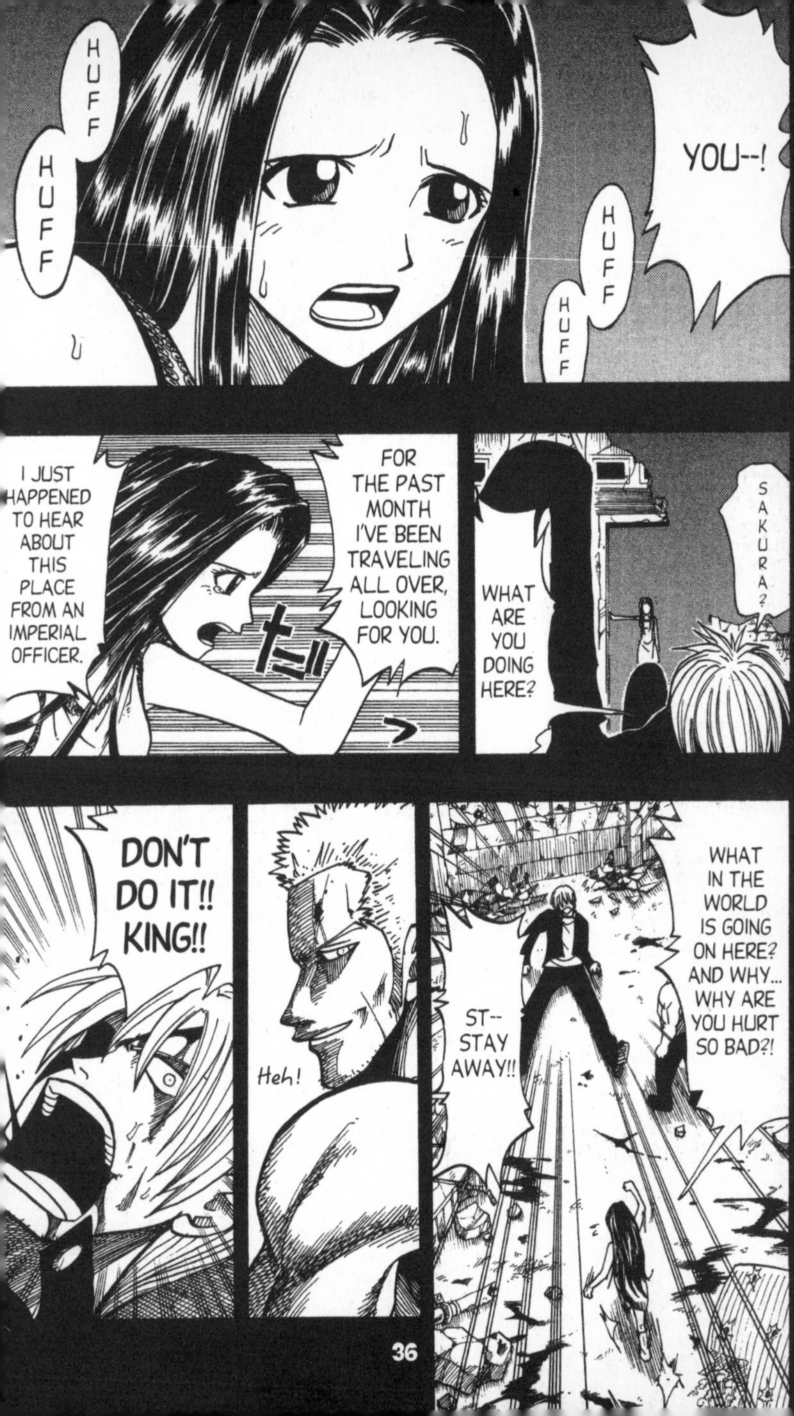
YOU--!
HUFF
HUFF
HUFF
HUFF
SAKURA?
WHAT ARE YOU DOING HERE?
FOR THE PAST MONTH I'VE BEEN TRAVELING ALL OVER, LOOKING FOR YOU.
I JUST HAPPENED TO HEAR ABOUT THIS PLACE FROM AN IMPERIAL OFFICER.
WHAT IN THE WORLD IS GOING ON HERE? AND WHY... WHY ARE YOU HURT SO BAD?!
ST-- STAY AWAY!!
Heh!
DON'T DO IT!! KING!!

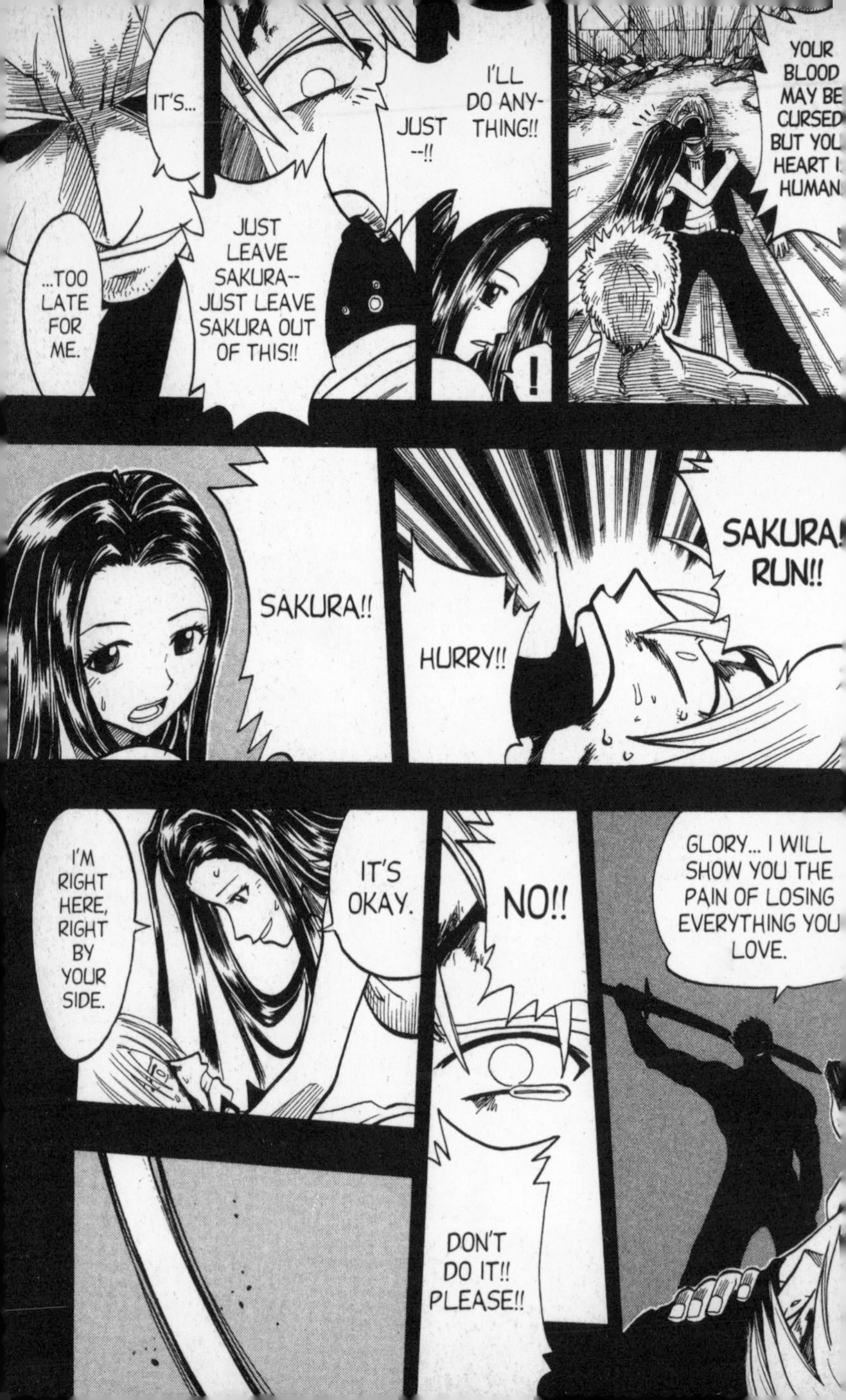
YOUR BLOOD MAY BE CURSED BUT YOU HEART I HUMAN
!
I'LL DO ANY-THING!!
JUST --!!
JUST LEAVE SAKURA-- JUST LEAVE SAKURA OUT OF THIS!!
IT'S...
...TOO LATE FOR ME.
SAKURA! RUN!!
HURRY!!
SAKURA!!
GLORY... I WILL SHOW YOU THE PAIN OF LOSING EVERYTHING YOU LOVE.
NO!!
DON'T DO IT!! PLEASE!!
IT'S OKAY.
I'M RIGHT HERE, RIGHT BY YOUR SIDE.

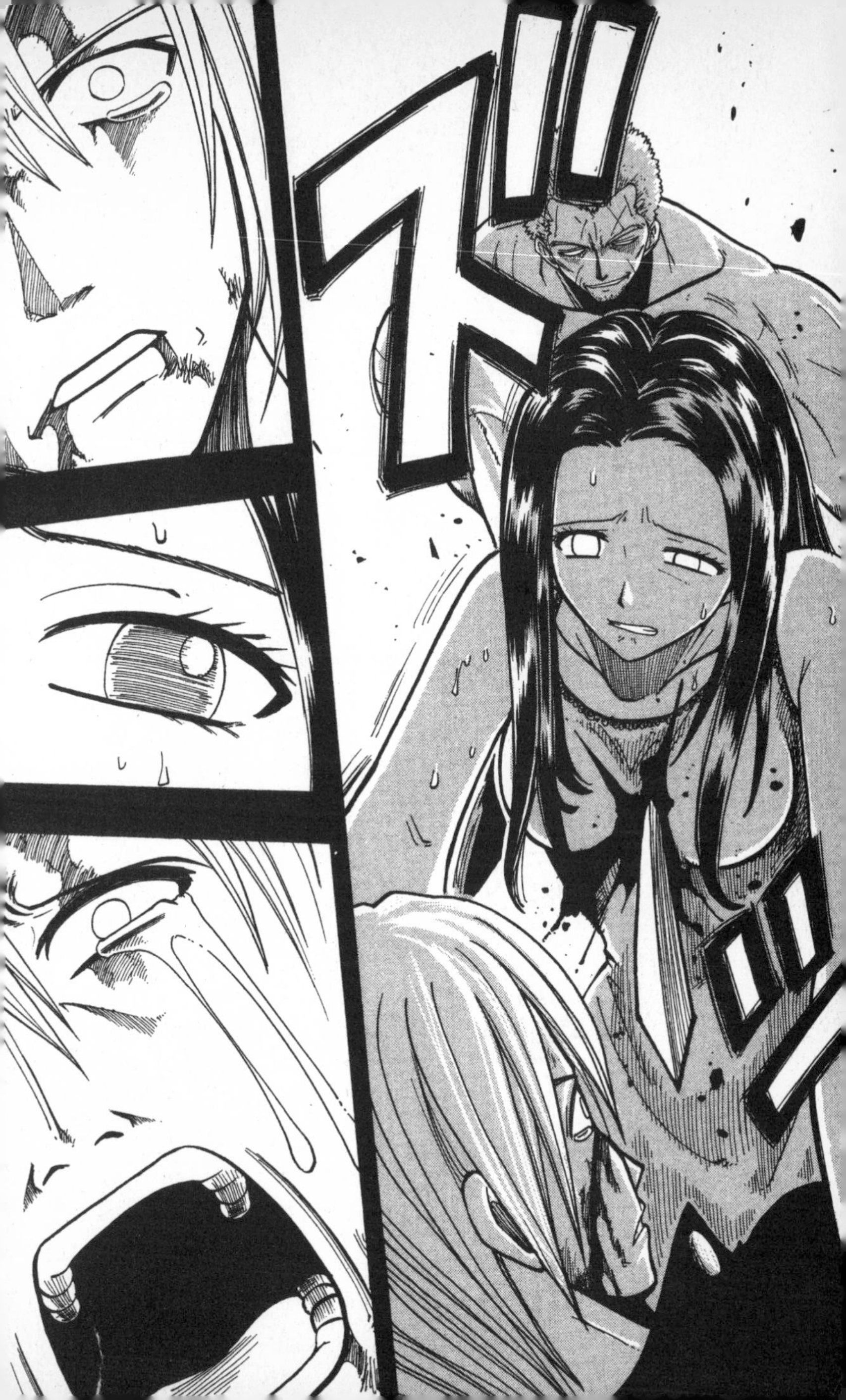

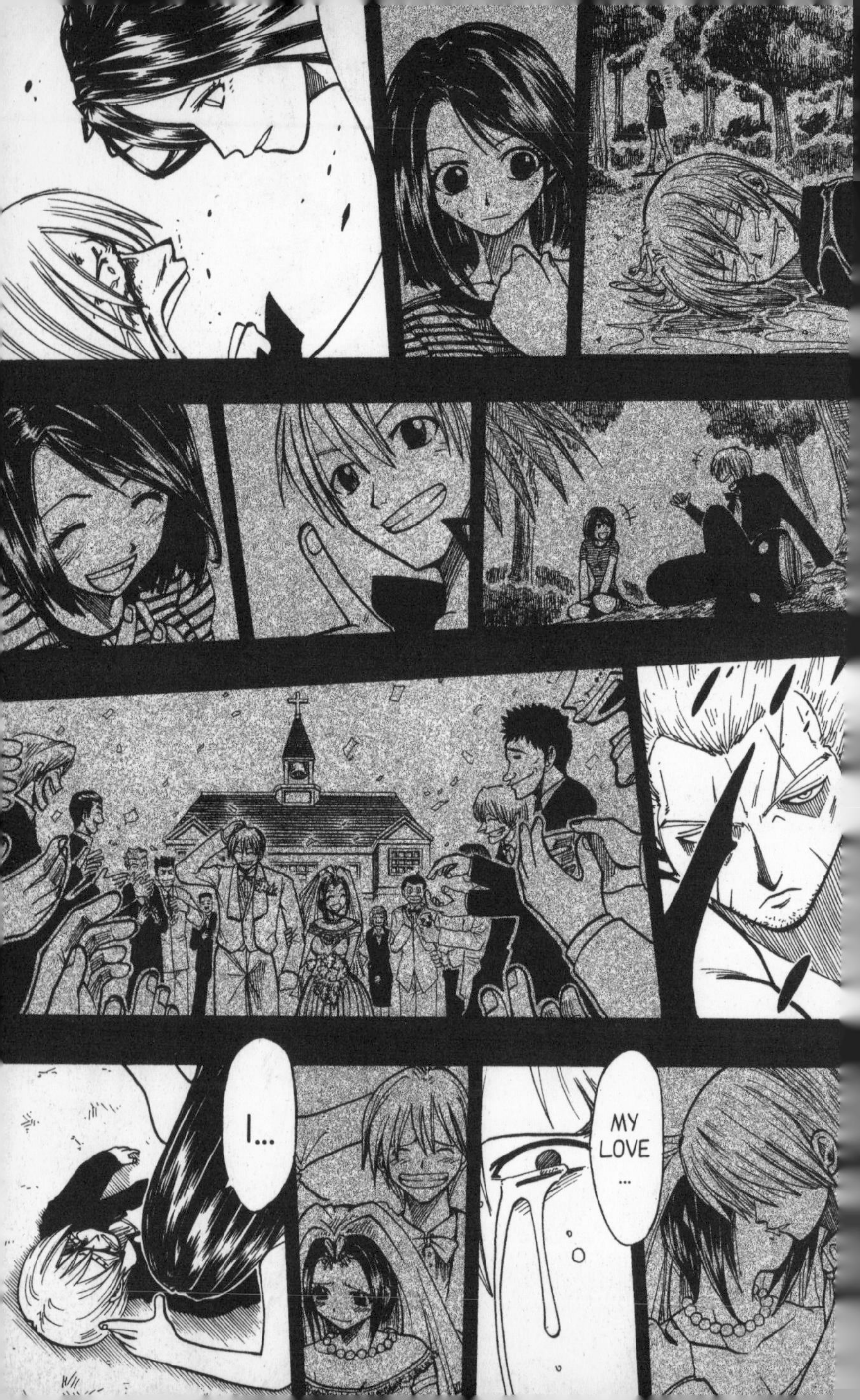
MY LOVE ...
I...

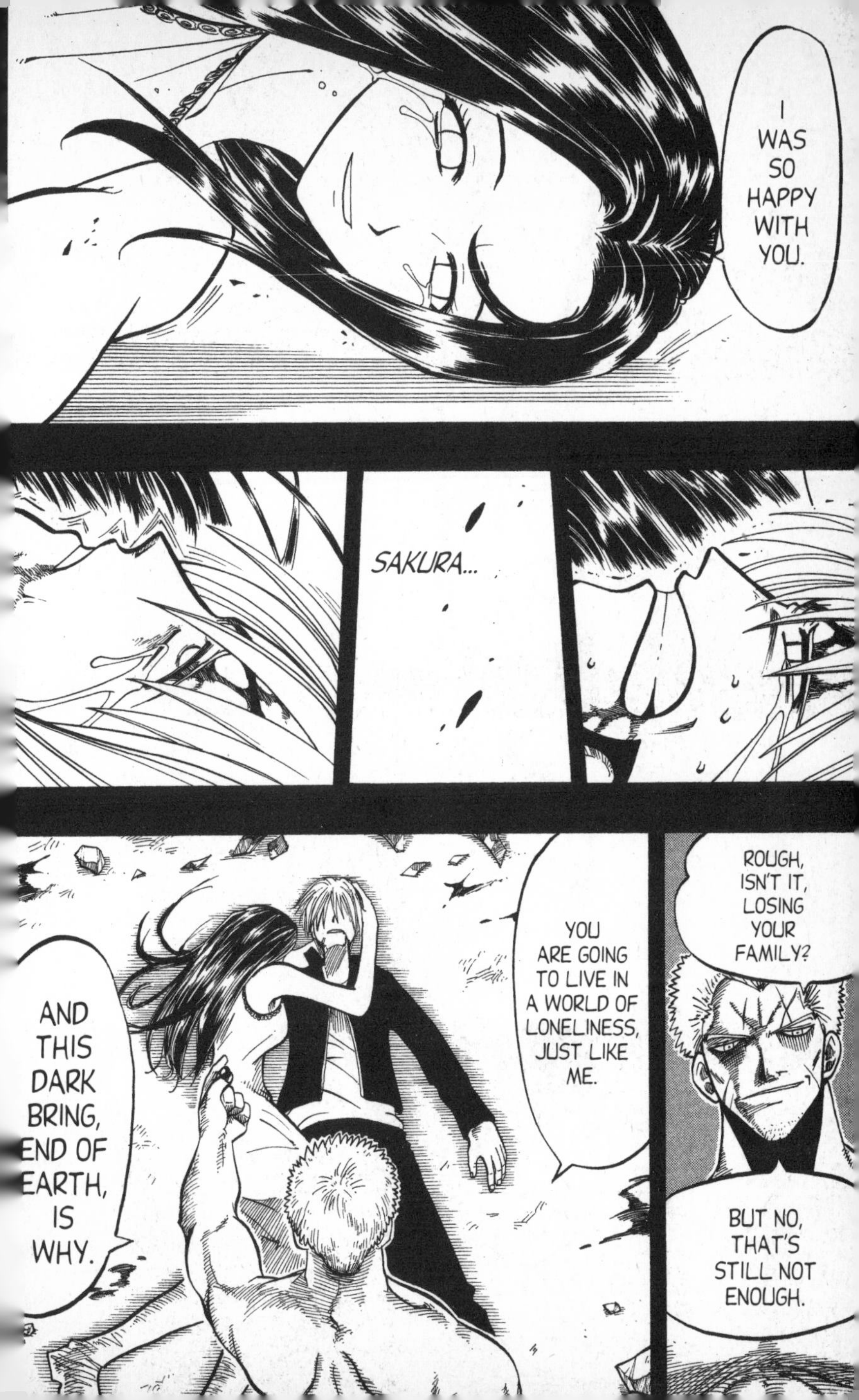
I WAS SO HAPPY WITH YOU.
SAKURA...
ROUGH, ISN'T IT, LOSING YOUR FAMILY?
BUT NO, THAT'S STILL NOT ENOUGH.
YOU ARE GOING TO LIVE IN A WORLD OF LONELINESS, JUST LIKE ME.
AND THIS DARK BRING, END OF EARTH, IS WHY.

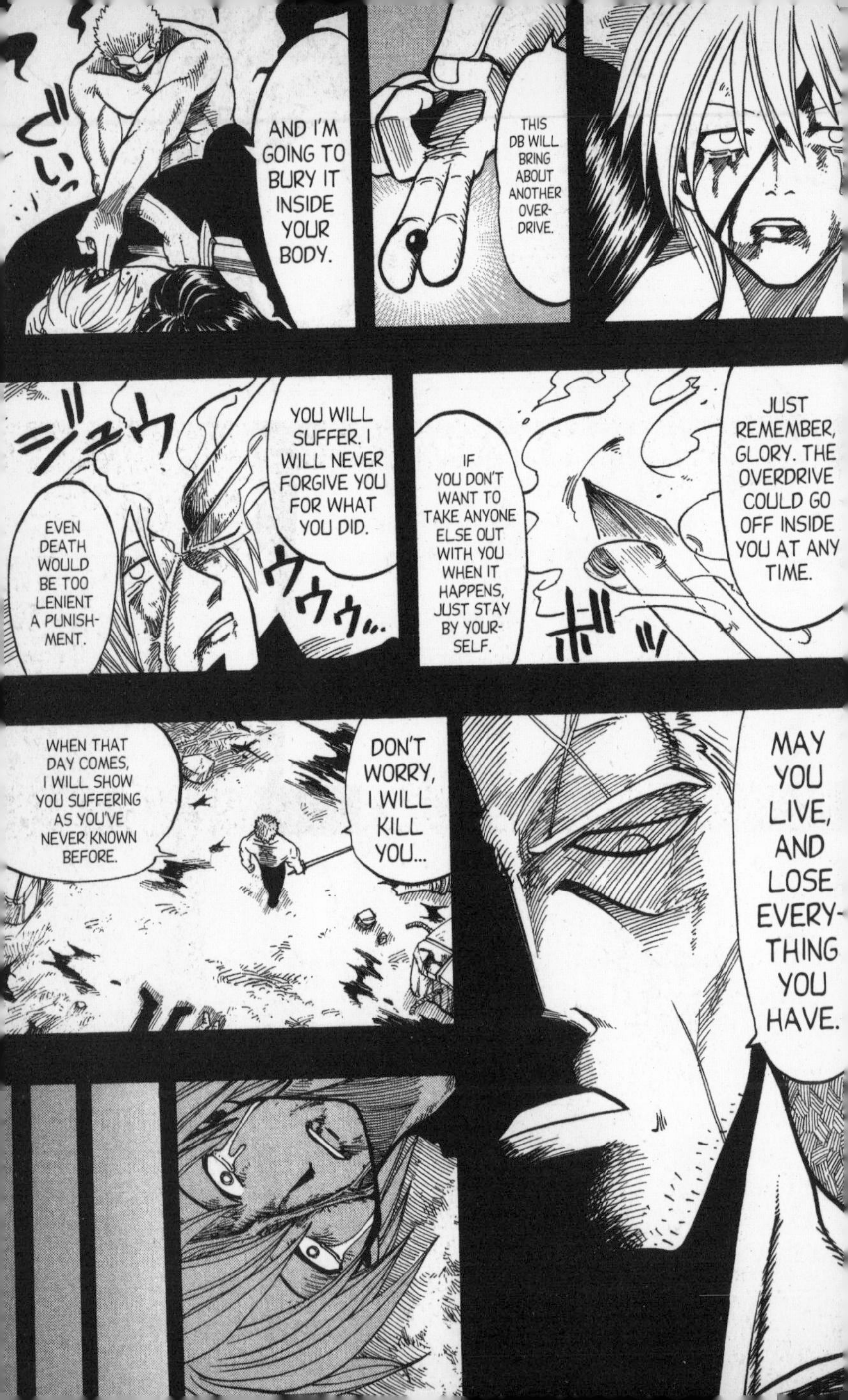
THIS DB WILL BRING ABOUT ANOTHER OVER-DRIVE.
AND I'M GOING TO BURY IT INSIDE YOUR BODY.
ぐいっ
JUST REMEMBER, GLORY. THE OVERDRIVE COULD GO OFF INSIDE YOU AT ANY TIME.
IF YOU DON'T WANT TO TAKE ANYONE ELSE OUT WITH YOU WHEN IT HAPPENS, JUST STAY BY YOUR-SELF.
ボッ
YOU WILL SUFFER. I WILL NEVER FORGIVE YOU FOR WHAT YOU DID.
ジュウ
ウウウ…
EVEN DEATH WOULD BE TOO LENIENT A PUNISH-MENT.
MAY YOU LIVE, AND LOSE EVERY-THING YOU HAVE.
DON'T WORRY, I WILL KILL YOU...
WHEN THAT DAY COMES, I WILL SHOW YOU SUFFERING AS YOU'VE NEVER KNOWN BEFORE.

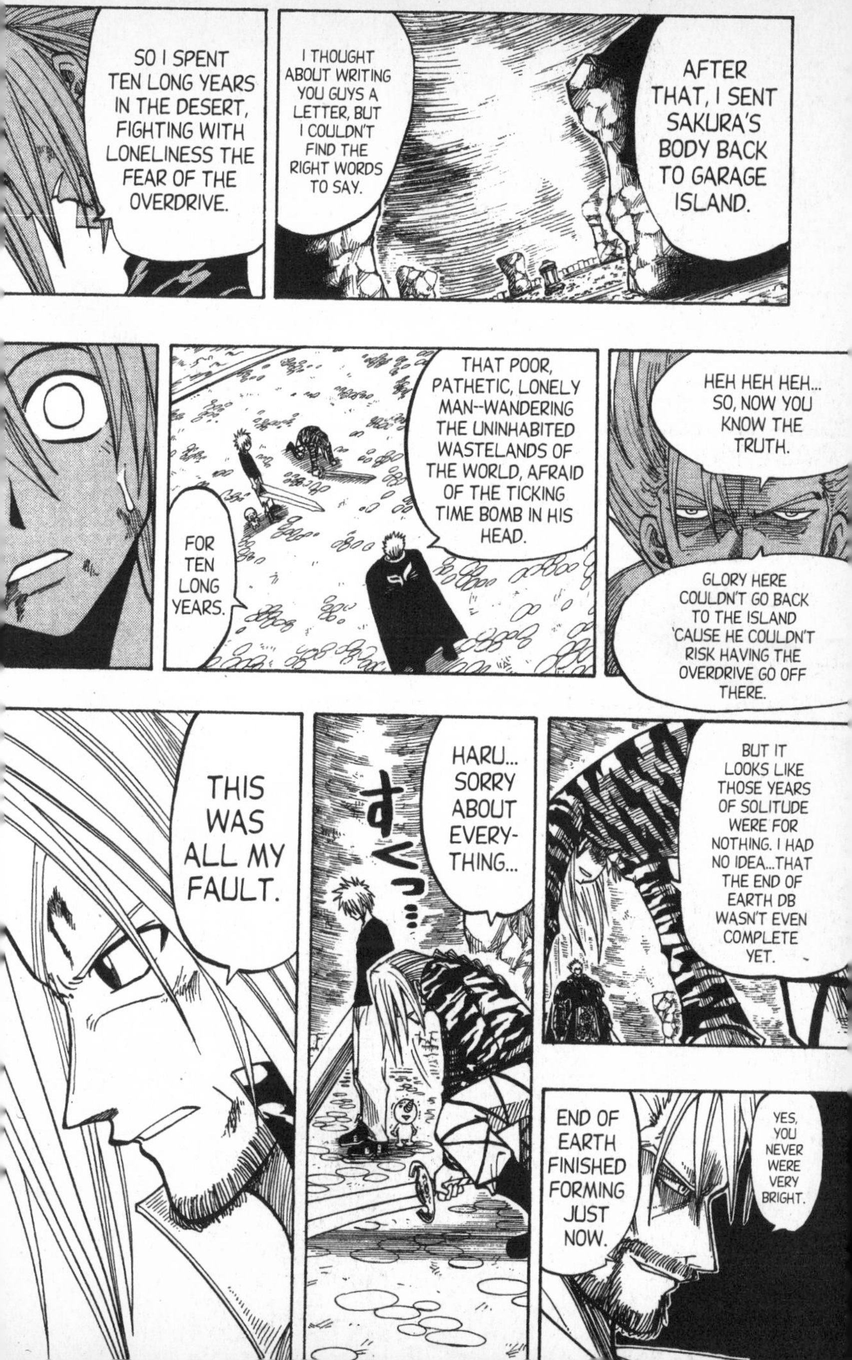
AFTER THAT, I SENT SAKURA'S BODY BACK TO GARAGE ISLAND.
I THOUGHT ABOUT WRITING YOU GUYS A LETTER, BUT I COULDN'T FIND THE RIGHT WORDS TO SAY.
SO I SPENT TEN LONG YEARS IN THE DESERT, FIGHTING WITH LONELINESS THE FEAR OF THE OVERDRIVE.
HEH HEH HEH... SO, NOW YOU KNOW THE TRUTH.
GLORY HERE COULDN'T GO BACK TO THE ISLAND 'CAUSE HE COULDN'T RISK HAVING THE OVERDRIVE GO OFF THERE.
THAT POOR, PATHETIC, LONELY MAN--WANDERING THE UNINHABITED WASTELANDS OF THE WORLD, AFRAID OF THE TICKING TIME BOMB IN HIS HEAD.
FOR TEN LONG YEARS.
BUT IT LOOKS LIKE THOSE YEARS OF SOLITUDE WERE FOR NOTHING. I HAD NO IDEA...THAT THE END OF EARTH DB WASN'T EVEN COMPLETE YET.
YES, YOU NEVER WERE VERY BRIGHT.
END OF EARTH FINISHED FORMING JUST NOW.
HARU... SORRY ABOUT EVERY-THING...
すくっ…
THIS WAS ALL MY FAULT.

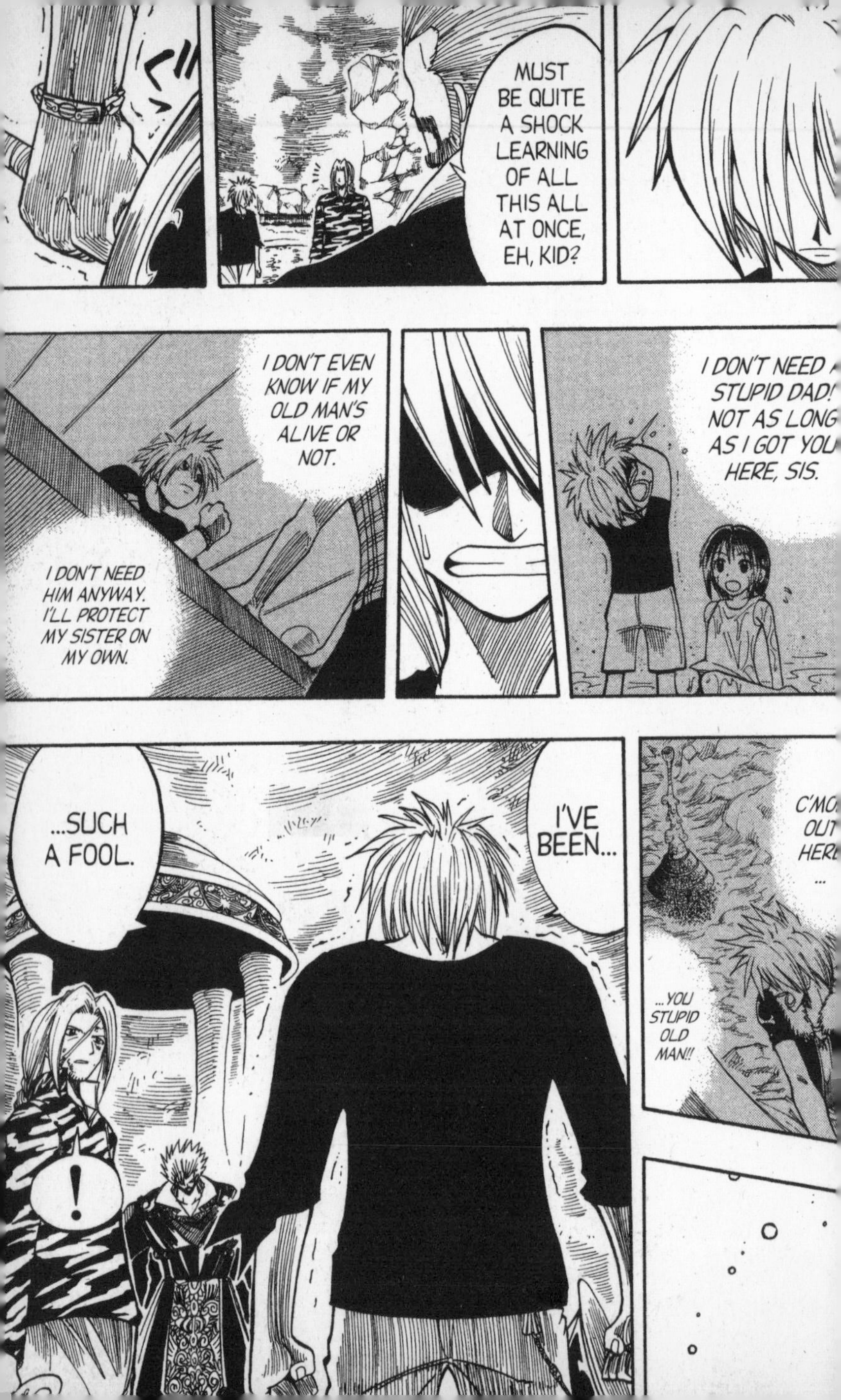

MUST BE QUITE A SHOCK LEARNING OF ALL THIS ALL AT ONCE, EH, KID?
I DON'T NEED STUPID DAD! NOT AS LONG AS I GOT YOU HERE, SIS.
I DON'T EVEN KNOW IF MY OLD MAN'S ALIVE OR NOT.
I DON'T NEED HIM ANYWAY. I'LL PROTECT MY SISTER ON MY OWN.
...YOU STUPID OLD MAN!!
I'VE BEEN...
...SUCH A FOOL.
!

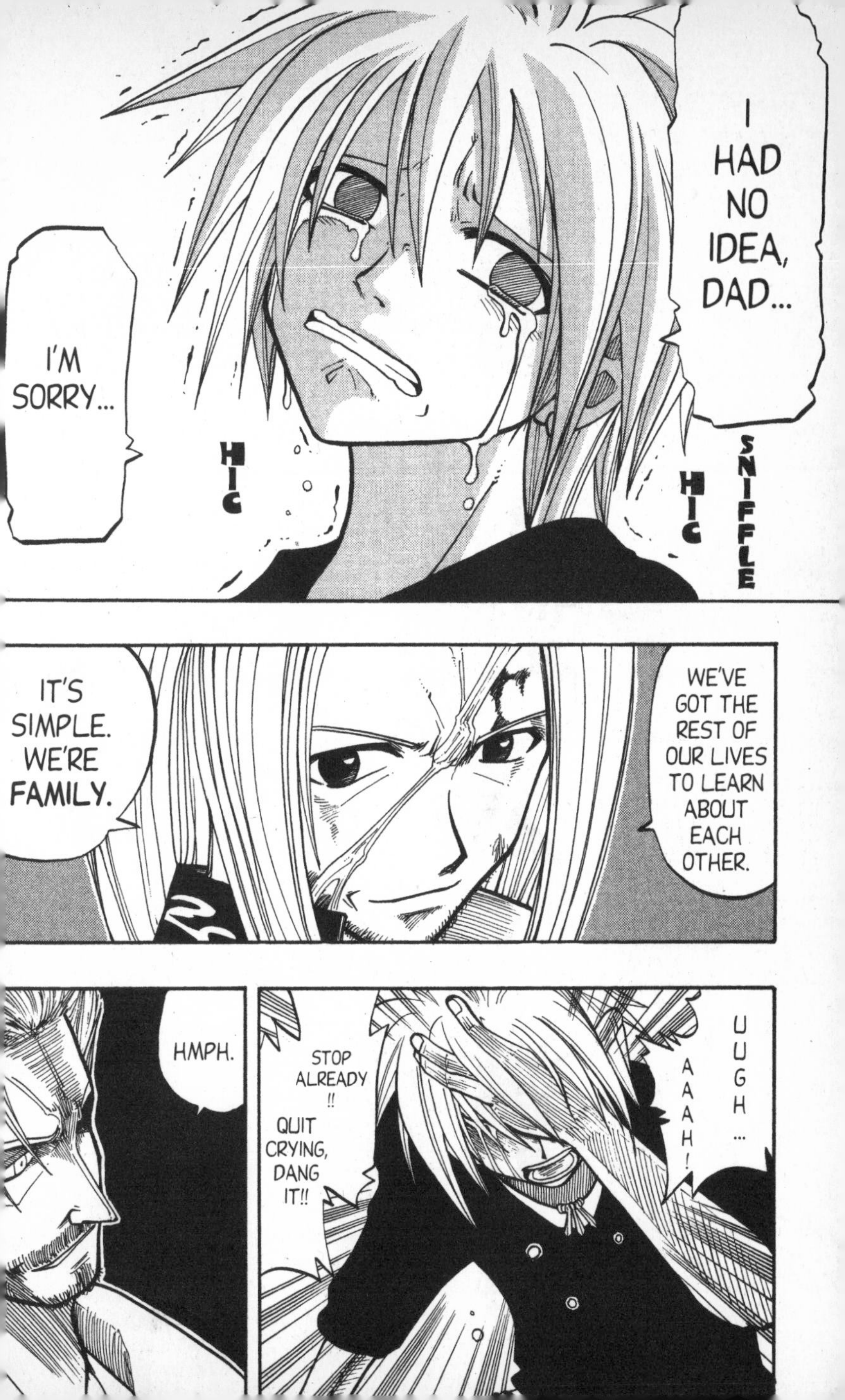
I HAD NO IDEA, DAD...
SNIFFLE
HIC
HIC
I'M SORRY...
WE'VE GOT THE REST OF OUR LIVES TO LEARN ABOUT EACH OTHER.
IT'S SIMPLE. WE'RE **FAMILY**.
UUGH...
AAAAH!
STOP ALREADY!!
QUIT CRYING, DANG IT!!
HMPH.

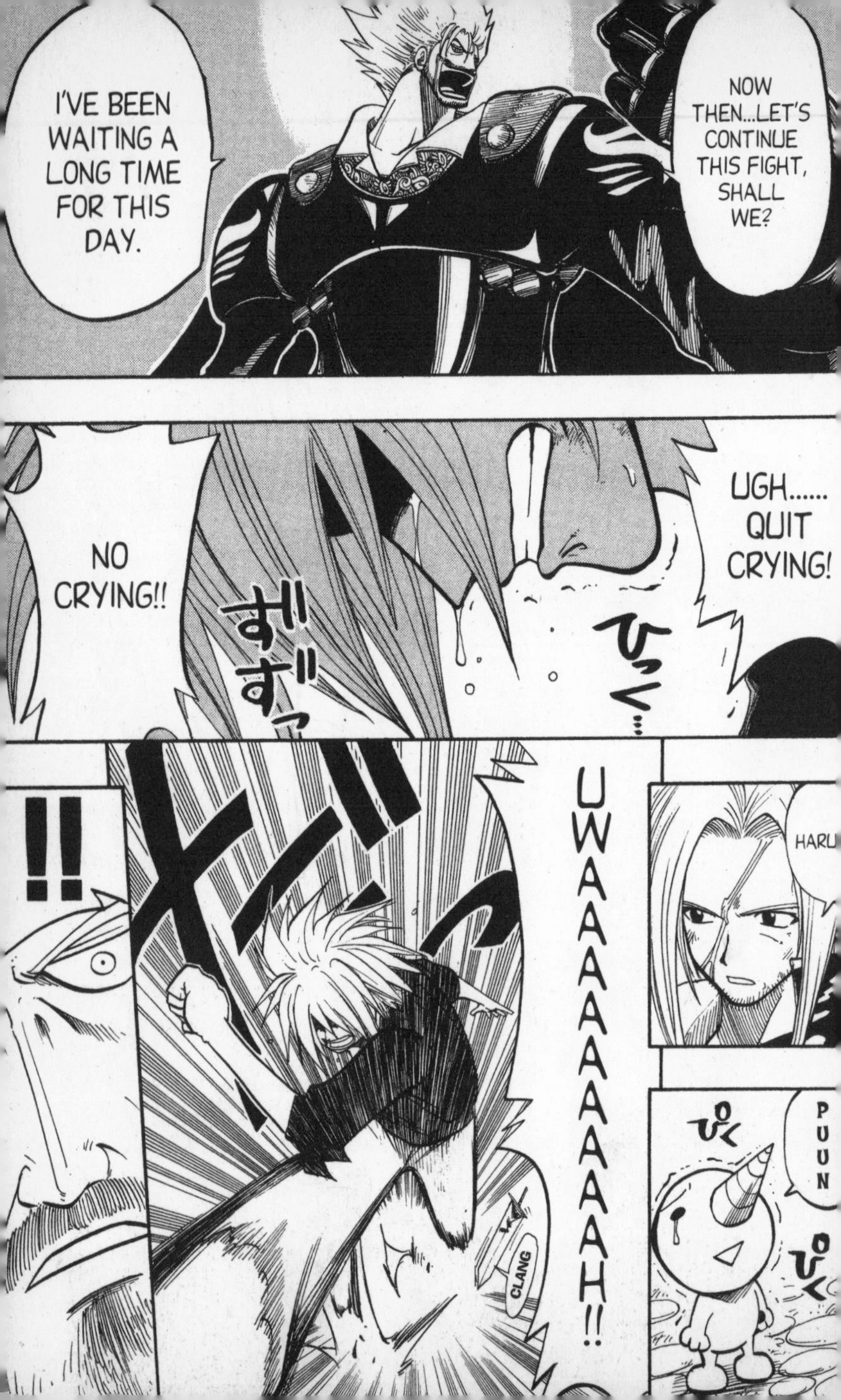
NOW THEN...LET'S CONTINUE THIS FIGHT, SHALL WE?
I'VE BEEN WAITING A LONG TIME FOR THIS DAY.
UGH...... QUIT CRYING!
ひっく…
ずずっ
NO CRYING!!
HARU
PUUN
ぴく
ぴく
UWAAAAAAAAAAH!!
CLANG
!!

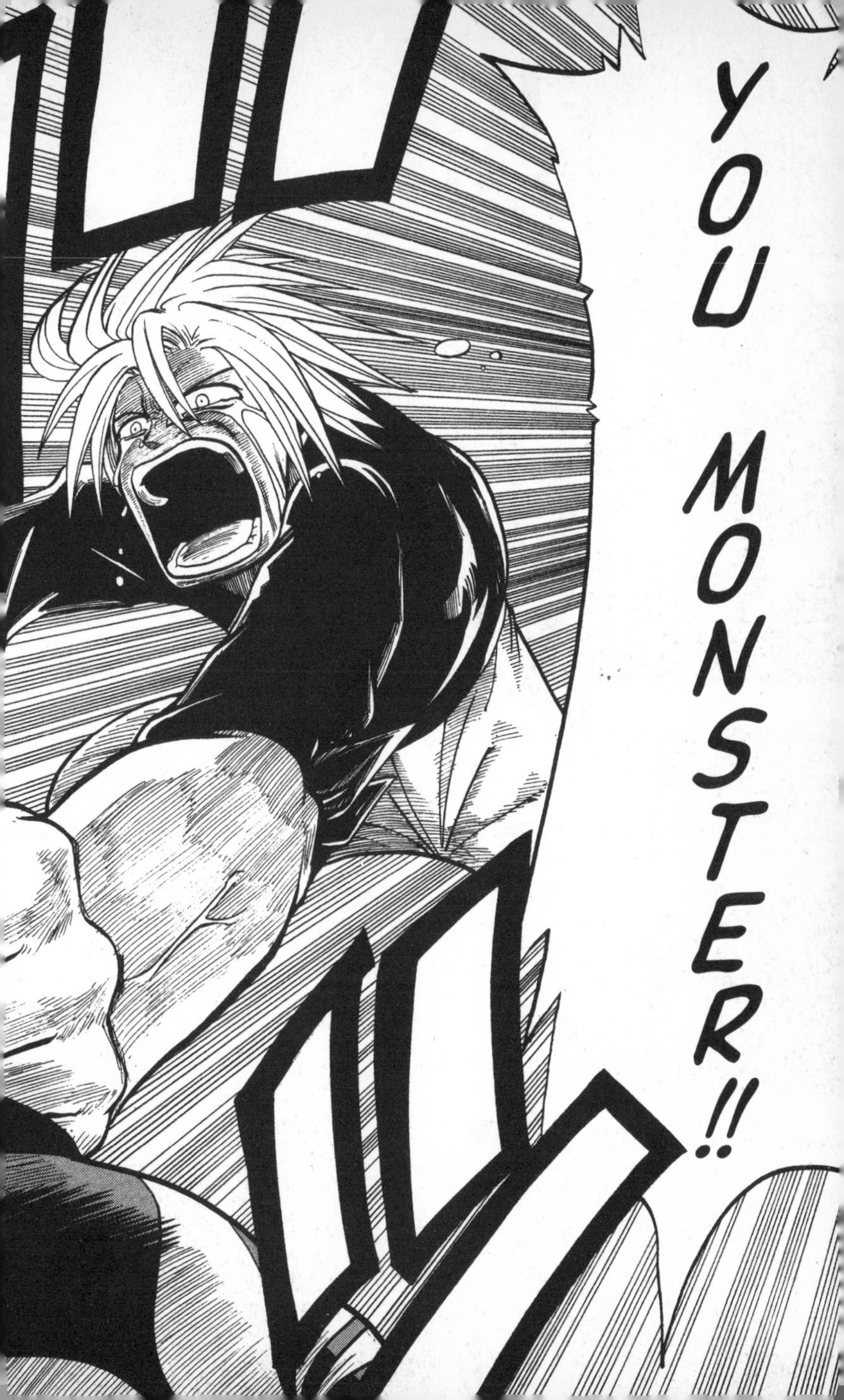
YOU MONSTER!!

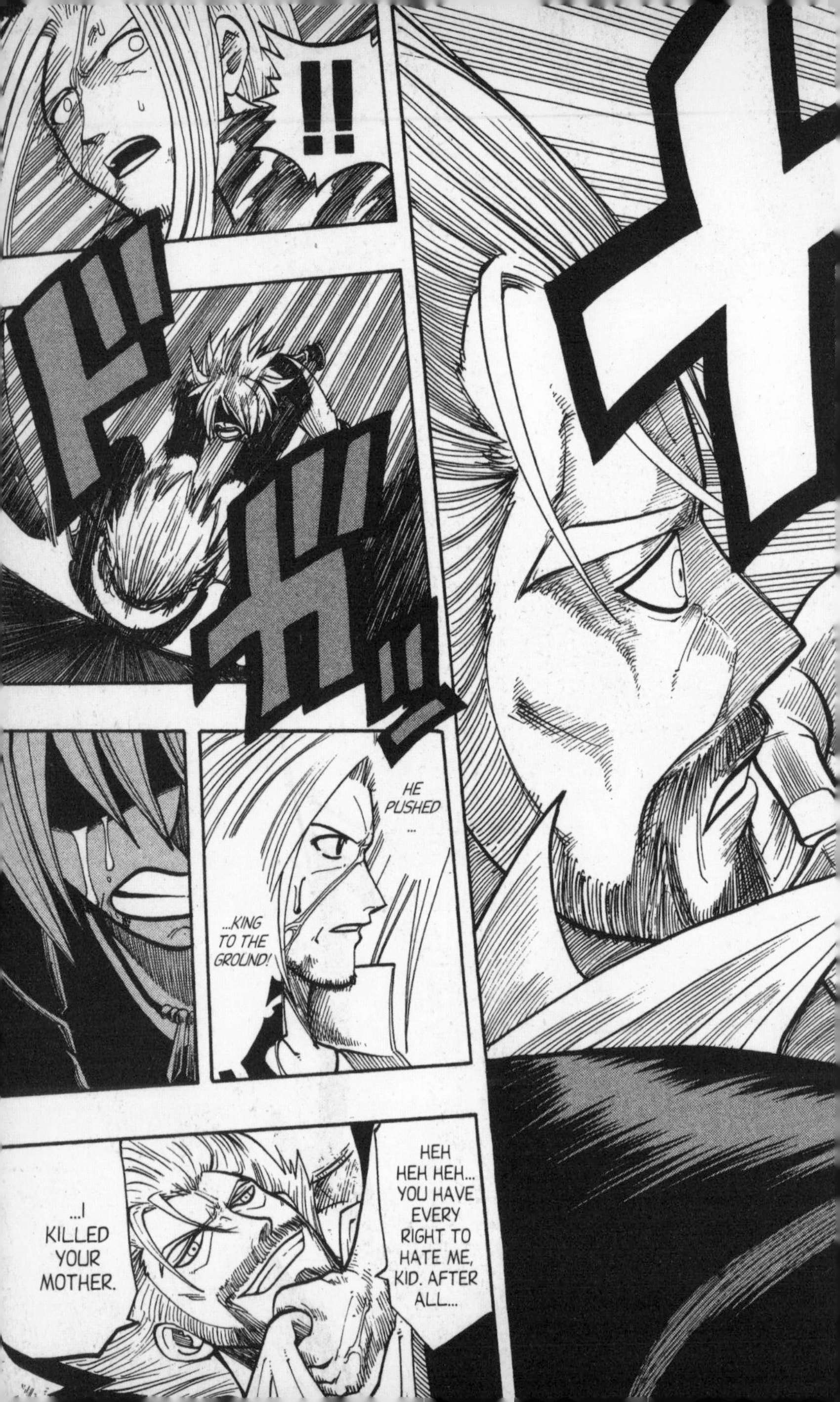
!!
HE PUSHED ...
...KING TO THE GROUND!
HEH HEH HEH... YOU HAVE EVERY RIGHT TO HATE ME, KID. AFTER ALL...
...I KILLED YOUR MOTHER.

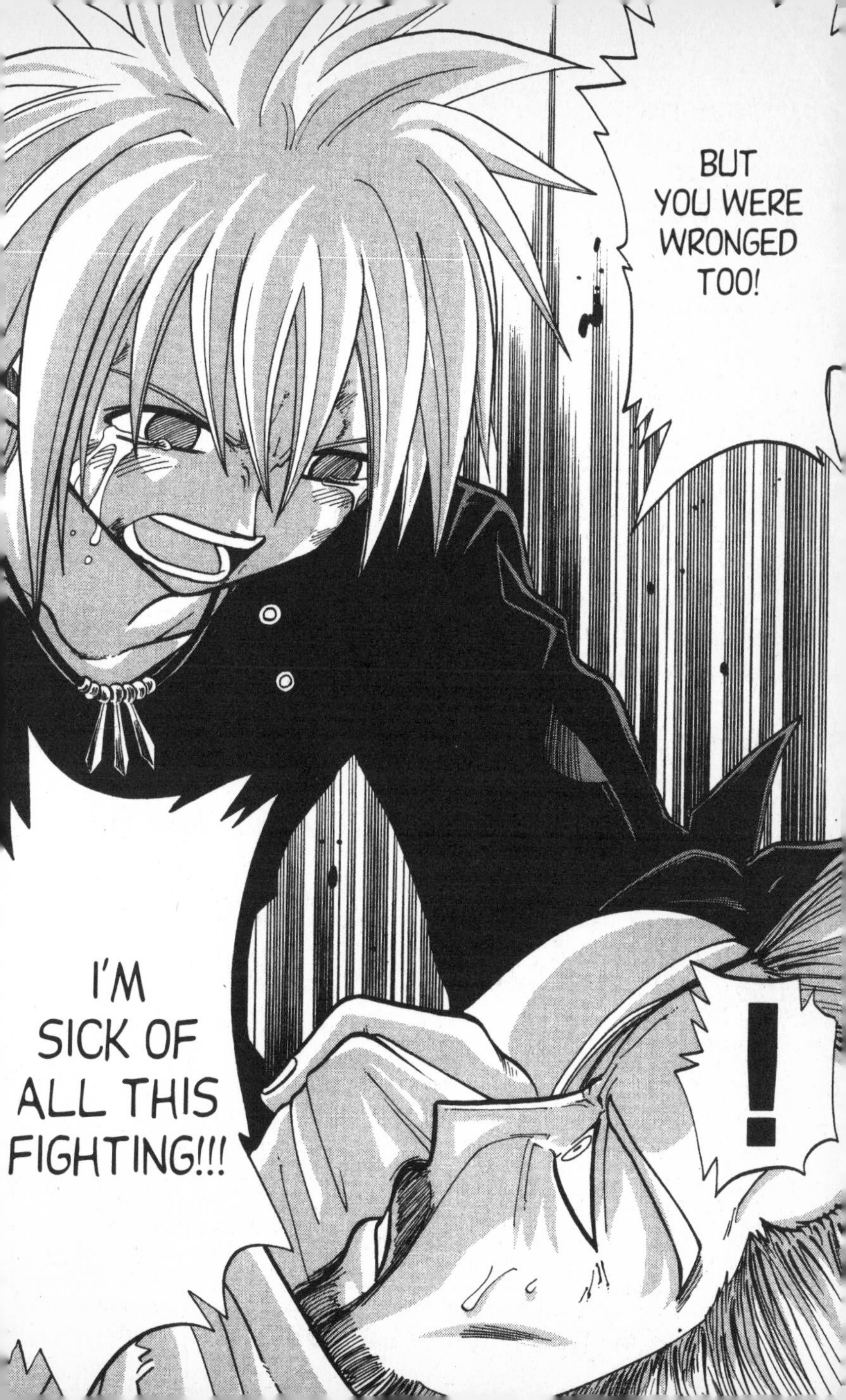
BUT YOU WERE WRONGED TOO!
I'M SICK OF ALL THIS FIGHTING!!!
!

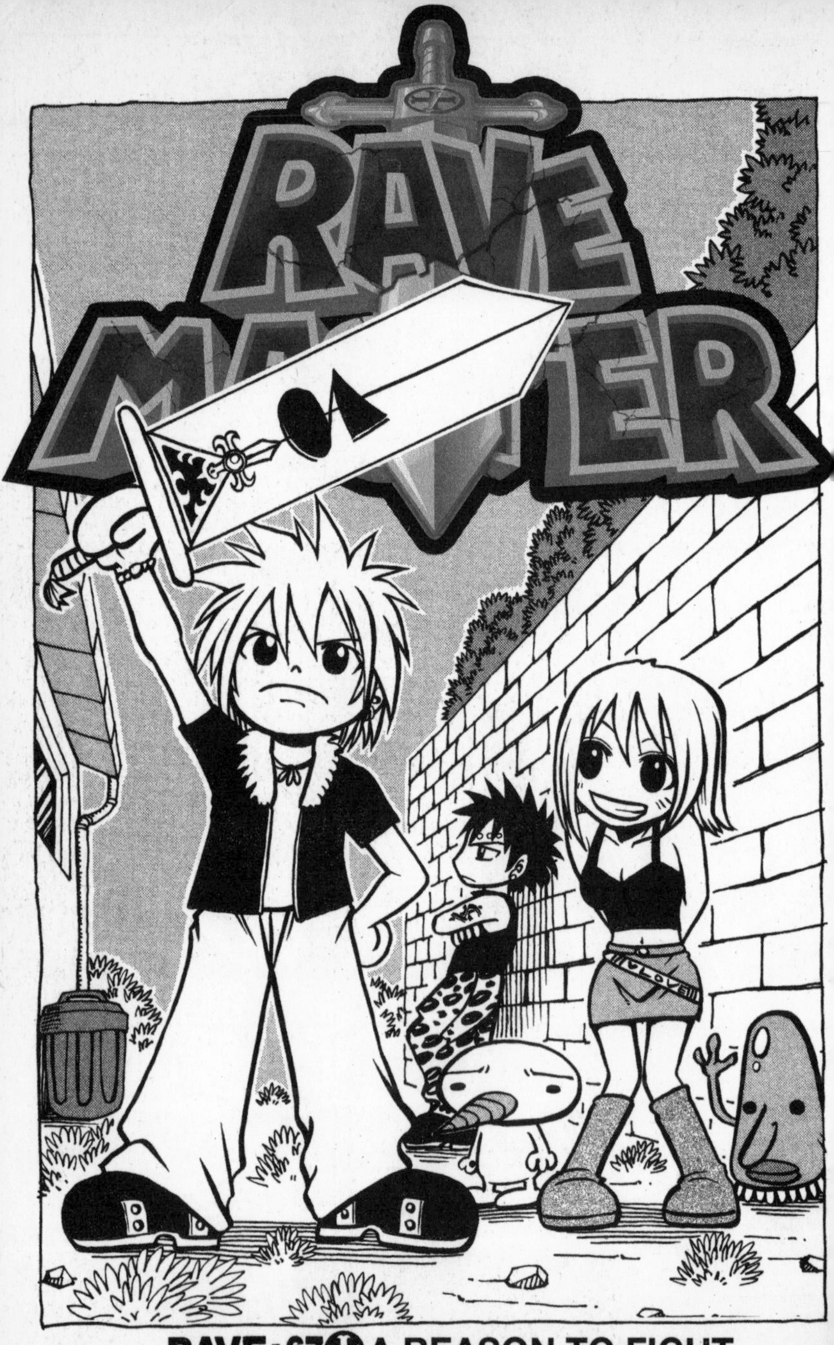
RAVE MASTER
LOVE

RAVE:67 A REASON TO FIGHT

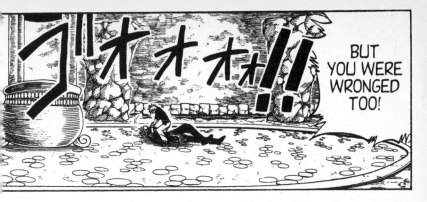

BUT YOU WERE WRONGED TOO!

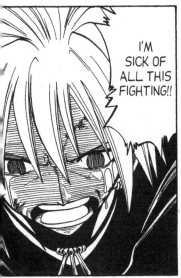

I'M SICK OF ALL THIS FIGHTING!!

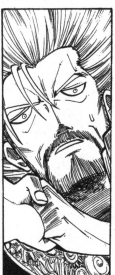

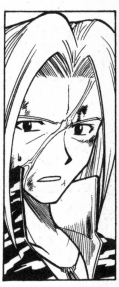

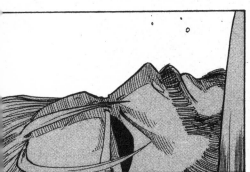

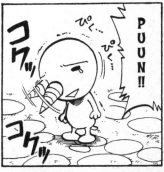

PUUN!!

50

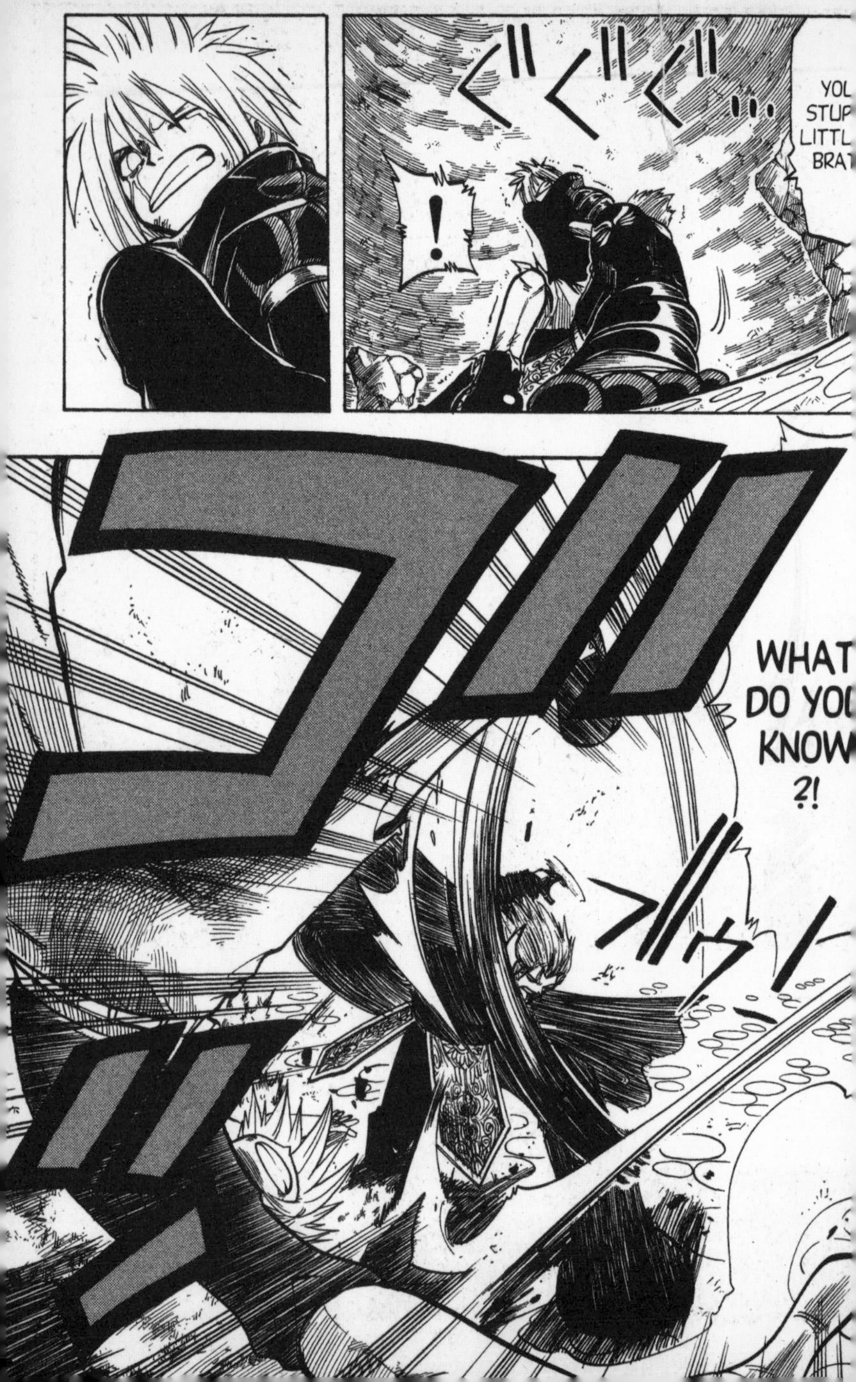
YOU
STUP
LITTL
BRAT
ぐぐぐ…
!
WHAT
DO YO
KNOW
?!

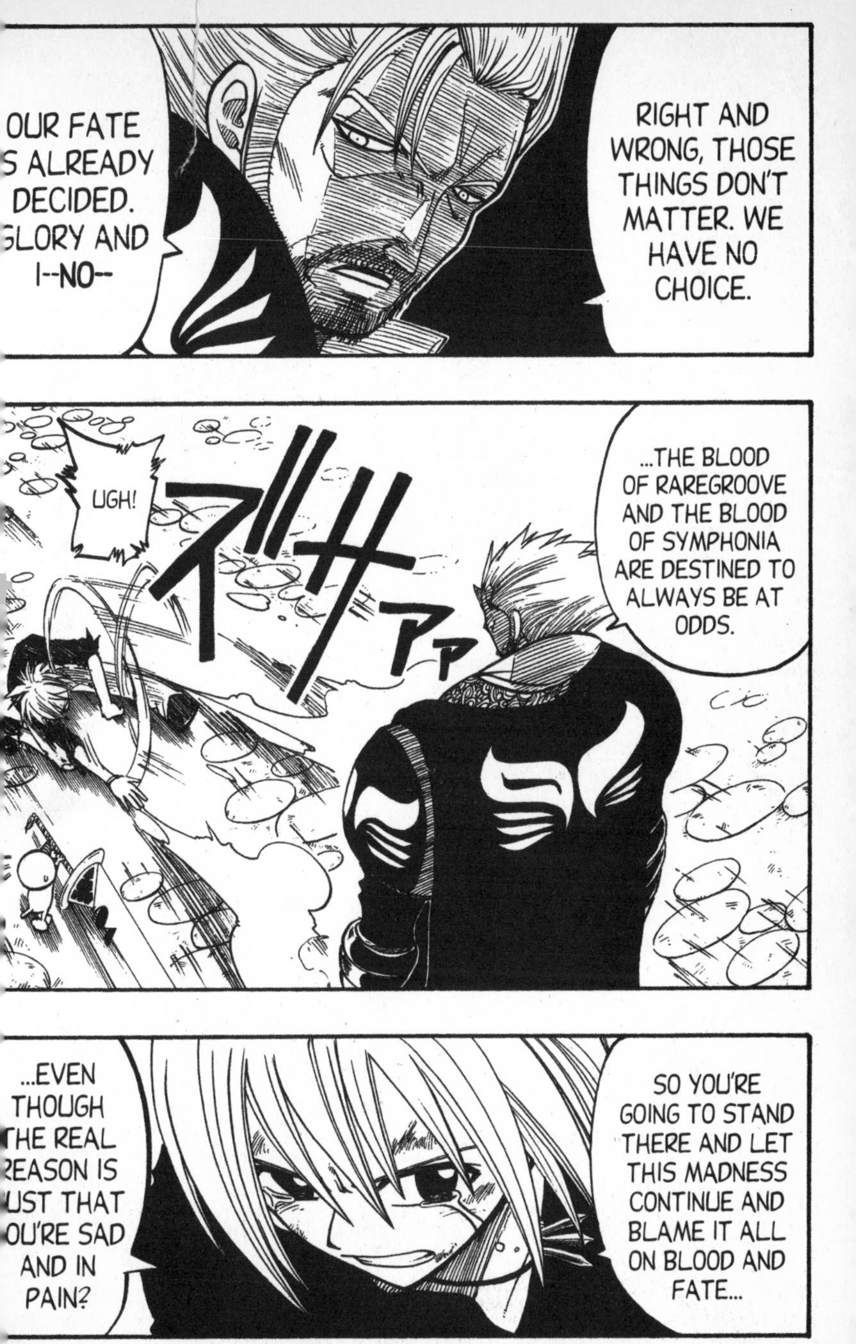
RIGHT AND WRONG, THOSE THINGS DON'T MATTER. WE HAVE NO CHOICE.
OUR FATE IS ALREADY DECIDED. GLORY AND I--NO--
...THE BLOOD OF RAREGROOVE AND THE BLOOD OF SYMPHONIA ARE DESTINED TO ALWAYS BE AT ODDS.
ズザァァ
UGH!
SO YOU'RE GOING TO STAND THERE AND LET THIS MADNESS CONTINUE AND BLAME IT ALL ON BLOOD AND FATE...
...EVEN THOUGH THE REAL REASON IS JUST THAT YOU'RE SAD AND IN PAIN?

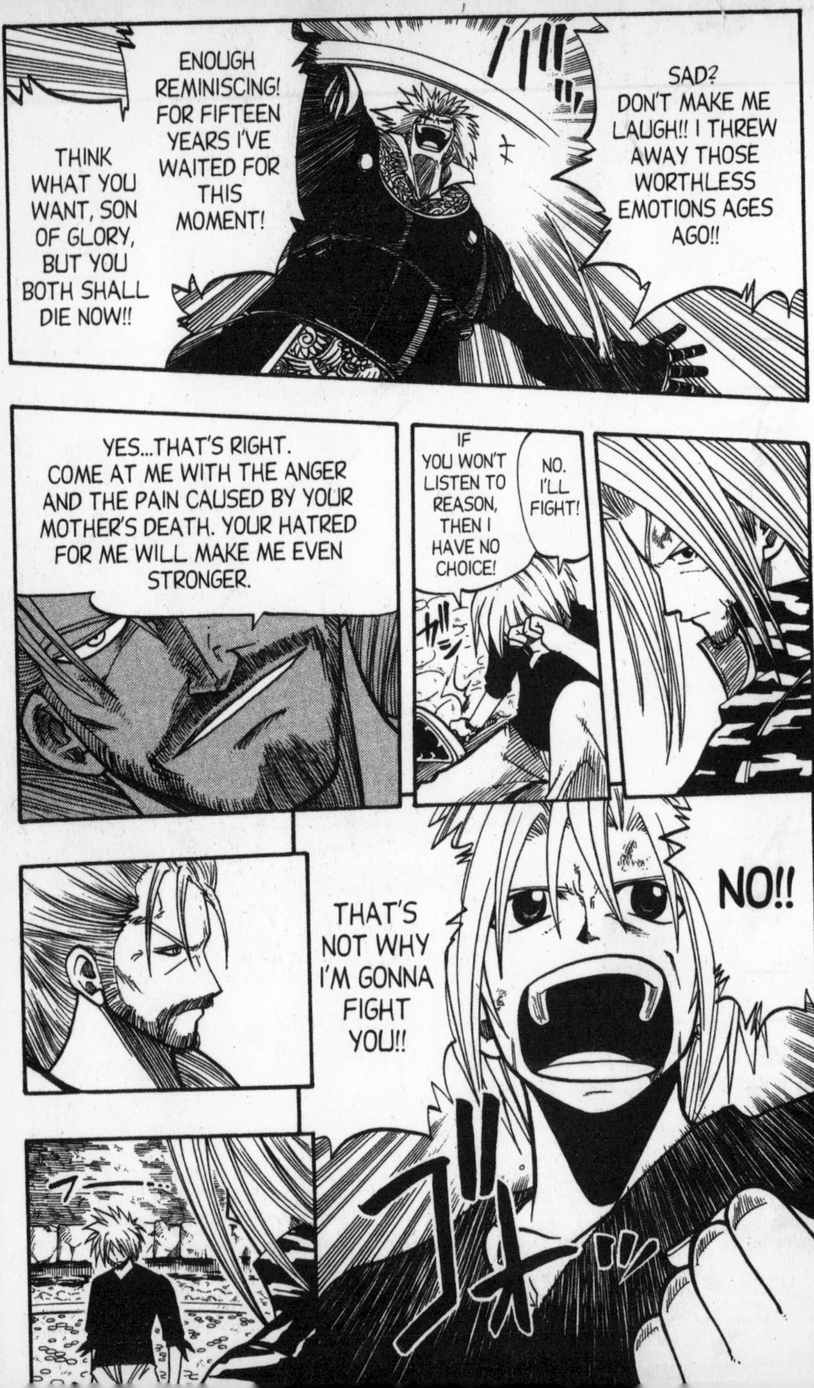
SAD? DON'T MAKE ME LAUGH!! I THREW AWAY THOSE WORTHLESS EMOTIONS AGES AGO!!
ENOUGH REMINISCING! FOR FIFTEEN YEARS I'VE WAITED FOR THIS MOMENT!
THINK WHAT YOU WANT, SON OF GLORY, BUT YOU BOTH SHALL DIE NOW!!
NO. I'LL FIGHT!
IF YOU WON'T LISTEN TO REASON, THEN I HAVE NO CHOICE!
YES...THAT'S RIGHT. COME AT ME WITH THE ANGER AND THE PAIN CAUSED BY YOUR MOTHER'S DEATH. YOUR HATRED FOR ME WILL MAKE ME EVEN STRONGER.
NO!!
THAT'S NOT WHY I'M GONNA FIGHT YOU!!

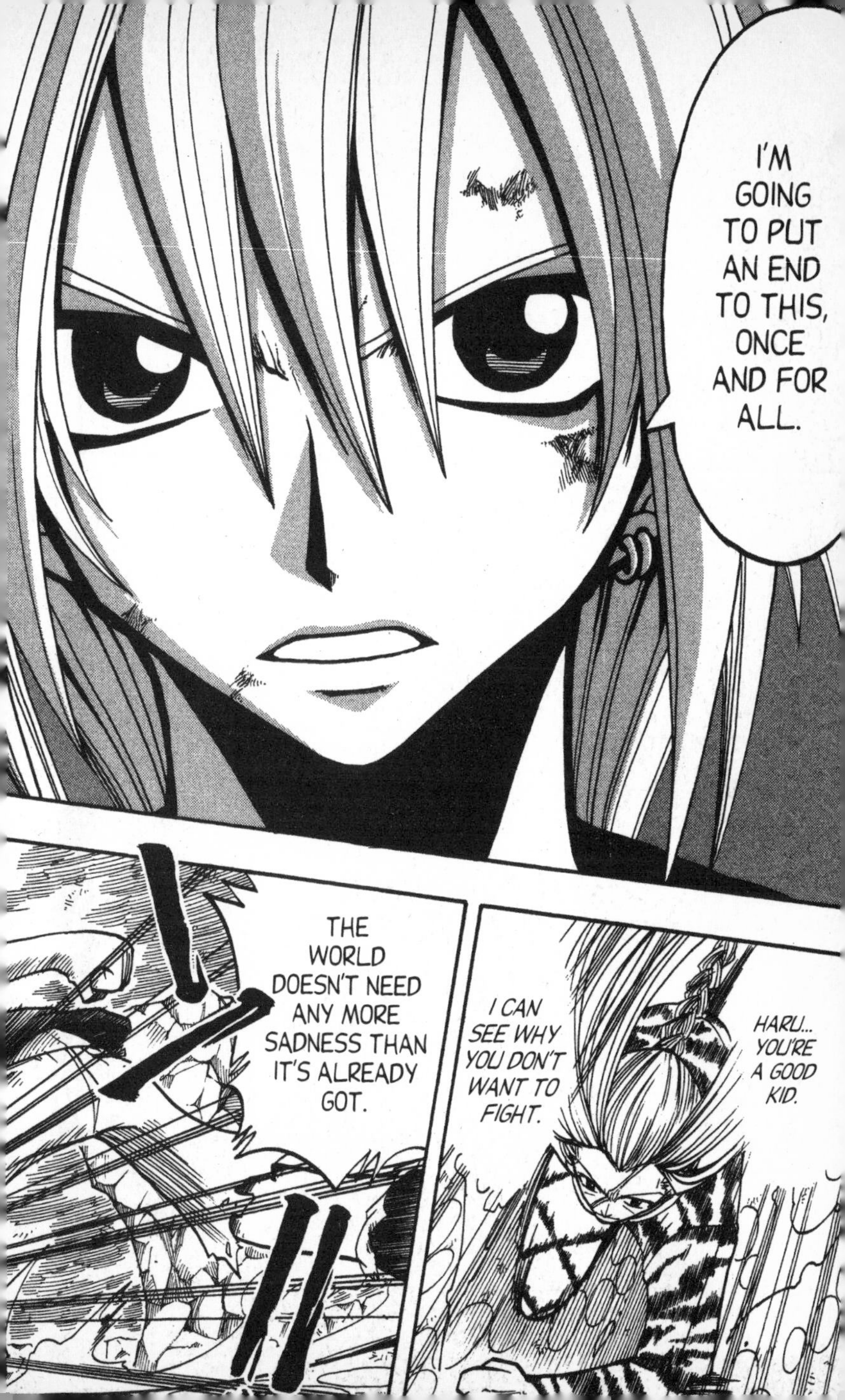
I'M GOING TO PUT AN END TO THIS, ONCE AND FOR ALL.
HARU... YOU'RE A GOOD KID.
I CAN SEE WHY YOU DON'T WANT TO FIGHT.
THE WORLD DOESN'T NEED ANY MORE SADNESS THAN IT'S ALREADY GOT.

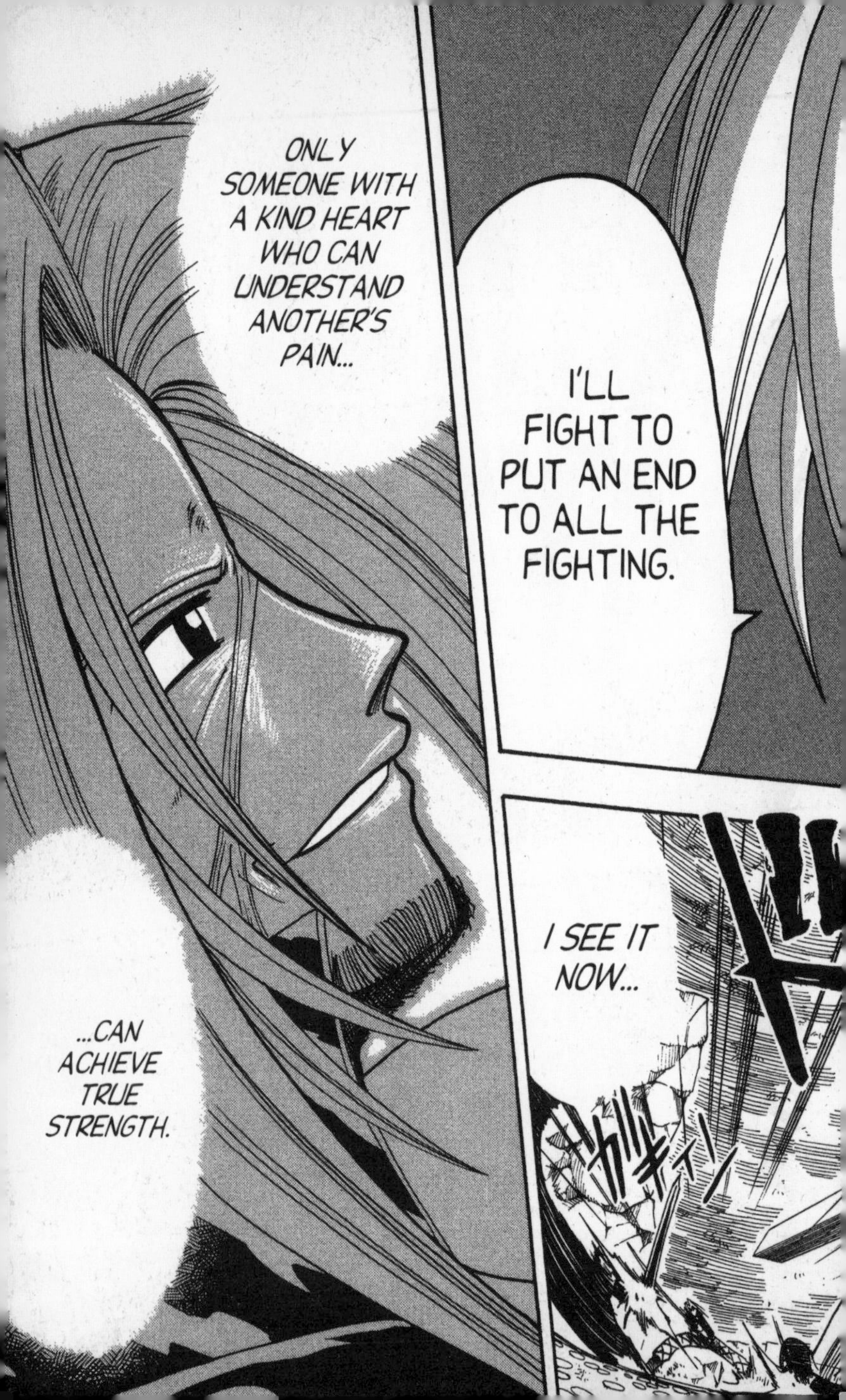
I'LL FIGHT TO PUT AN END TO ALL THE FIGHTING.
I SEE IT NOW...
ONLY SOMEONE WITH A KIND HEART WHO CAN UNDERSTAND ANOTHER'S PAIN...
...CAN ACHIEVE TRUE STRENGTH.

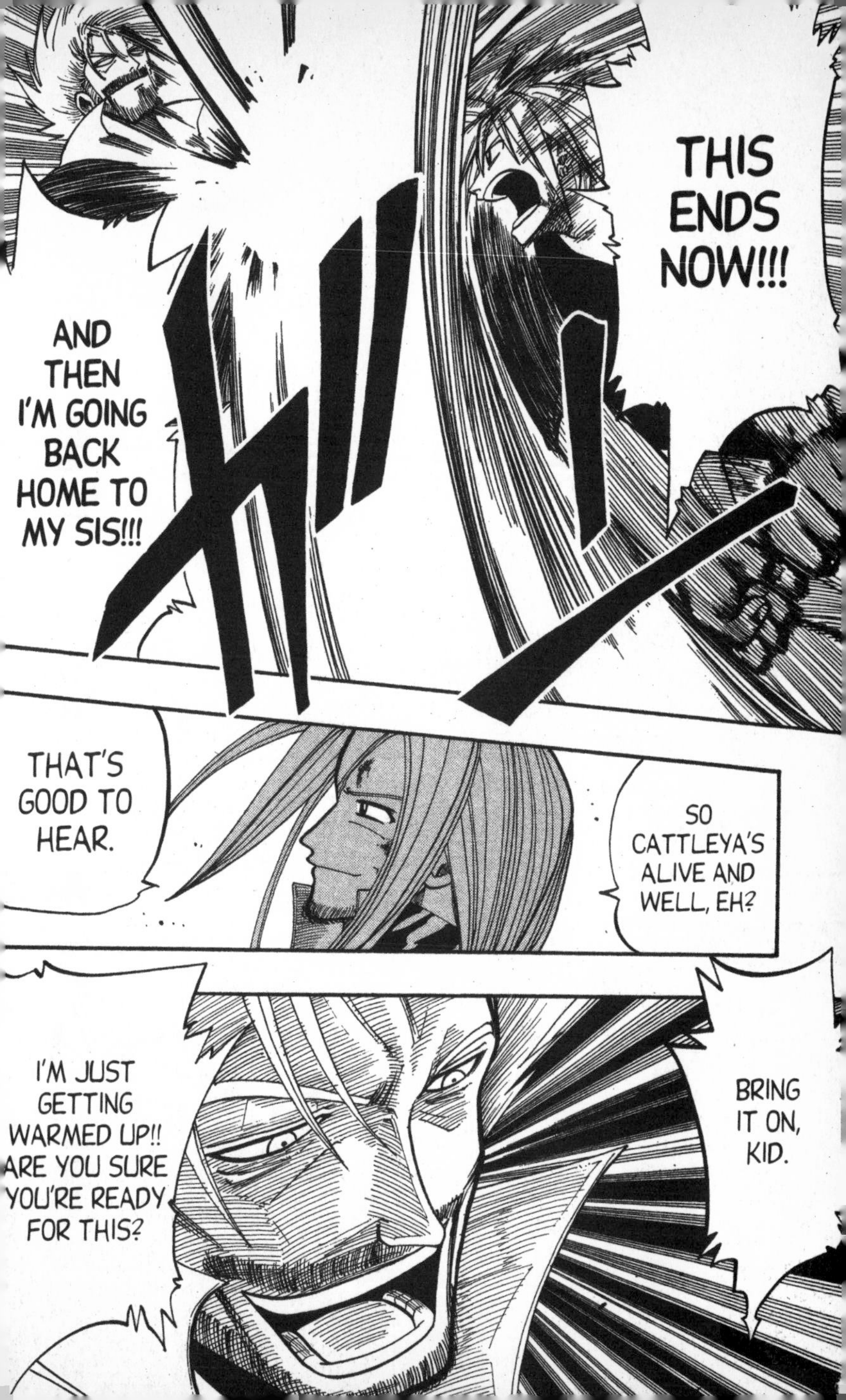
THIS ENDS NOW!!!
AND THEN I'M GOING BACK HOME TO MY SIS!!!
SO CATTLEYA'S ALIVE AND WELL, EH?
THAT'S GOOD TO HEAR.
BRING IT ON, KID.
I'M JUST GETTING WARMED UP!! ARE YOU SURE YOU'RE READY FOR THIS?

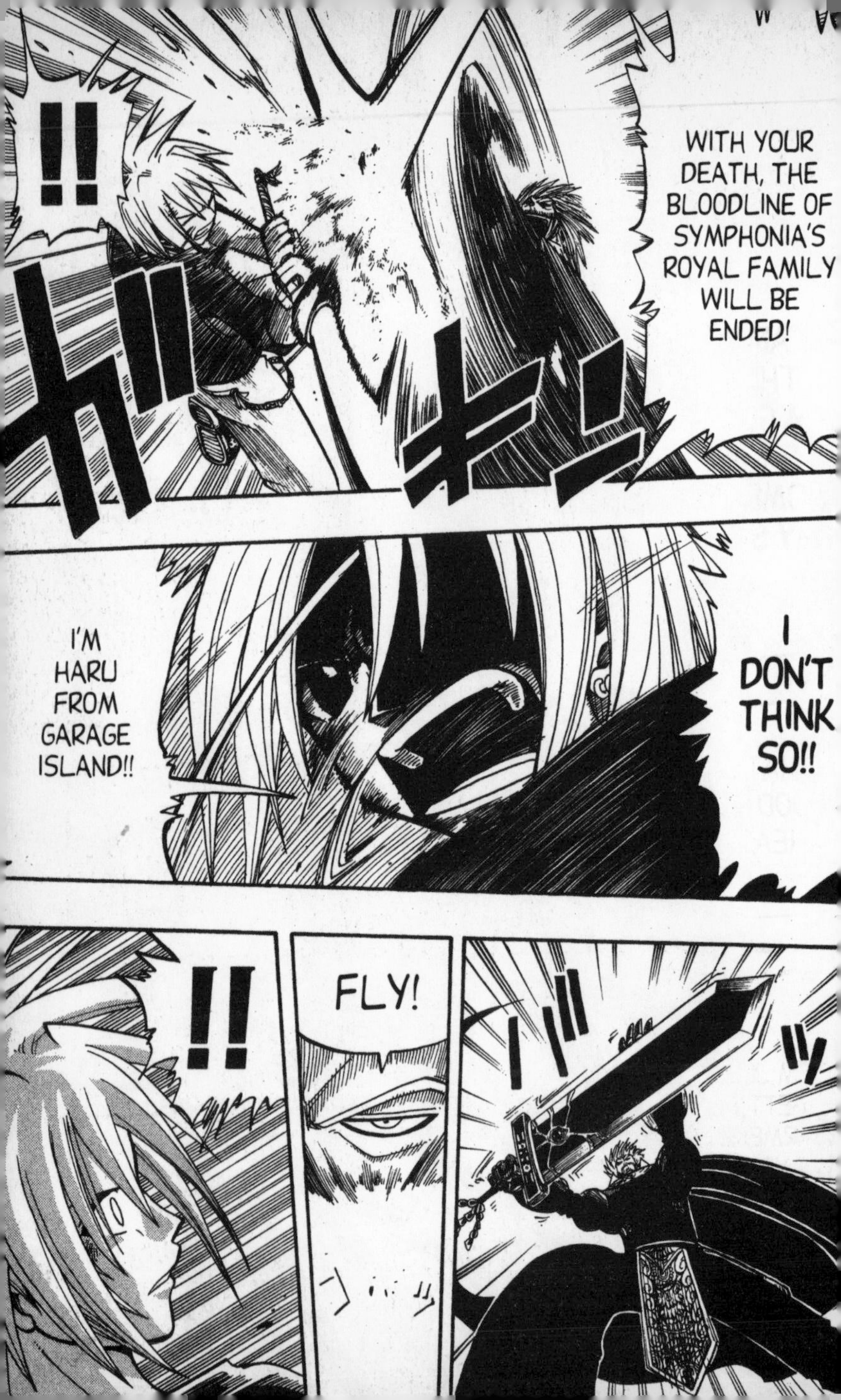
WITH YOUR DEATH, THE BLOODLINE OF SYMPHONIA'S ROYAL FAMILY WILL BE ENDED!
!!
I DON'T THINK SO!!
I'M HARU FROM GARAGE ISLAND!!
FLY!
!!

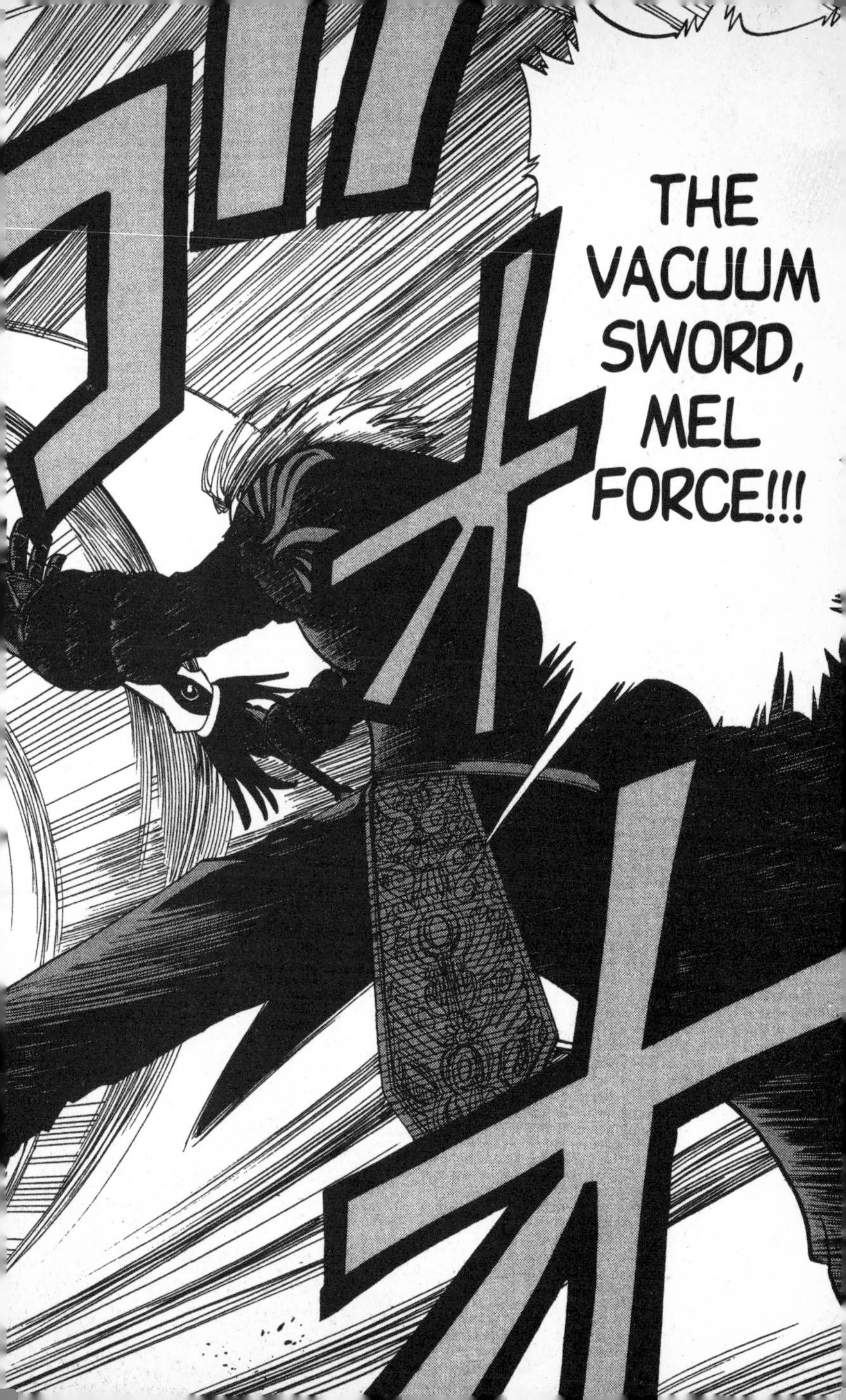
THE VACUUM SWORD, MEL FORCE!!!

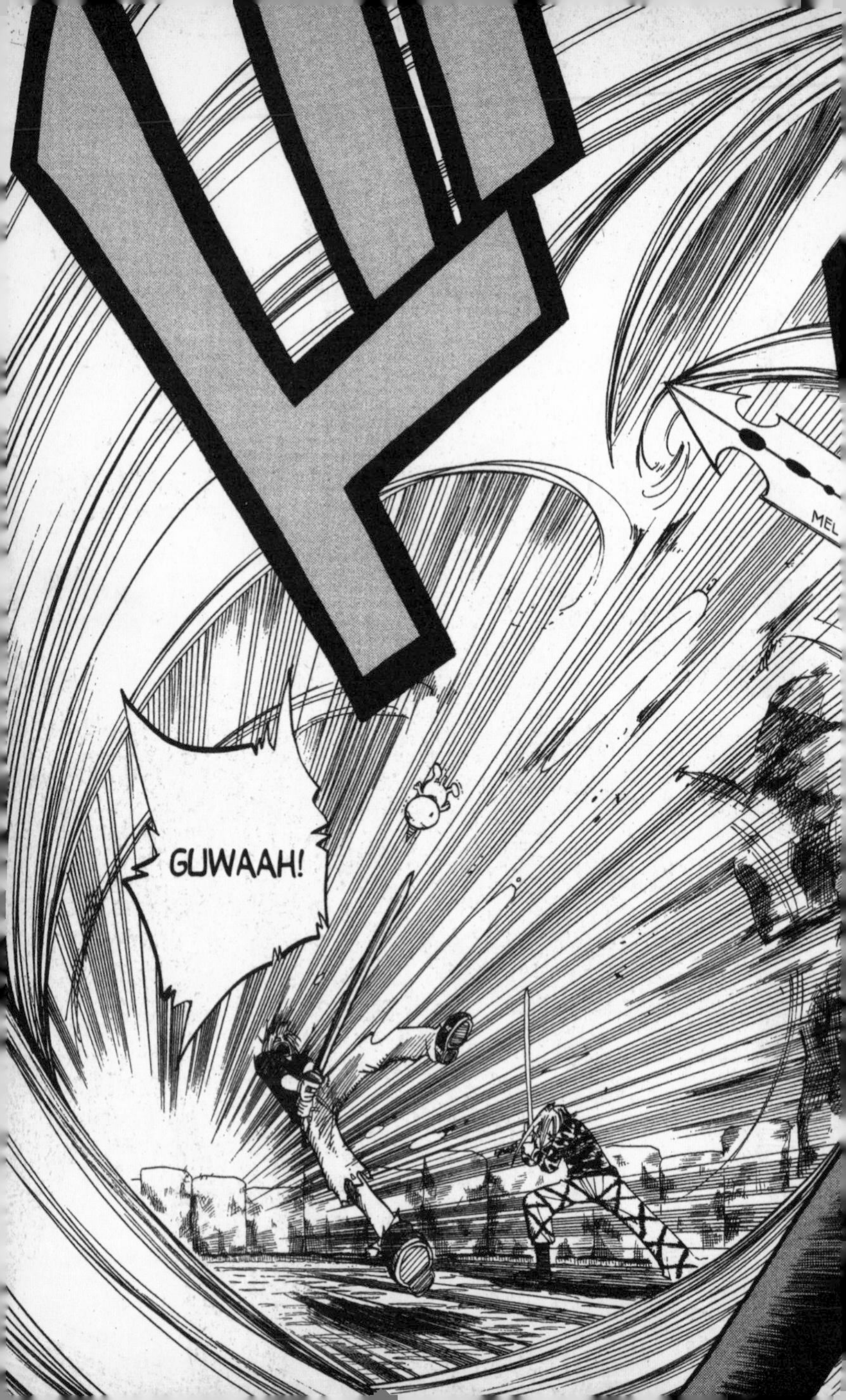
MEL
GUWAAH!

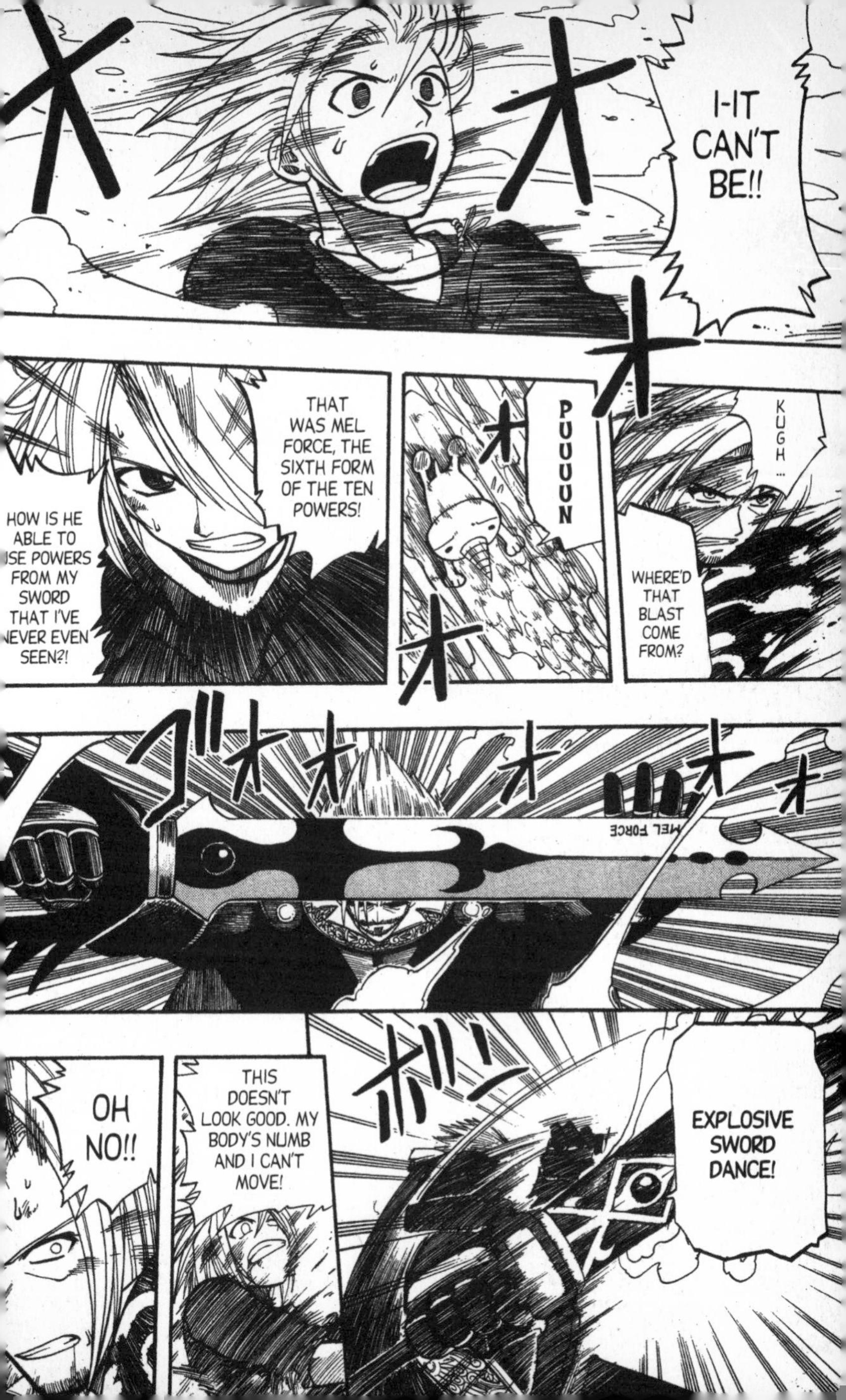
I-IT CAN'T BE!!
KUGH...
WHERE'D THAT BLAST COME FROM?
PUUUUUN
THAT WAS MEL FORCE, THE SIXTH FORM OF THE TEN POWERS!
HOW IS HE ABLE TO USE POWERS FROM MY SWORD THAT I'VE NEVER EVEN SEEN?!
MEL FORCE
EXPLOSIVE SWORD DANCE!
THIS DOESN'T LOOK GOOD. MY BODY'S NUMB AND I CAN'T MOVE!
OH NO!!

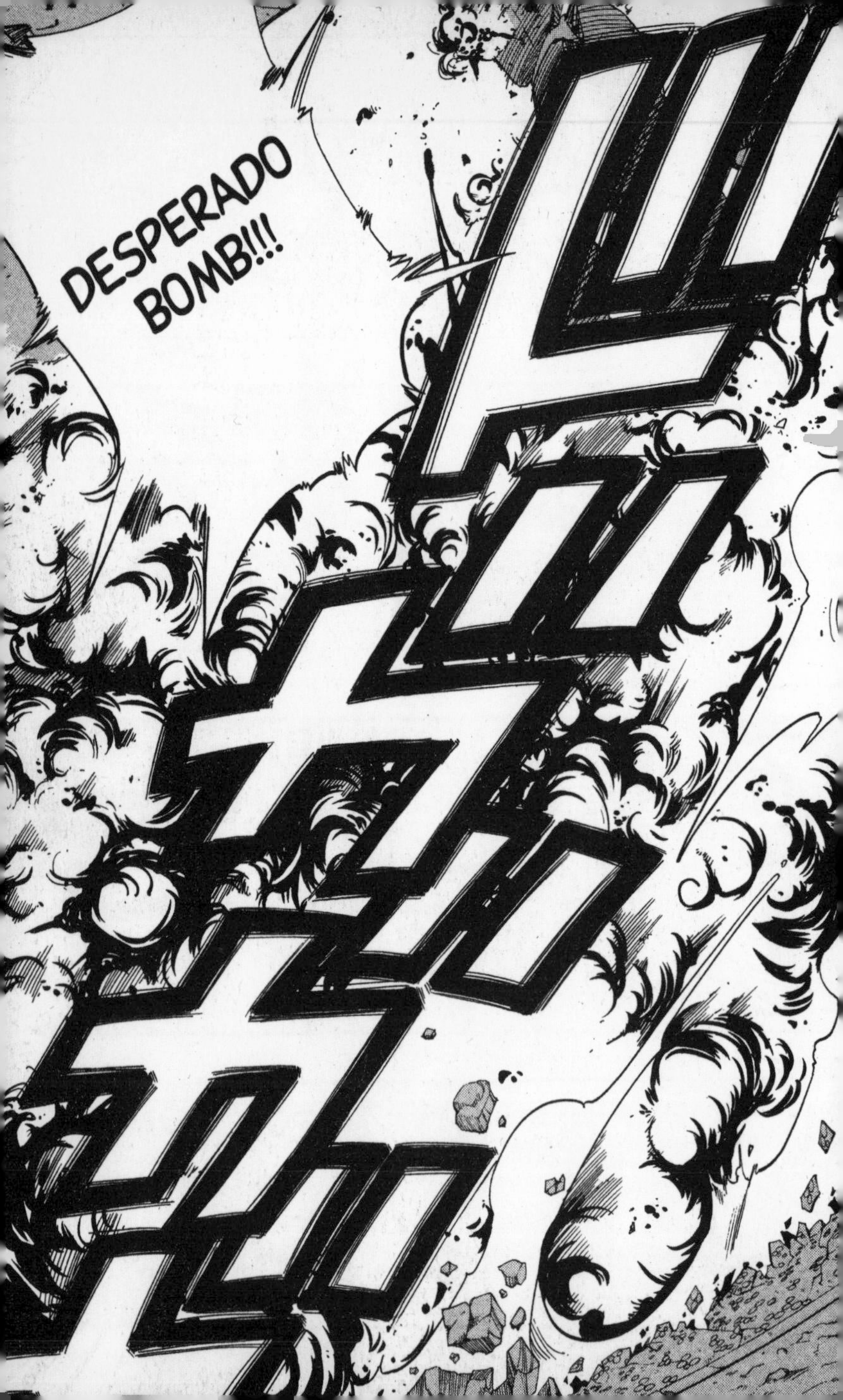
DESPERADO BOMB!!!

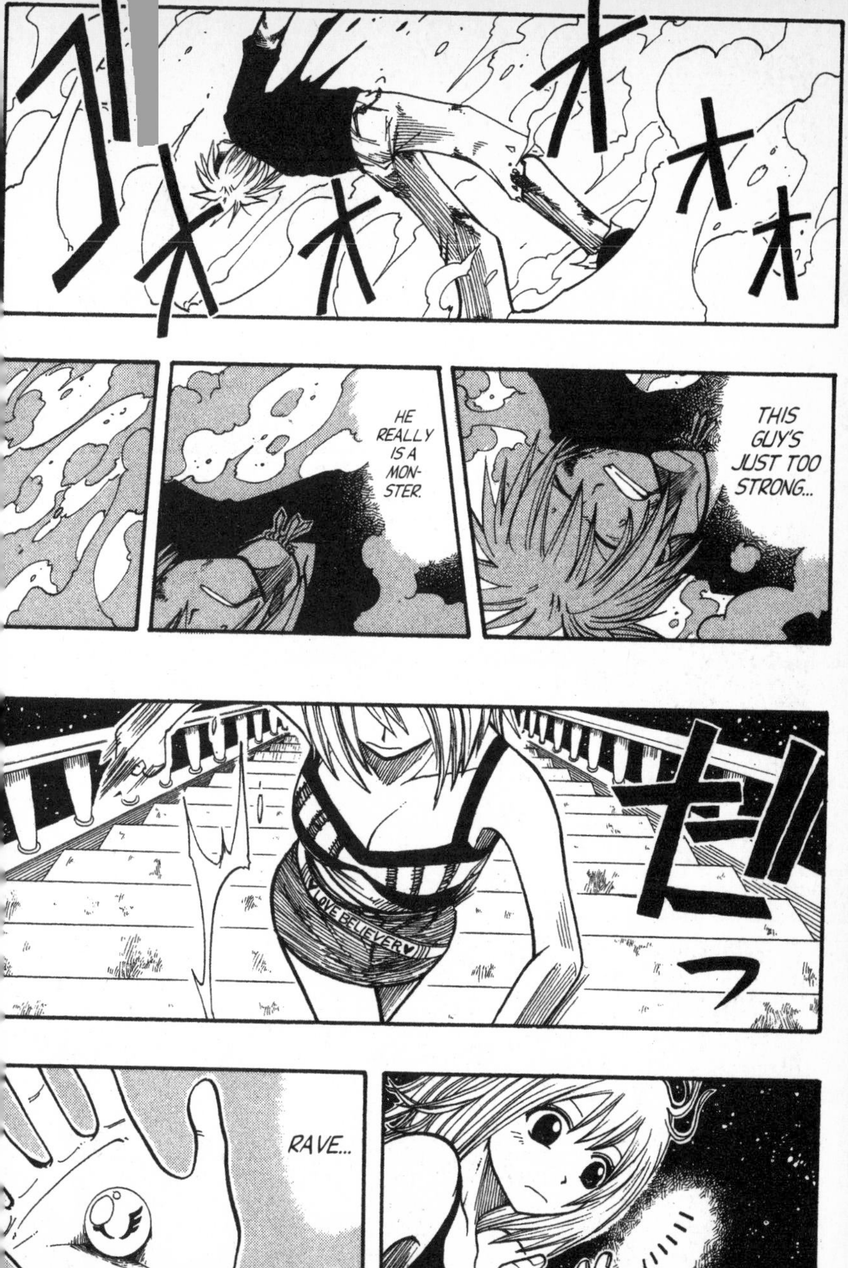
THIS GUY'S JUST TOO STRONG...
HE REALLY IS A MON-STER.
♥LOVE BELIEVER♥
RAVE...

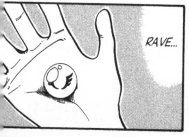

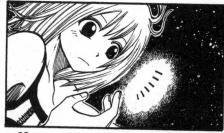

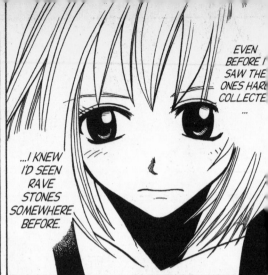

EVEN BEFORE I SAW THE ONES HAR COLLECTE ...
...I KNEW I'D SEEN RAVE STONES SOMEWHERE BEFORE.
AND I REMEMBER THIS TOWER TOO.
BUT I DON'T THINK I'VE EVER BEEN INSIDE IT.
たっ たっ たっ たっ
ぶるぶるっ
ARGH! I'M TIRED OF THINKIN'!
!
BING
I FOUND IT!
ピキ ピキキ
ピキ ピキキ ピキ ピキ

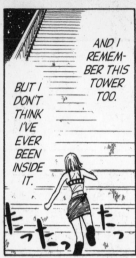

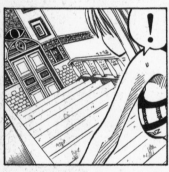

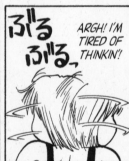

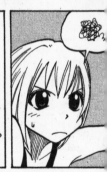

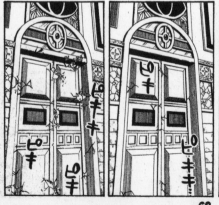

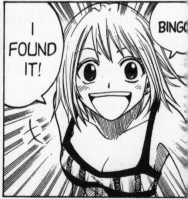

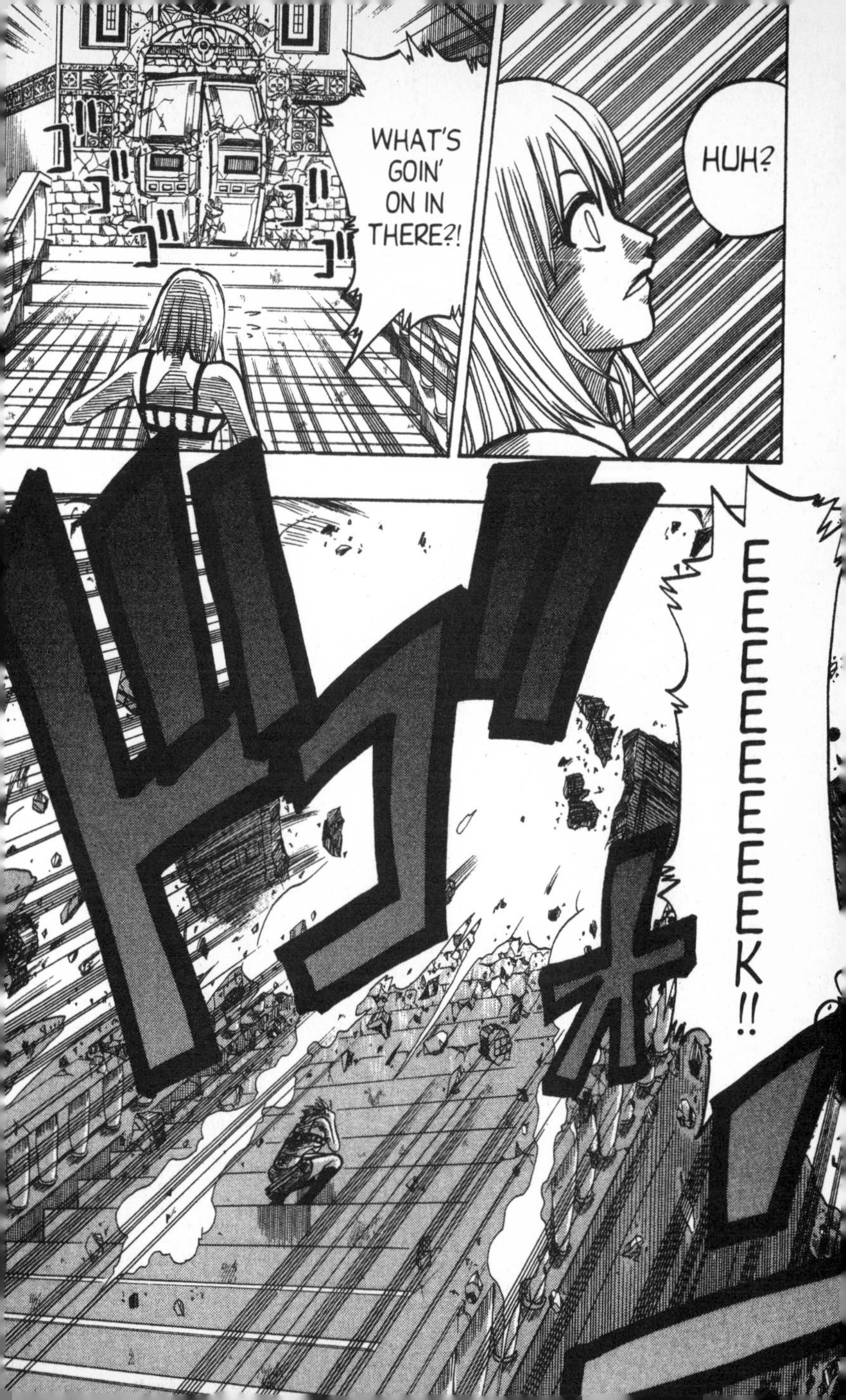
HUH?
WHAT'S GOIN' ON IN THERE?!
EEEEEEEEK!!

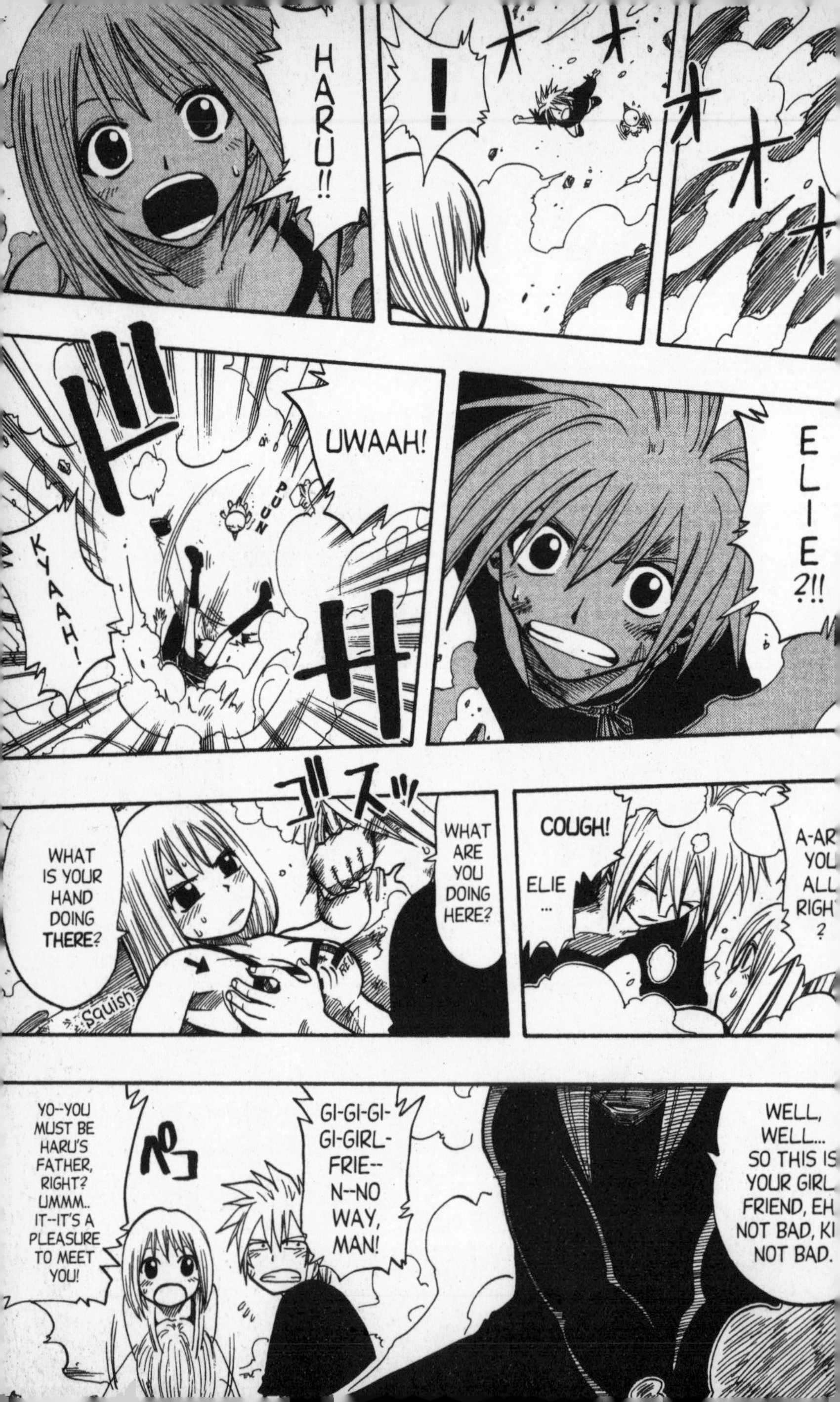
!
HARU!!
ELIE?!!
UWAAH!
PUUN
KYAAAH!
A-AR YOU ALL RIGH ?
COUGH!
ELIE ...
WHAT ARE YOU DOING HERE?
WHAT IS YOUR HAND DOING THERE?
Squish
WELL, WELL... SO THIS IS YOUR GIRL FRIEND, EH NOT BAD, KI NOT BAD.
GI-GI-GI-GI-GIRL-FRIE--N--NO WAY, MAN!
YO--YOU MUST BE HARU'S FATHER, RIGHT? UMMM.. IT--IT'S A PLEASURE TO MEET YOU!

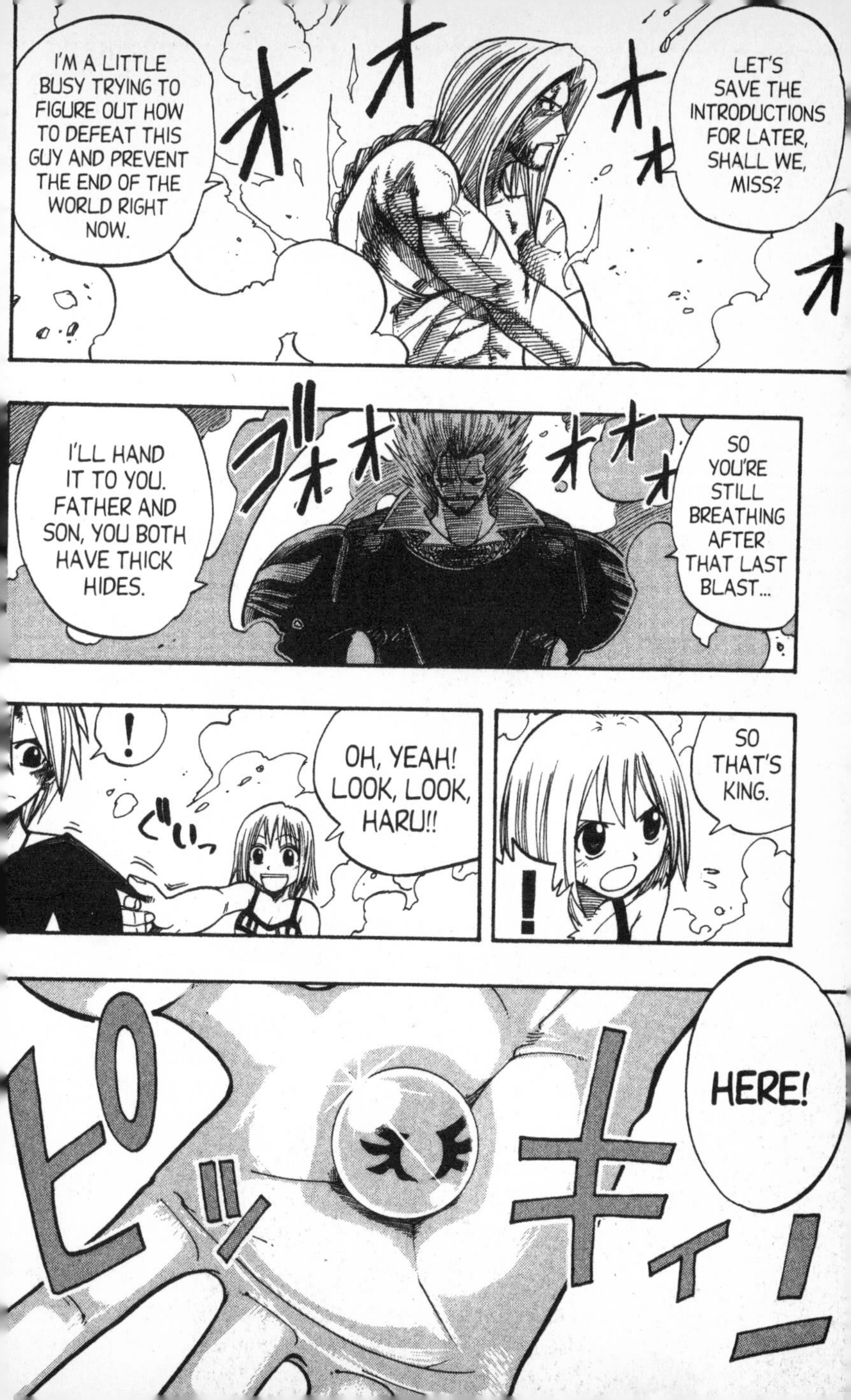
LET'S SAVE THE INTRODUCTIONS FOR LATER, SHALL WE, MISS?
I'M A LITTLE BUSY TRYING TO FIGURE OUT HOW TO DEFEAT THIS GUY AND PREVENT THE END OF THE WORLD RIGHT NOW.
SO YOU'RE STILL BREATHING AFTER THAT LAST BLAST...
I'LL HAND IT TO YOU. FATHER AND SON, YOU BOTH HAVE THICK HIDES.
SO THAT'S KING.
!
OH, YEAH! LOOK, LOOK, HARU!!
!
HERE!

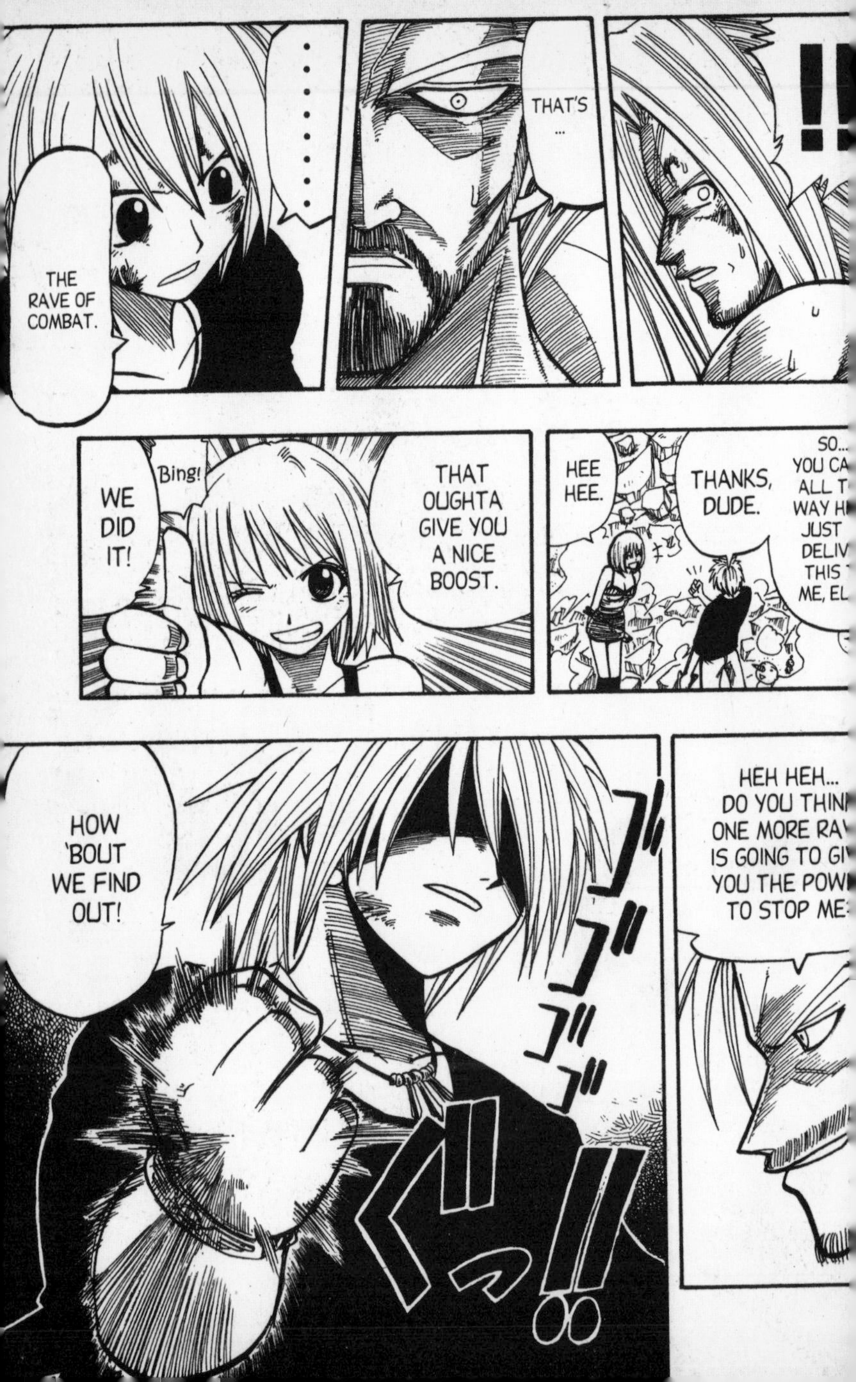
!!
THAT'S ...
......
THE RAVE OF COMBAT.
SO... YOU CA ALL T WAY H JUST DELIV THIS T ME, EL
THANKS, DUDE.
HEE HEE.
THAT OUGHTA GIVE YOU A NICE BOOST.
Bing!
WE DID IT!
HEH HEH... DO YOU THIN ONE MORE RA IS GOING TO GI YOU THE POW TO STOP ME
ゴゴゴゴ
ぐっ!!
HOW 'BOUT WE FIND OUT!

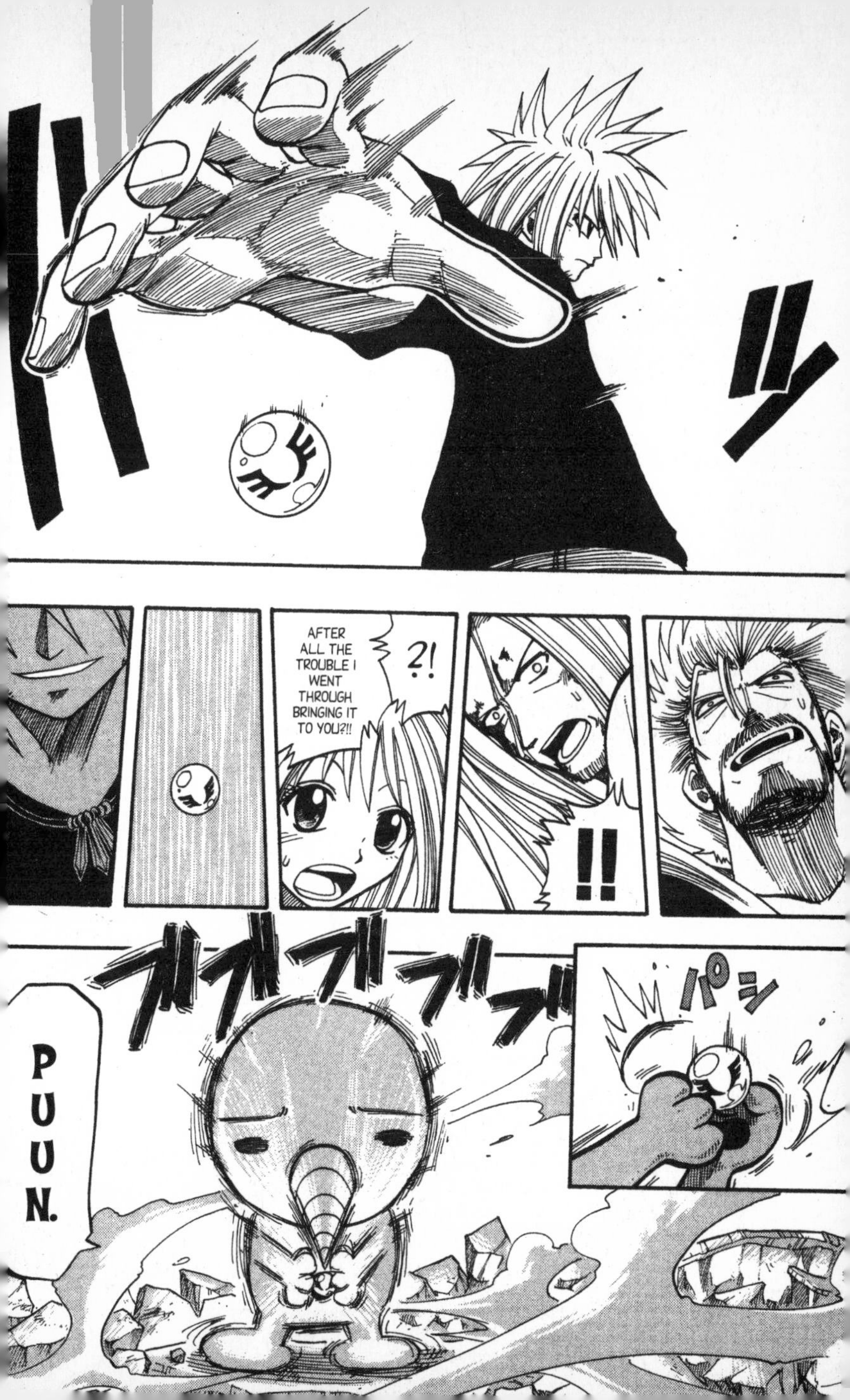
!!
?!
AFTER ALL THE TROUBLE I WENT THROUGH BRINGING IT TO YOU?!!
PUUN.

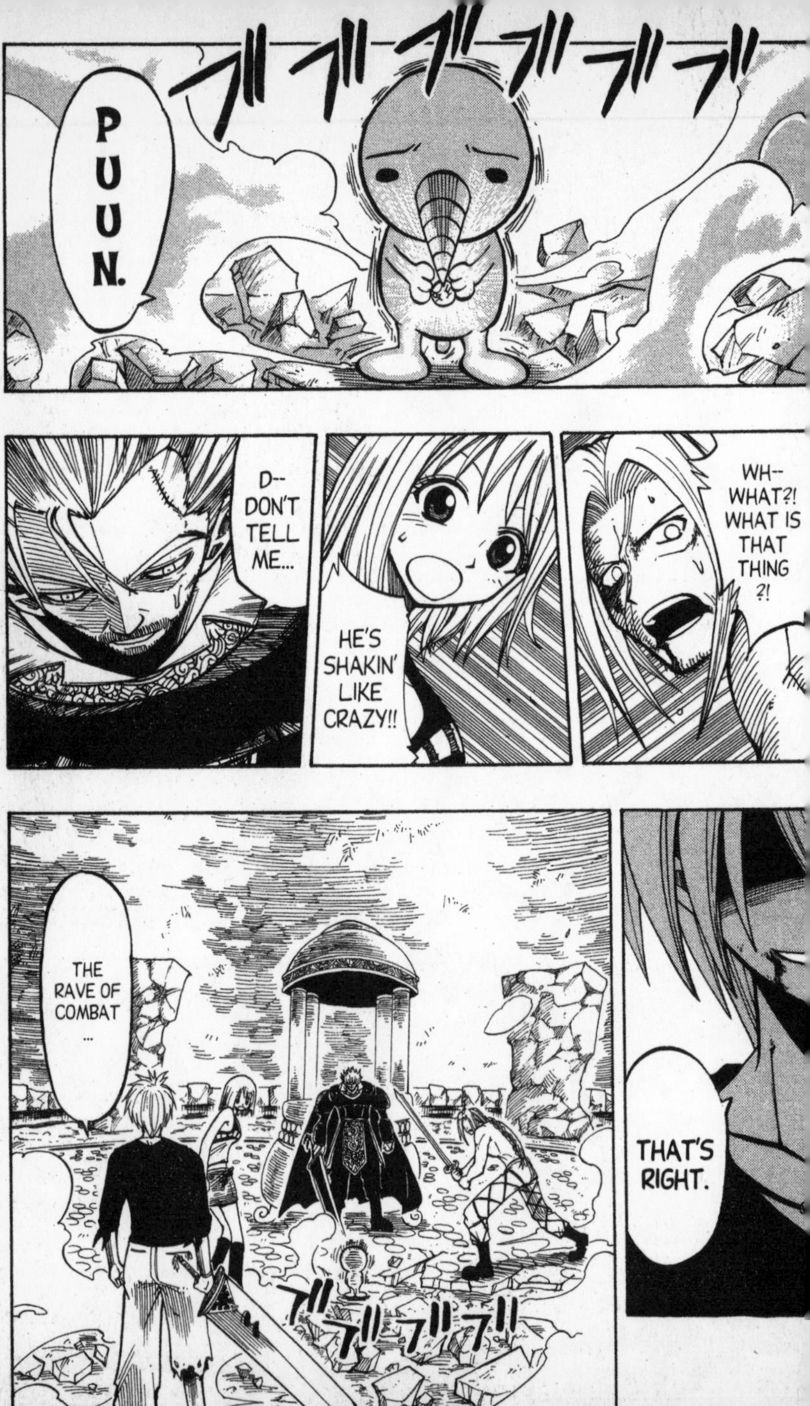
ブブブブブブ
PUUN.
WH-- WHAT?! WHAT IS THAT THING ?!
HE'S SHAKIN' LIKE CRAZY!!
D-- DON'T TELL ME...
THAT'S RIGHT.
THE RAVE OF COMBAT ...
ブブブブ

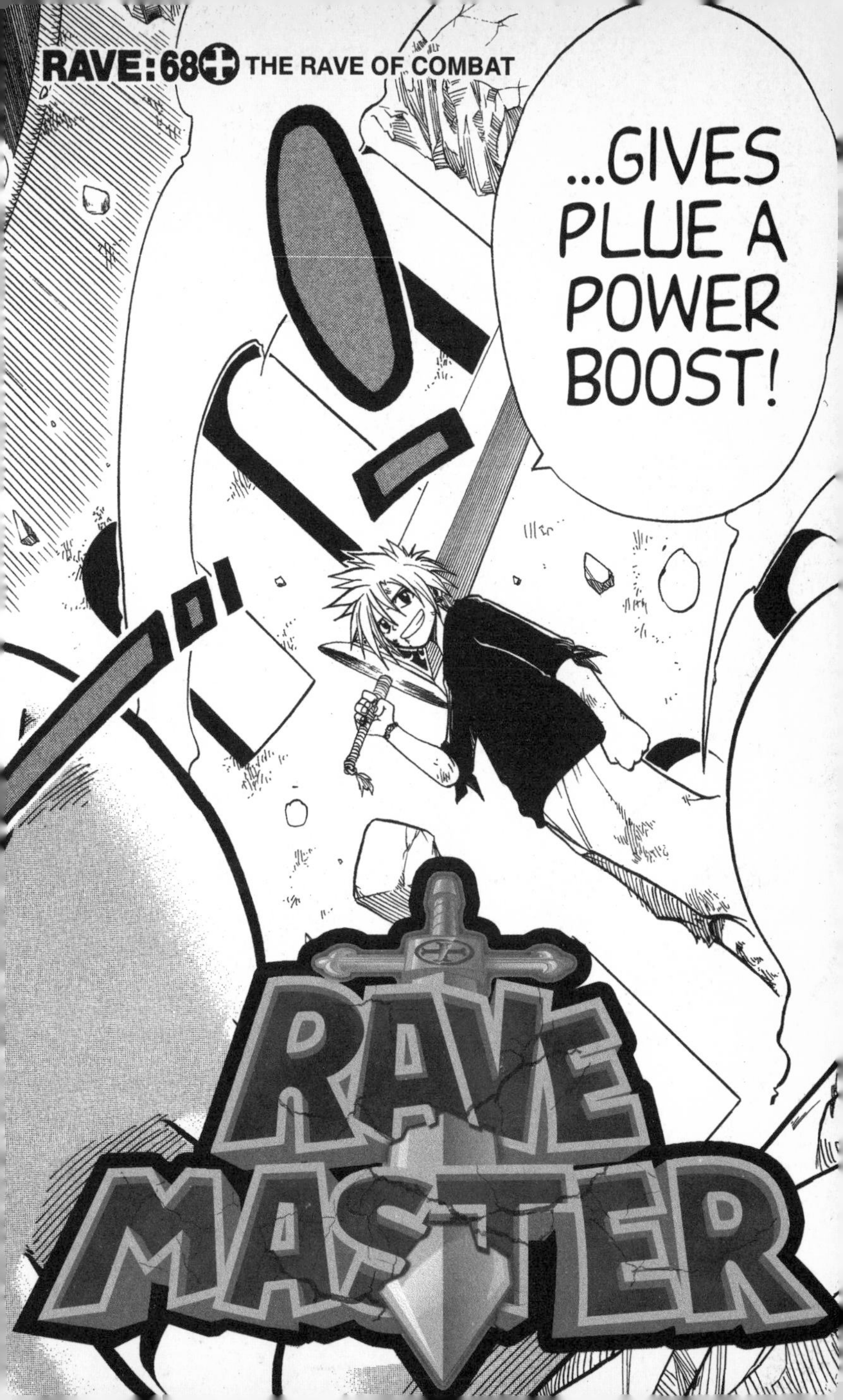
RAVE:68 THE RAVE OF COMBAT
...GIVES PLUE A POWER BOOST!
RAVE MASTER

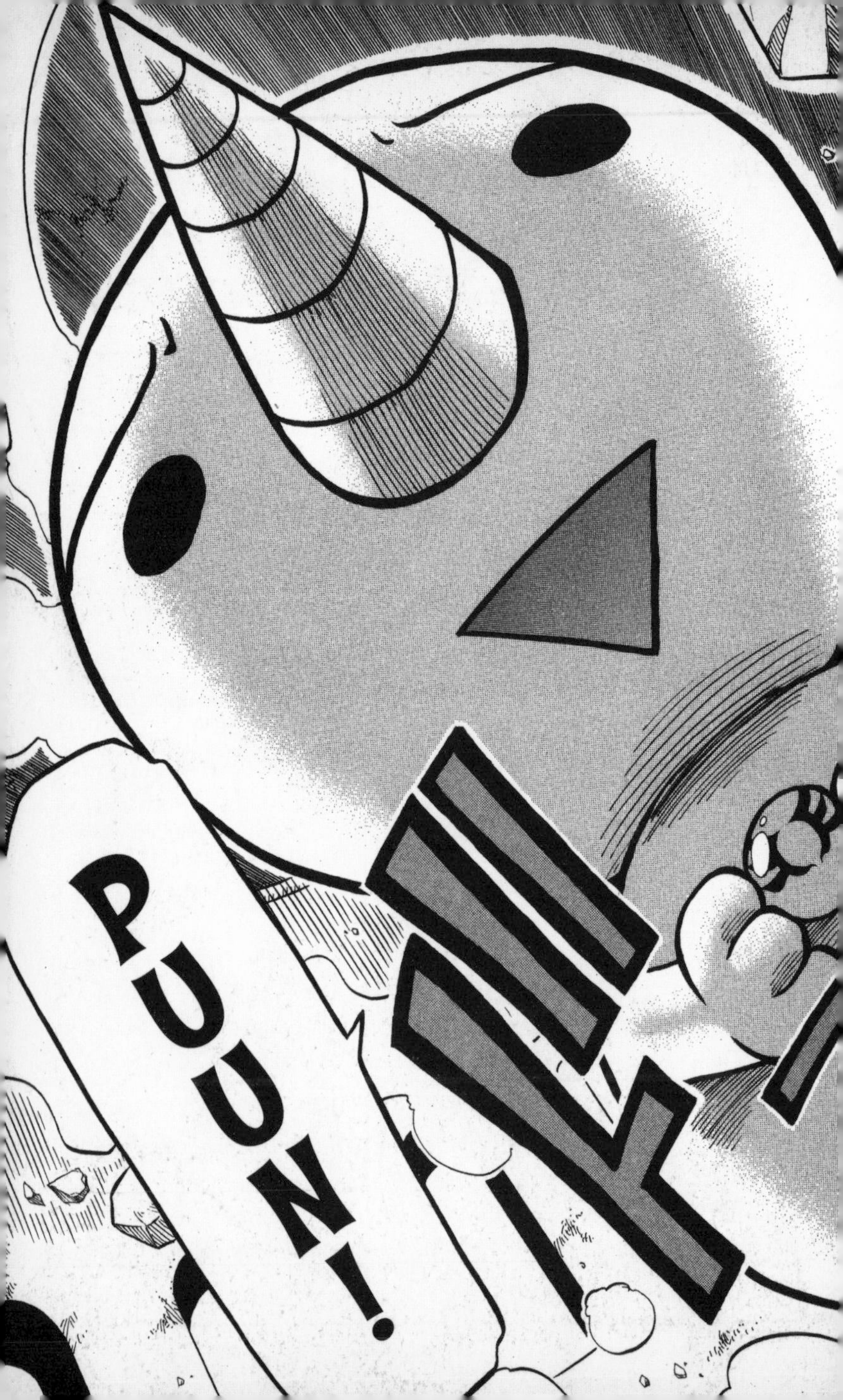
PUUN!

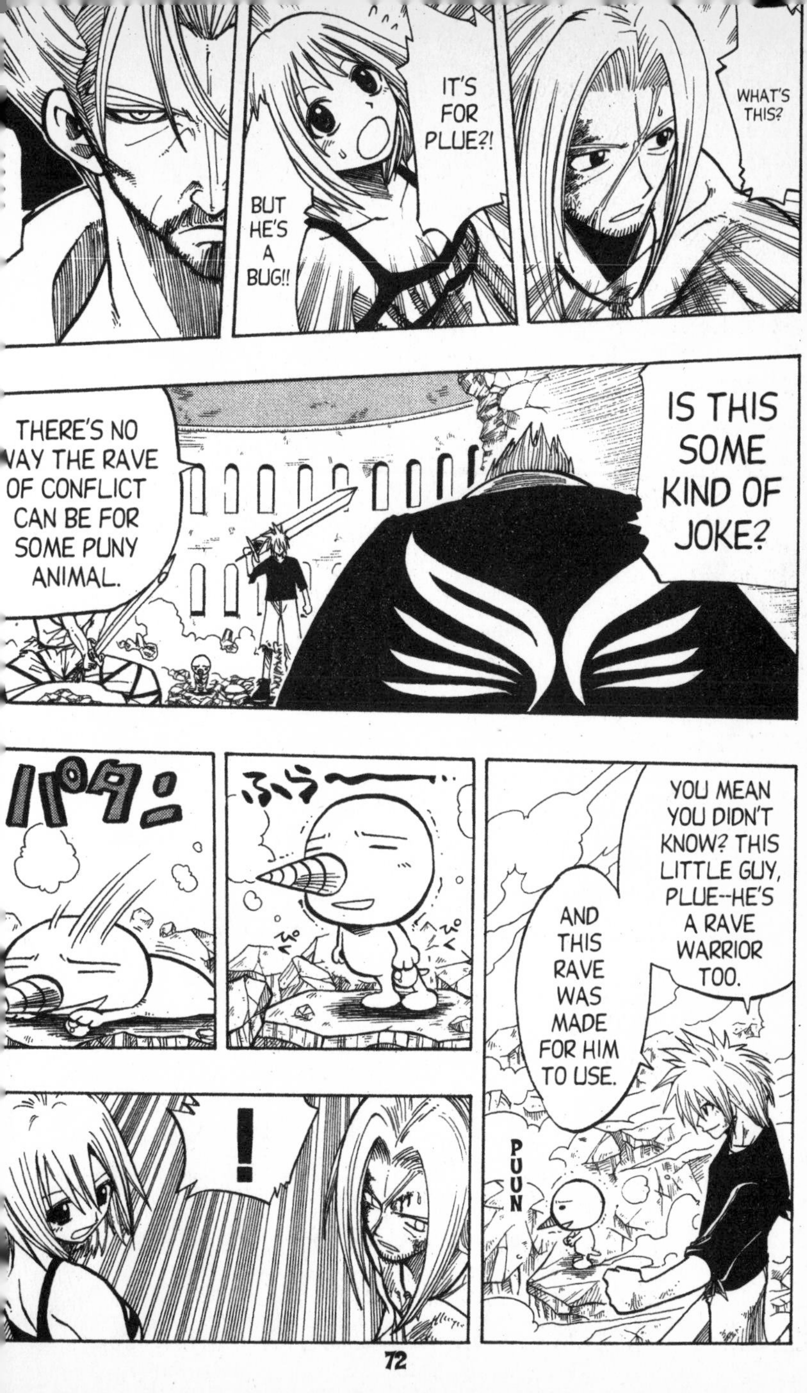
WHAT'S THIS?
IT'S FOR PLUE?!
BUT HE'S A BUG!!
IS THIS SOME KIND OF JOKE?
THERE'S NO WAY THE RAVE OF CONFLICT CAN BE FOR SOME PUNY ANIMAL.
YOU MEAN YOU DIDN'T KNOW? THIS LITTLE GUY, PLUE--HE'S A RAVE WARRIOR TOO.
AND THIS RAVE WAS MADE FOR HIM TO USE.
PUUN
ふら〜〜
パタン
!

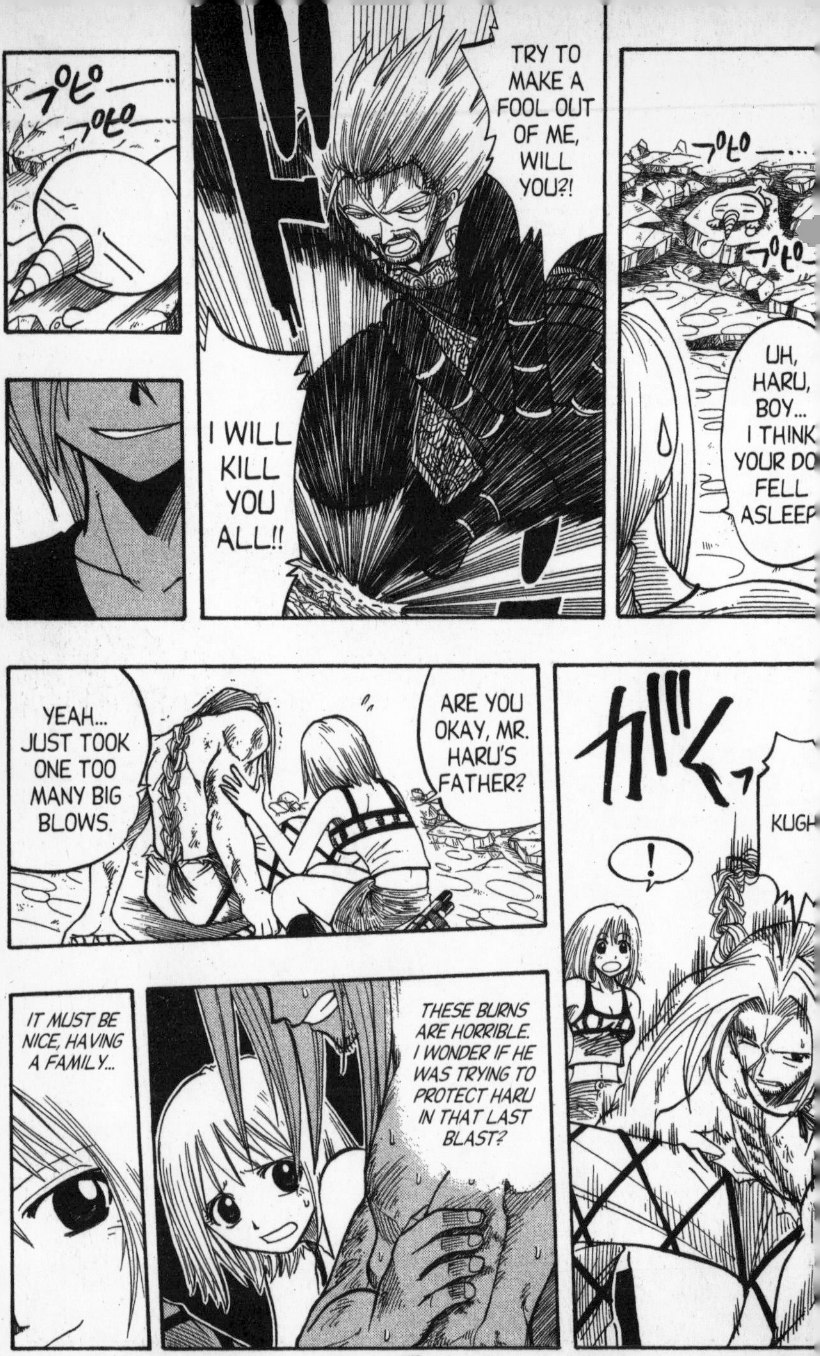
プピ—…
プピ—
UH, HARU, BOY... I THINK YOUR DO FELL ASLEEP
TRY TO MAKE A FOOL OUT OF ME, WILL YOU?!
I WILL KILL YOU ALL!!
プピ—…
プピ—…
がくっ
KUGH
!
ARE YOU OKAY, MR. HARU'S FATHER?
YEAH... JUST TOOK ONE TOO MANY BIG BLOWS.
THESE BURNS ARE HORRIBLE. I WONDER IF HE WAS TRYING TO PROTECT HARU IN THAT LAST BLAST?
IT MUST BE NICE, HAVING A FAMILY...

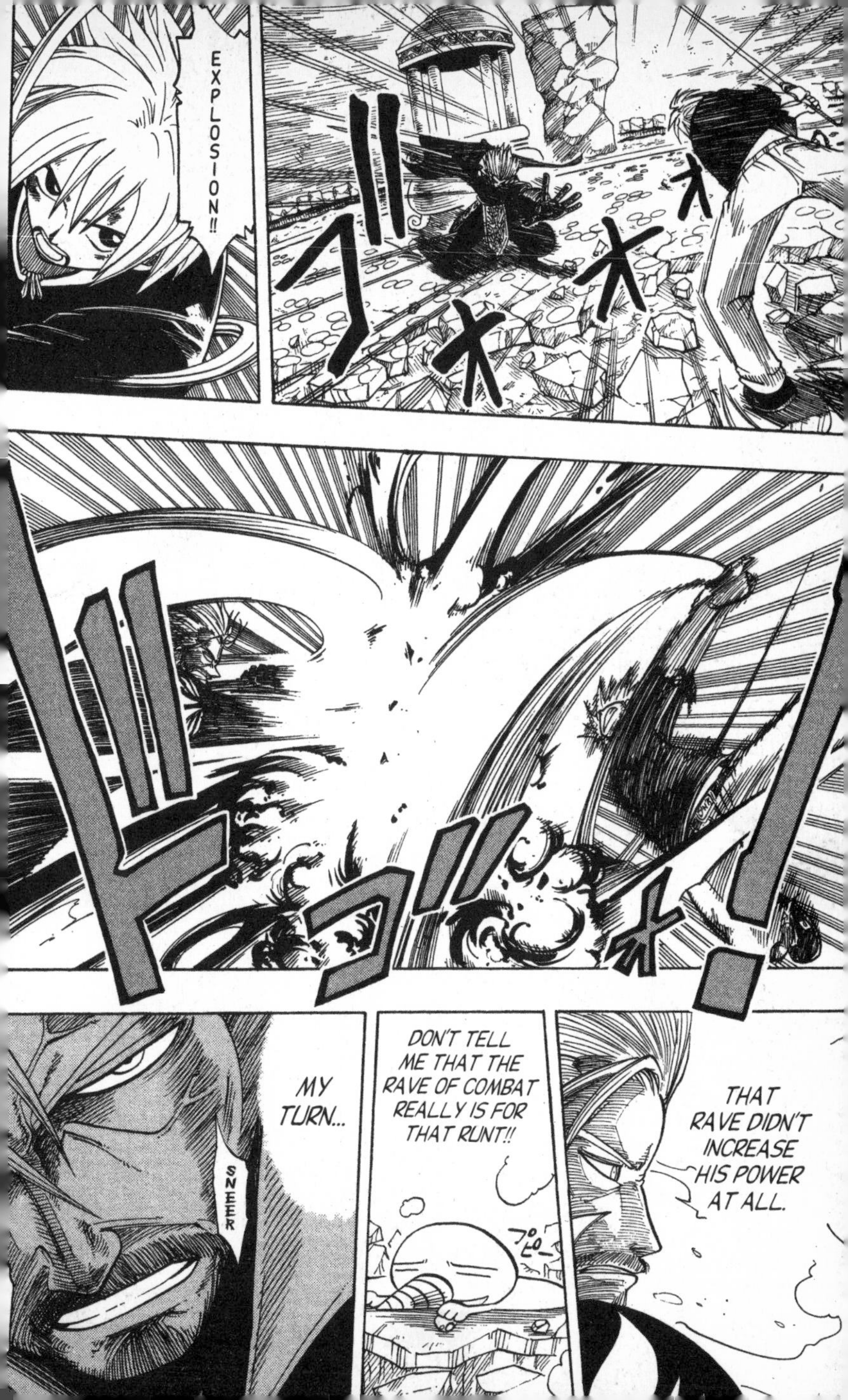
EXPLOSION!!
THAT RAVE DIDN'T INCREASE HIS POWER AT ALL.
DON'T TELL ME THAT THE RAVE OF COMBAT REALLY IS FOR THAT RUNT!!
MY TURN...
SNEER

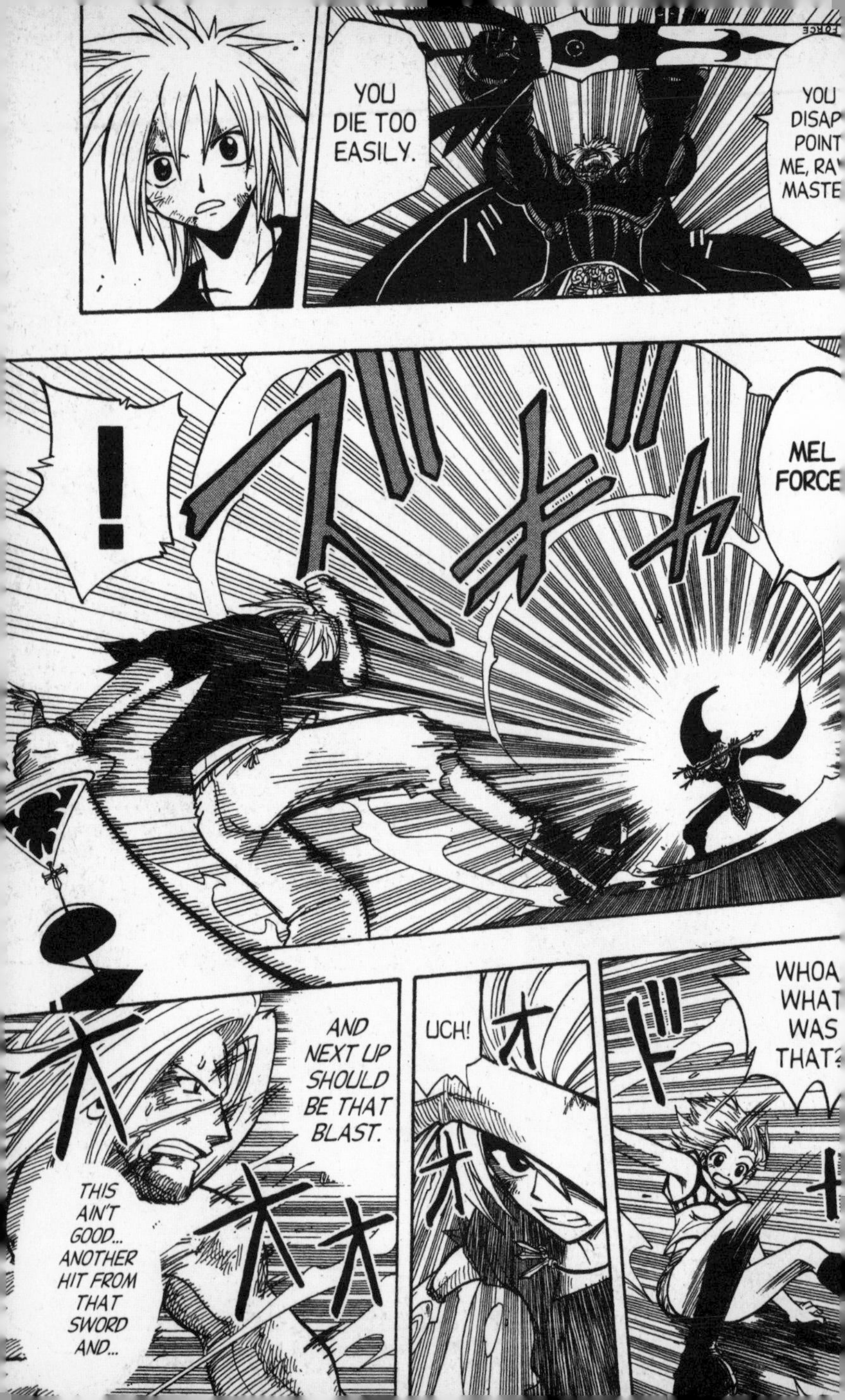
YOU DISAP POINT ME, RA MASTE
YOU DIE TOO EASILY.
MEL FORCE
!
WHOA WHAT WAS THAT?
UCH!
AND NEXT UP SHOULD BE THAT BLAST.
THIS AIN'T GOOD... ANOTHER HIT FROM THAT SWORD AND...

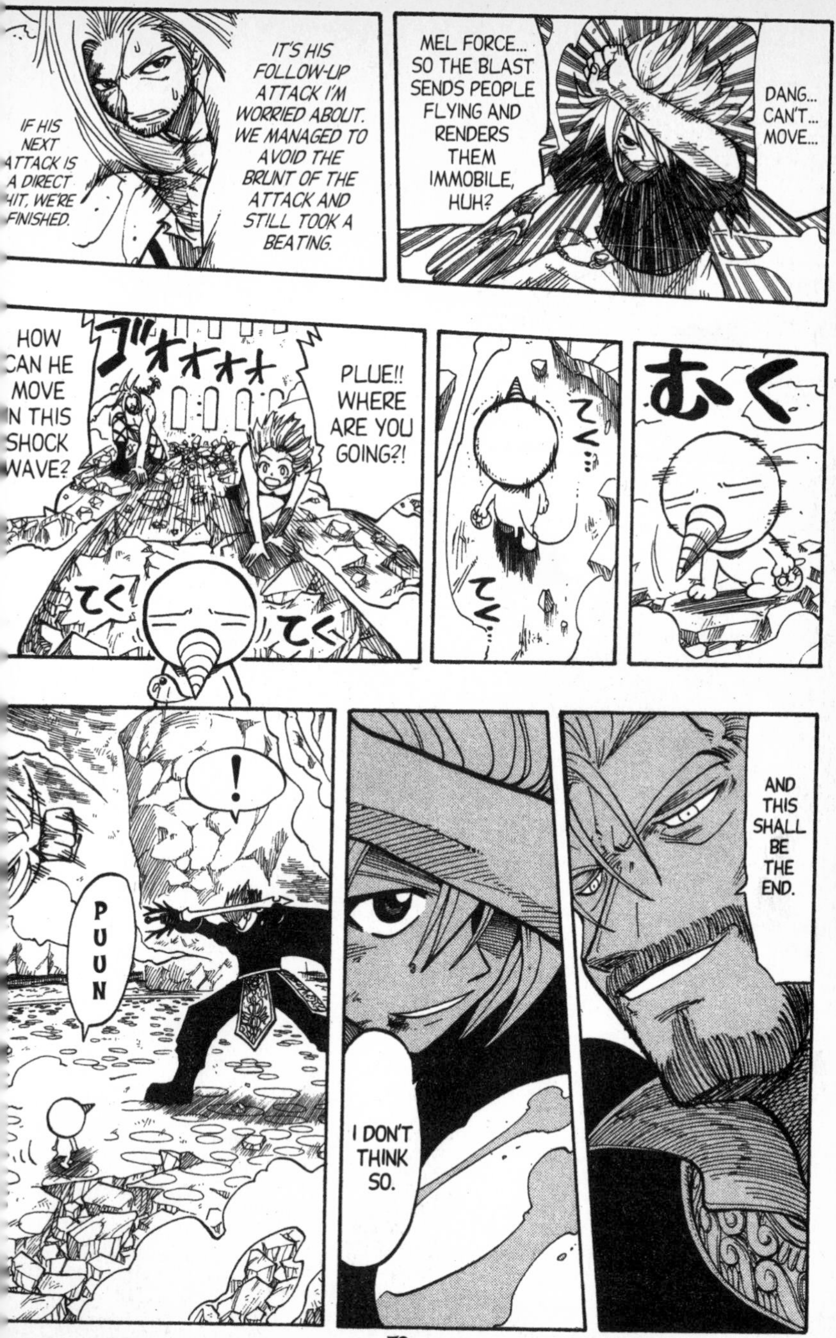
DANG... CAN'T... MOVE...
MEL FORCE... SO THE BLAST SENDS PEOPLE FLYING AND RENDERS THEM IMMOBILE, HUH?
IT'S HIS FOLLOW-UP ATTACK I'M WORRIED ABOUT. WE MANAGED TO AVOID THE BRUNT OF THE ATTACK AND STILL TOOK A BEATING.
IF HIS NEXT ATTACK IS A DIRECT HIT, WE'RE FINISHED.
むく
てく...
てく...
PLUE!! WHERE ARE YOU GOING?!
ゴオオオオ
HOW CAN HE MOVE IN THIS SHOCK WAVE?
てく
てく
AND THIS SHALL BE THE END.
I DON'T THINK SO.
!
PUUN

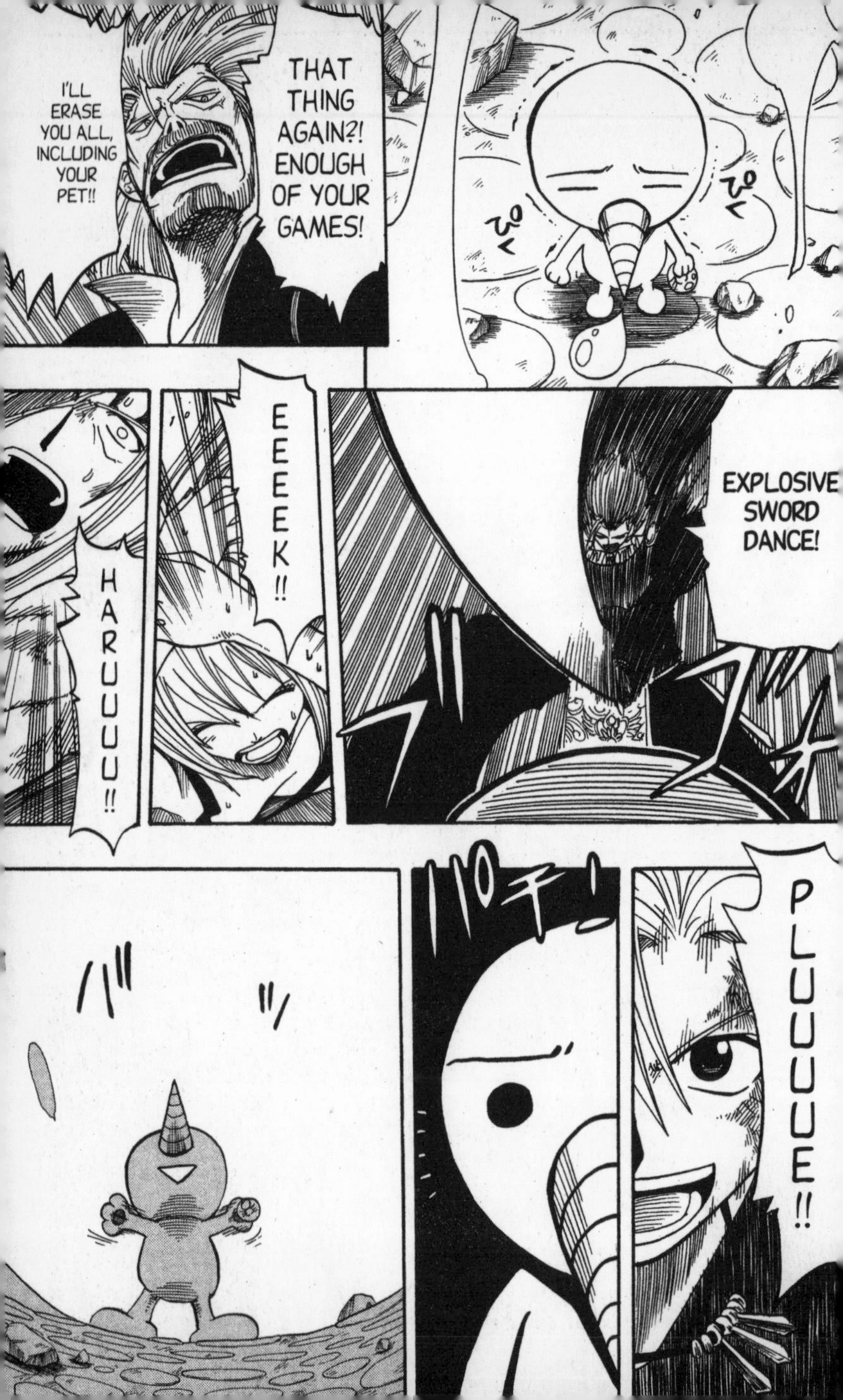
THAT THING AGAIN?! ENOUGH OF YOUR GAMES!
I'LL ERASE YOU ALL, INCLUDING YOUR PET!!
EXPLOSIVE SWORD DANCE!
EEEEEK!!
HARUUUUU!!
PLUUUUUE!!

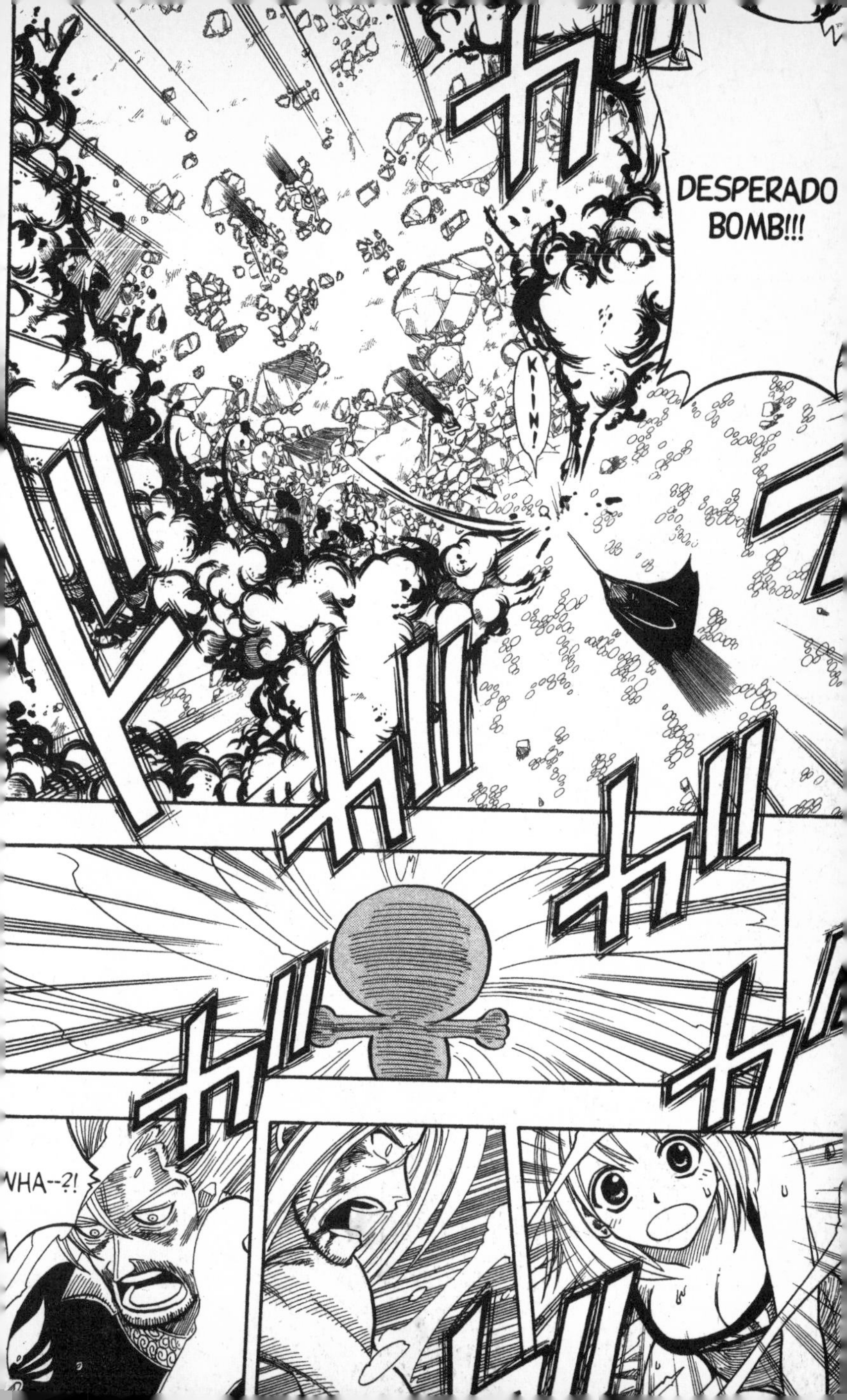
DESPERADO BOMB!!!
KIIN!
WHA--?!

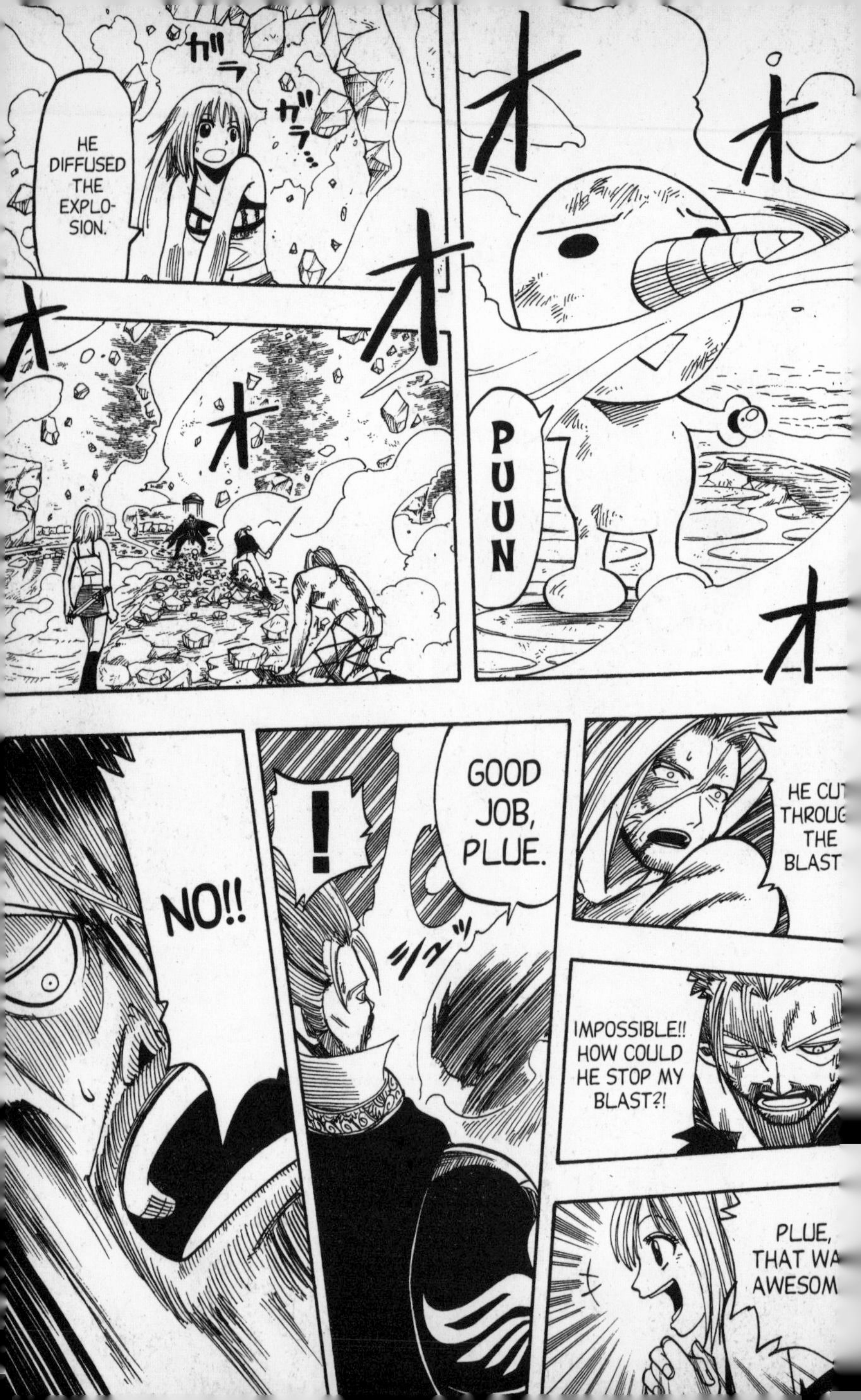
オ
オ
PUUN
オ
ガラ
ガラ
HE DIFFUSED THE EXPLOSION.
オ
オ
オ
HE CUT THROUG THE BLAST
IMPOSSIBLE!! HOW COULD HE STOP MY BLAST?!
PLUE, THAT WA AWESOM
GOOD JOB, PLUE.
!
NO!!

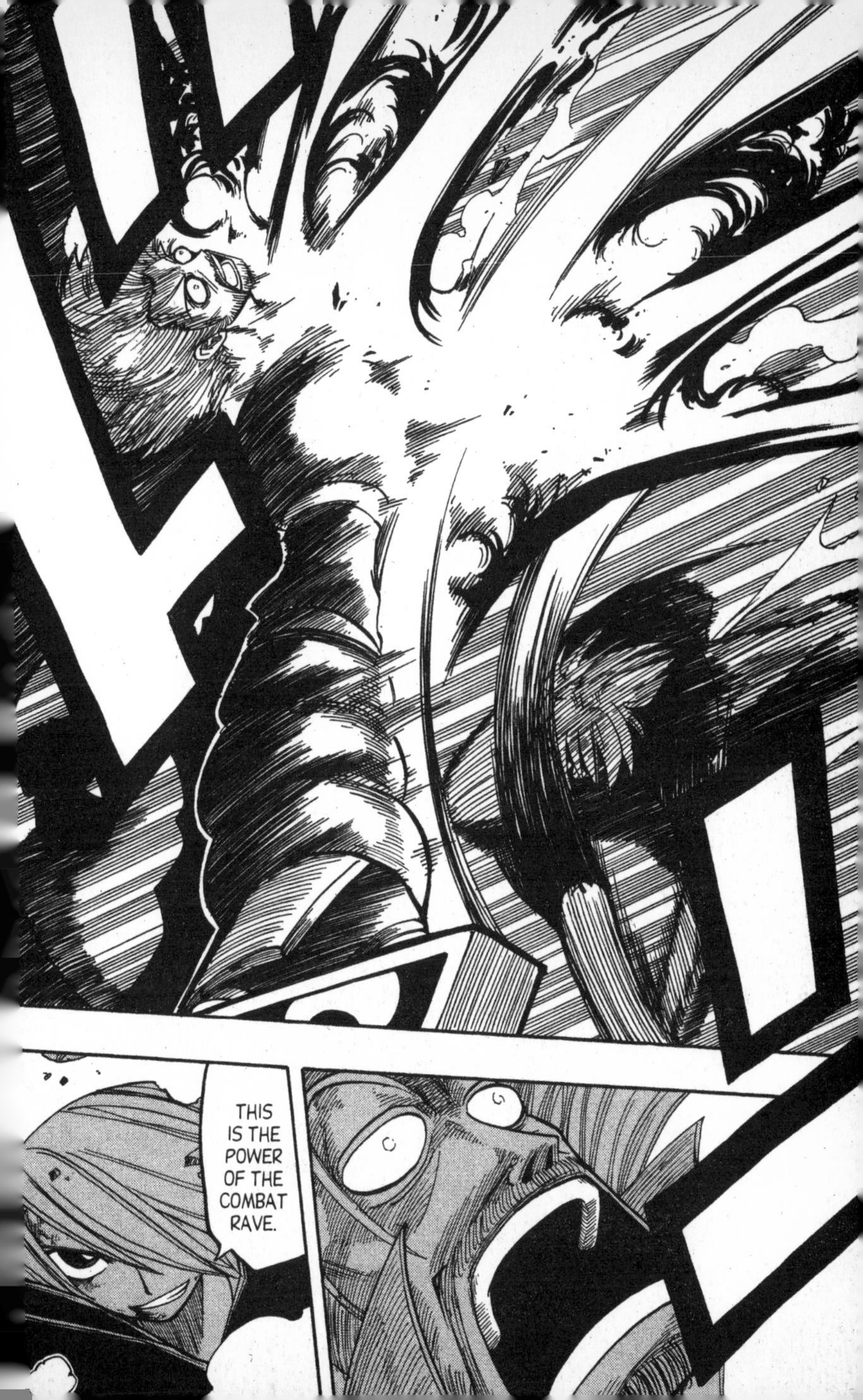
THIS IS THE POWER OF THE COMBAT RAVE.

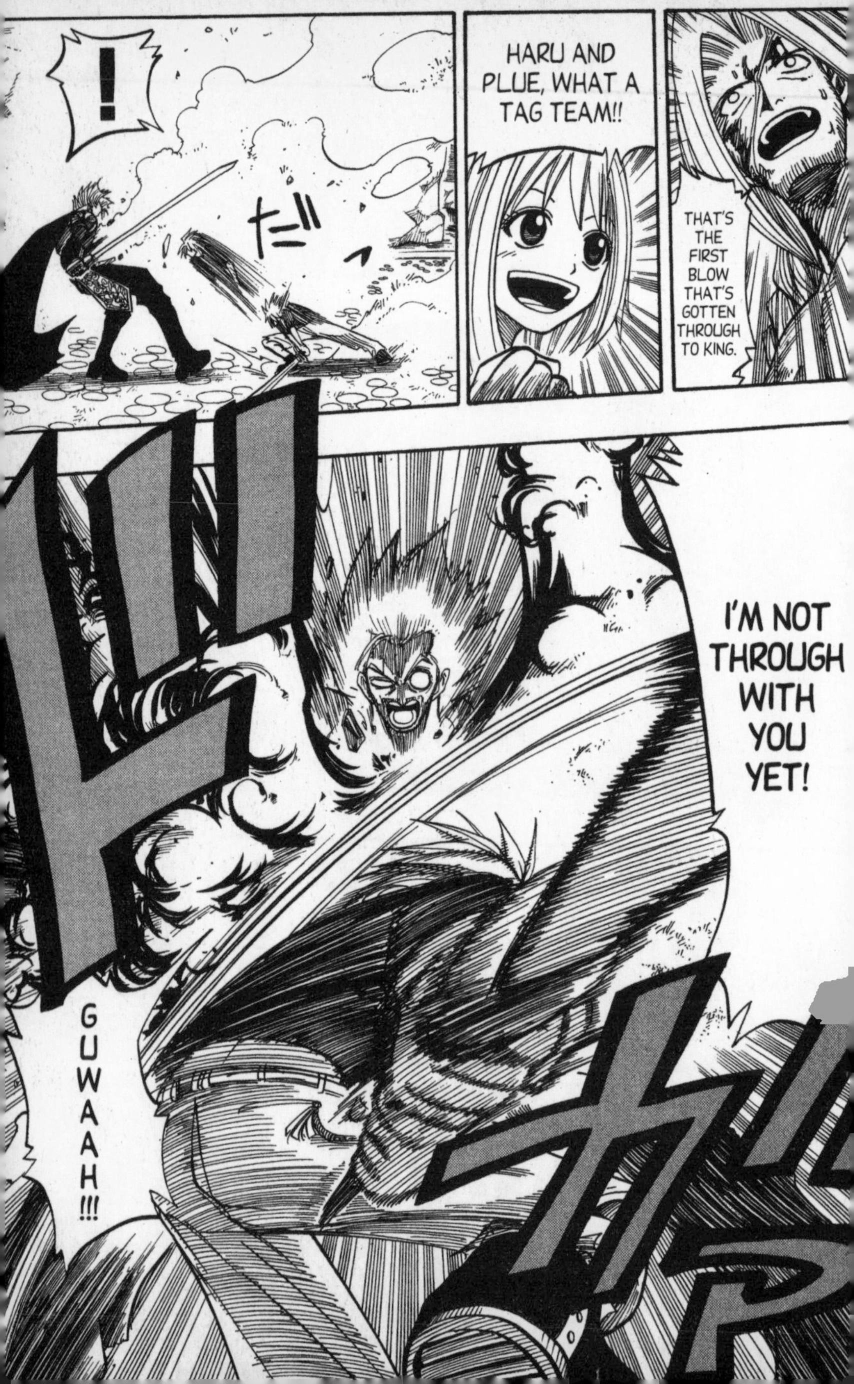
THAT'S THE FIRST BLOW THAT'S GOTTEN THROUGH TO KING.
HARU AND PLUE, WHAT A TAG TEAM!!
!
I'M NOT THROUGH WITH YOU YET!
GUWAAAH!!!

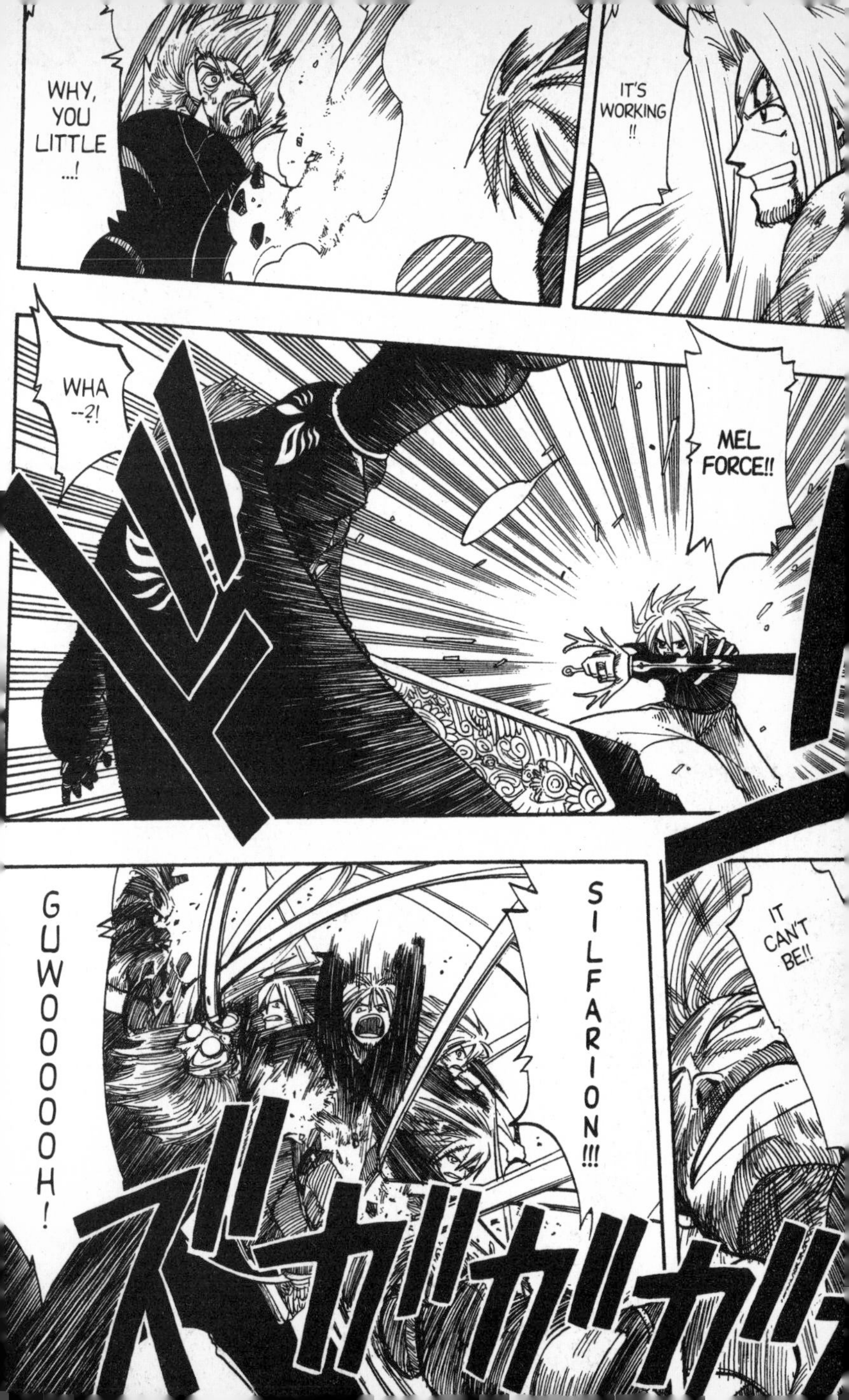
IT'S WORKING!!
WHY, YOU LITTLE ...!
MEL FORCE!!
WHA--?!
IT CAN'T BE!!
SILFARION!!!
GUWOOOOOOH!

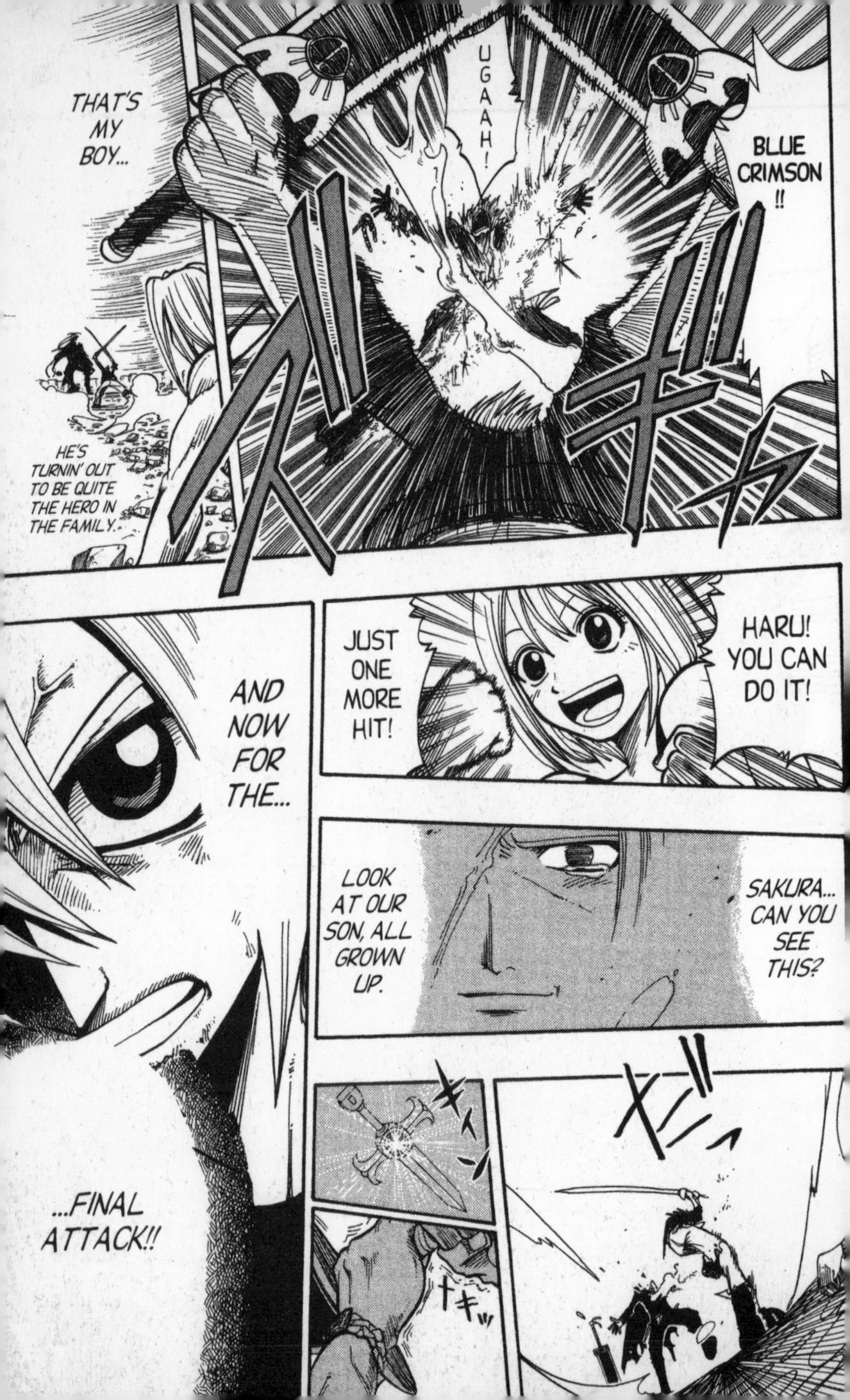
BLUE CRIMSON !!
UGAAH!
THAT'S MY BOY...
HE'S TURNIN' OUT TO BE QUITE THE HERO IN THE FAMILY...
HARU! YOU CAN DO IT!
JUST ONE MORE HIT!
SAKURA... CAN YOU SEE THIS?
LOOK AT OUR SON, ALL GROWN UP.
AND NOW FOR THE...
...FINAL ATTACK!!

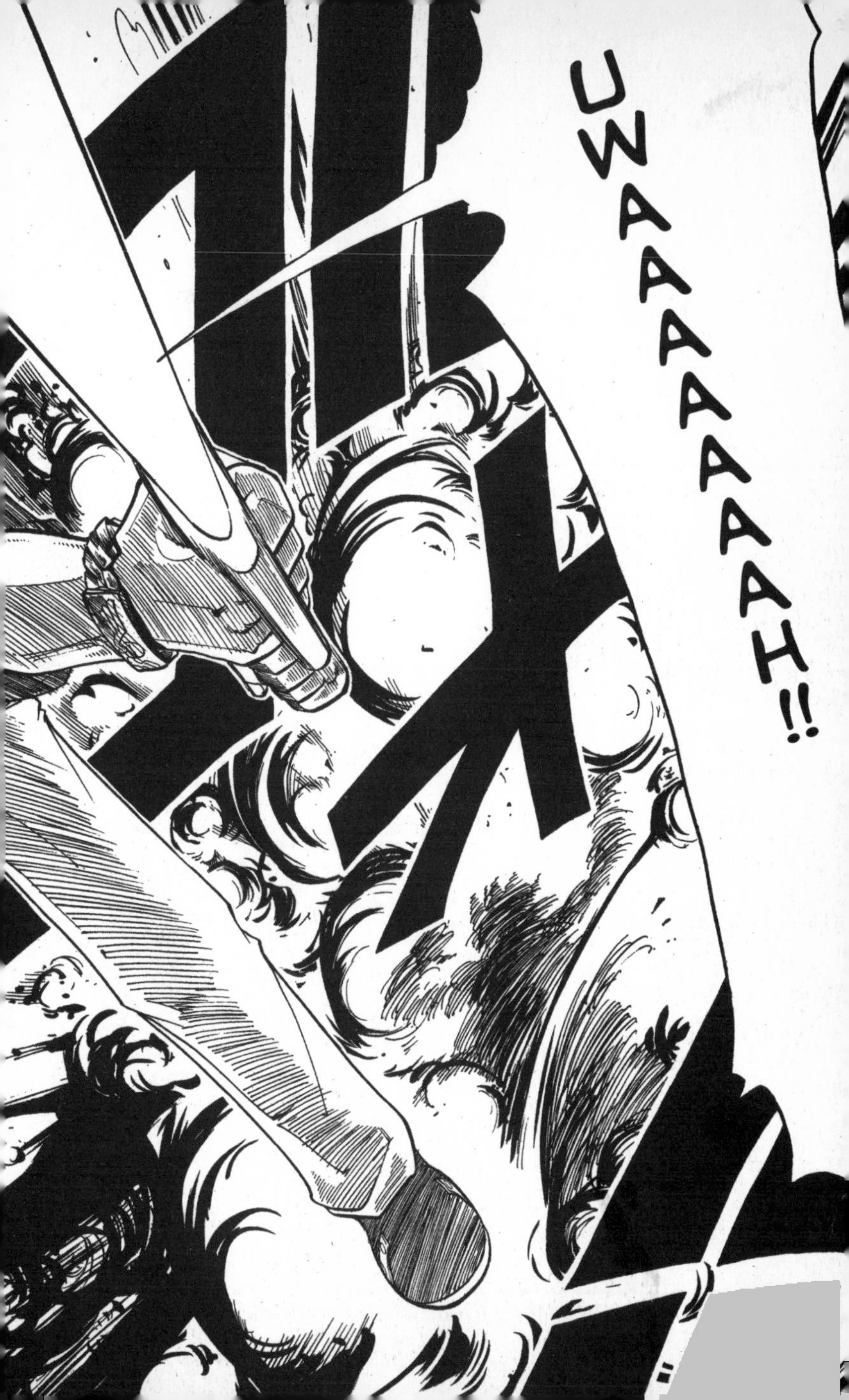
UWAAAAAAH!!

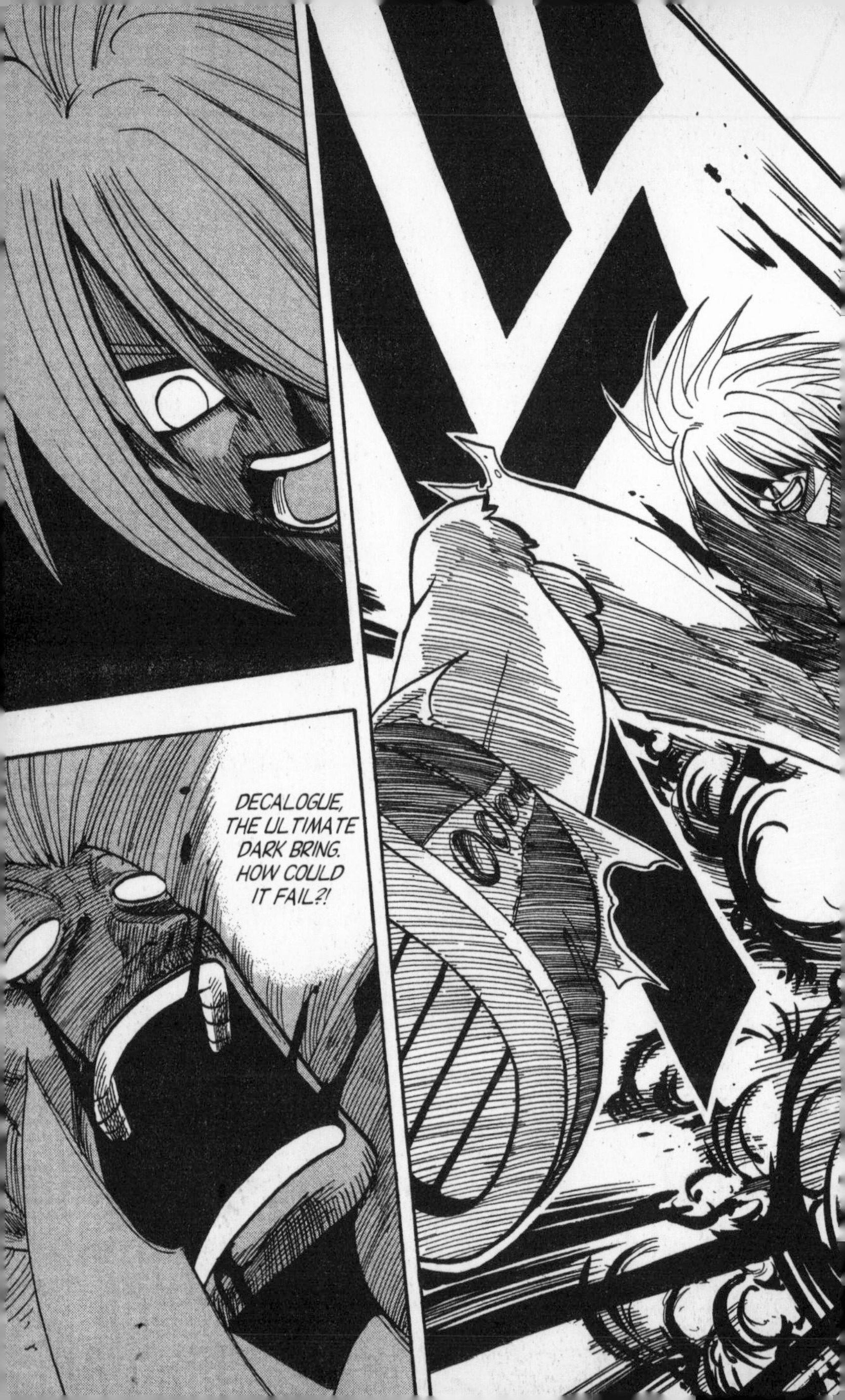
DECALOGUE, THE ULTIMATE DARK BRING. HOW COULD IT FAIL?!

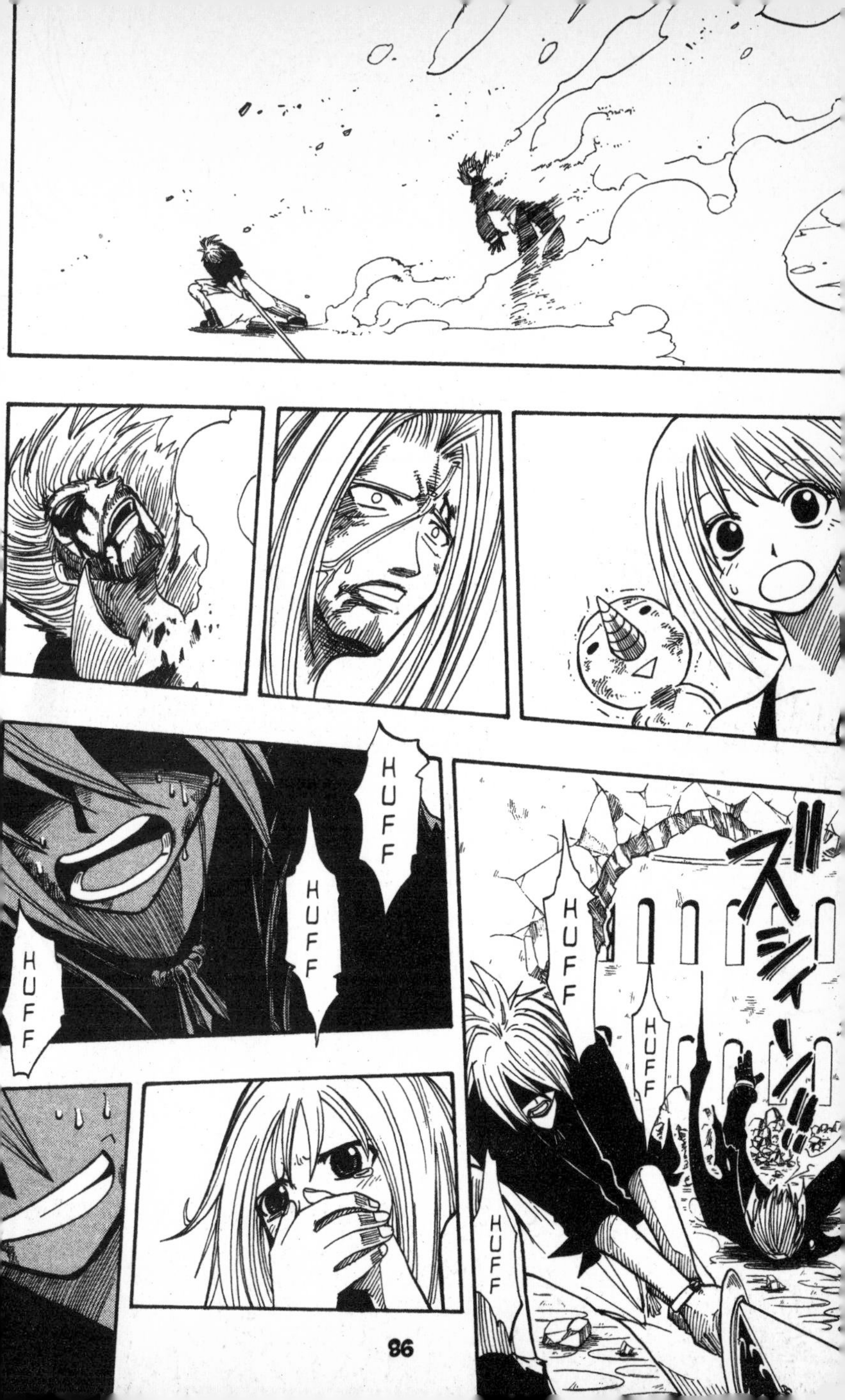
ズシィーン!!
HUFF
HUFF
HUFF
HUFF
HUFF
HUFF

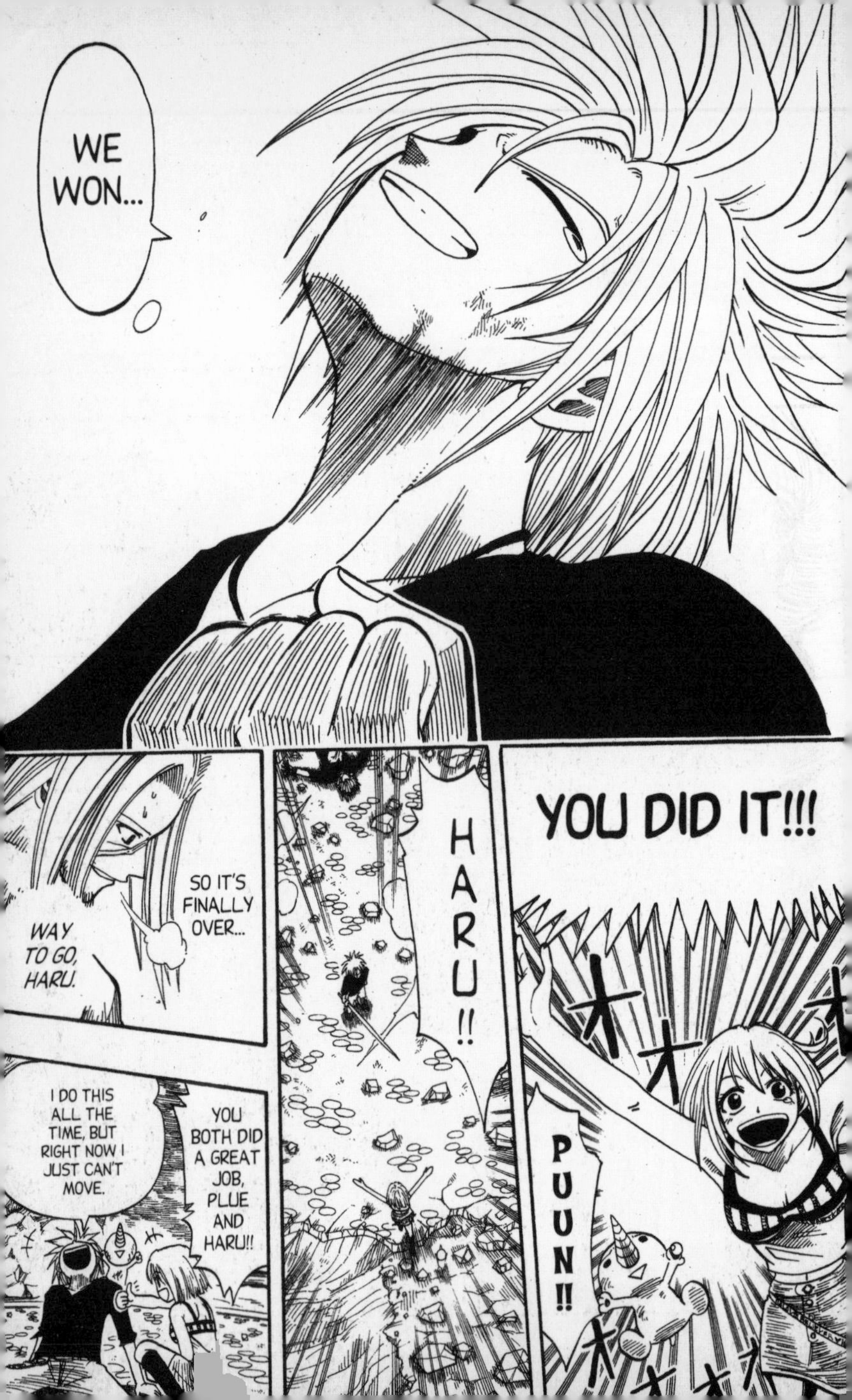
WE WON...
YOU DID IT!!!
PUUN!!
HARU!!
SO IT'S FINALLY OVER...
WAY TO GO, HARU.
YOU BOTH DID A GREAT JOB, PLUE AND HARU!!
I DO THIS ALL THE TIME, BUT RIGHT NOW I JUST CAN'T MOVE.

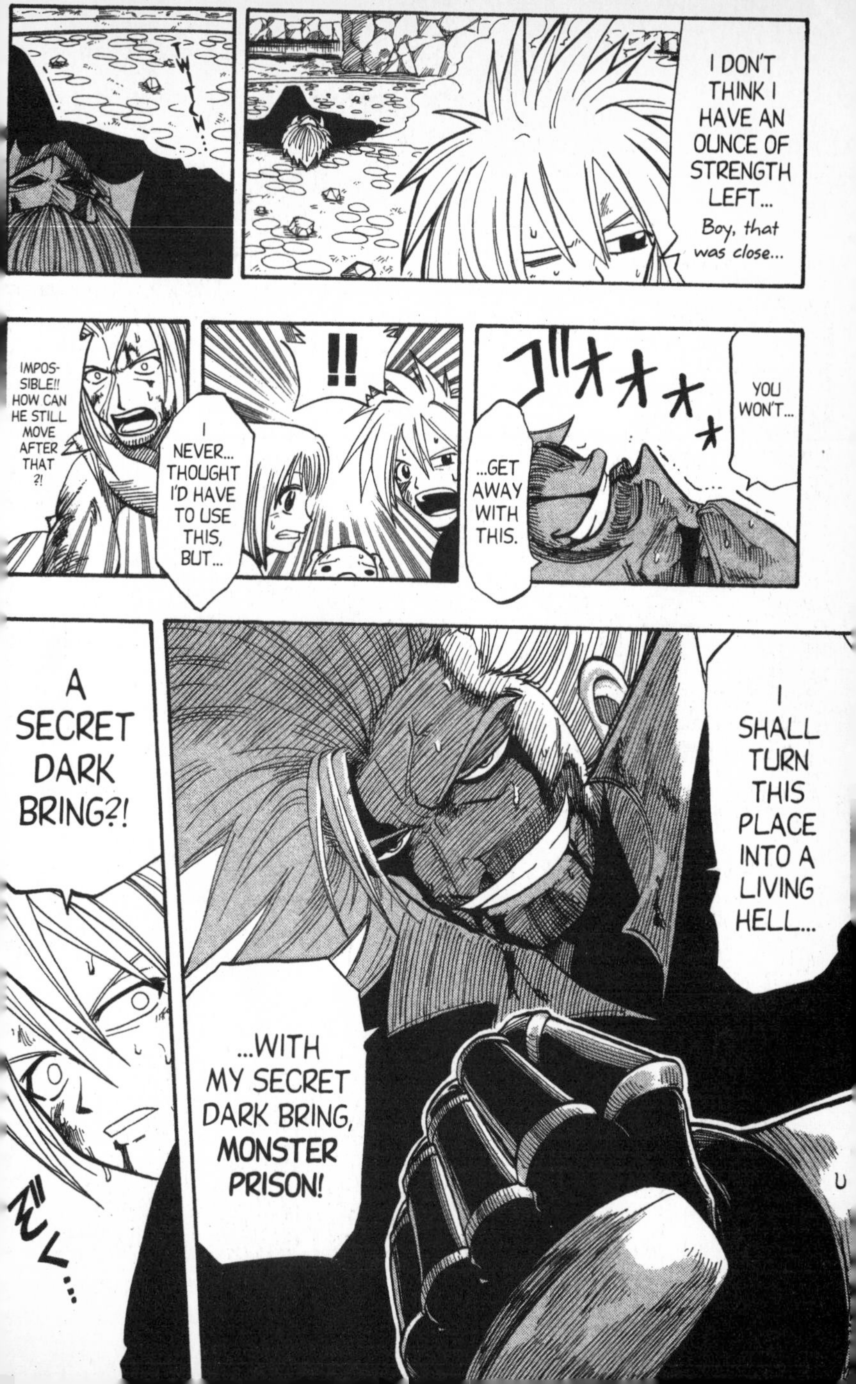
I DON'T THINK I HAVE AN OUNCE OF STRENGTH LEFT...
Boy, that was close...
TWITCH...
YOU WON'T...
...GET AWAY WITH THIS.
!!
I NEVER... THOUGHT I'D HAVE TO USE THIS, BUT...
IMPOSSIBLE!! HOW CAN HE STILL MOVE AFTER THAT?!
I SHALL TURN THIS PLACE INTO A LIVING HELL...
...WITH MY SECRET DARK BRING, MONSTER PRISON!
A SECRET DARK BRING?!

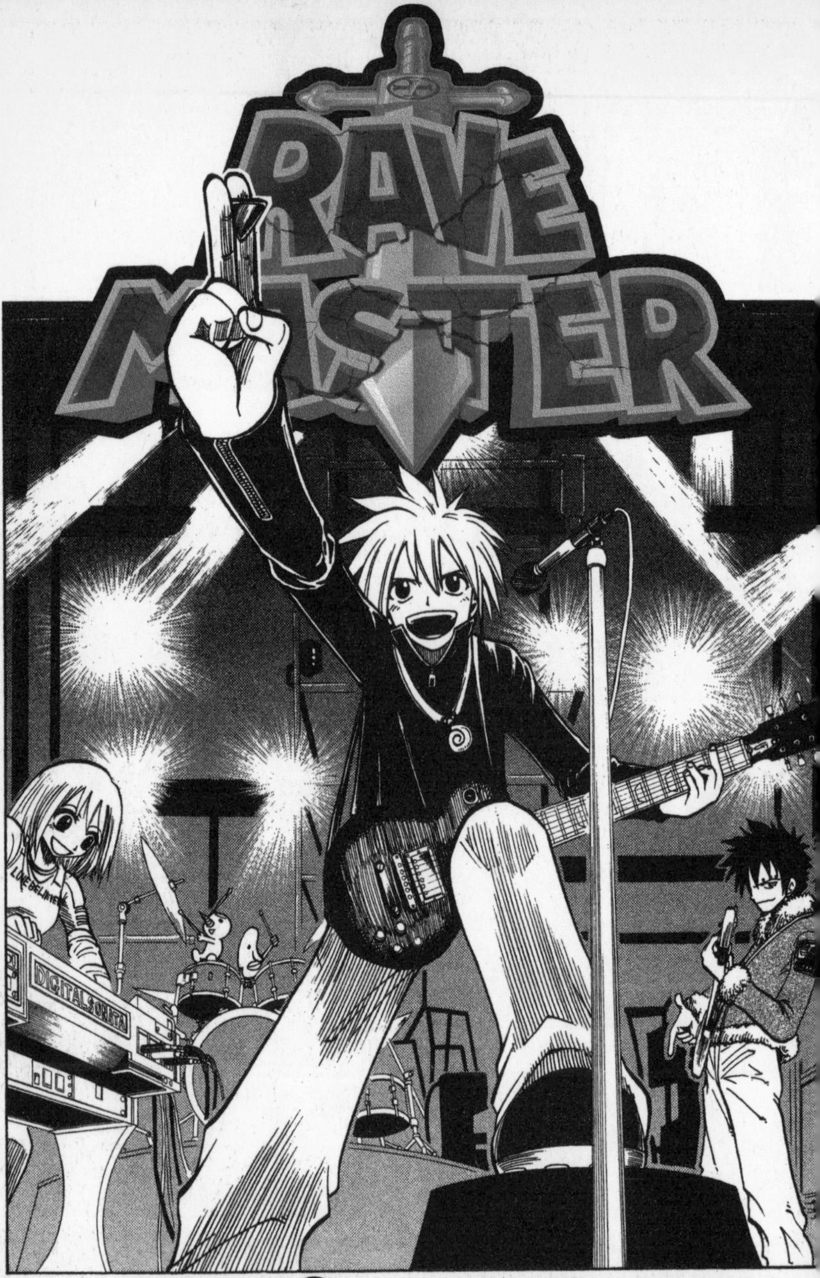
RAVE MASTER
DIGITAL SONATA

RAVE:69 ✚ EVIL RUNS RECKLESS

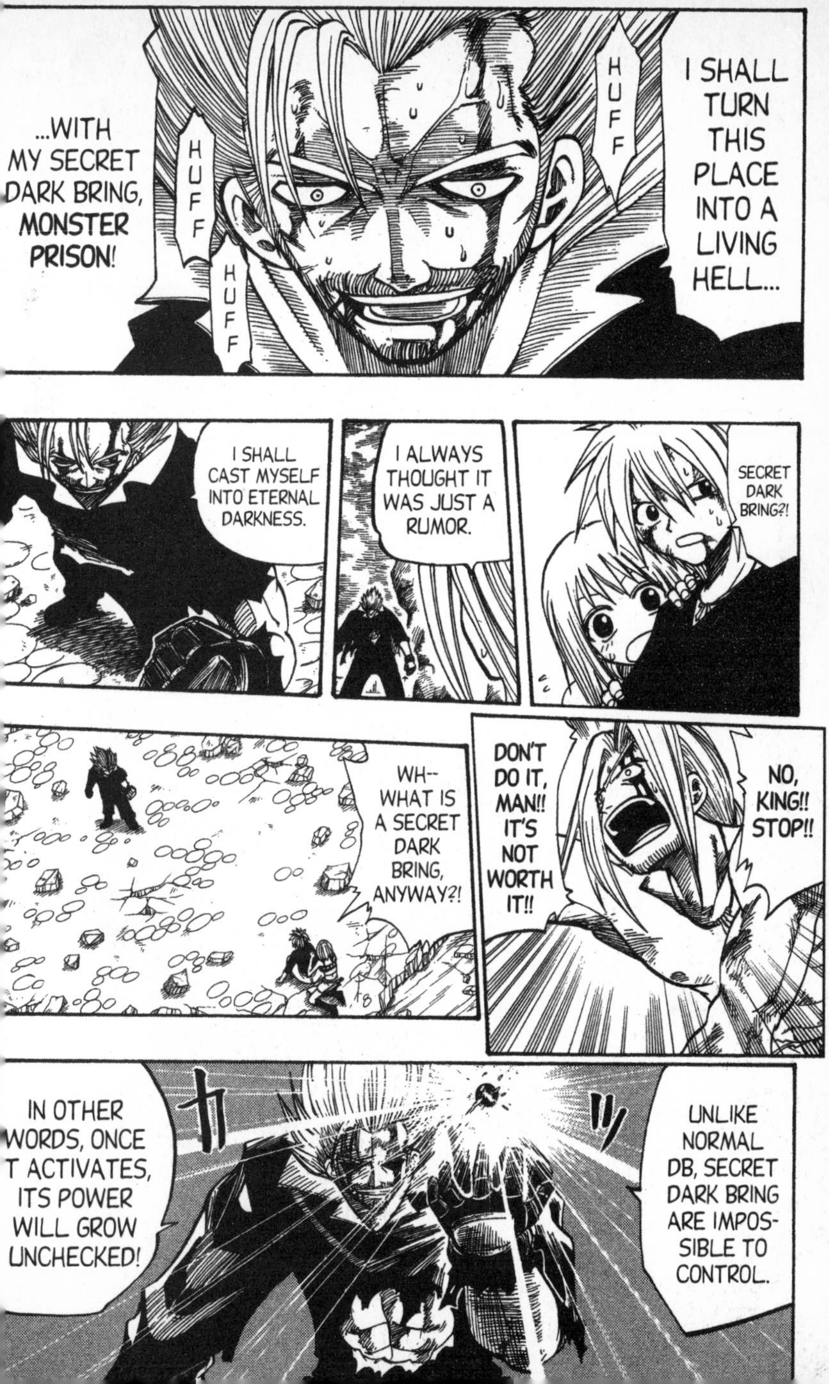
I SHALL TURN THIS PLACE INTO A LIVING HELL...
HUFF
HUFF
HUFF
...WITH MY SECRET DARK BRING, MONSTER PRISON!
SECRET DARK BRING?!
I ALWAYS THOUGHT IT WAS JUST A RUMOR.
I SHALL CAST MYSELF INTO ETERNAL DARKNESS.
NO, KING!! STOP!!
DON'T DO IT, MAN!! IT'S NOT WORTH IT!!
WH-- WHAT IS A SECRET DARK BRING, ANYWAY?!
UNLIKE NORMAL DB, SECRET DARK BRING ARE IMPOSSIBLE TO CONTROL.
IN OTHER WORDS, ONCE T ACTIVATES, ITS POWER WILL GROW UNCHECKED!

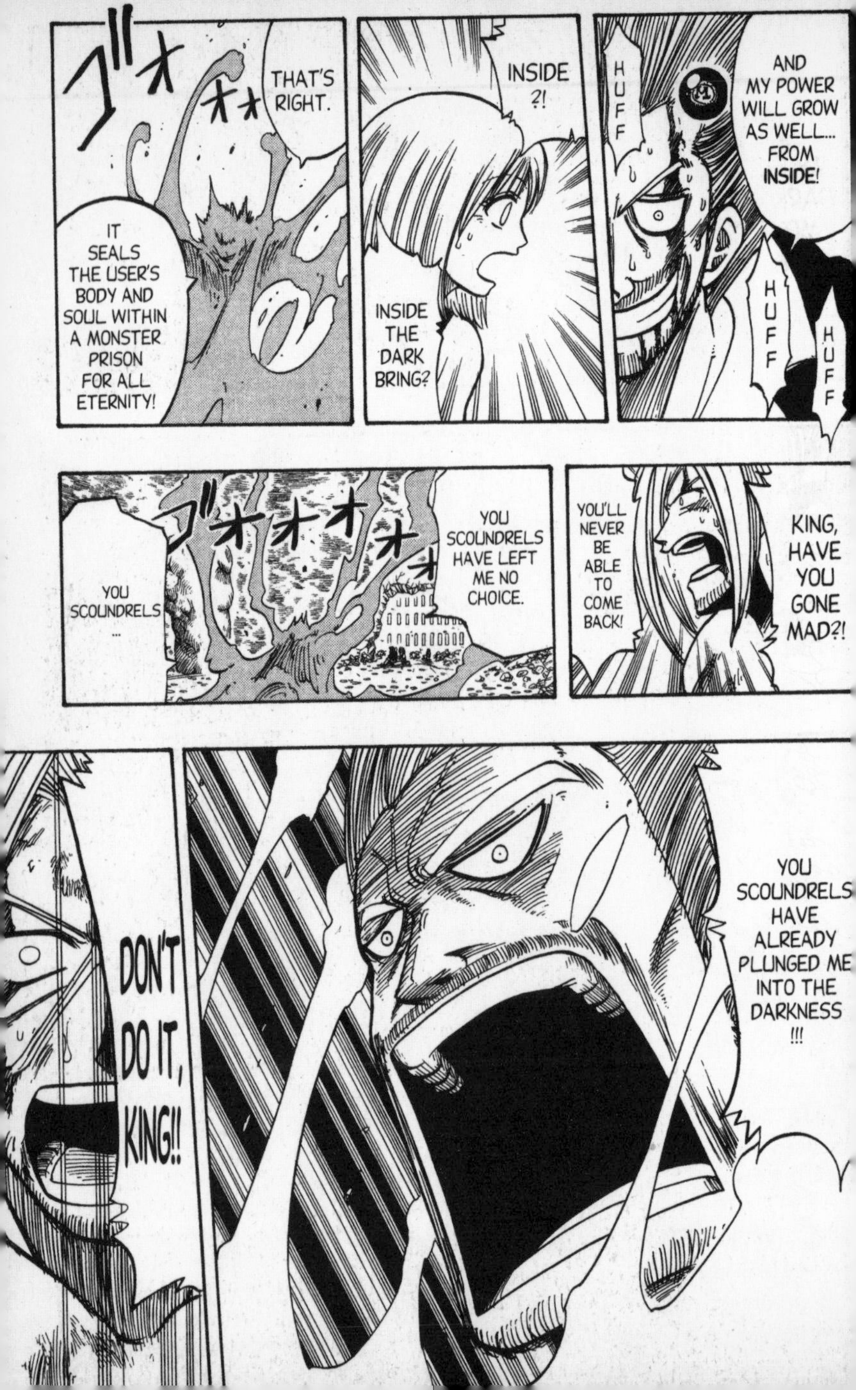
AND MY POWER WILL GROW AS WELL... FROM INSIDE!
HUFF
HUFF
HUFF
INSIDE ?!
INSIDE THE DARK BRING?
THAT'S RIGHT.
IT SEALS THE USER'S BODY AND SOUL WITHIN A MONSTER PRISON FOR ALL ETERNITY!
KING, HAVE YOU GONE MAD?!
YOU'LL NEVER BE ABLE TO COME BACK!
YOU SCOUNDRELS HAVE LEFT ME NO CHOICE.
YOU SCOUNDRELS ...
YOU SCOUNDRELS HAVE ALREADY PLUNGED ME INTO THE DARKNESS !!!
DON'T DO IT, KING!!

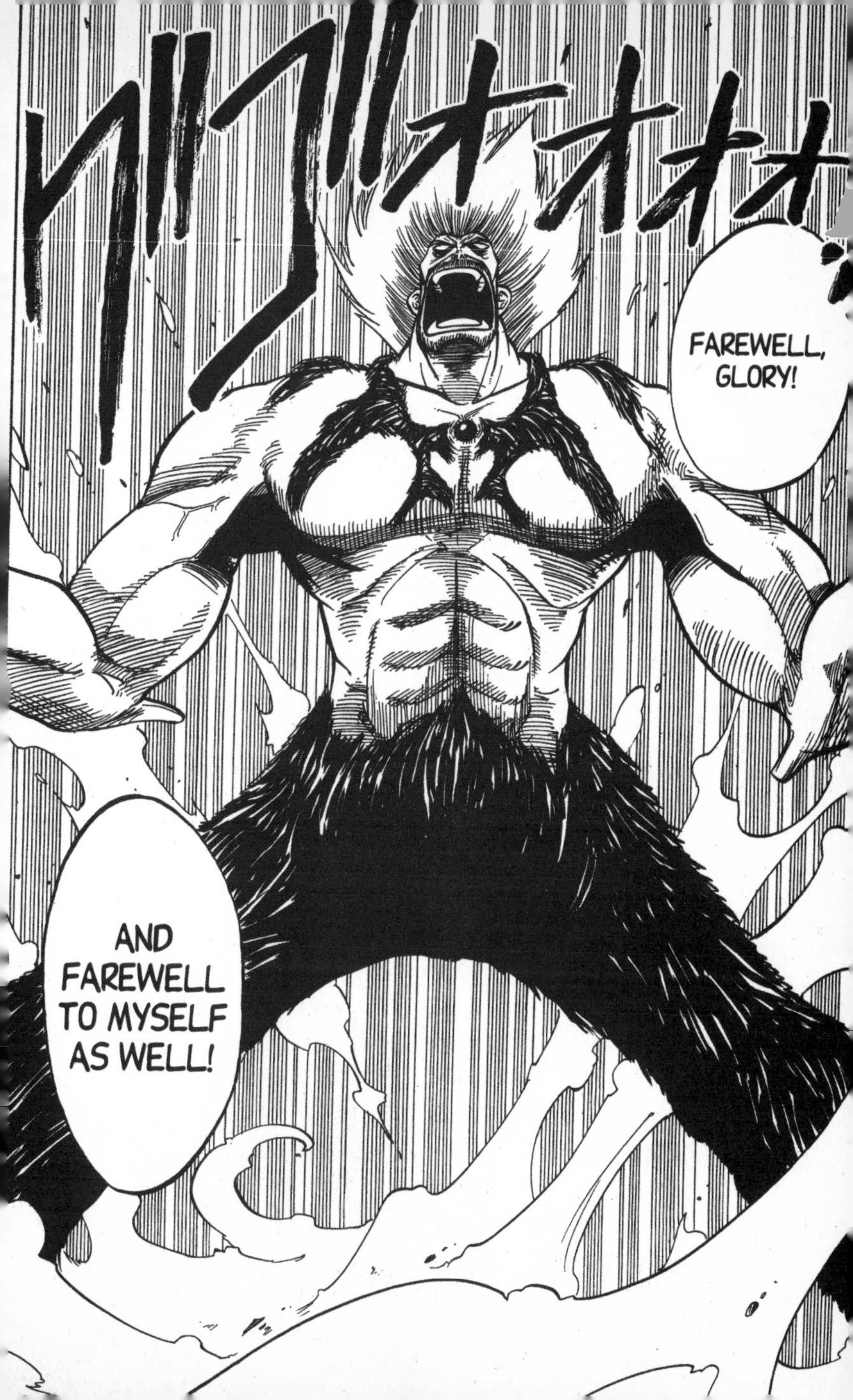
FAREWELL, GLORY!
AND FAREWELL TO MYSELF AS WELL!

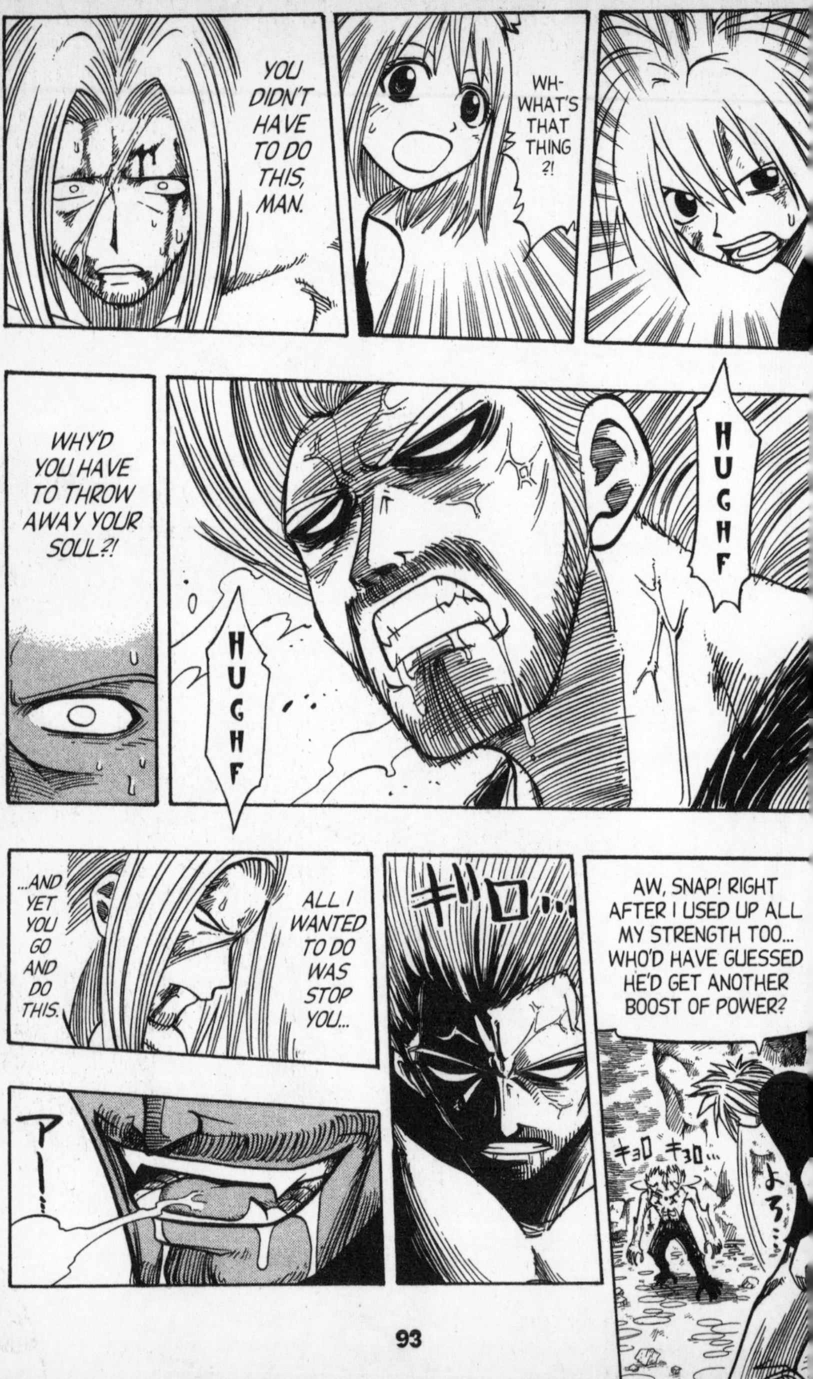
WH- WHAT'S THAT THING ?!
YOU DIDN'T HAVE TO DO THIS, MAN.
HUGHF
HUGHF
WHY'D YOU HAVE TO THROW AWAY YOUR SOUL?!
AW, SNAP! RIGHT AFTER I USED UP ALL MY STRENGTH TOO... WHO'D HAVE GUESSED HE'D GET ANOTHER BOOST OF POWER?
キョロ キョロ...
よろ...
ギロ...
ALL I WANTED TO DO WAS STOP YOU...
...AND YET YOU GO AND DO THIS.
アー...

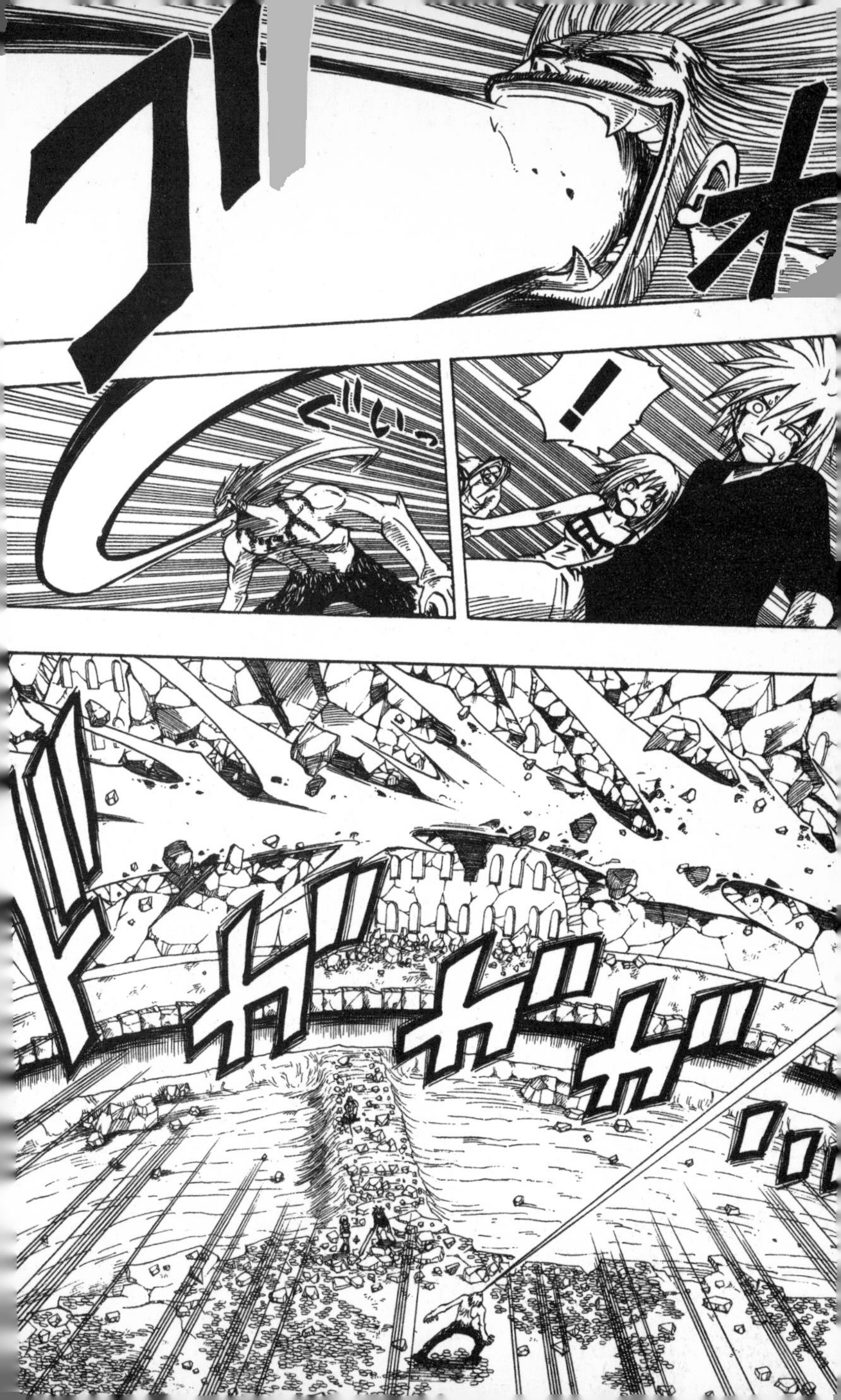

ブオ
!
ぐいーっ
ドオ゛オ゛オ゛

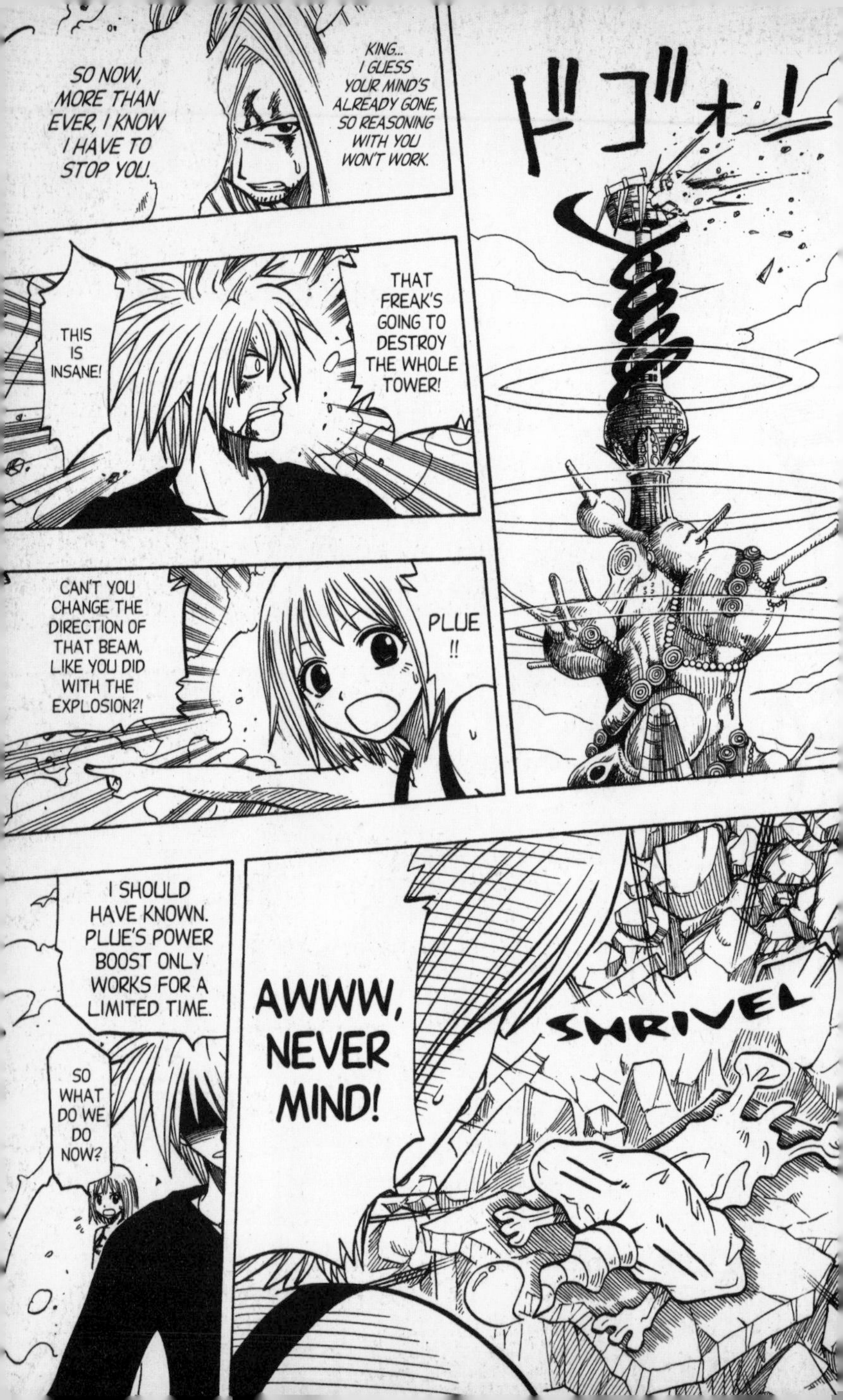
ドゴォ！
KING... I GUESS YOUR MIND'S ALREADY GONE, SO REASONING WITH YOU WON'T WORK.
SO NOW, MORE THAN EVER, I KNOW I HAVE TO STOP YOU.
THAT FREAK'S GOING TO DESTROY THE WHOLE TOWER!
THIS IS INSANE!
PLUE !!
CAN'T YOU CHANGE THE DIRECTION OF THAT BEAM, LIKE YOU DID WITH THE EXPLOSION?!
AWWW, NEVER MIND!
SHRIVEL
I SHOULD HAVE KNOWN. PLUE'S POWER BOOST ONLY WORKS FOR A LIMITED TIME.
SO WHAT DO WE DO NOW?

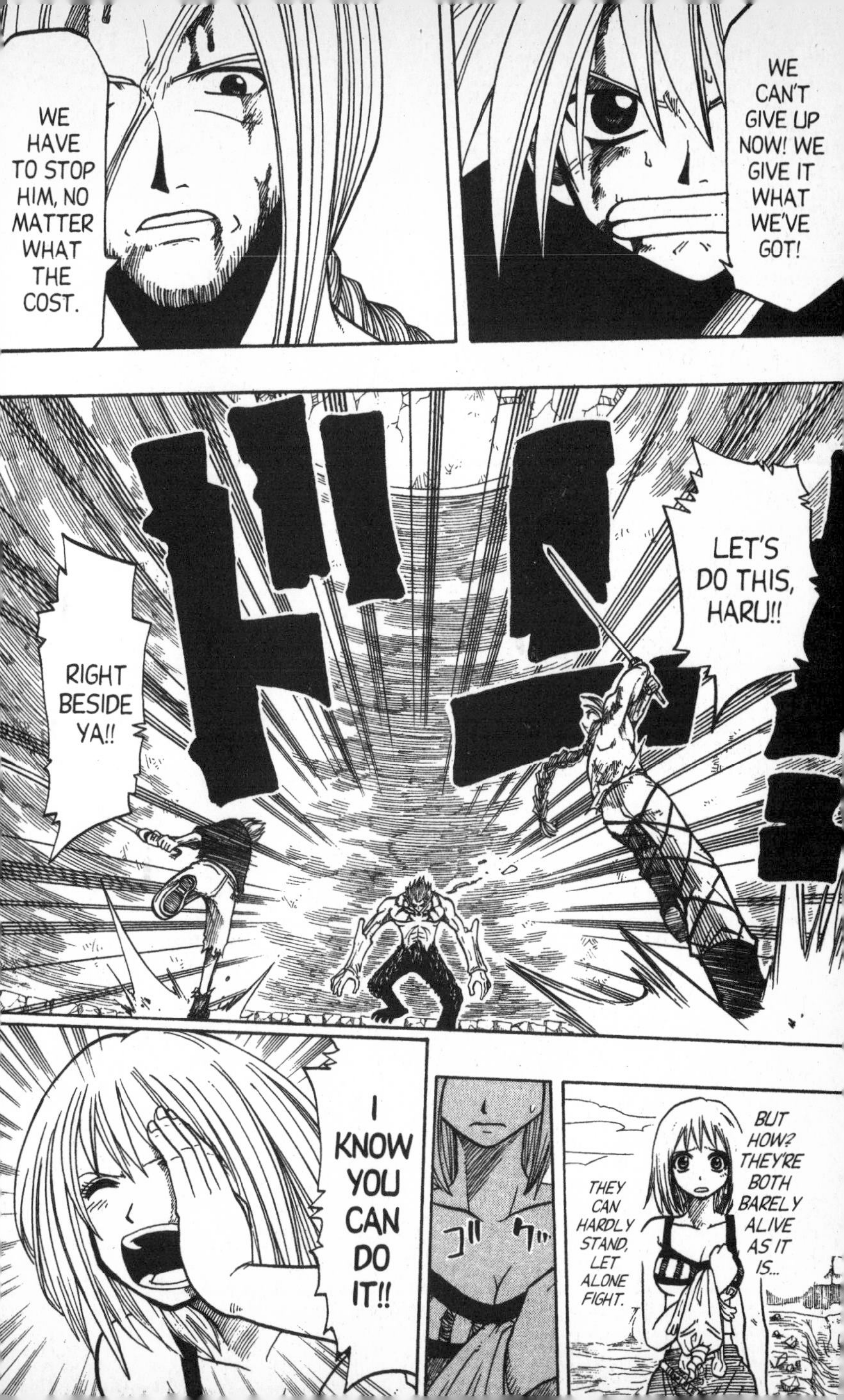
WE CAN'T GIVE UP NOW! WE GIVE IT WHAT WE'VE GOT!
WE HAVE TO STOP HIM, NO MATTER WHAT THE COST.
LET'S DO THIS, HARU!!
RIGHT BESIDE YA!!
BUT HOW? THEY'RE BOTH BARELY ALIVE AS IT IS...
THEY CAN HARDLY STAND, LET ALONE FIGHT.
I KNOW YOU CAN DO IT!!

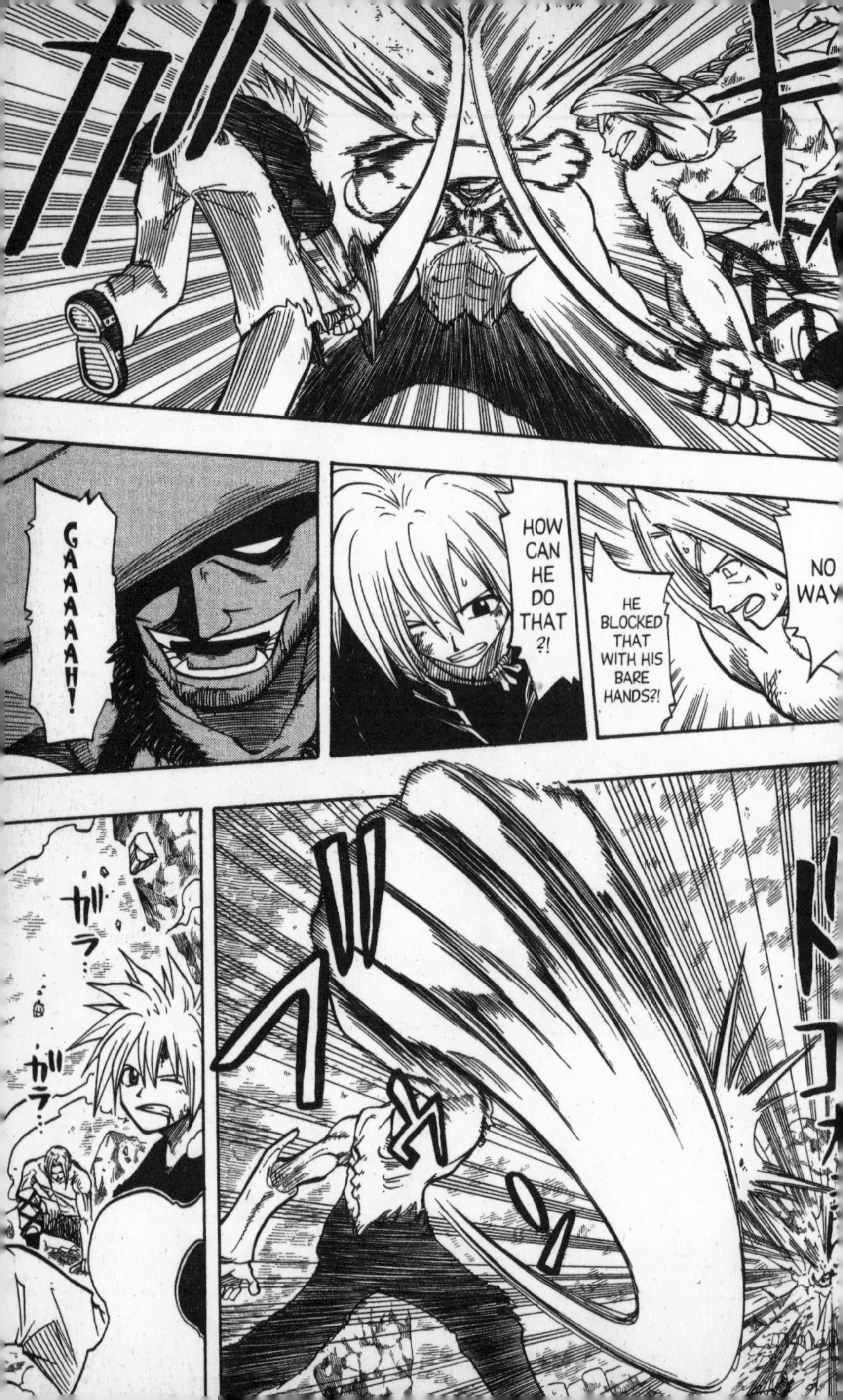
NO WAY
HE BLOCKED THAT WITH HIS BARE HANDS?!
HOW CAN HE DO THAT ?!
GAAAAAAH!

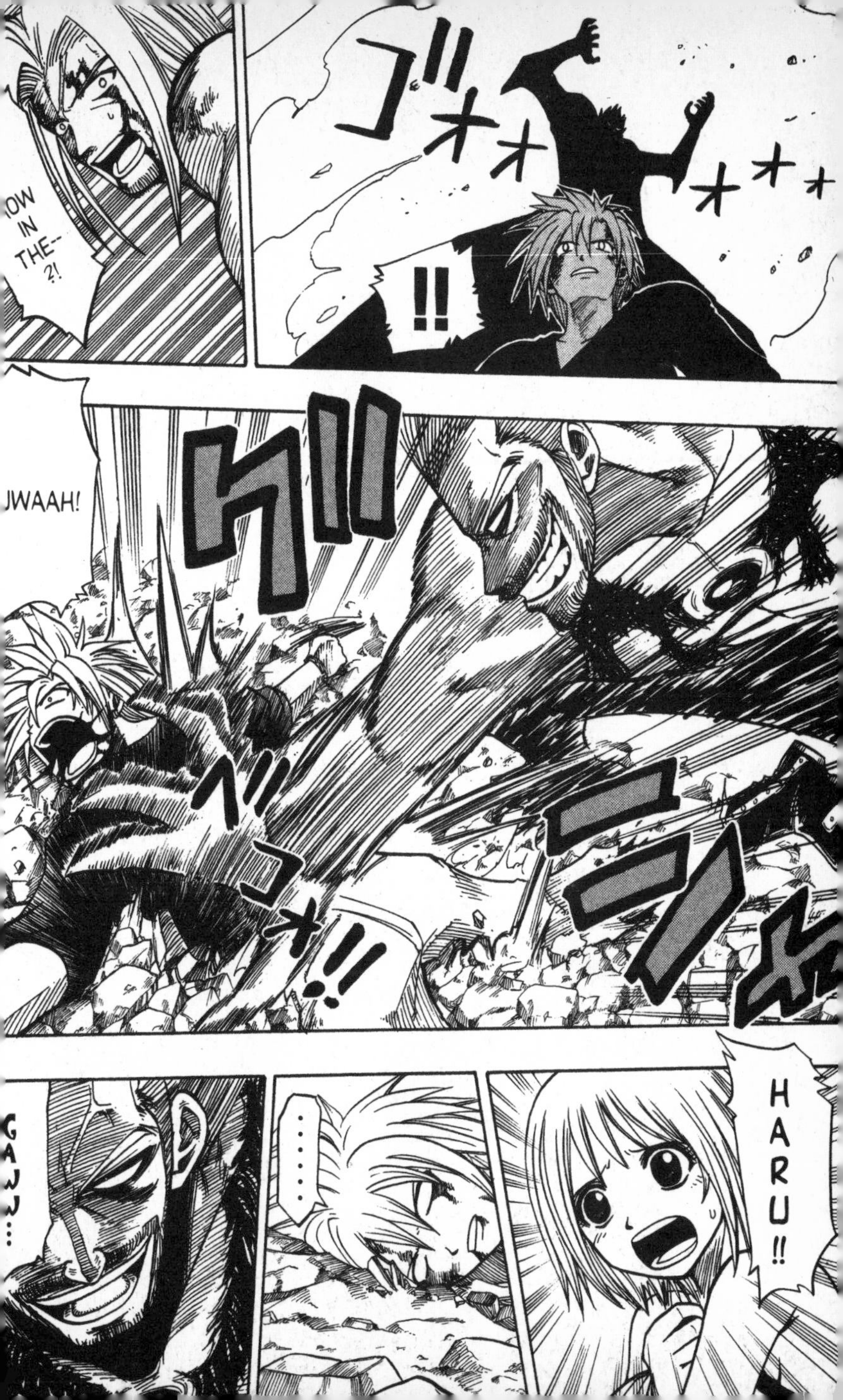
ゴオオオォォォ
!!
OW IN THE--?!
JWAAH!
HARU!!
......
GAWW...

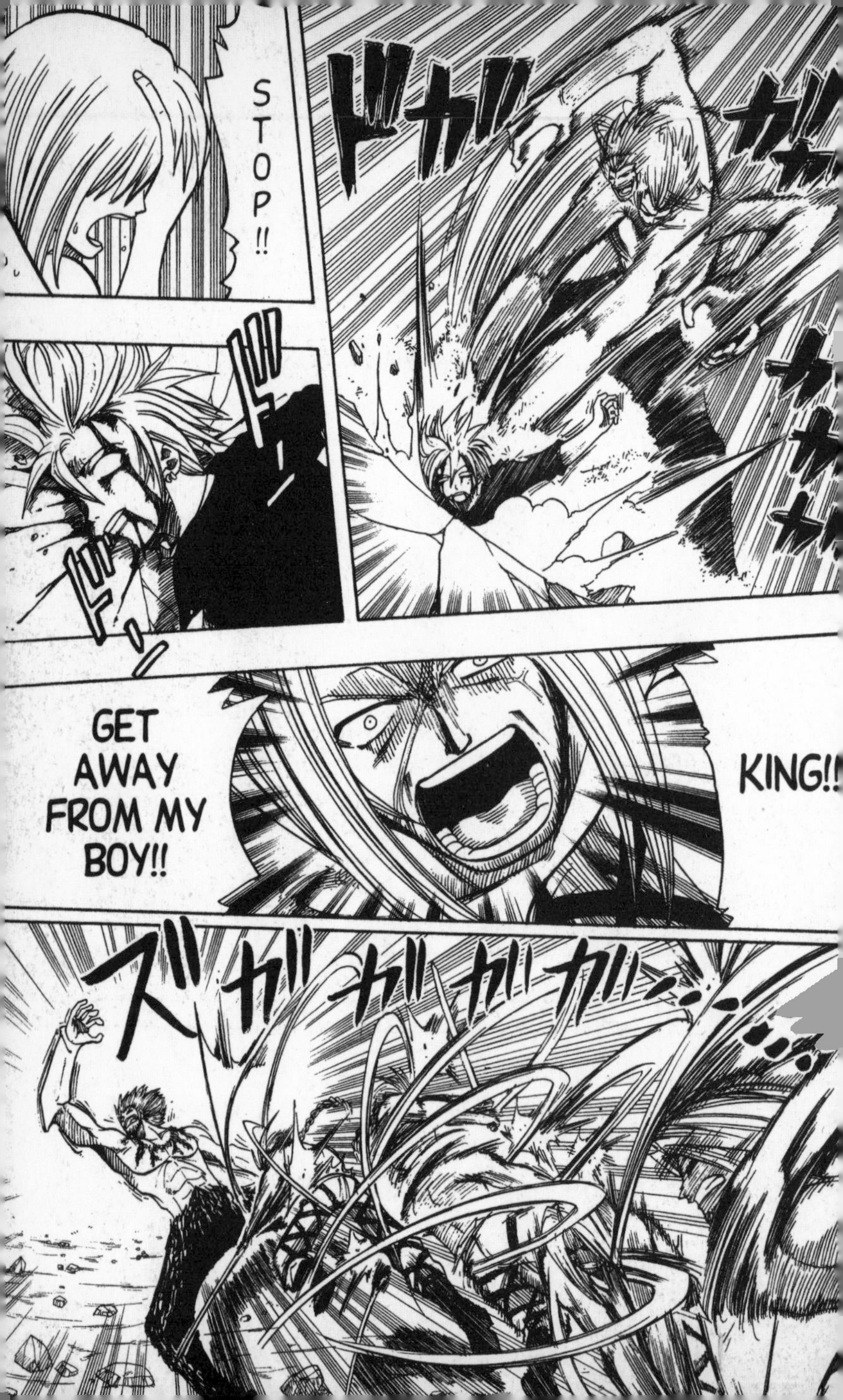
STOP!!
KING!!
GET AWAY FROM MY BOY!!

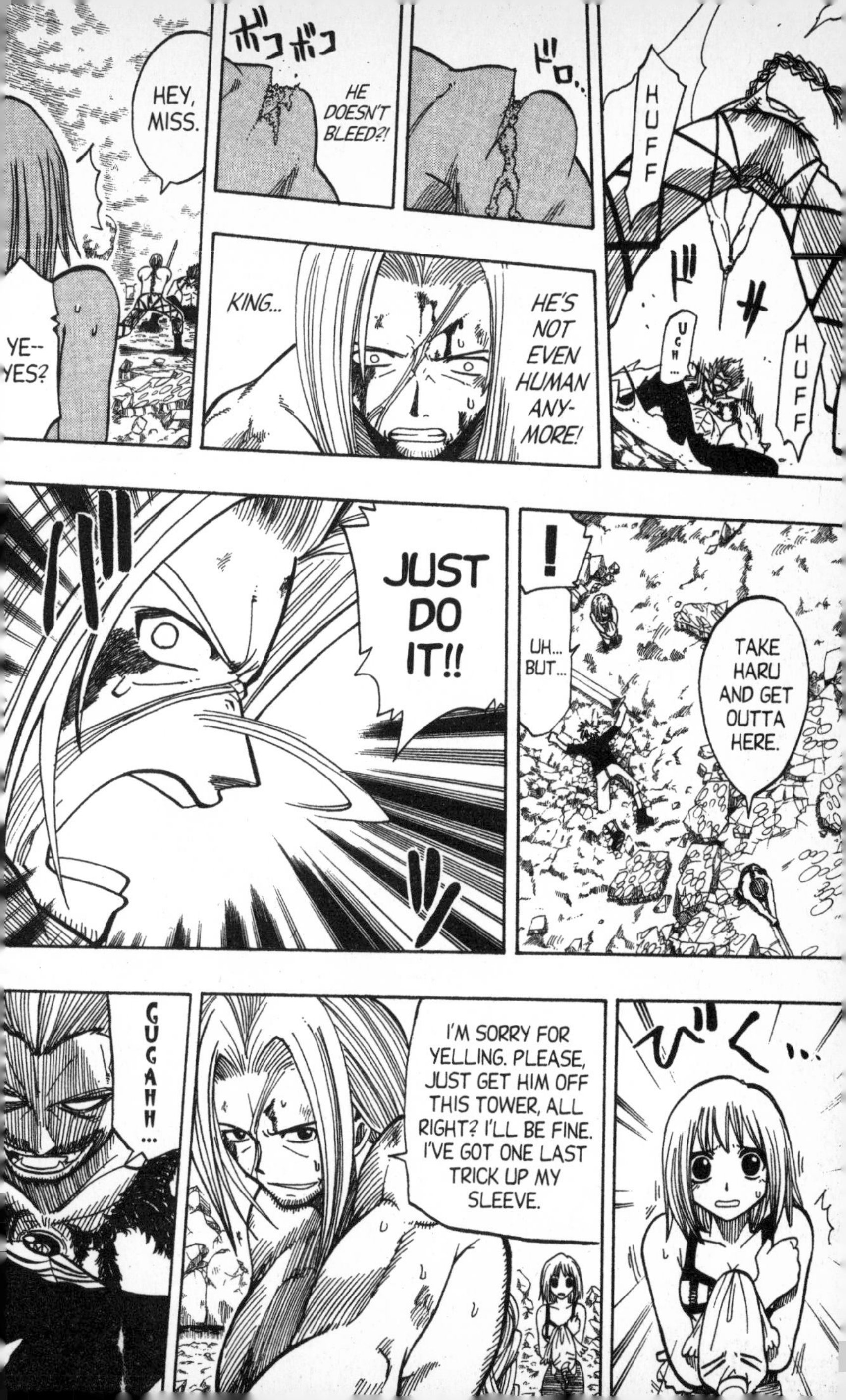
HUFF
UGH...
HUFF
ドド
ドロ...
ボコボコ
HE DOESN'T BLEED?!
HE'S NOT EVEN HUMAN ANYMORE!
KING...
HEY, MISS.
YE-- YES?
TAKE HARU AND GET OUTTA HERE.
!
UH... BUT...
JUST DO IT!!
びく...
I'M SORRY FOR YELLING. PLEASE, JUST GET HIM OFF THIS TOWER, ALL RIGHT? I'LL BE FINE. I'VE GOT ONE LAST TRICK UP MY SLEEVE.
GUGAHH...

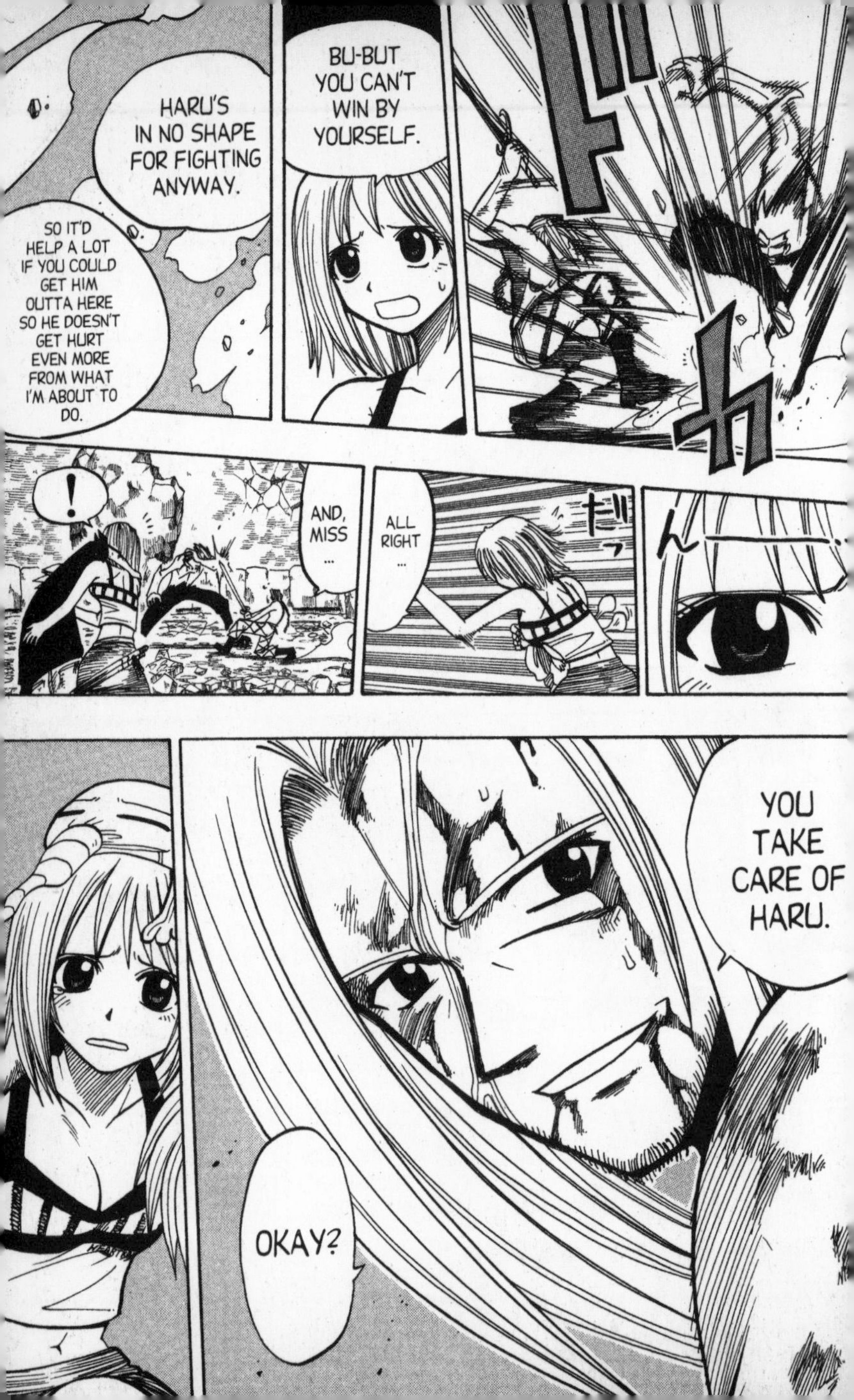
BU-BUT YOU CAN'T WIN BY YOURSELF.
HARU'S IN NO SHAPE FOR FIGHTING ANYWAY.
SO IT'D HELP A LOT IF YOU COULD GET HIM OUTTA HERE SO HE DOESN'T GET HURT EVEN MORE FROM WHAT I'M ABOUT TO DO.
ALL RIGHT ...
AND, MISS ...
!
YOU TAKE CARE OF HARU.
OKAY?

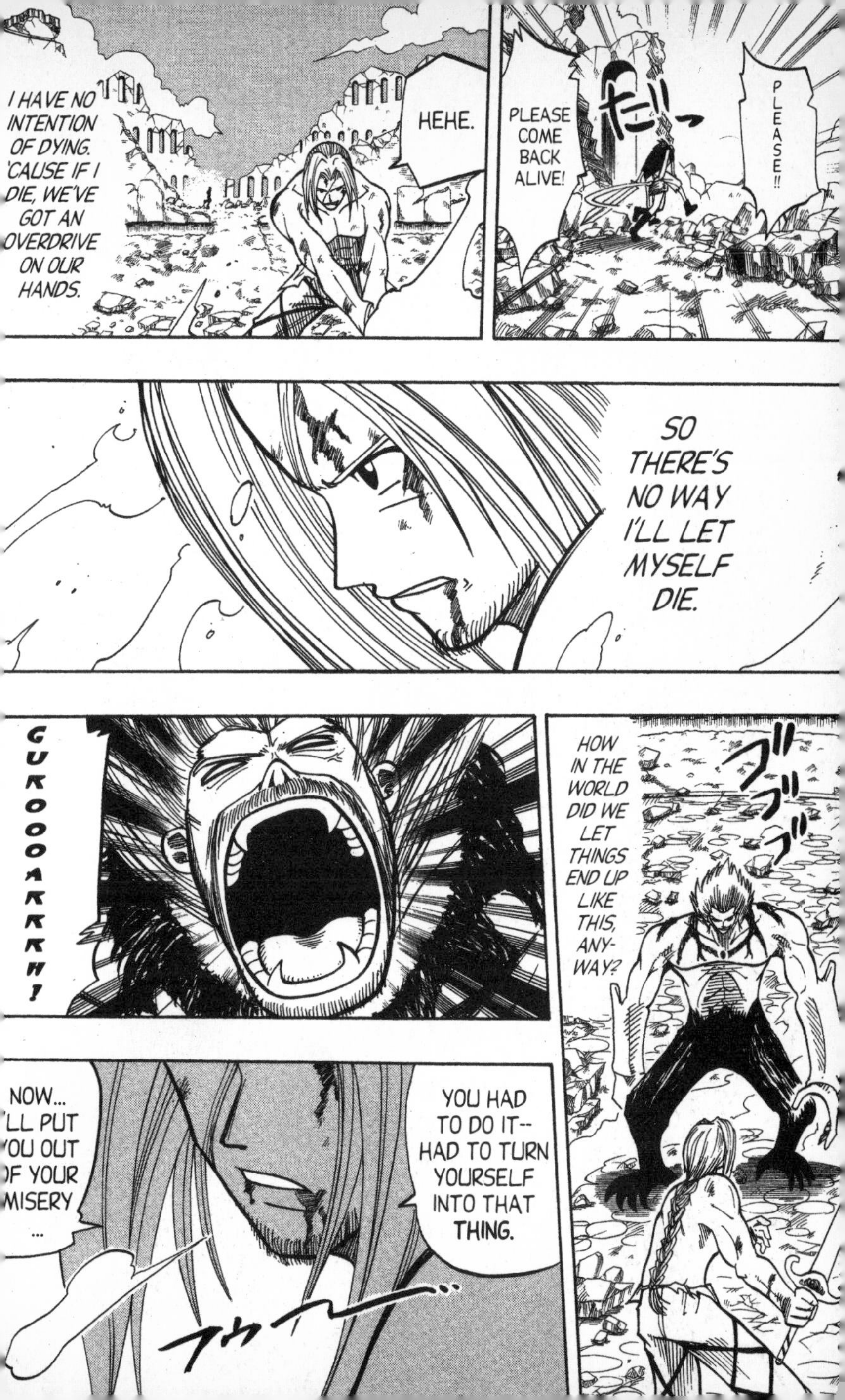
PLEASE COME BACK ALIVE!
PLEASE!!
HEHE.
I HAVE NO INTENTION OF DYING. 'CAUSE IF I DIE, WE'VE GOT AN OVERDRIVE ON OUR HANDS.
SO THERE'S NO WAY I'LL LET MYSELF DIE.
HOW IN THE WORLD DID WE LET THINGS END UP LIKE THIS, ANY-WAY?
GUROOOOARRRRH!
YOU HAD TO DO IT-- HAD TO TURN YOURSELF INTO THAT THING.
NOW... LL PUT OU OUT F YOUR MISERY ...

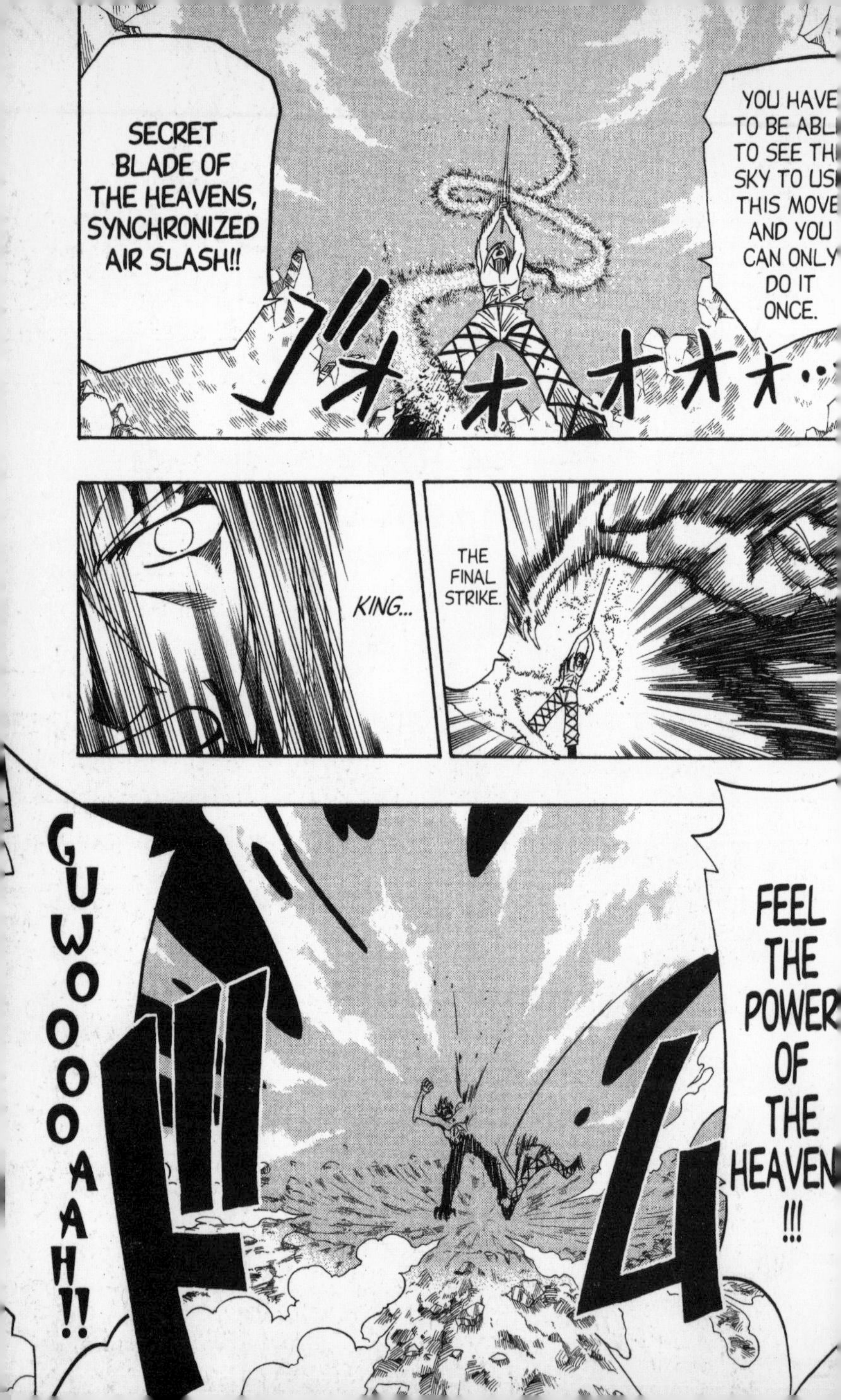
YOU HAVE TO BE ABL TO SEE TH SKY TO US THIS MOVE AND YOU CAN ONLY DO IT ONCE.
SECRET BLADE OF THE HEAVENS, SYNCHRONIZED AIR SLASH!!
THE FINAL STRIKE.
KING...
FEEL THE POWER OF THE HEAVEN !!!
GUWOOOOAAH!!

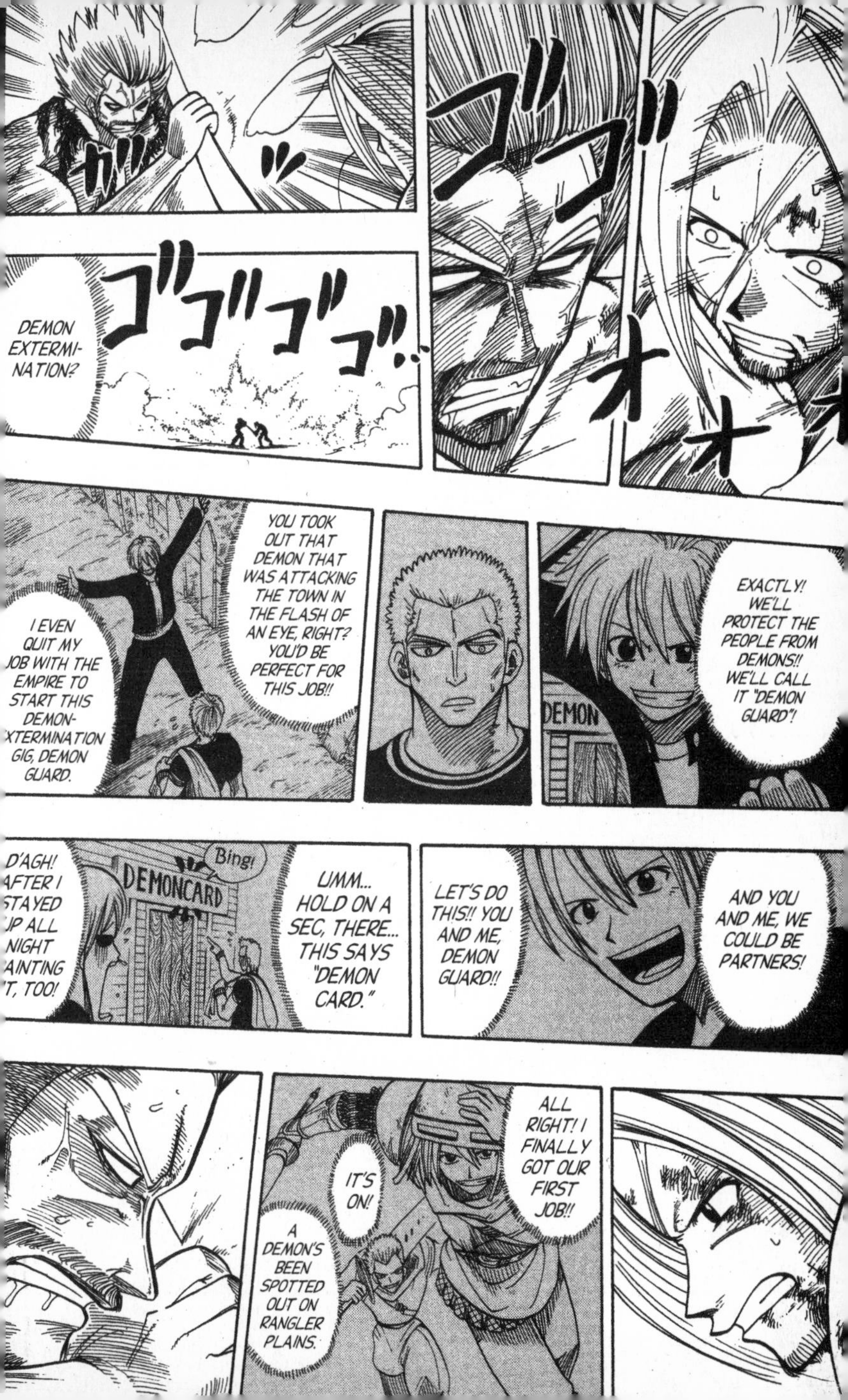
DEMON EXTERMINATION?
YOU TOOK OUT THAT DEMON THAT WAS ATTACKING THE TOWN IN THE FLASH OF AN EYE, RIGHT? YOU'D BE PERFECT FOR THIS JOB!!
I EVEN QUIT MY JOB WITH THE EMPIRE TO START THIS DEMON-XTERMINATION GIG, DEMON GUARD.
EXACTLY! WE'LL PROTECT THE PEOPLE FROM DEMONS!! WE'LL CALL IT "DEMON GUARD"!
DEMON
AND YOU AND ME, WE COULD BE PARTNERS!
LET'S DO THIS!! YOU AND ME, DEMON GUARD!!
UMM... HOLD ON A SEC, THERE... THIS SAYS "DEMON CARD."
Bing!
DEMONCARD
D'AGH! AFTER I STAYED UP ALL NIGHT AINTING T, TOO!
ALL RIGHT! I FINALLY GOT OUR FIRST JOB!!
IT'S ON!
A DEMON'S BEEN SPOTTED OUT ON RANGLER PLAINS.

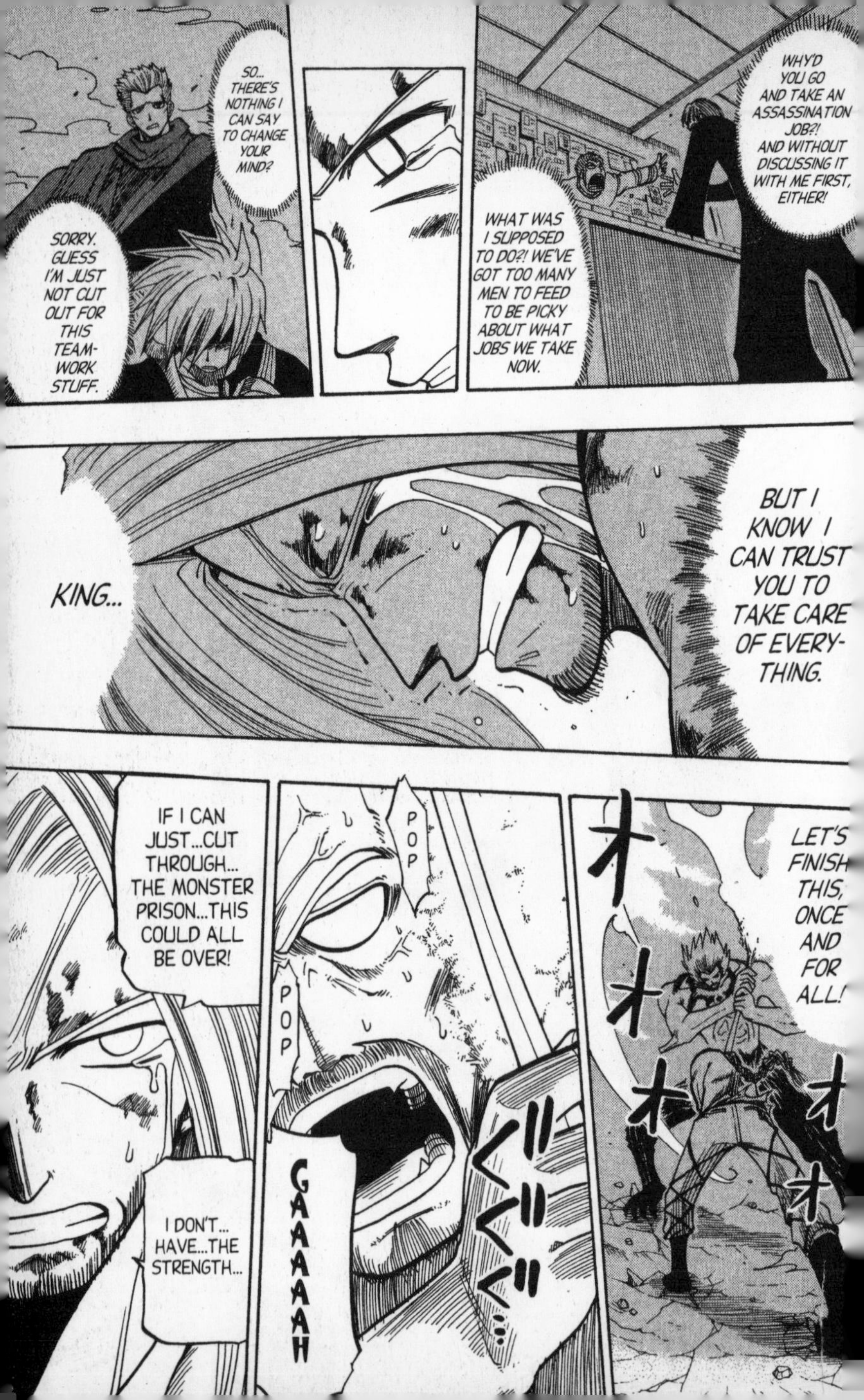
WHY'D YOU GO AND TAKE AN ASSASSINATION JOB?! AND WITHOUT DISCUSSING IT WITH ME FIRST, EITHER!
WHAT WAS I SUPPOSED TO DO?! WE'VE GOT TOO MANY MEN TO FEED TO BE PICKY ABOUT WHAT JOBS WE TAKE NOW.
SO... THERE'S NOTHING I CAN SAY TO CHANGE YOUR MIND?
SORRY. GUESS I'M JUST NOT CUT OUT FOR THIS TEAM-WORK STUFF.
BUT I KNOW I CAN TRUST YOU TO TAKE CARE OF EVERY-THING.
KING...
オオ
オオオ
LET'S FINISH THIS, ONCE AND FOR ALL!
POP
POP
POP
POP
ぐぐぐ...
GAAAAAH
IF I CAN JUST...CUT THROUGH... THE MONSTER PRISON...THIS COULD ALL BE OVER!
I DON'T... HAVE...THE STRENGTH...

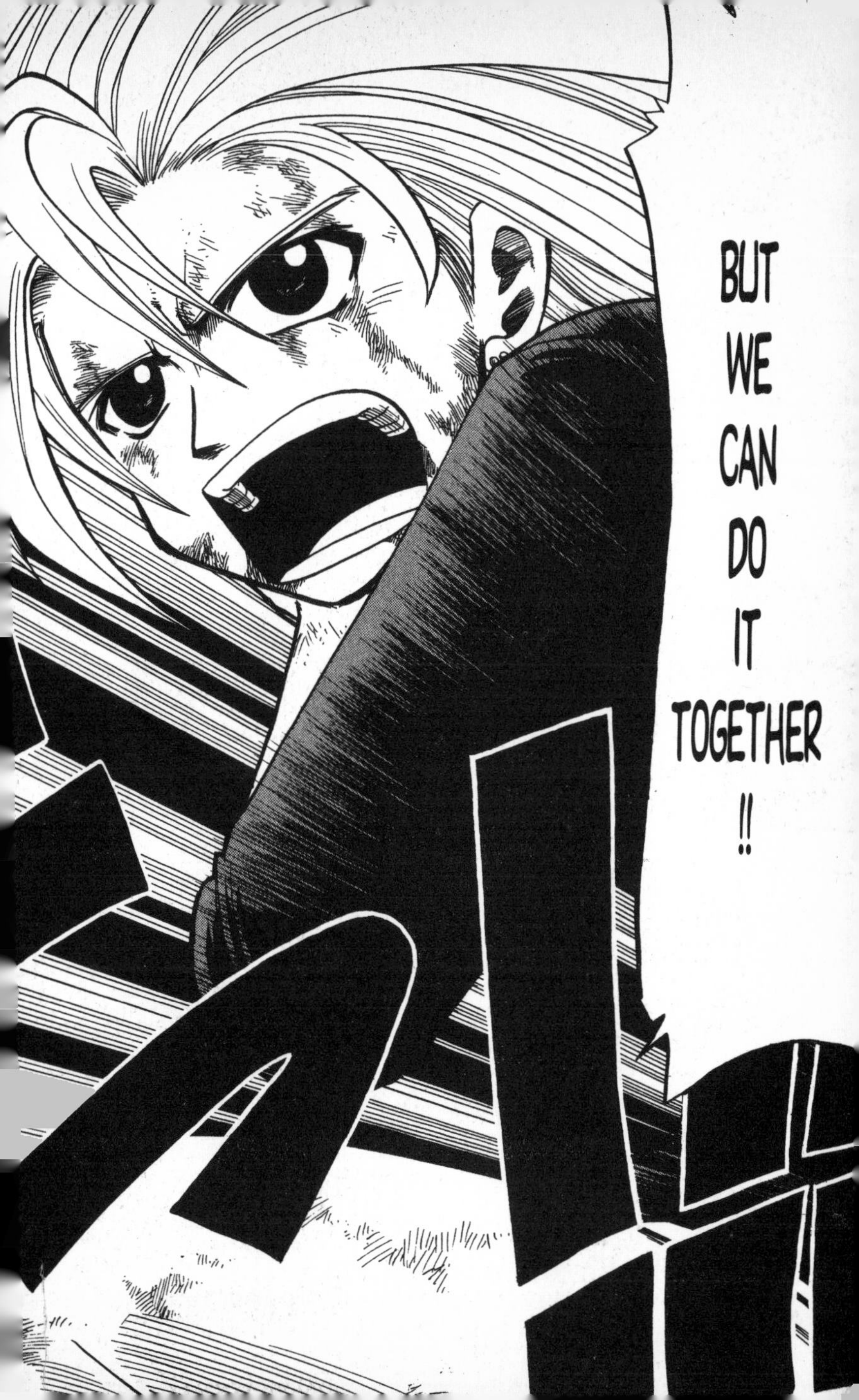
BUT WE CAN DO IT TOGETHER!!

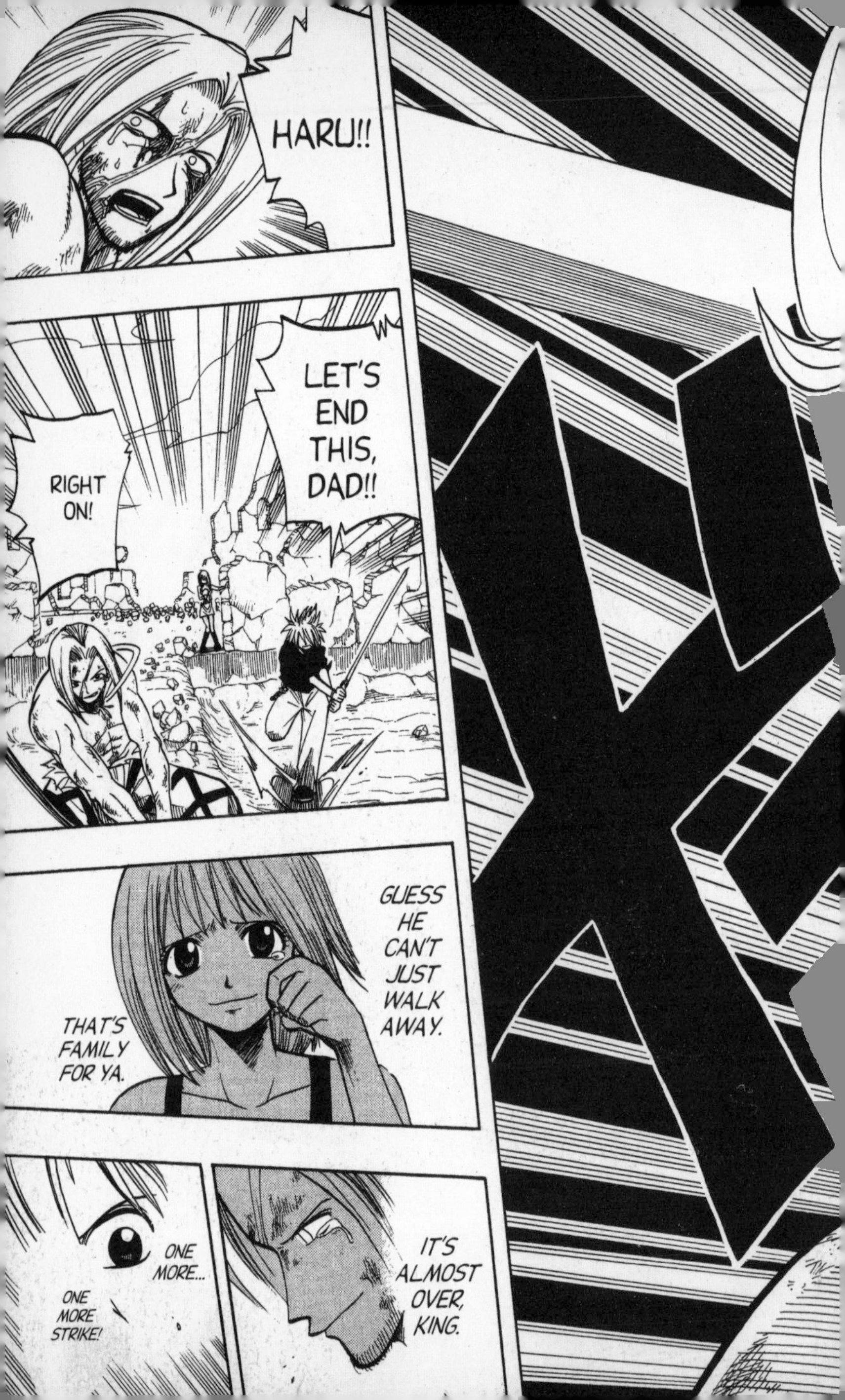
HARU!!
LET'S END THIS, DAD!!
RIGHT ON!
GUESS HE CAN'T JUST WALK AWAY.
THAT'S FAMILY FOR YA.
IT'S ALMOST OVER, KING.
ONE MORE...
ONE MORE STRIKE!

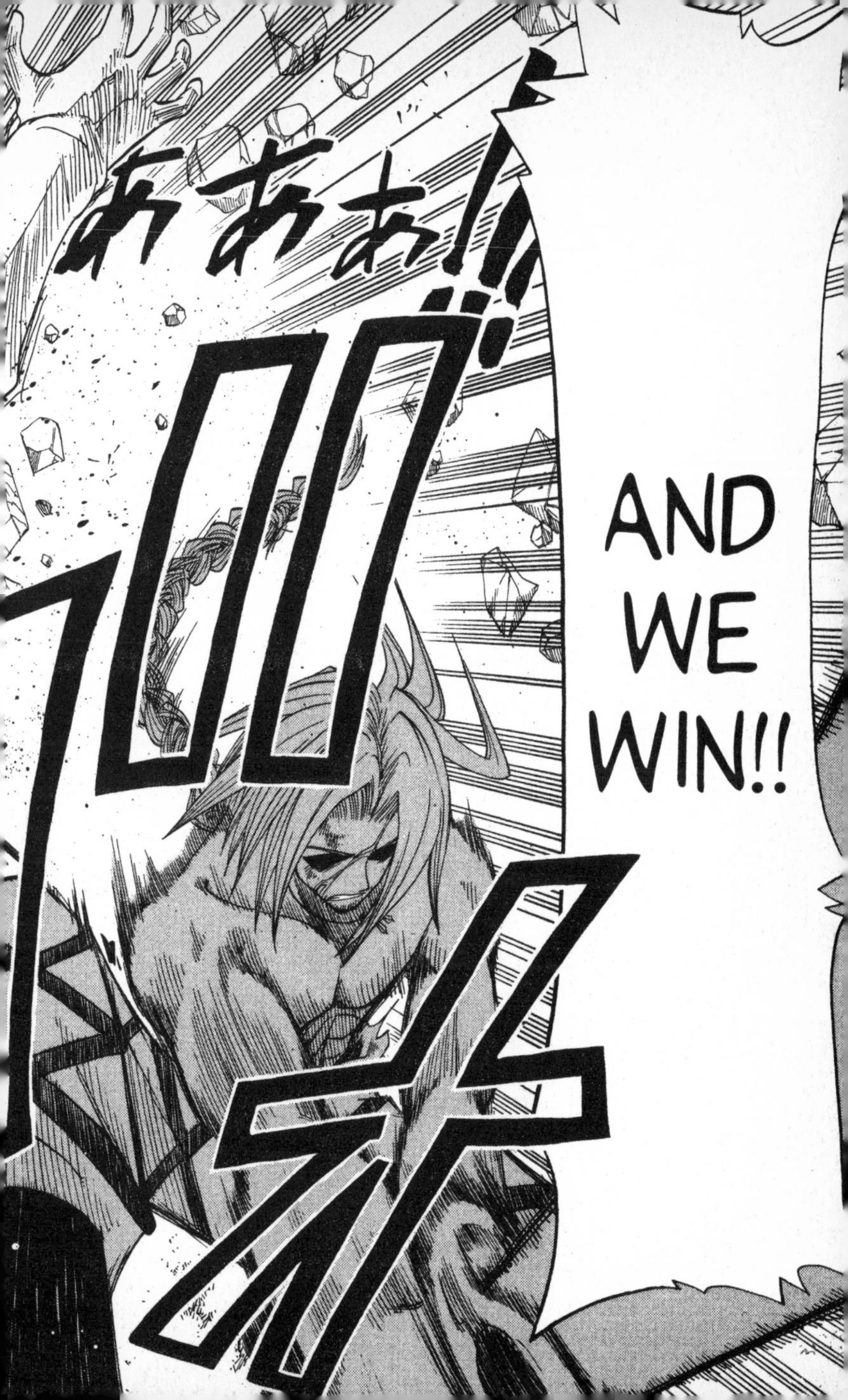
AND WE WIN!!
あああ!!!

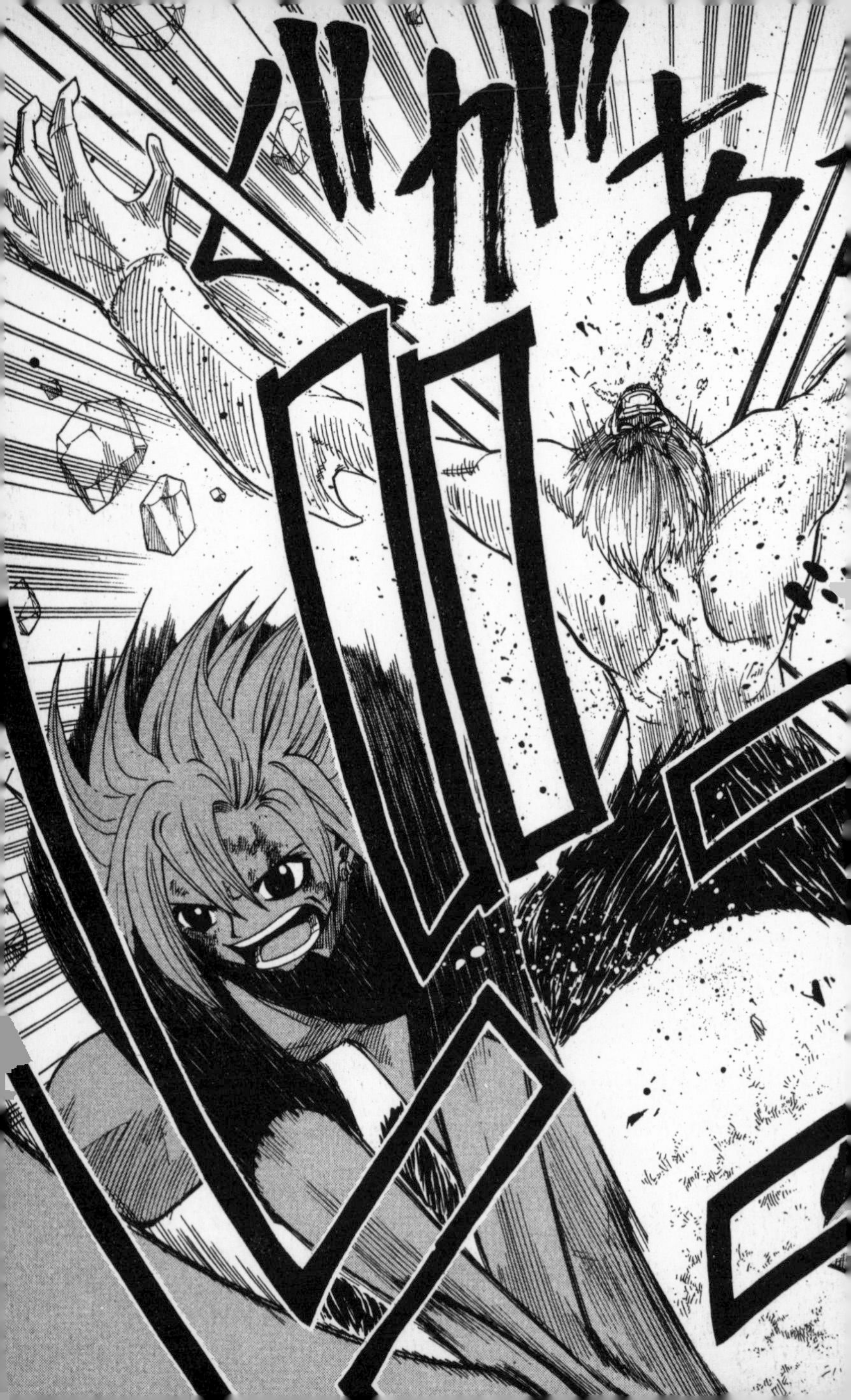

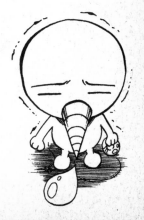

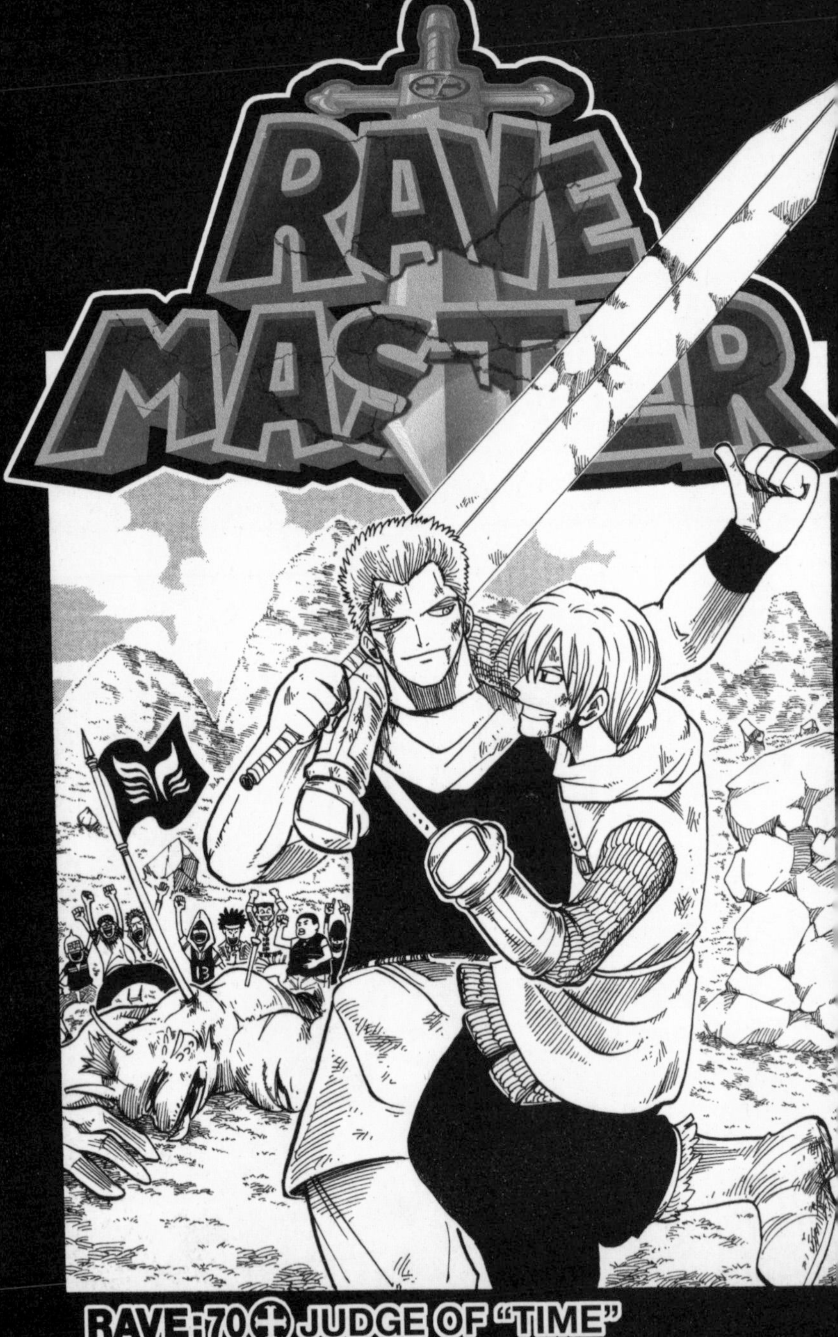
RAVE MASTER

RAVE:70 ✚ JUDGE OF "TIME"

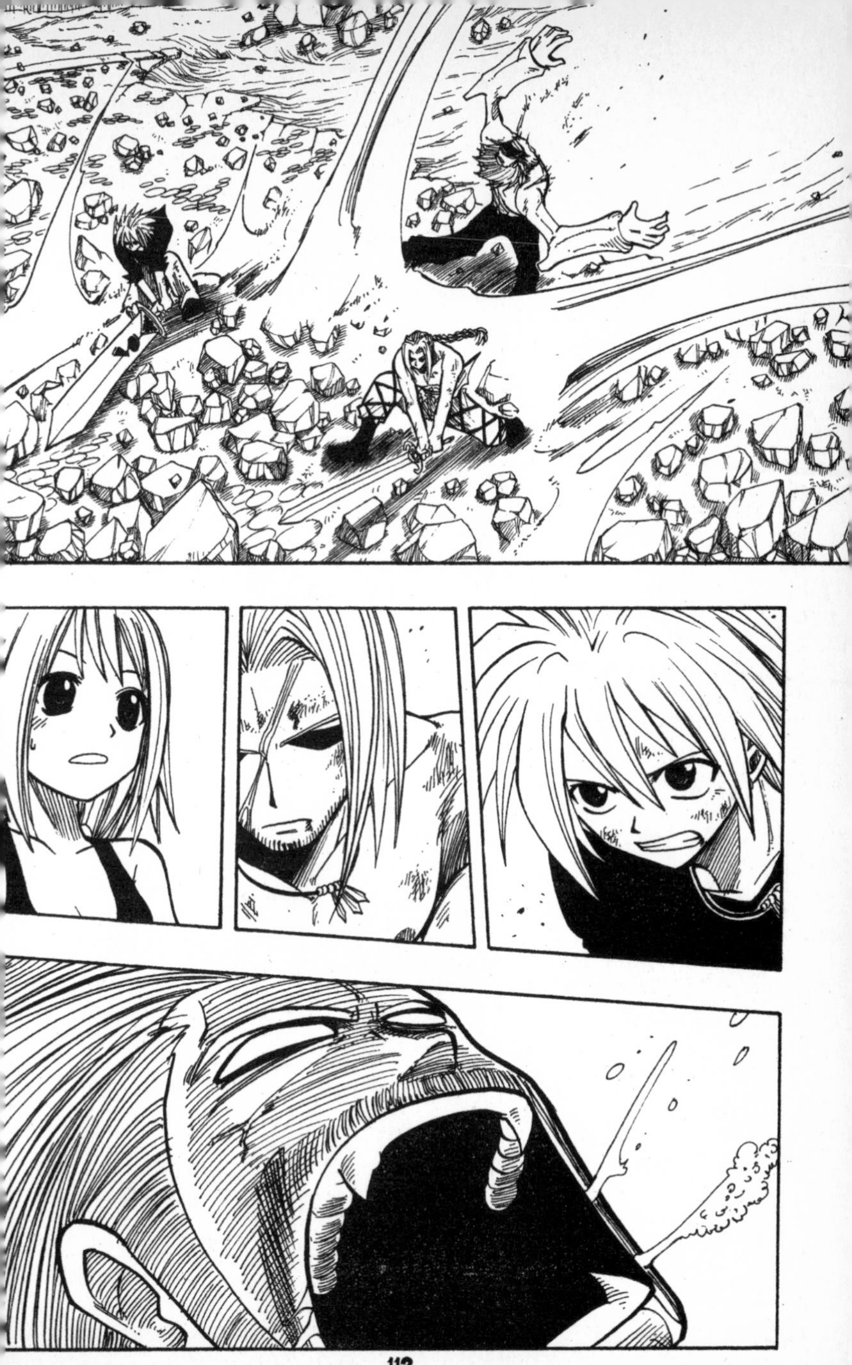

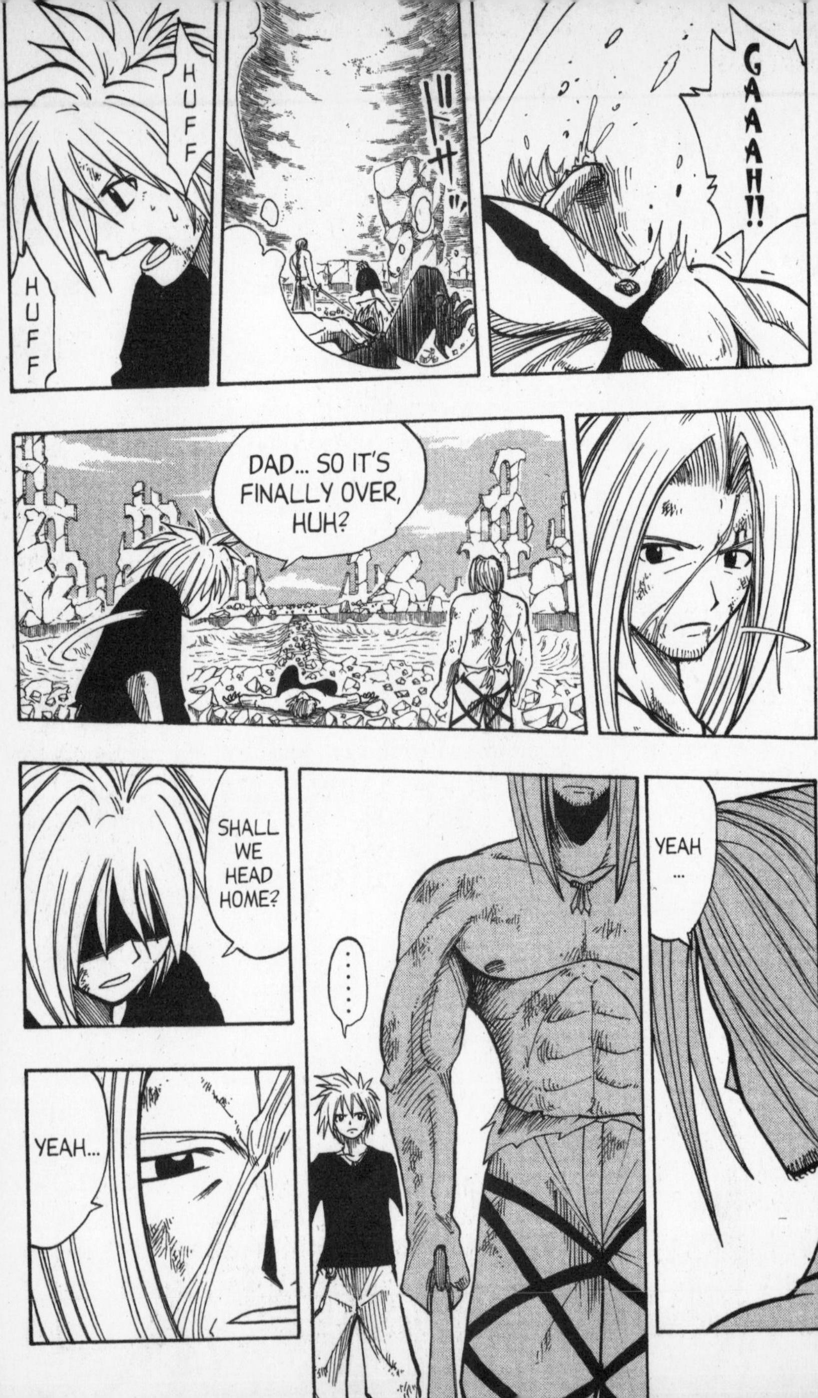
GAAAH!!
HUFF HUFF
DAD... SO IT'S FINALLY OVER, HUH?
YEAH ...
......
SHALL WE HEAD HOME?
YEAH...

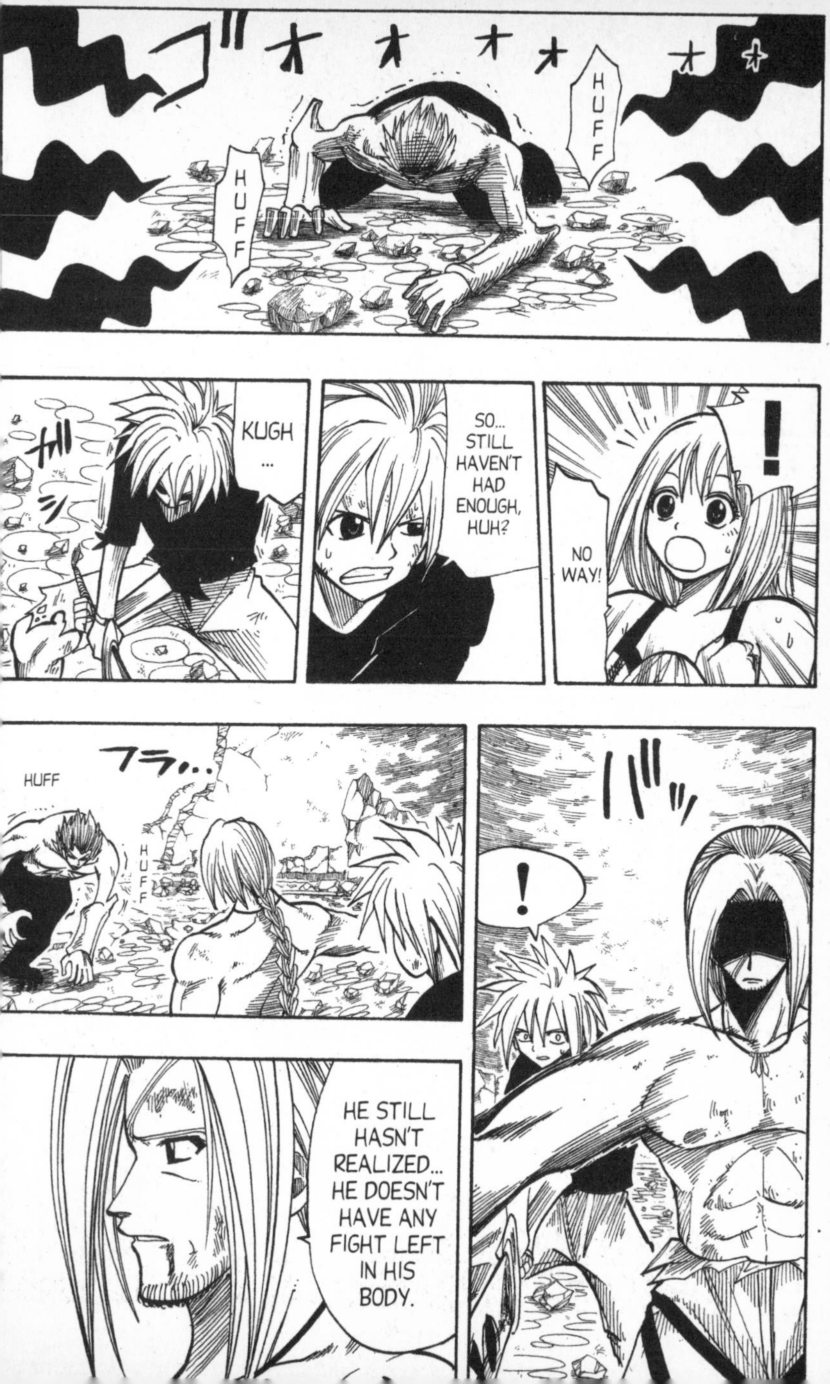
ゴオオオオオ
HUFF
HUFF
HUFF
HUFF
!
NO WAY!
SO... STILL HAVEN'T HAD ENOUGH, HUH?
KUGH ...
バッ
!
フラ…
HUFF
HUFF
HE STILL HASN'T REALIZED... HE DOESN'T HAVE ANY FIGHT LEFT IN HIS BODY.

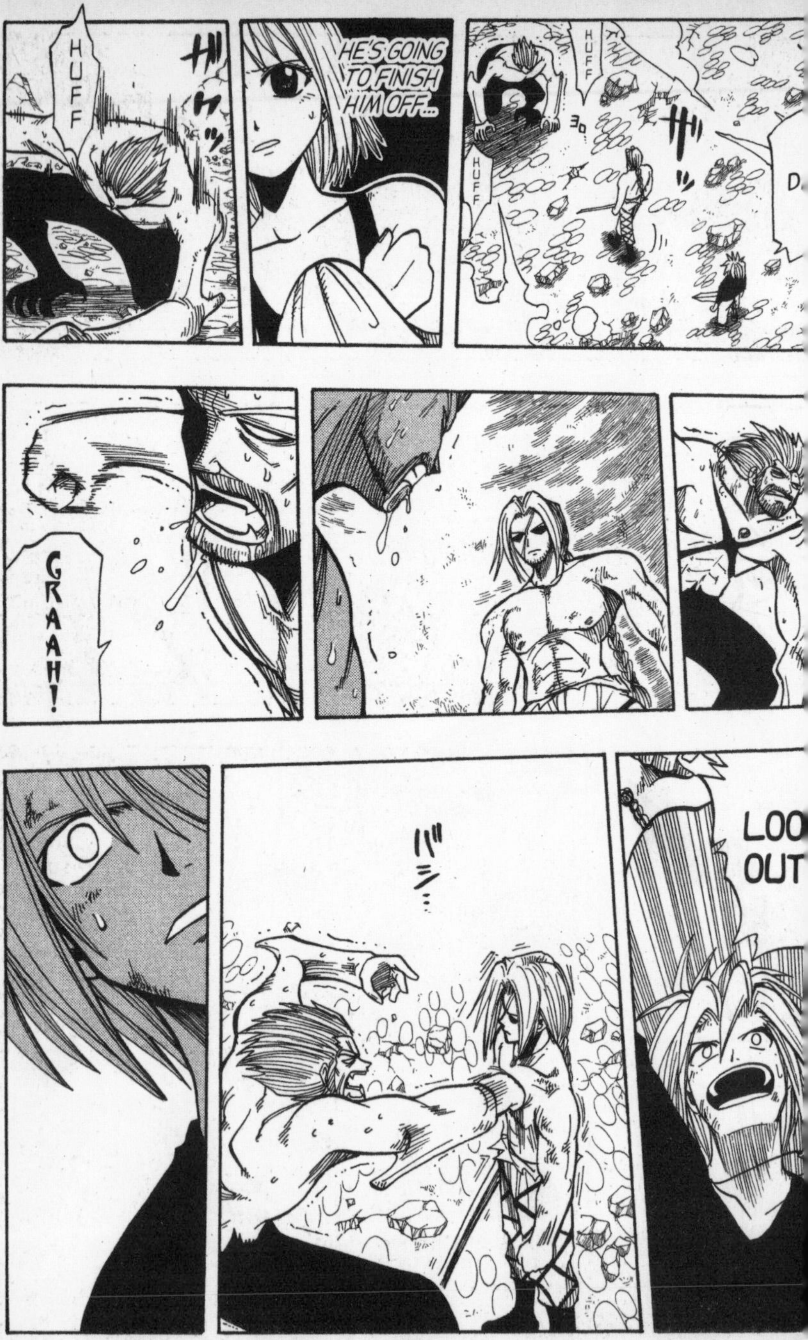
HUFF
HUFF
HE'S GOING TO FINISH HIM OFF...
HUFF
GRAAAH!
LOO
OUT

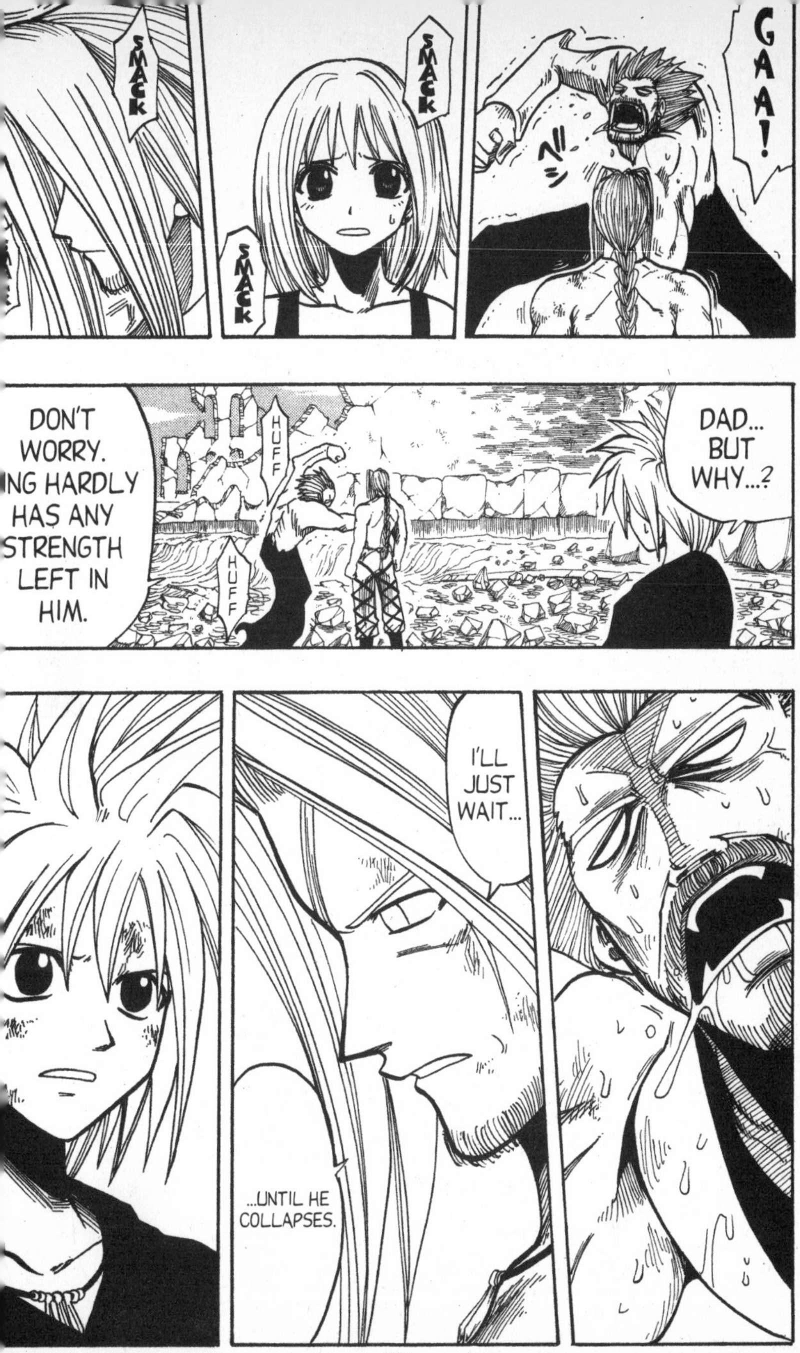
GAAA!
SMACK
SMACK
SMACK
DAD... BUT WHY...?
HUFF
HUFF
DON'T WORRY. NG HARDLY HAS ANY STRENGTH LEFT IN HIM.
I'LL JUST WAIT...
...UNTIL HE COLLAPSES.

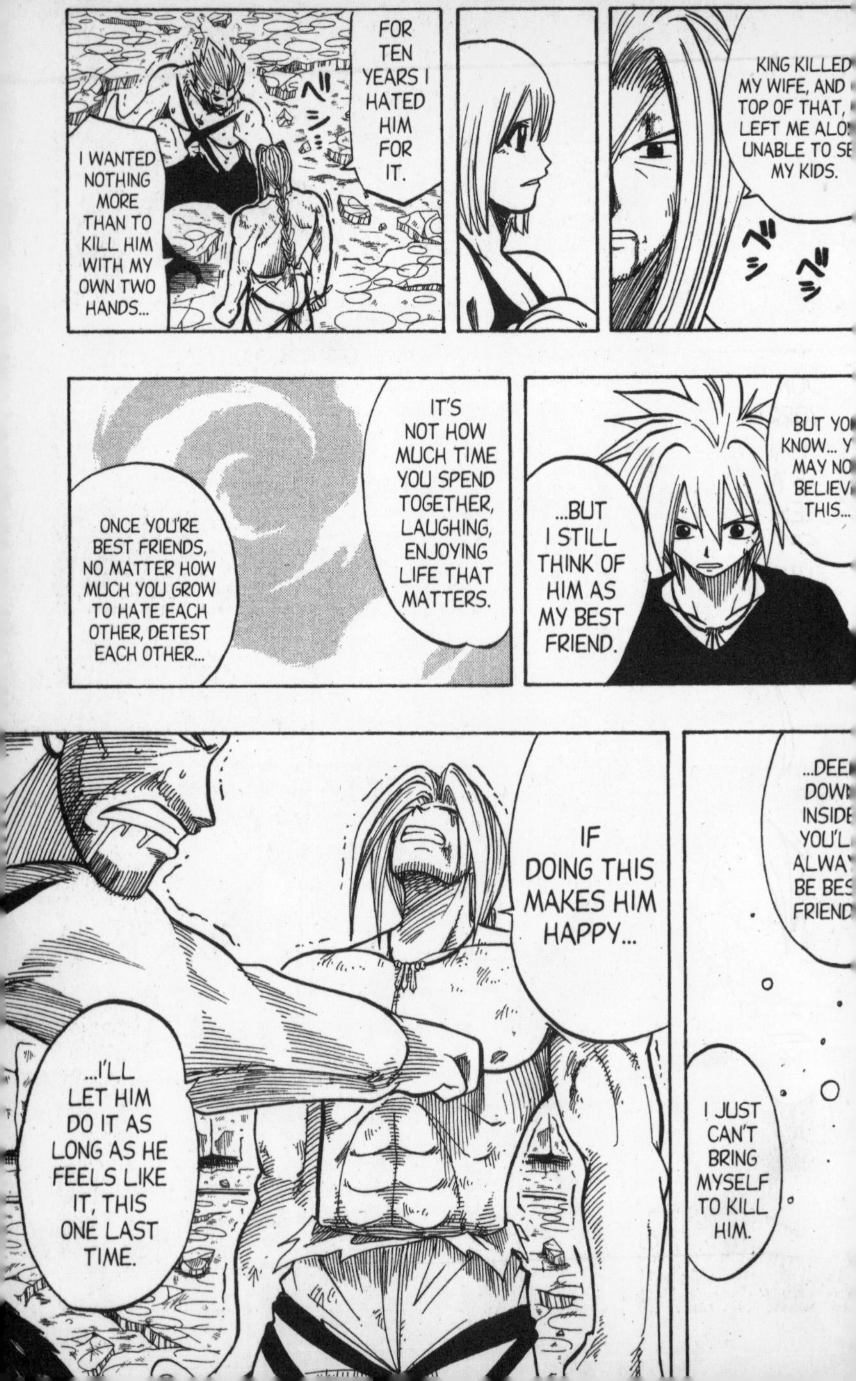
KING KILLED MY WIFE, AND TOP OF THAT, LEFT ME ALO UNABLE TO SE MY KIDS.
ベシ ベシ
FOR TEN YEARS I HATED HIM FOR IT.
I WANTED NOTHING MORE THAN TO KILL HIM WITH MY OWN TWO HANDS...
ベシ
BUT YO KNOW... Y MAY NO BELIEV THIS...
...BUT I STILL THINK OF HIM AS MY BEST FRIEND.
IT'S NOT HOW MUCH TIME YOU SPEND TOGETHER, LAUGHING, ENJOYING LIFE THAT MATTERS.
ONCE YOU'RE BEST FRIENDS, NO MATTER HOW MUCH YOU GROW TO HATE EACH OTHER, DETEST EACH OTHER...
...DEE DOW INSIDE YOU'L ALWAY BE BES FRIEND
I JUST CAN'T BRING MYSELF TO KILL HIM.
IF DOING THIS MAKES HIM HAPPY...
...I'LL LET HIM DO IT AS LONG AS HE FEELS LIKE IT, THIS ONE LAST TIME.

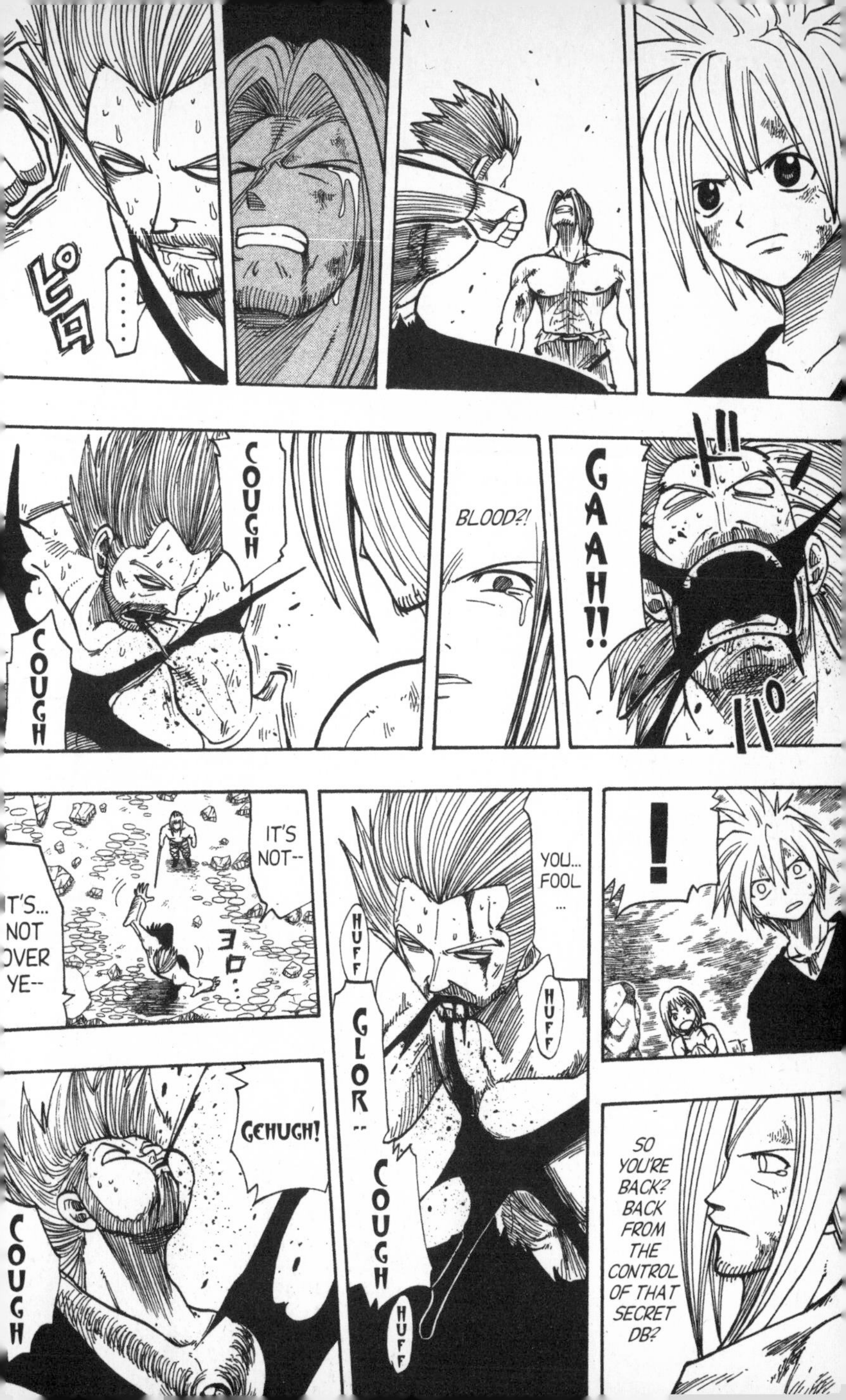
......
GAAH!!
BLOOD?!
COUGH
COUGH
!
YOU... FOOL ...
HUFF
HUFF
GLOR--
COUGH
HUFF
IT'S NOT--
IT'S... NOT OVER YE--
ヨロ...
SO YOU'RE BACK? BACK FROM THE CONTROL OF THAT SECRET DB?
GEHUGH!
COUGH

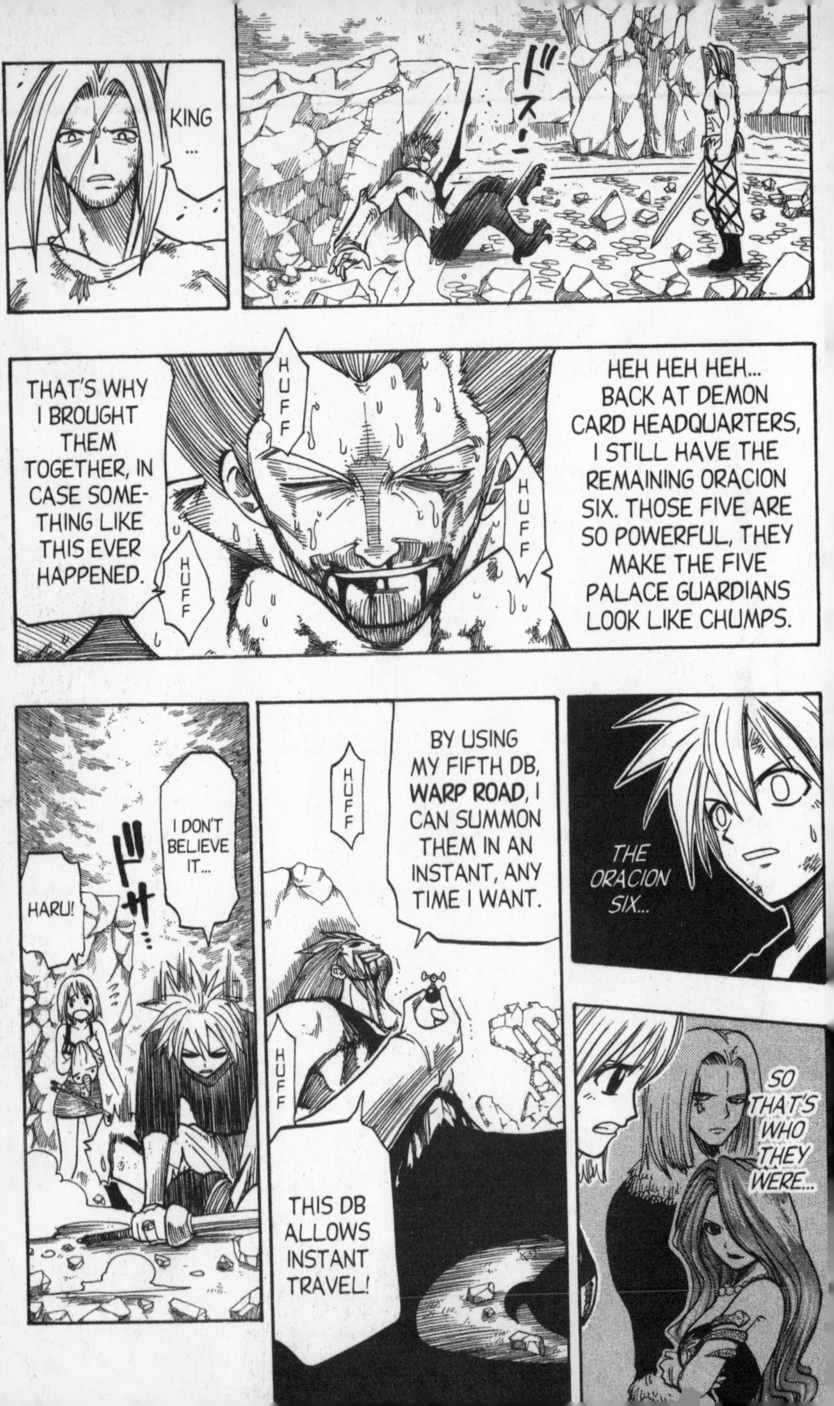
ドス
KING ...
HEH HEH HEH... BACK AT DEMON CARD HEADQUARTERS, I STILL HAVE THE REMAINING ORACION SIX. THOSE FIVE ARE SO POWERFUL, THEY MAKE THE FIVE PALACE GUARDIANS LOOK LIKE CHUMPS.
HUFF
HUFF
HUFF
THAT'S WHY I BROUGHT THEM TOGETHER, IN CASE SOME-THING LIKE THIS EVER HAPPENED.
THE ORACION SIX...
SO THAT'S WHO THEY WERE...
HUFF
BY USING MY FIFTH DB, **WARP ROAD**, I CAN SUMMON THEM IN AN INSTANT, ANY TIME I WANT.
HUFF
THIS DB ALLOWS INSTANT TRAVEL!
I DON'T BELIEVE IT...
HARU!

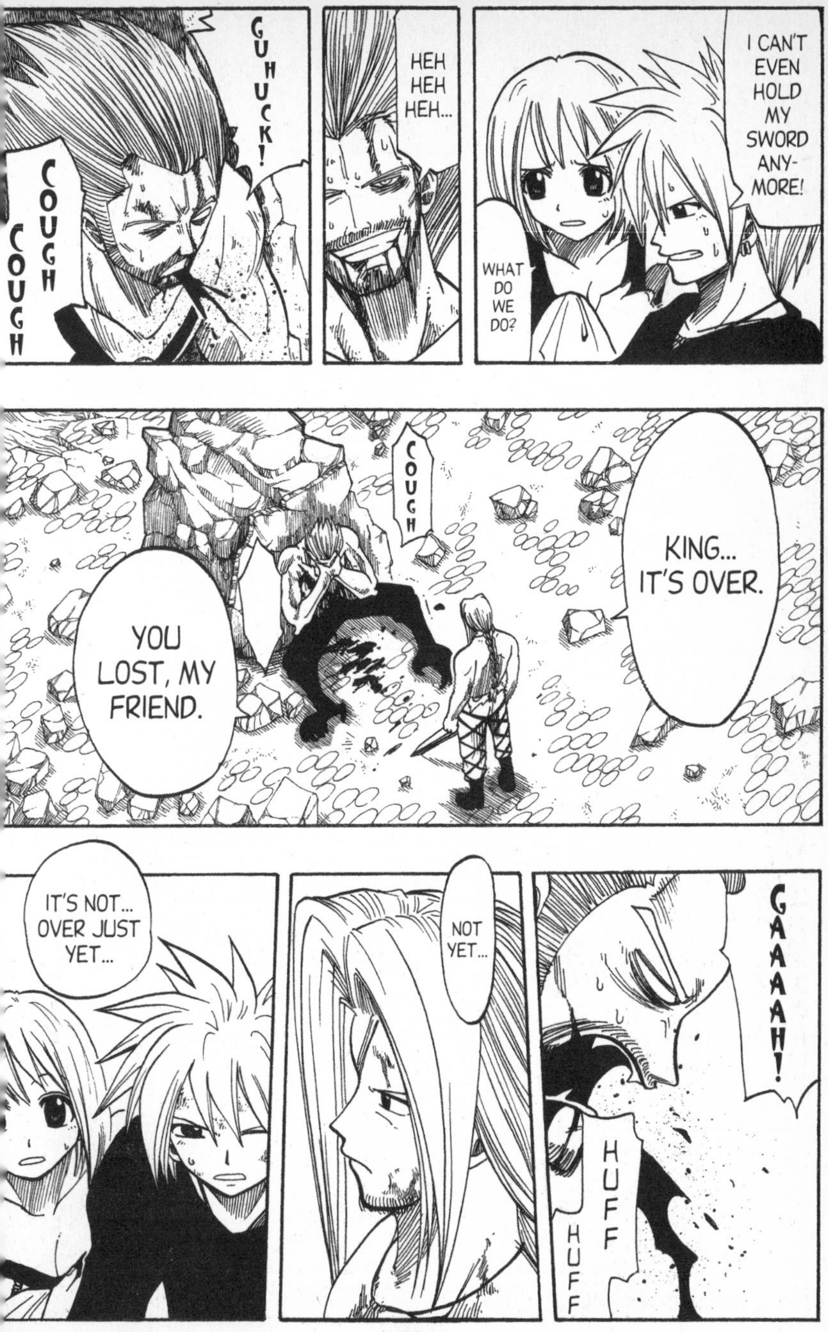
I CAN'T EVEN HOLD MY SWORD ANY-MORE!
WHAT DO WE DO?
HEH HEH HEH...
GUHUCK!
COUGH COUGH
KING... IT'S OVER.
COUGH
YOU LOST, MY FRIEND.
GAAAAH!
HUFF HUFF
NOT YET...
IT'S NOT... OVER JUST YET...

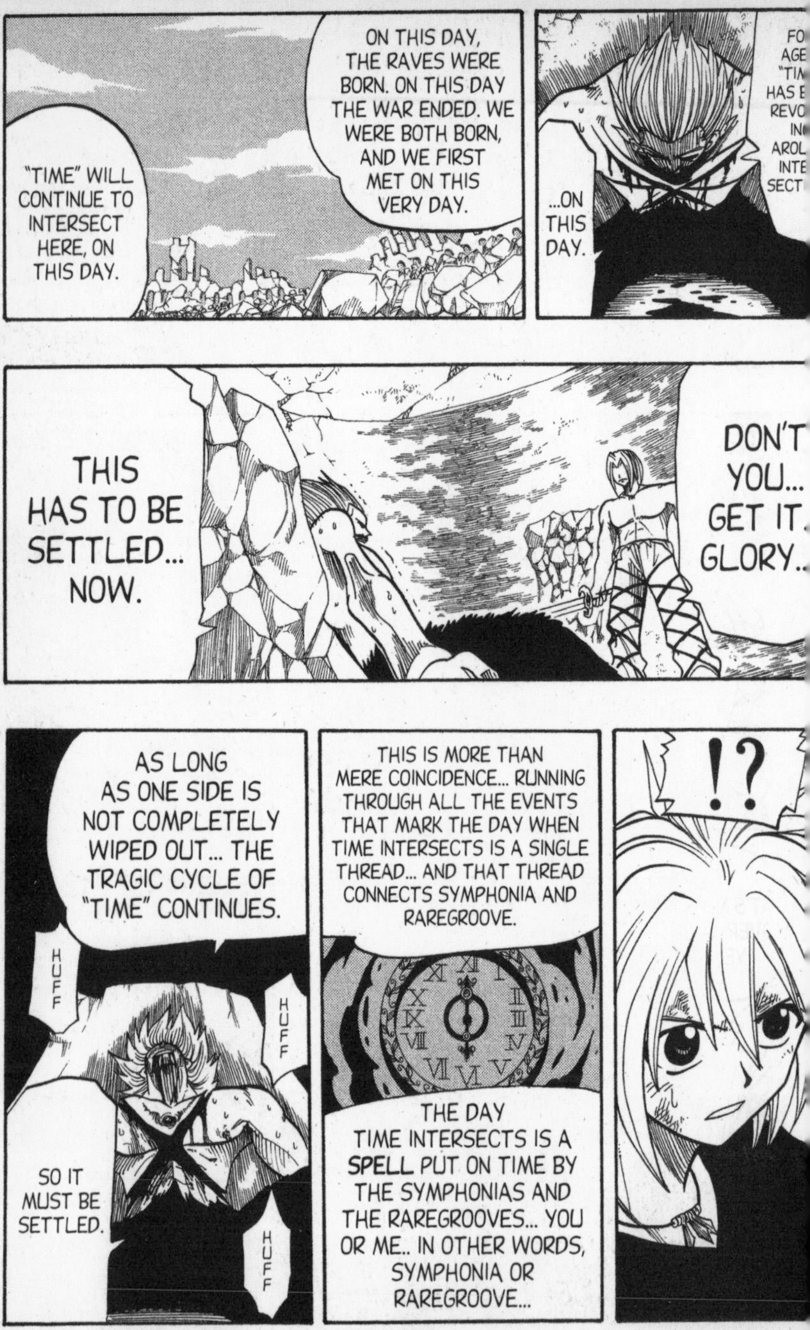

...ON THIS DAY.
ON THIS DAY, THE RAVES WERE BORN. ON THIS DAY THE WAR ENDED. WE WERE BOTH BORN, AND WE FIRST MET ON THIS VERY DAY.
"TIME" WILL CONTINUE TO INTERSECT HERE, ON THIS DAY.
DON'T YOU... GET IT. GLORY...
THIS HAS TO BE SETTLED... NOW.
!?
THIS IS MORE THAN MERE COINCIDENCE... RUNNING THROUGH ALL THE EVENTS THAT MARK THE DAY WHEN TIME INTERSECTS IS A SINGLE THREAD... AND THAT THREAD CONNECTS SYMPHONIA AND RAREGROOVE.
THE DAY TIME INTERSECTS IS A SPELL PUT ON TIME BY THE SYMPHONIAS AND THE RAREGROOVES... YOU OR ME.. IN OTHER WORDS, SYMPHONIA OR RAREGROOVE...
AS LONG AS ONE SIDE IS NOT COMPLETELY WIPED OUT... THE TRAGIC CYCLE OF "TIME" CONTINUES.
HUFF
HUFF
SO IT MUST BE SETTLED.
HUFF

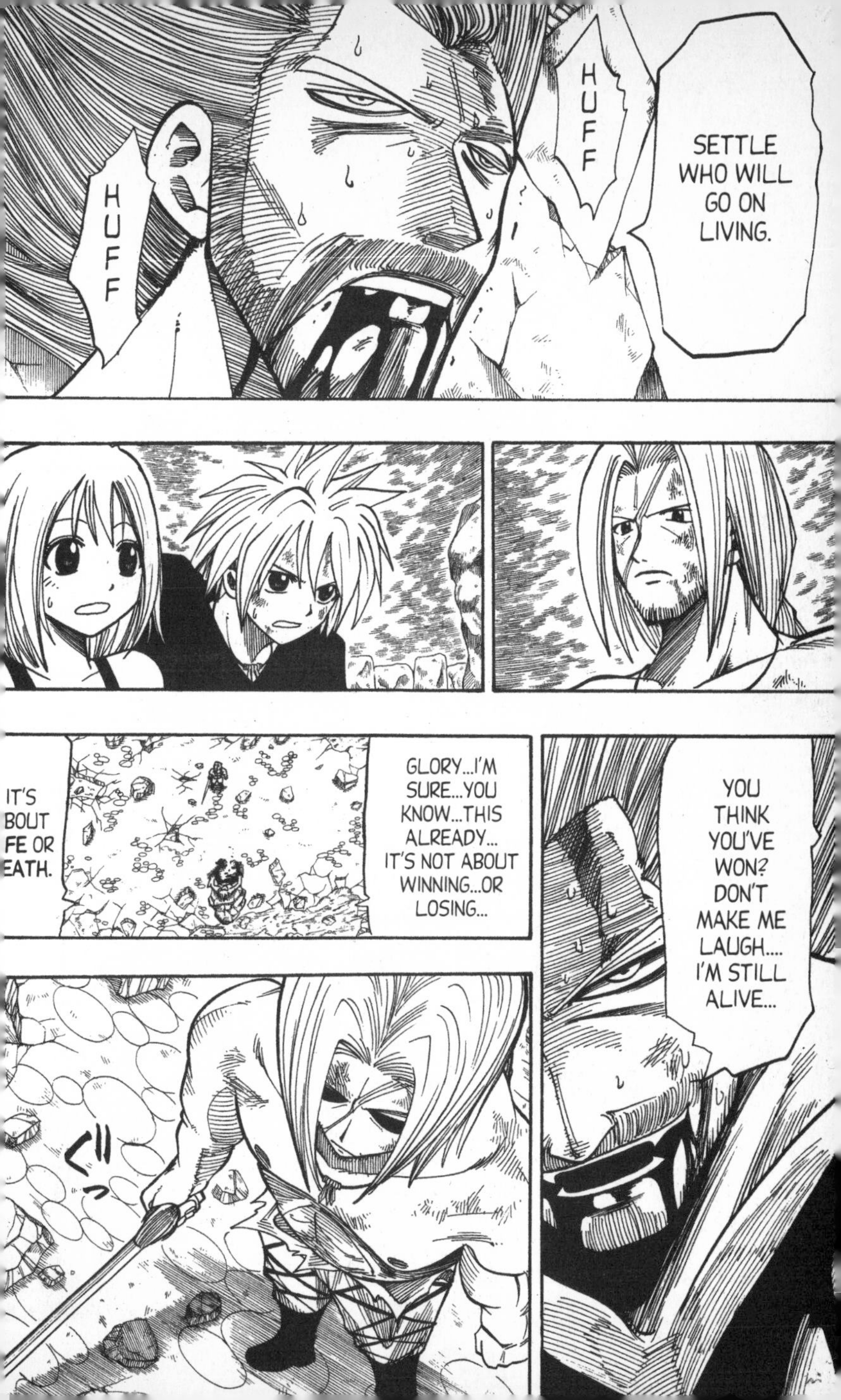
SETTLE WHO WILL GO ON LIVING.
HUFF HUFF
HUFF HUFF
YOU THINK YOU'VE WON? DON'T MAKE ME LAUGH.... I'M STILL ALIVE...
GLORY...I'M SURE...YOU KNOW...THIS ALREADY... IT'S NOT ABOUT WINNING...OR LOSING...
IT'S BOUT FE OR EATH.
ぐっ

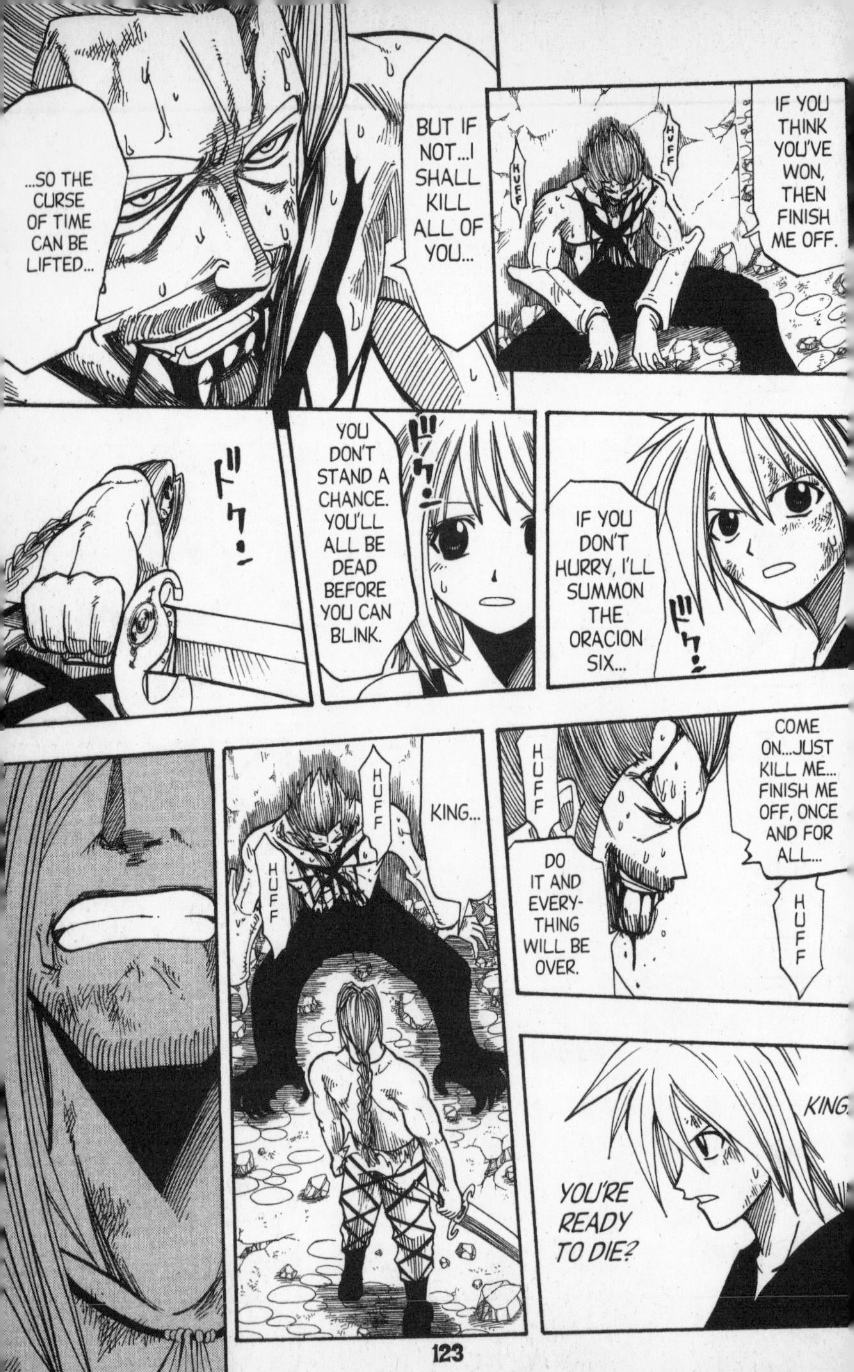

IF YOU THINK YOU'VE WON, THEN FINISH ME OFF.
HUFF
HUFF
BUT IF NOT...I SHALL KILL ALL OF YOU...
...SO THE CURSE OF TIME CAN BE LIFTED...
IF YOU DON'T HURRY, I'LL SUMMON THE ORACION SIX...
ドク!
YOU DON'T STAND A CHANCE. YOU'LL ALL BE DEAD BEFORE YOU CAN BLINK.
ドク!
ドク!
COME ON...JUST KILL ME... FINISH ME OFF, ONCE AND FOR ALL...
HUFF
HUFF
DO IT AND EVERY-THING WILL BE OVER.
KING.
YOU'RE READY TO DIE?
KING...
HUFF
HUFF

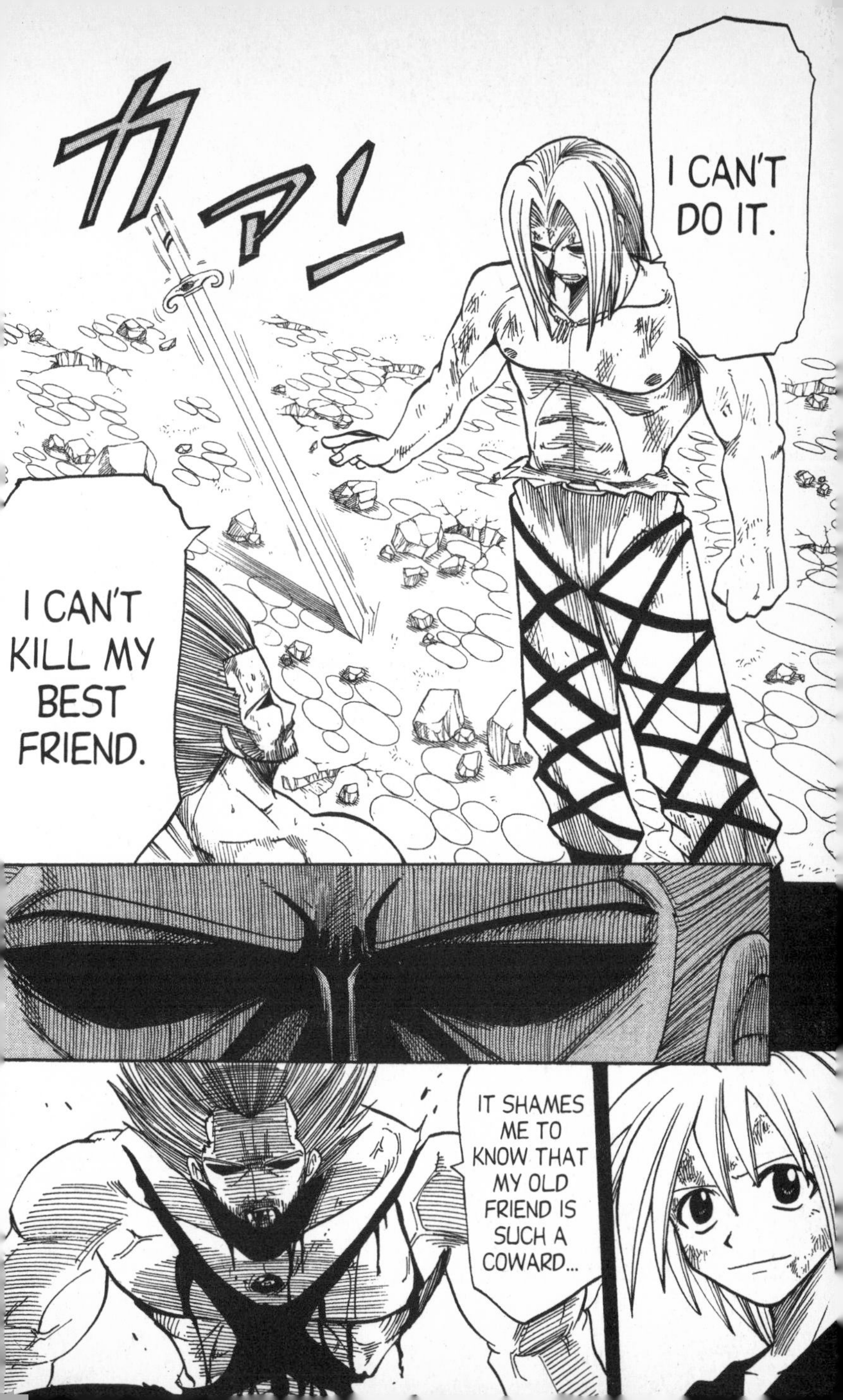
I CAN'T DO IT.
カァン
I CAN'T KILL MY BEST FRIEND.
IT SHAMES ME TO KNOW THAT MY OLD FRIEND IS SUCH A COWARD...

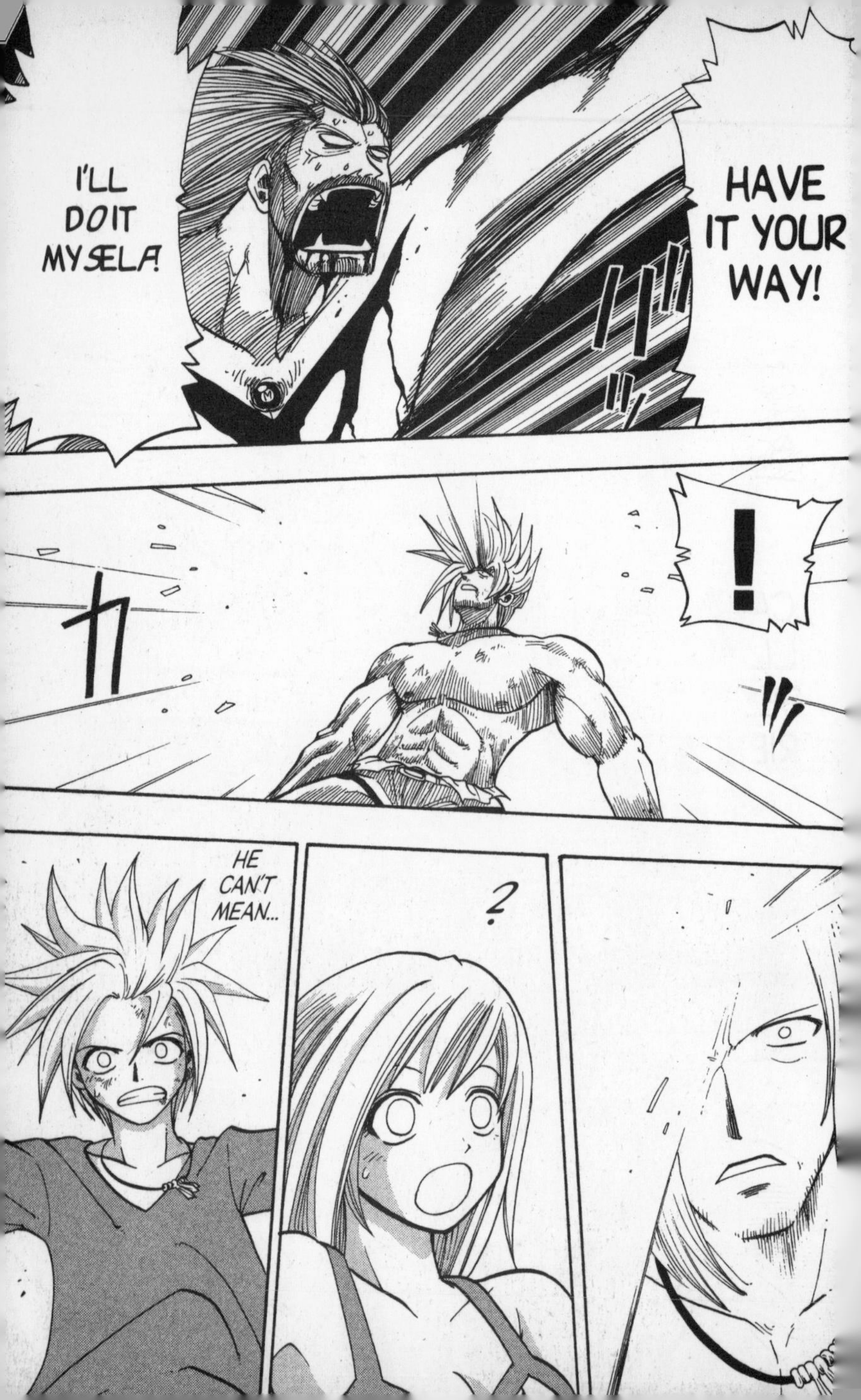

HAVE IT YOUR WAY!
I'LL DO IT MYSELF!
!
カ
?
HE CAN'T MEAN...

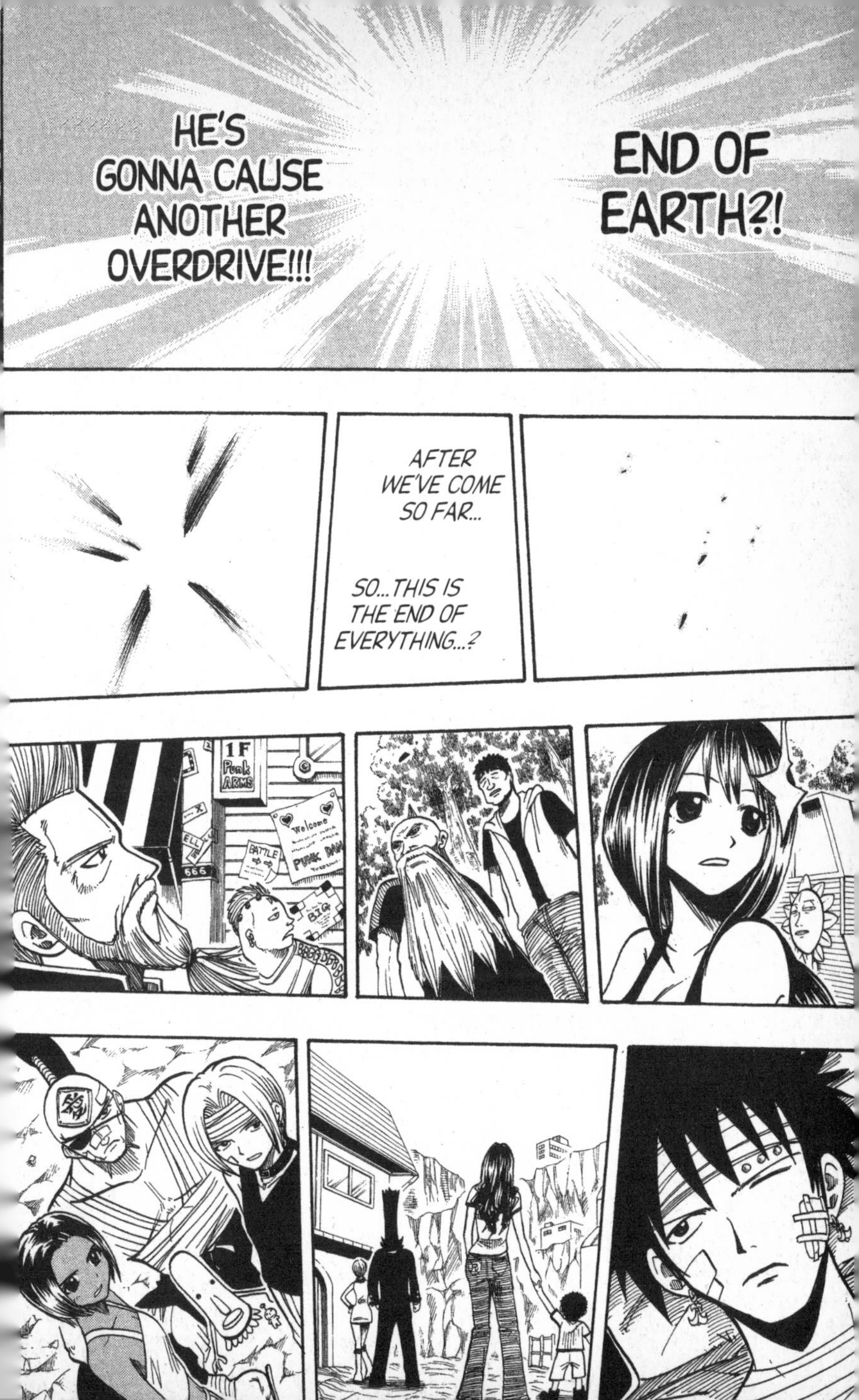
END OF EARTH?!
HE'S GONNA CAUSE ANOTHER OVERDRIVE!!!
AFTER WE'VE COME SO FAR...
SO...THIS IS THE END OF EVERYTHING...?
1F
Punk ARMS
Welcome
BATTLE
666

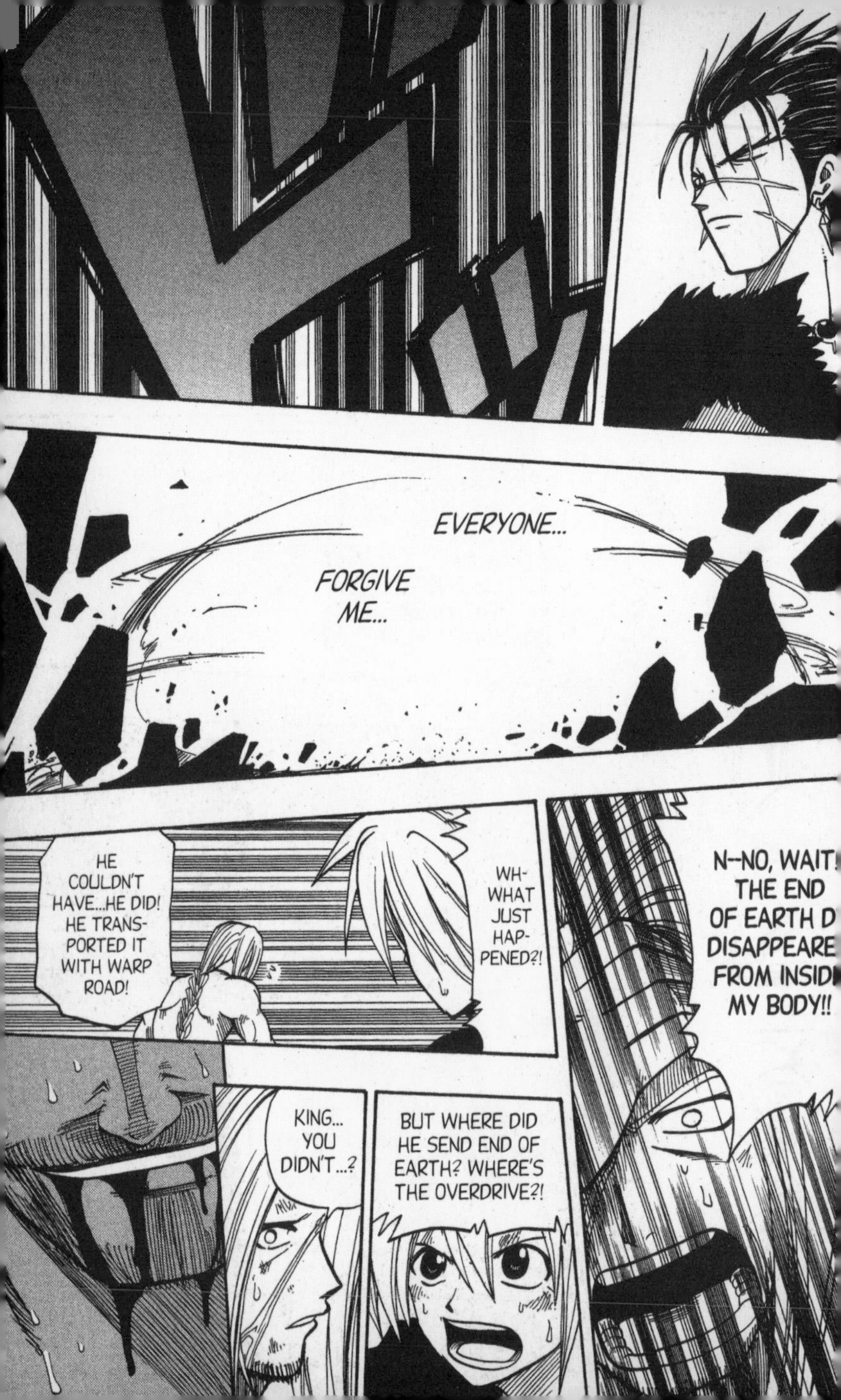
EVERYONE...
FORGIVE ME...
N--NO, WAIT! THE END OF EARTH D DISAPPEARE FROM INSID MY BODY!!
WH-WHAT JUST HAP-PENED?!
HE COULDN'T HAVE...HE DID! HE TRANS-PORTED IT WITH WARP ROAD!
BUT WHERE DID HE SEND END OF EARTH? WHERE'S THE OVERDRIVE?!
KING... YOU DIDN'T...?

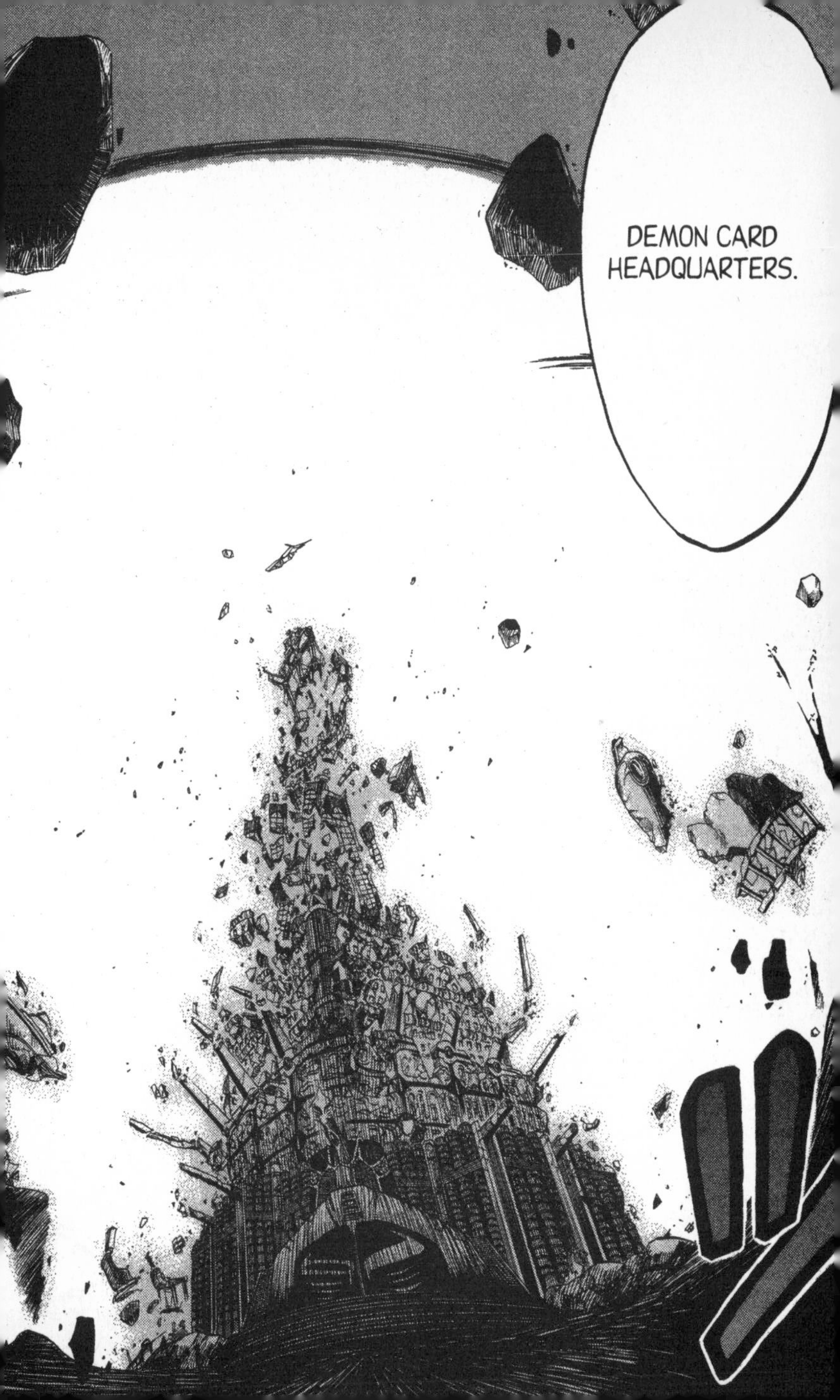
DEMON CARD HEADQUARTERS.

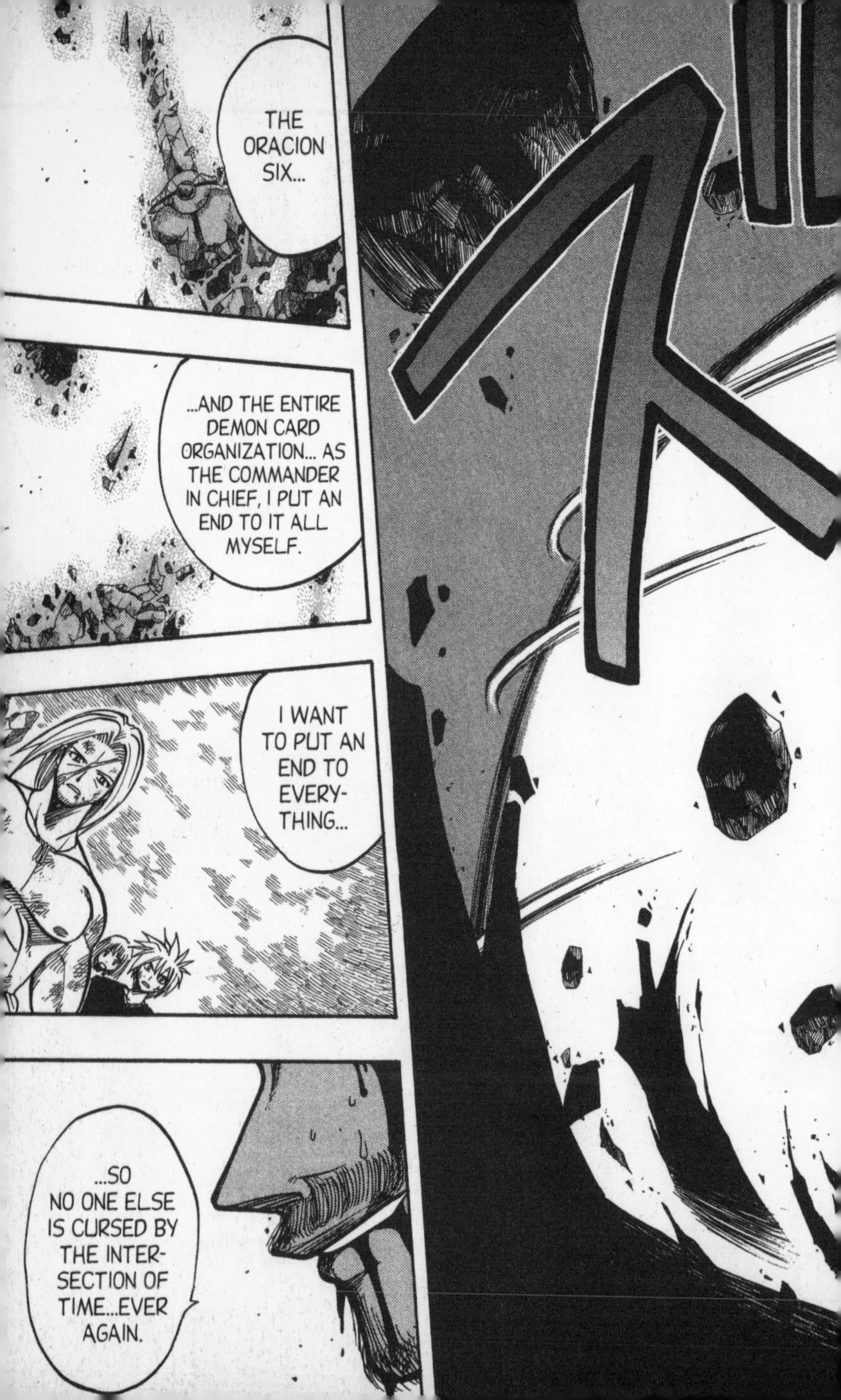
THE ORACION SIX...
...AND THE ENTIRE DEMON CARD ORGANIZATION... AS THE COMMANDER IN CHIEF, I PUT AN END TO IT ALL MYSELF.
I WANT TO PUT AN END TO EVERYTHING...
...SO NO ONE ELSE IS CURSED BY THE INTERSECTION OF TIME...EVER AGAIN.

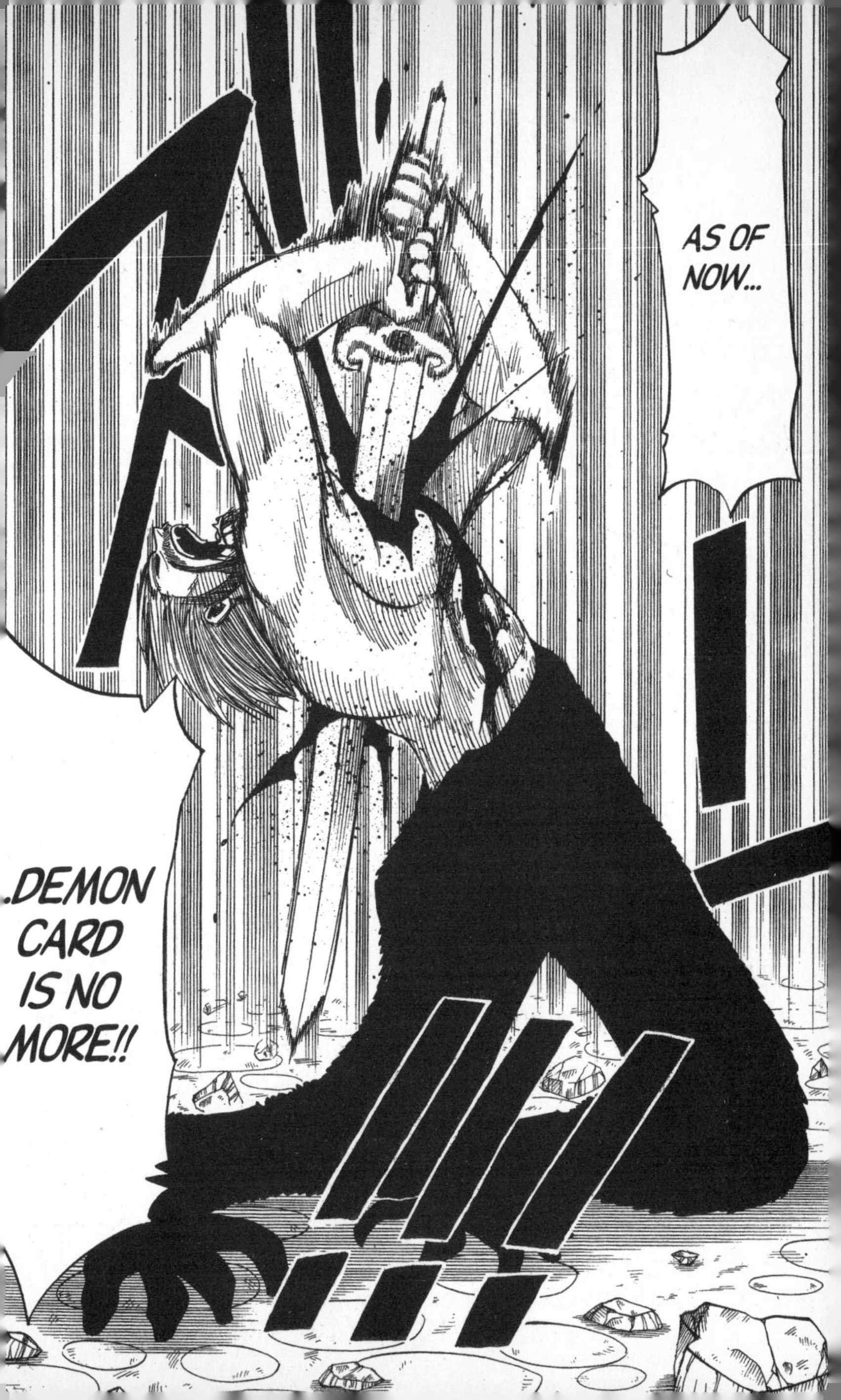
AS OF NOW...
.DEMON CARD IS NO MORE!!

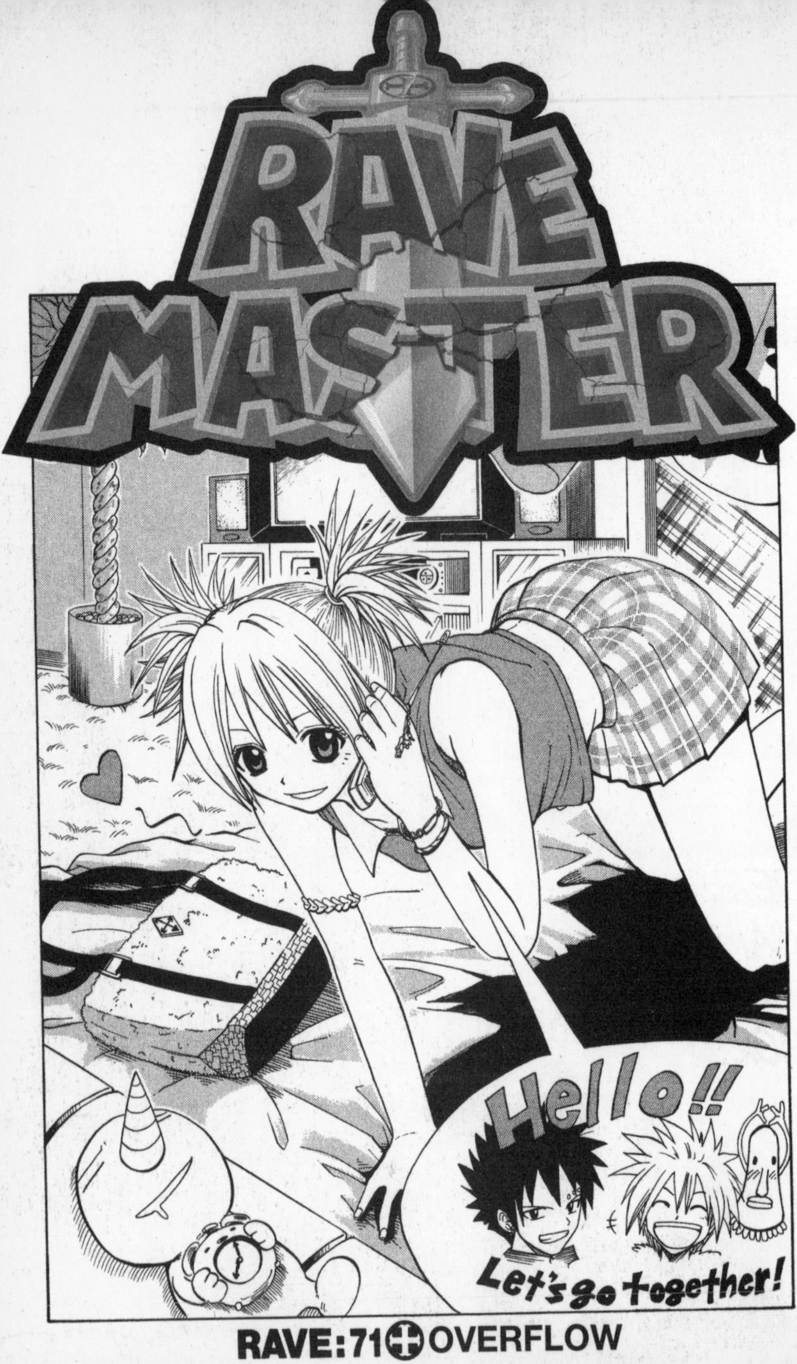
RAVE MASTER
Hello!!
Let's go together!

RAVE:71 ✠ OVERFLOW

KING!!
YOU DIDN'T...
YOU DIDN'T HAVE TO KILL YOURSELF!

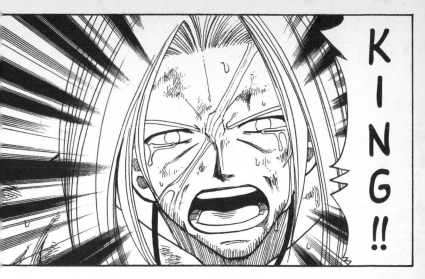

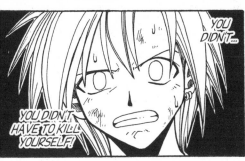

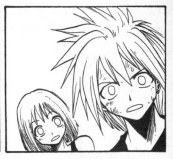

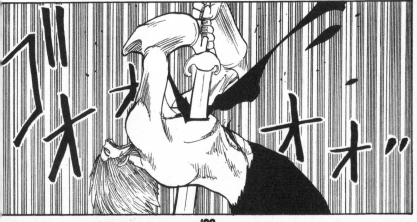

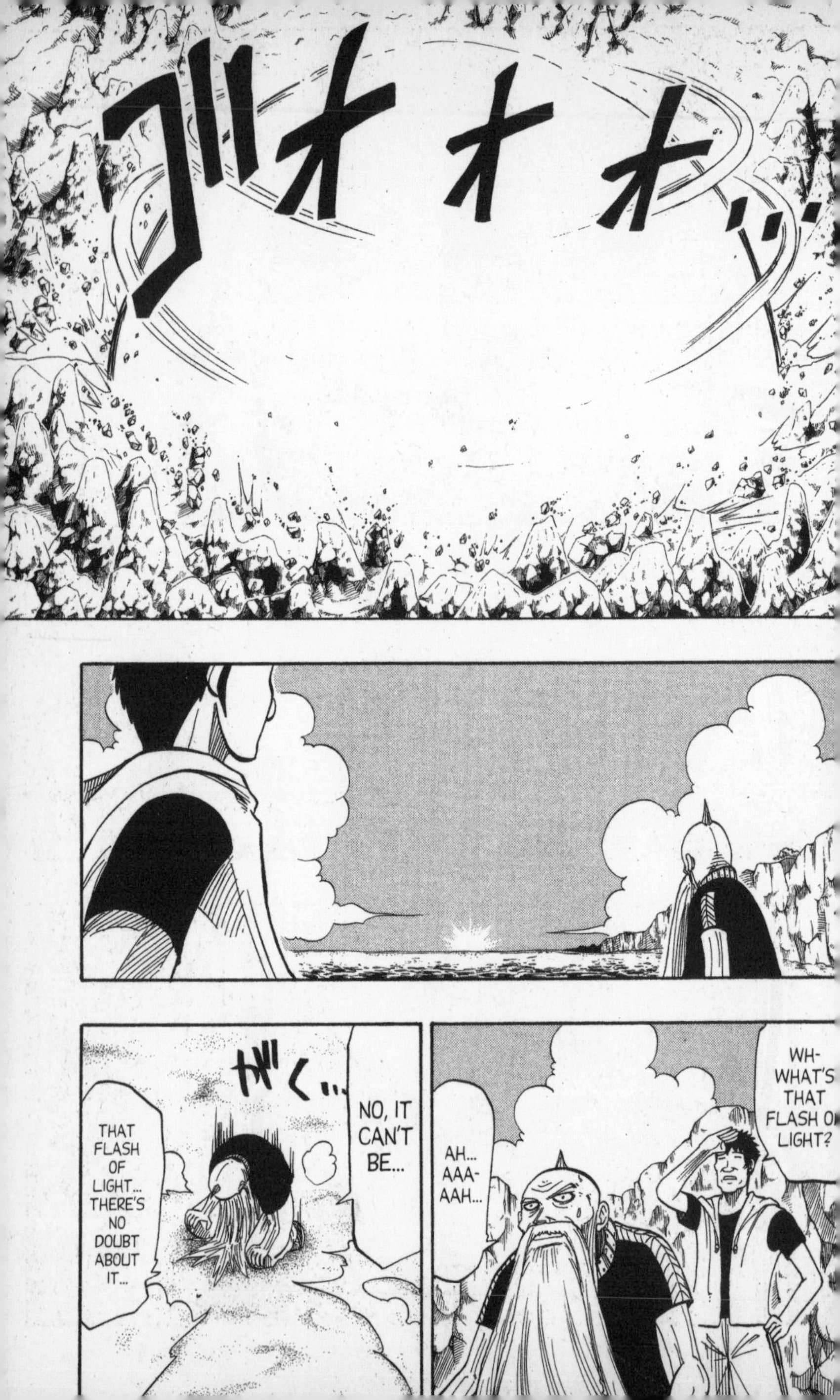
ゴオオオッ
WH- WHAT'S THAT FLASH O LIGHT?
AH... AAA-AAH...
がく…
NO, IT CAN'T BE...
THAT FLASH OF LIGHT... THERE'S NO DOUBT ABOUT IT...

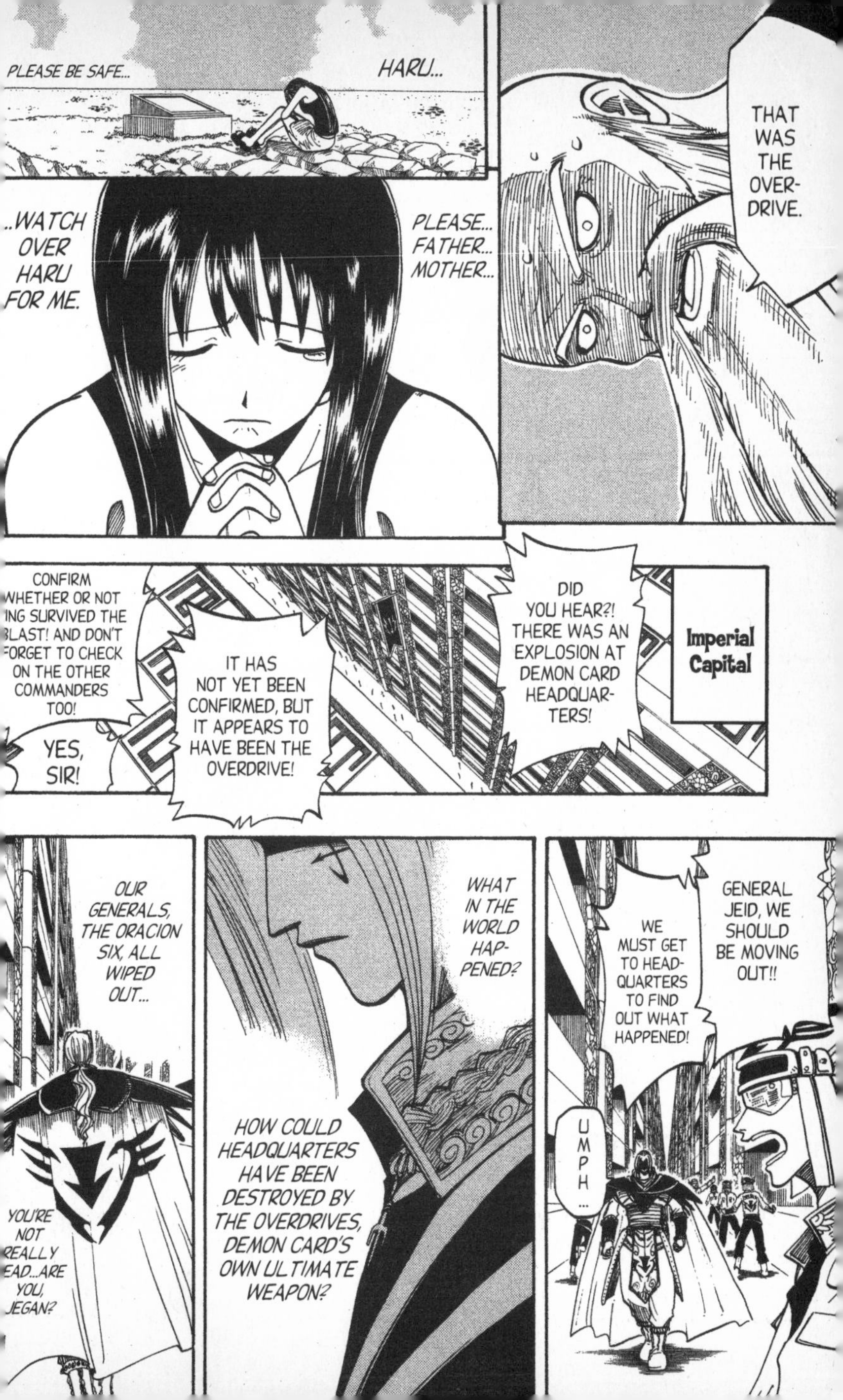

THAT WAS THE OVER-DRIVE.
HARU...
PLEASE BE SAFE...
PLEASE... FATHER... MOTHER...
..WATCH OVER HARU FOR ME.
Imperial Capital
DID YOU HEAR?! THERE WAS AN EXPLOSION AT DEMON CARD HEADQUAR-TERS!
IT HAS NOT YET BEEN CONFIRMED, BUT IT APPEARS TO HAVE BEEN THE OVERDRIVE!
CONFIRM WHETHER OR NOT ING SURVIVED THE BLAST! AND DON'T FORGET TO CHECK ON THE OTHER COMMANDERS TOO!
YES, SIR!
GENERAL JEID, WE SHOULD BE MOVING OUT!!
WE MUST GET TO HEAD-QUARTERS TO FIND OUT WHAT HAPPENED!
UMPH...
WHAT IN THE WORLD HAP-PENED?
HOW COULD HEADQUARTERS HAVE BEEN DESTROYED BY THE OVERDRIVES, DEMON CARD'S OWN ULTIMATE WEAPON?
OUR GENERALS, THE ORACION SIX, ALL WIPED OUT...
YOU'RE NOT REALLY EAD...ARE YOU, JEGAN?

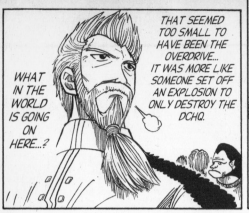

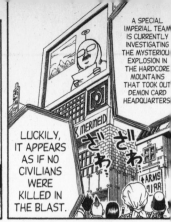

A SPECIAL IMPERIAL TEAM IS CURRENTLY INVESTIGATING THE MYSTERIOU EXPLOSION IN THE HARDCORE MOUNTAINS THAT TOOK OUT DEMON CARD HEADQUARTERS
MERMEID
ざわ ざわ
ARMS
LUCKILY, IT APPEARS AS IF NO CIVILIANS WERE KILLED IN THE BLAST.
THAT SEEMED TOO SMALL TO HAVE BEEN THE OVERDRIVE... IT WAS MORE LIKE SOMEONE SET OFF AN EXPLOSION TO ONLY DESTROY THE DCHQ.
WHAT IN THE WORLD IS GOING ON HERE...?
I SAW IT...
I HAD A VISION. THAT FLASH O LIGHT...A EXPLO-SION.
IT CAME FROM THE NORTH. I THINK IT WAS THE OVER-DRIVE.
NORTH? THE HARDCORE MOUNTAINS LIE IN THAT DIRECTION!
MOUNTAINS... YES. I SAW A HUGE FORTRESS GOING UP IN FLAMES.
A FORTRESS? THAT'S DEMON CARD HEAD-QUARTERS!

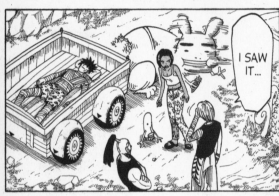

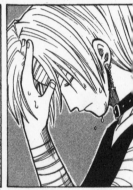

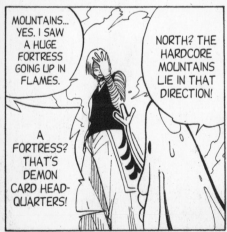

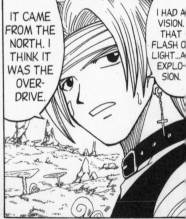

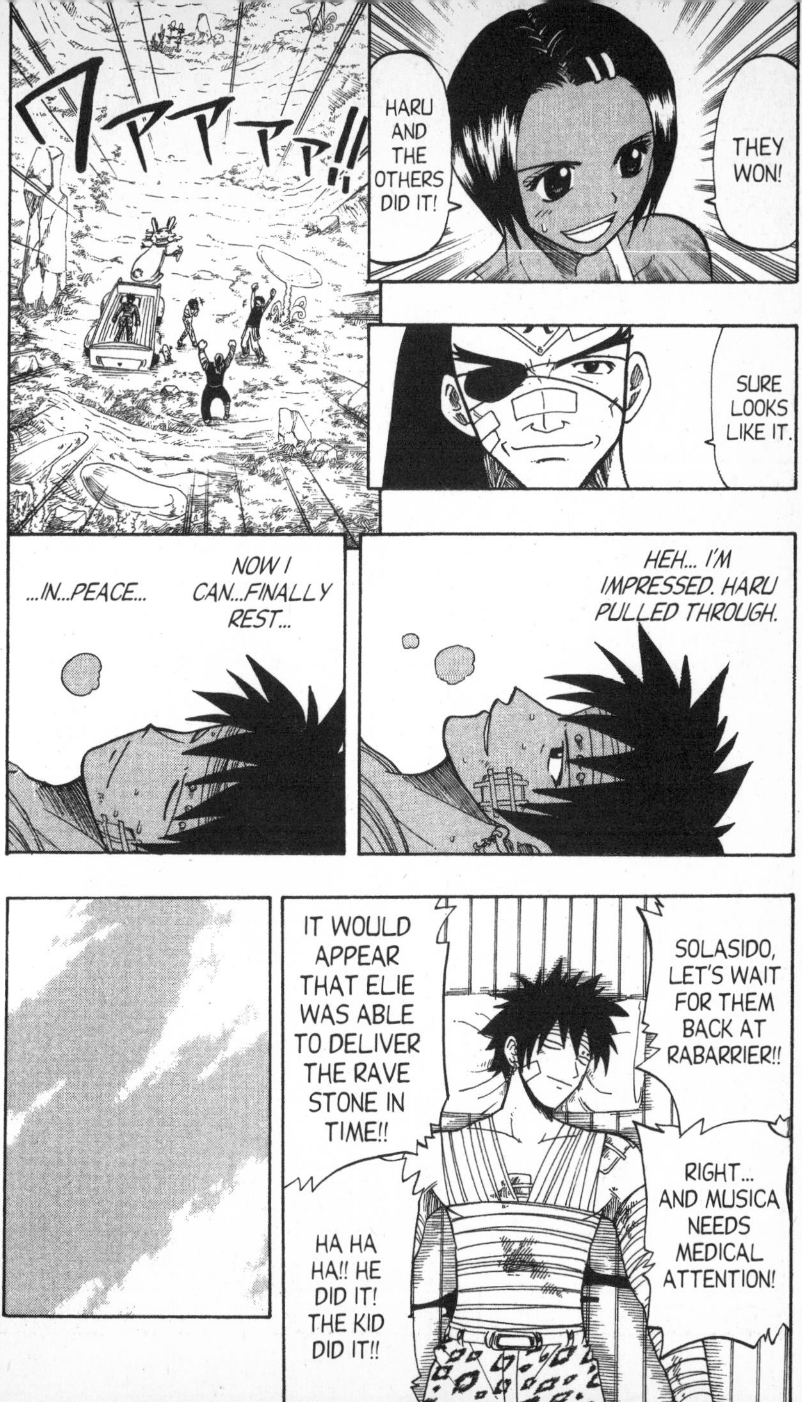
THEY WON!
HARU AND THE OTHERS DID IT!
SURE LOOKS LIKE IT.
ワアアアア!!
HEH... I'M IMPRESSED. HARU PULLED THROUGH.
NOW I CAN...FINALLY REST...
...IN...PEACE...
SOLASIDO, LET'S WAIT FOR THEM BACK AT RABARRIER!!
IT WOULD APPEAR THAT ELIE WAS ABLE TO DELIVER THE RAVE STONE IN TIME!!
RIGHT... AND MUSICA NEEDS MEDICAL ATTENTION!
HA HA HA!! HE DID IT! THE KID DID IT!!

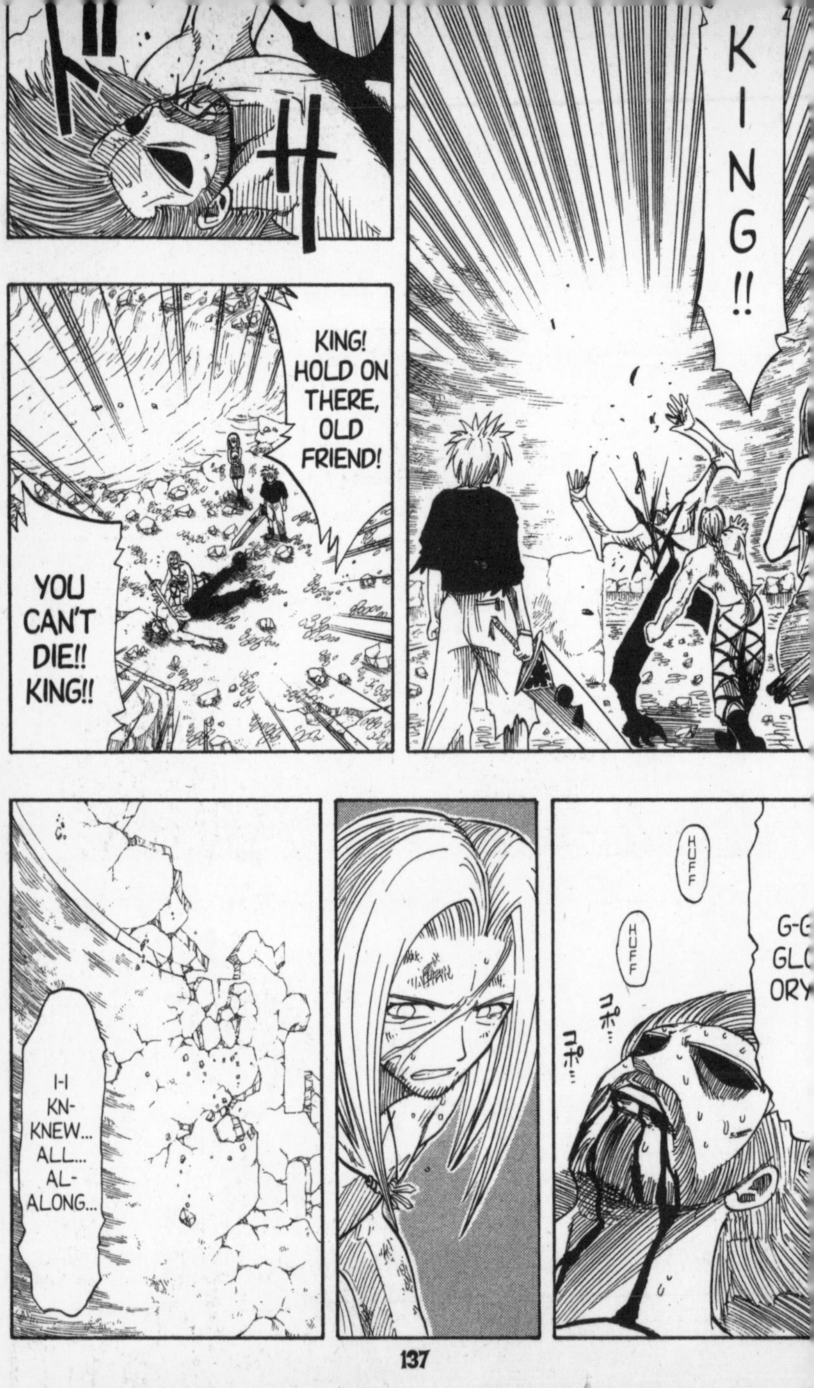
KING!!
KING! HOLD ON THERE, OLD FRIEND!
YOU CAN'T DIE!! KING!!
HUFF
HUFF
コポ…
コポ…
G-G GLO ORY
I-I KN- KNEW... ALL... AL- ALONG...

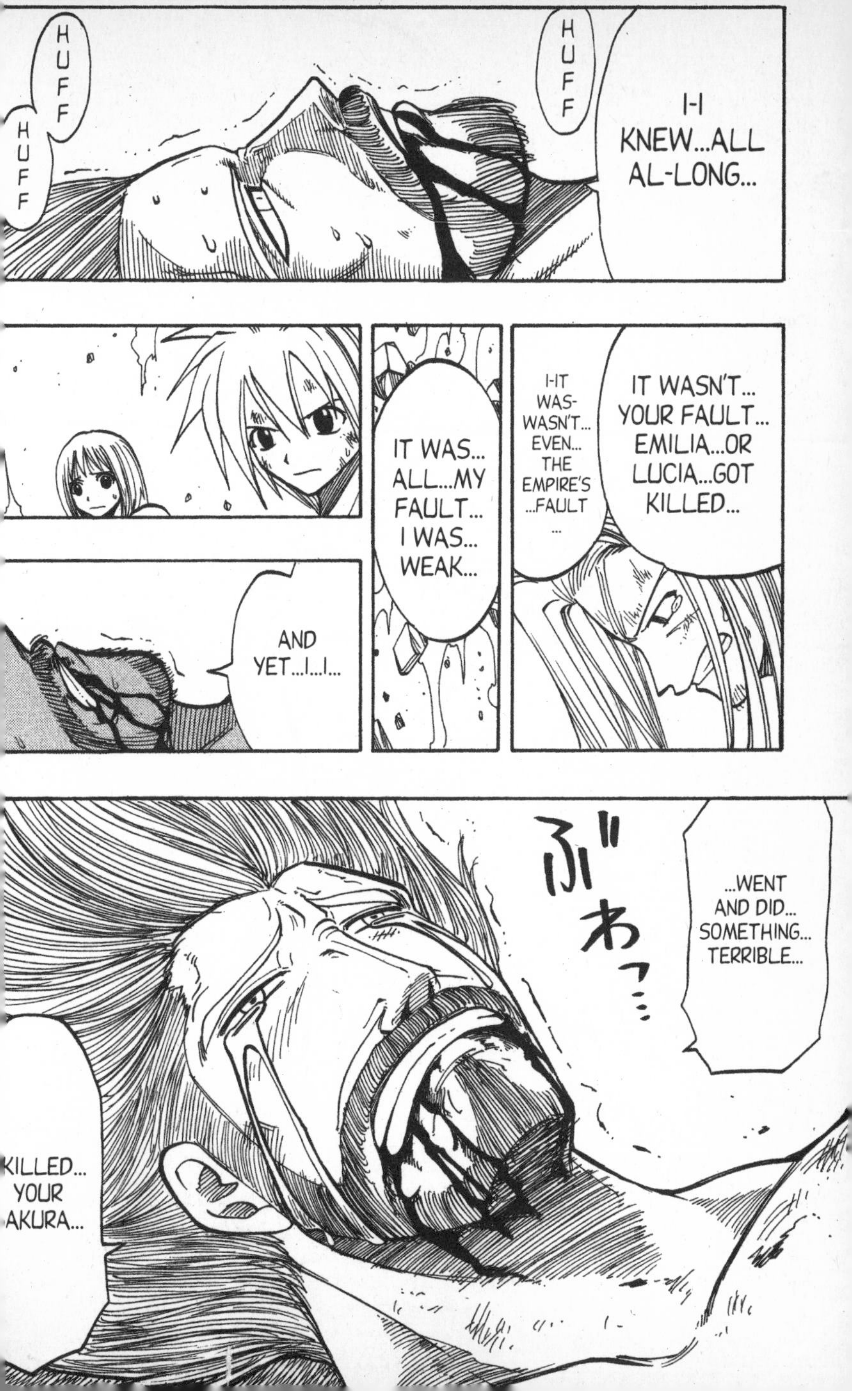
I-I KNEW...ALL AL-LONG...
HUFF
HUFF HUFF
IT WASN'T... YOUR FAULT... EMILIA...OR LUCIA...GOT KILLED...
I-IT WAS- WASN'T... EVEN... THE EMPIRE'S ...FAULT ...
IT WAS... ALL...MY FAULT... I WAS... WEAK...
AND YET...I...I...
...WENT AND DID... SOMETHING... TERRIBLE...
ぶわっ
KILLED... YOUR AKURA...

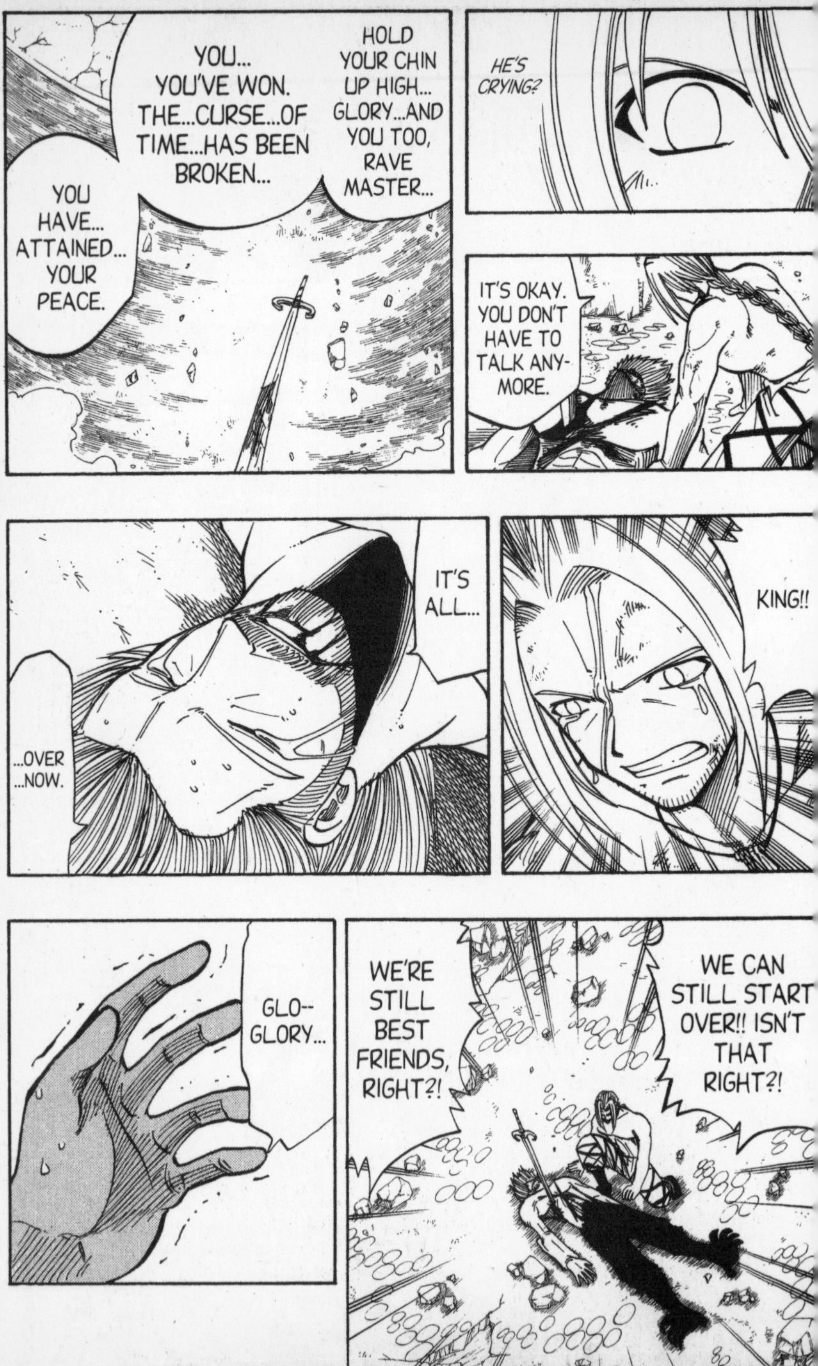
YOU... YOU'VE WON. THE...CURSE...OF TIME...HAS BEEN BROKEN...
HOLD YOUR CHIN UP HIGH... GLORY...AND YOU TOO, RAVE MASTER...
YOU HAVE... ATTAINED... YOUR PEACE.
HE'S CRYING?
IT'S OKAY. YOU DON'T HAVE TO TALK ANY-MORE.
IT'S ALL...
...OVER ...NOW.
KING!!
GLO-- GLORY...
WE'RE STILL BEST FRIENDS, RIGHT?!
WE CAN STILL START OVER!! ISN'T THAT RIGHT?!

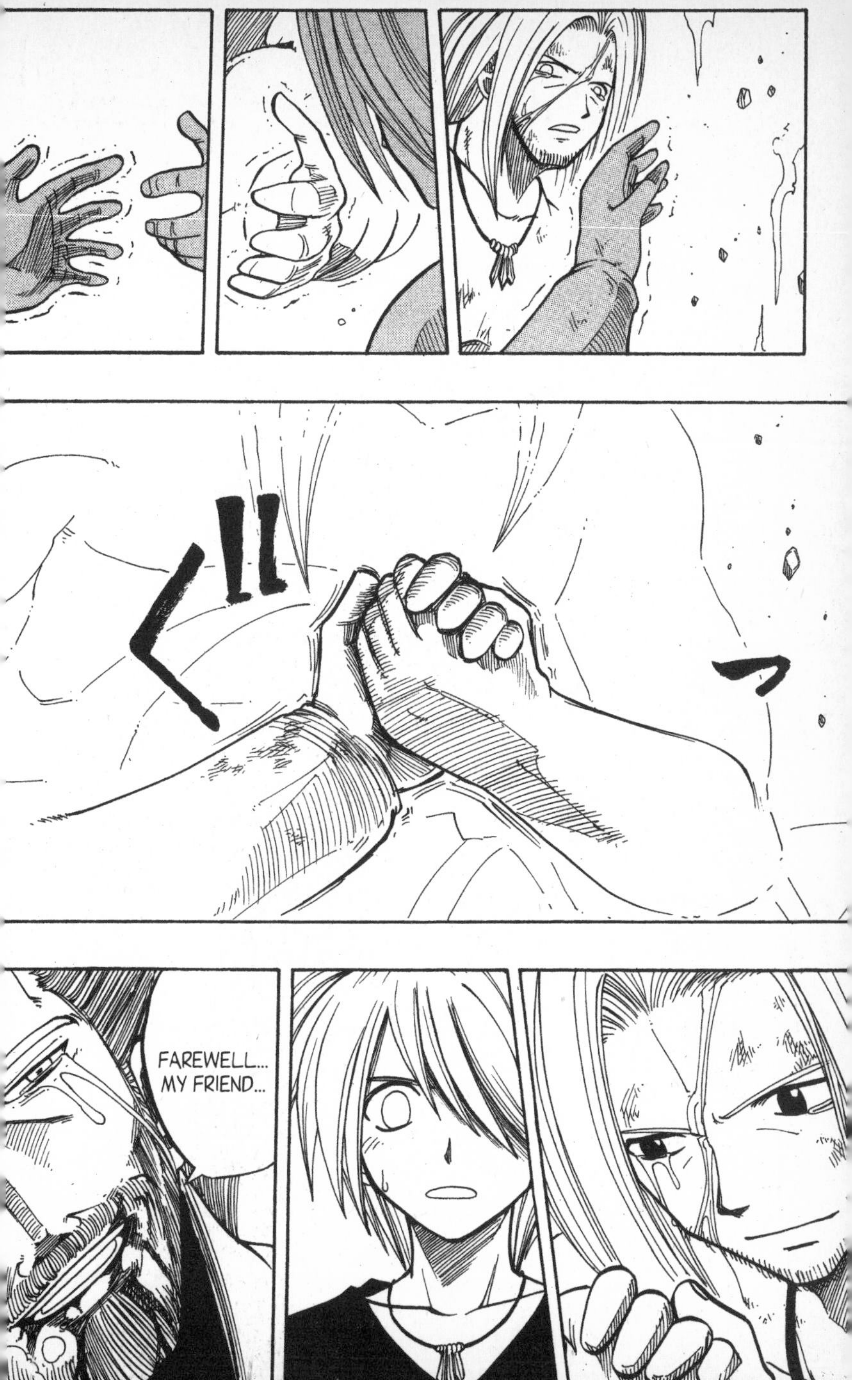
FAREWELL... MY FRIEND...

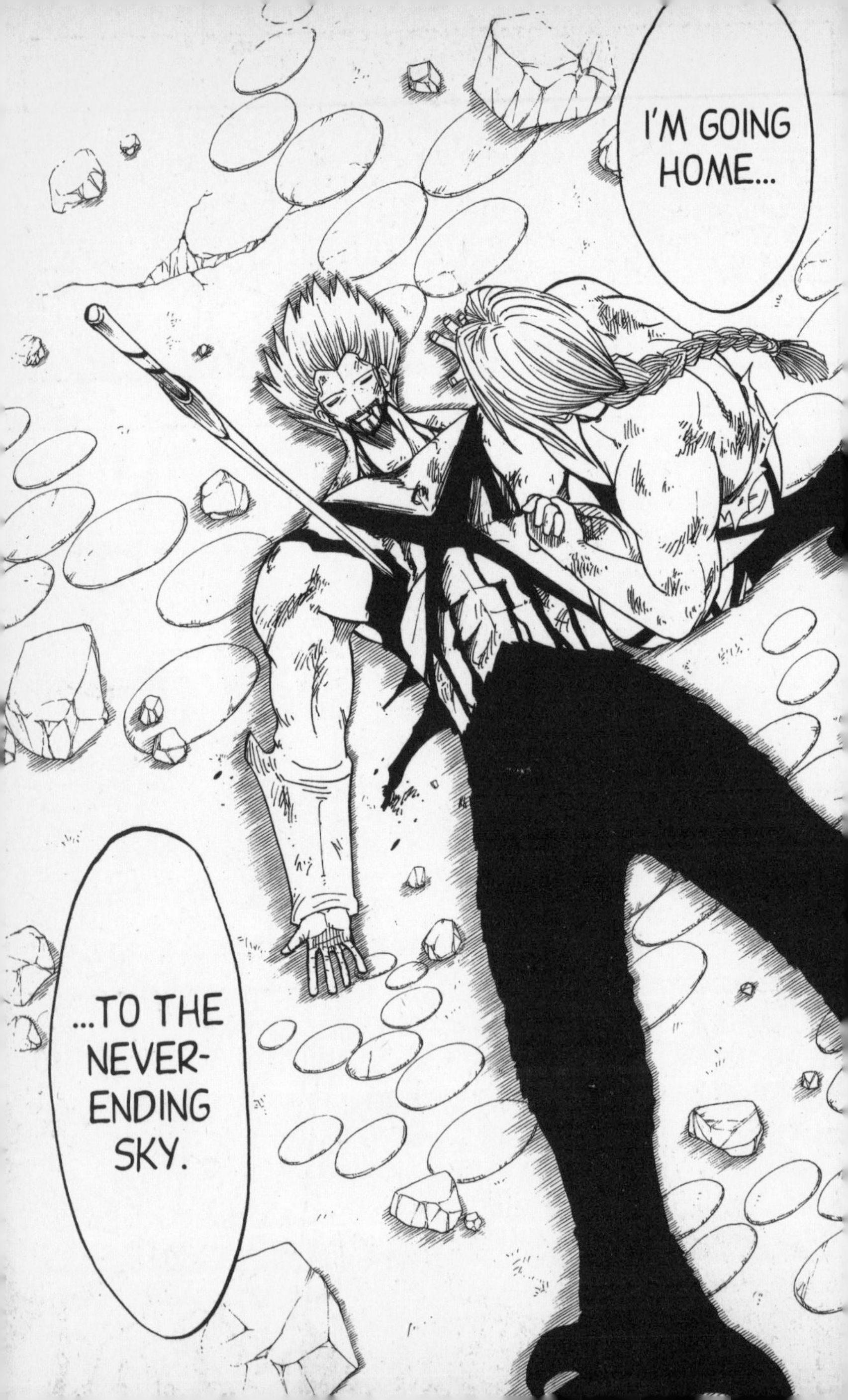
I'M GOING HOME...
...TO THE NEVER-ENDING SKY.

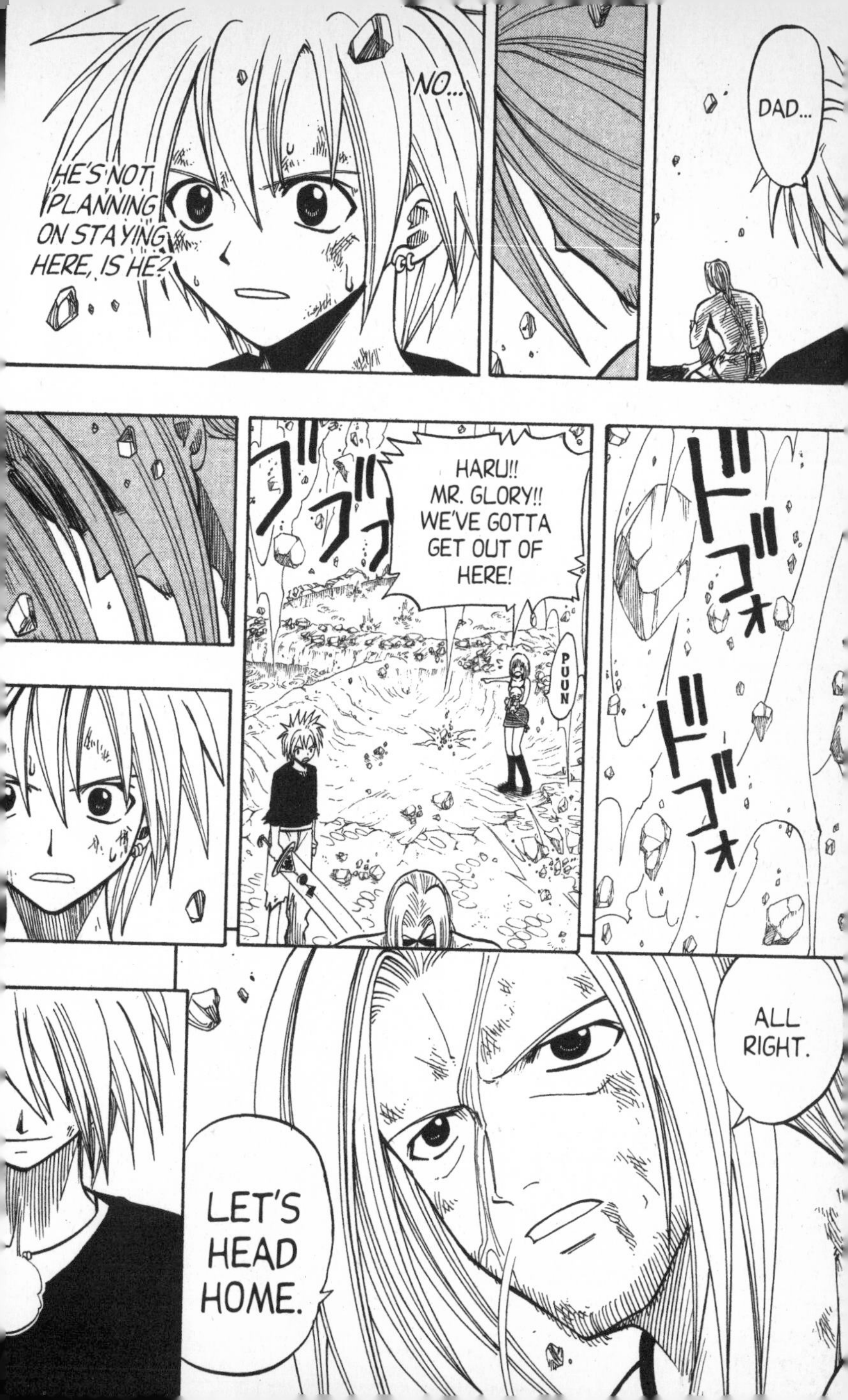
DAD...
NO...
HE'S NOT PLANNING ON STAYING HERE, IS HE?
ドゴォ
ドゴォ
HARU!! MR. GLORY!! WE'VE GOTTA GET OUT OF HERE!
PUUN
ブブッ
ALL RIGHT.
LET'S HEAD HOME.

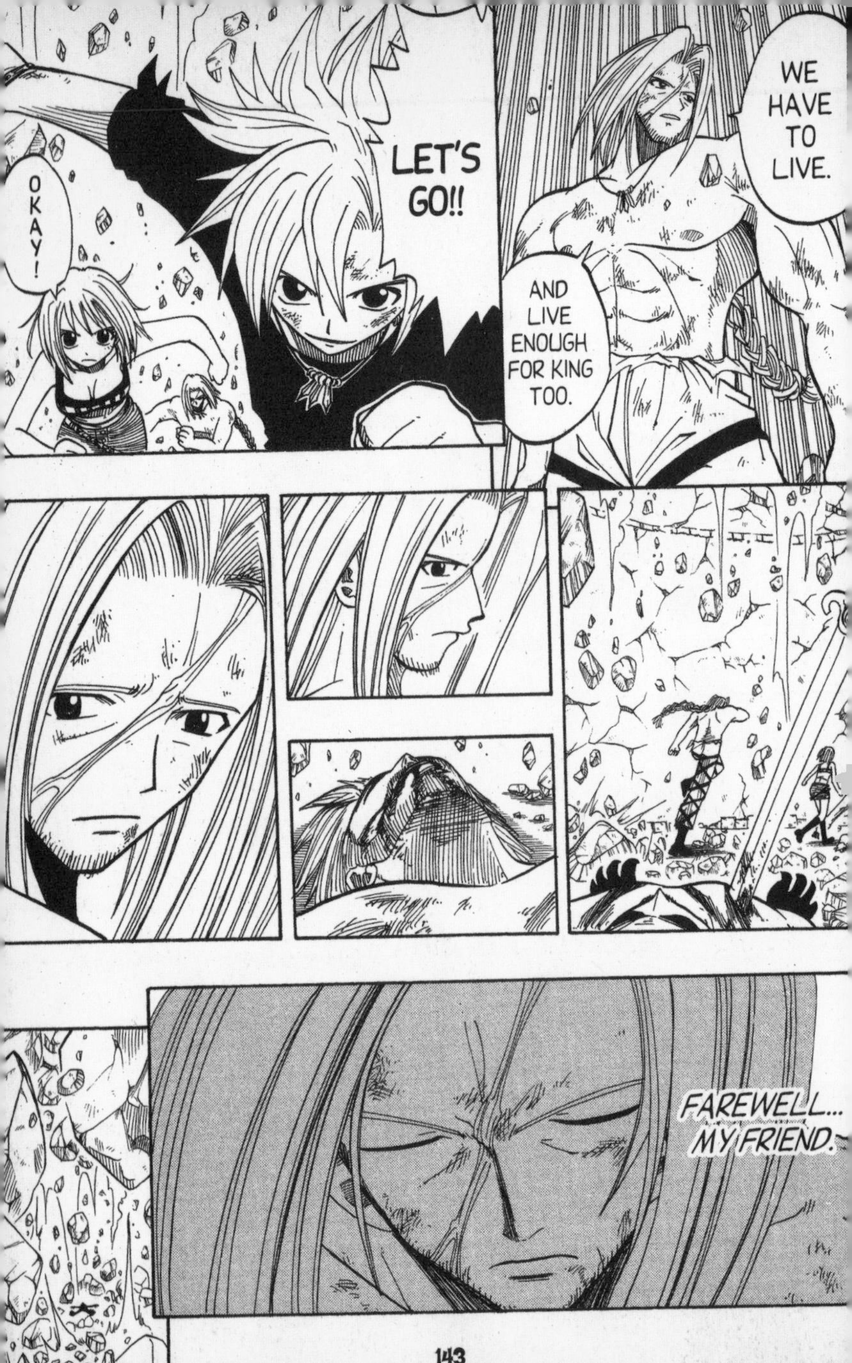
WE HAVE TO LIVE.
AND LIVE ENOUGH FOR KING TOO.
LET'S GO!!
OKAY!
FAREWELL... MY FRIEND.

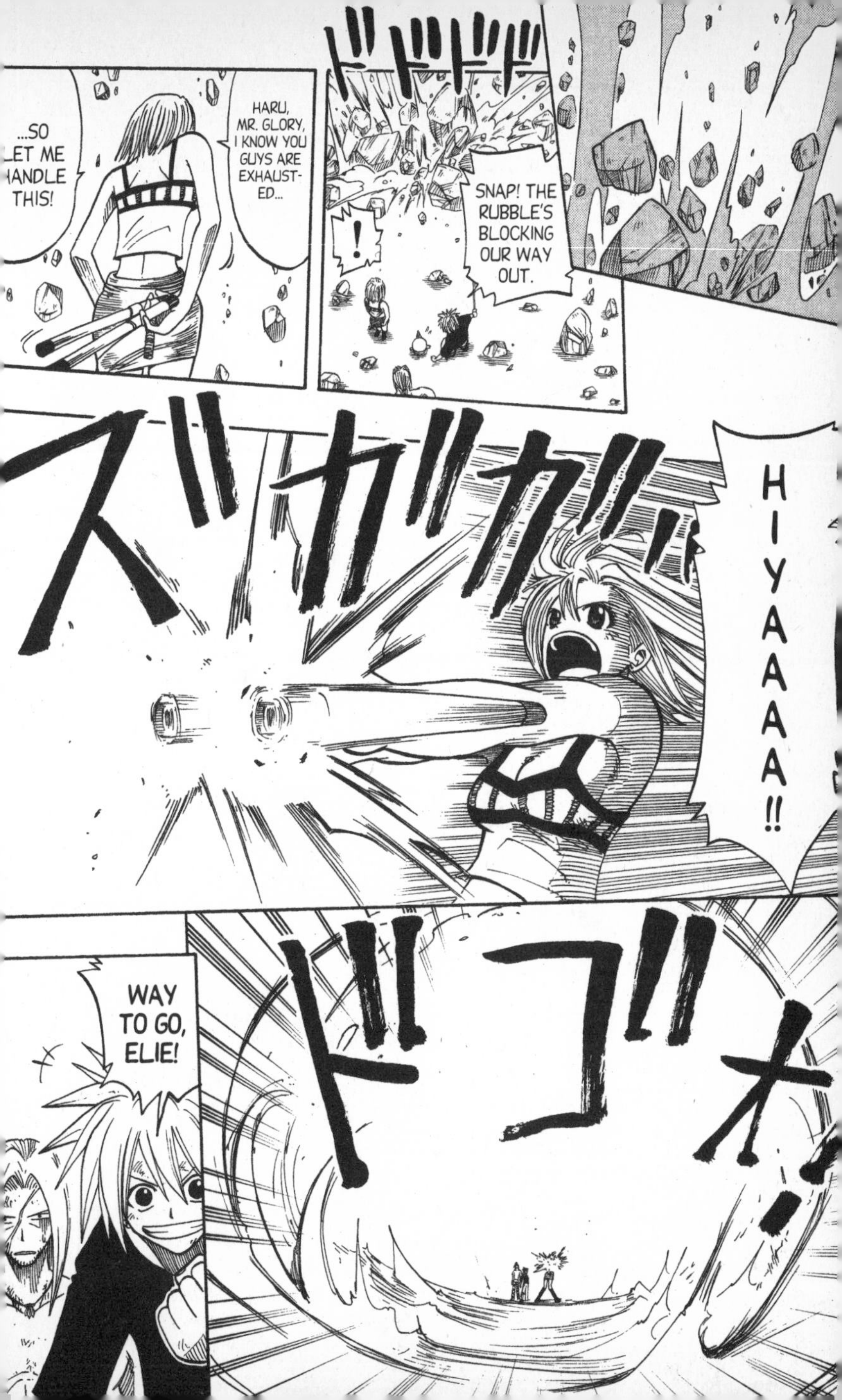

ドドドド
SNAP! THE RUBBLE'S BLOCKING OUR WAY OUT.
!
HARU, MR. GLORY, I KNOW YOU GUYS ARE EXHAUST-ED...
...SO LET ME HANDLE THIS!
HIYAAAAA!!
ズガガ
ドゴォ
WAY TO GO, ELIE!

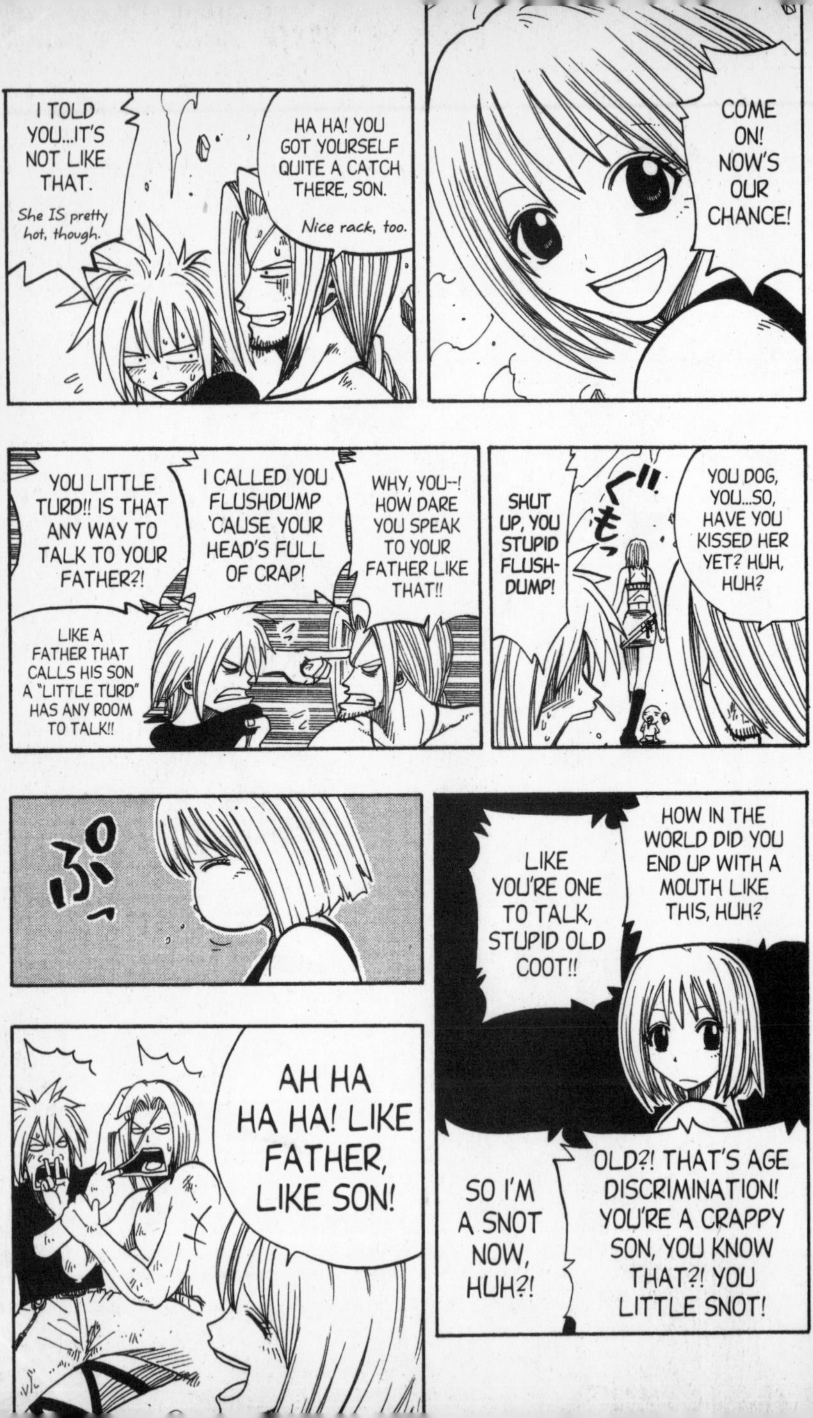
COME ON! NOW'S OUR CHANCE!
HA HA! YOU GOT YOURSELF QUITE A CATCH THERE, SON.
Nice rack, too.
I TOLD YOU...IT'S NOT LIKE THAT.
She IS pretty hot, though.
YOU DOG, YOU...SO, HAVE YOU KISSED HER YET? HUH, HUH?
SHUT UP, YOU STUPID FLUSH-DUMP!
WHY, YOU--! HOW DARE YOU SPEAK TO YOUR FATHER LIKE THAT!!
I CALLED YOU FLUSHDUMP 'CAUSE YOUR HEAD'S FULL OF CRAP!
YOU LITTLE TURD!! IS THAT ANY WAY TO TALK TO YOUR FATHER?!
LIKE A FATHER THAT CALLS HIS SON A "LITTLE TURD" HAS ANY ROOM TO TALK!!
HOW IN THE WORLD DID YOU END UP WITH A MOUTH LIKE THIS, HUH?
LIKE YOU'RE ONE TO TALK, STUPID OLD COOT!!
OLD?! THAT'S AGE DISCRIMINATION! YOU'RE A CRAPPY SON, YOU KNOW THAT?! YOU LITTLE SNOT!
SO I'M A SNOT NOW, HUH?!
AH HA HA HA! LIKE FATHER, LIKE SON!

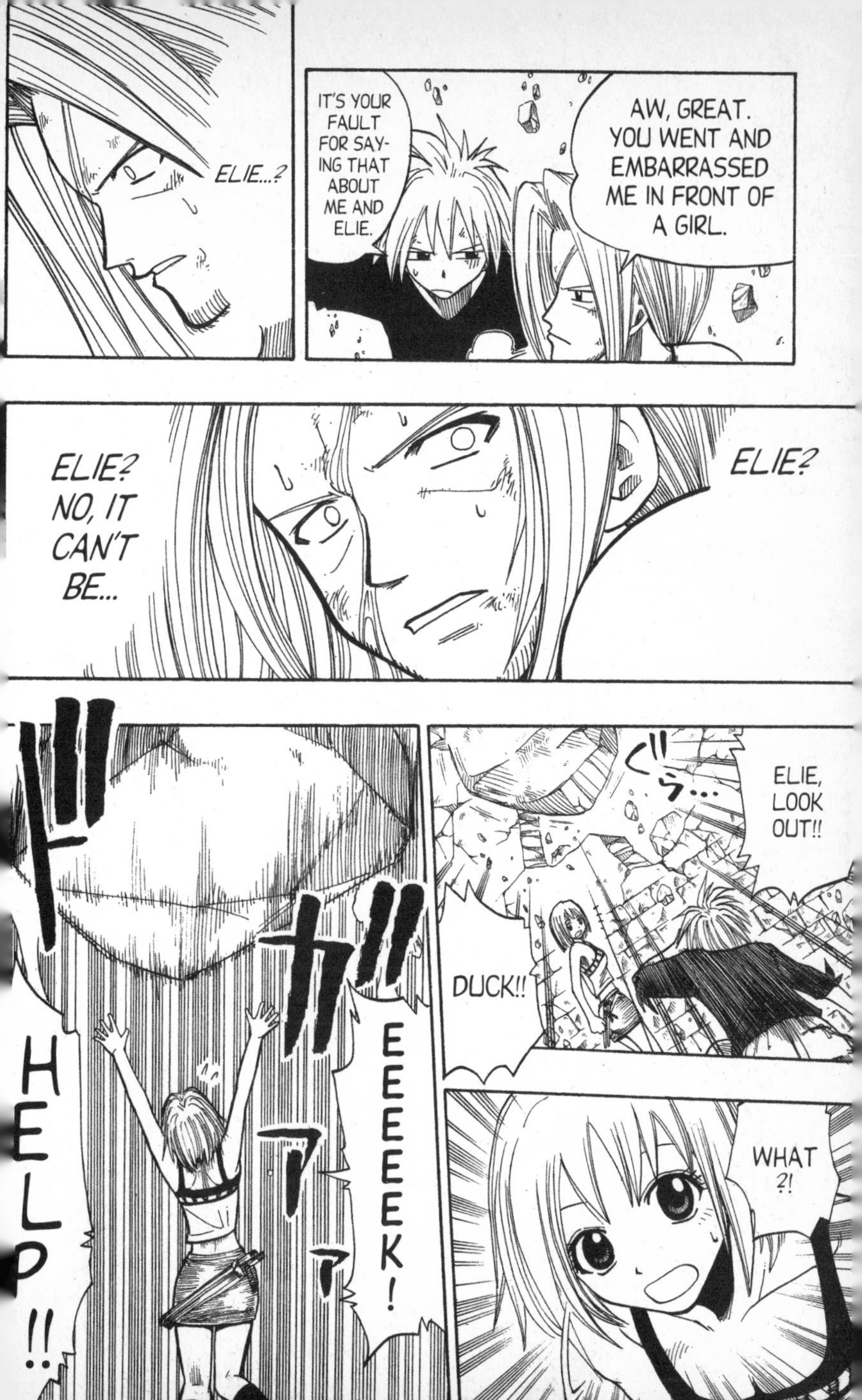
AW, GREAT. YOU WENT AND EMBARRASSED ME IN FRONT OF A GIRL.
IT'S YOUR FAULT FOR SAYING THAT ABOUT ME AND ELIE.
ELIE...?
ELIE?
ELIE? NO, IT CAN'T BE...
ぐら…
ELIE, LOOK OUT!!
DUCK!!
WHAT?!
ドガ
EEEEEEK!
アァ
HELP!!

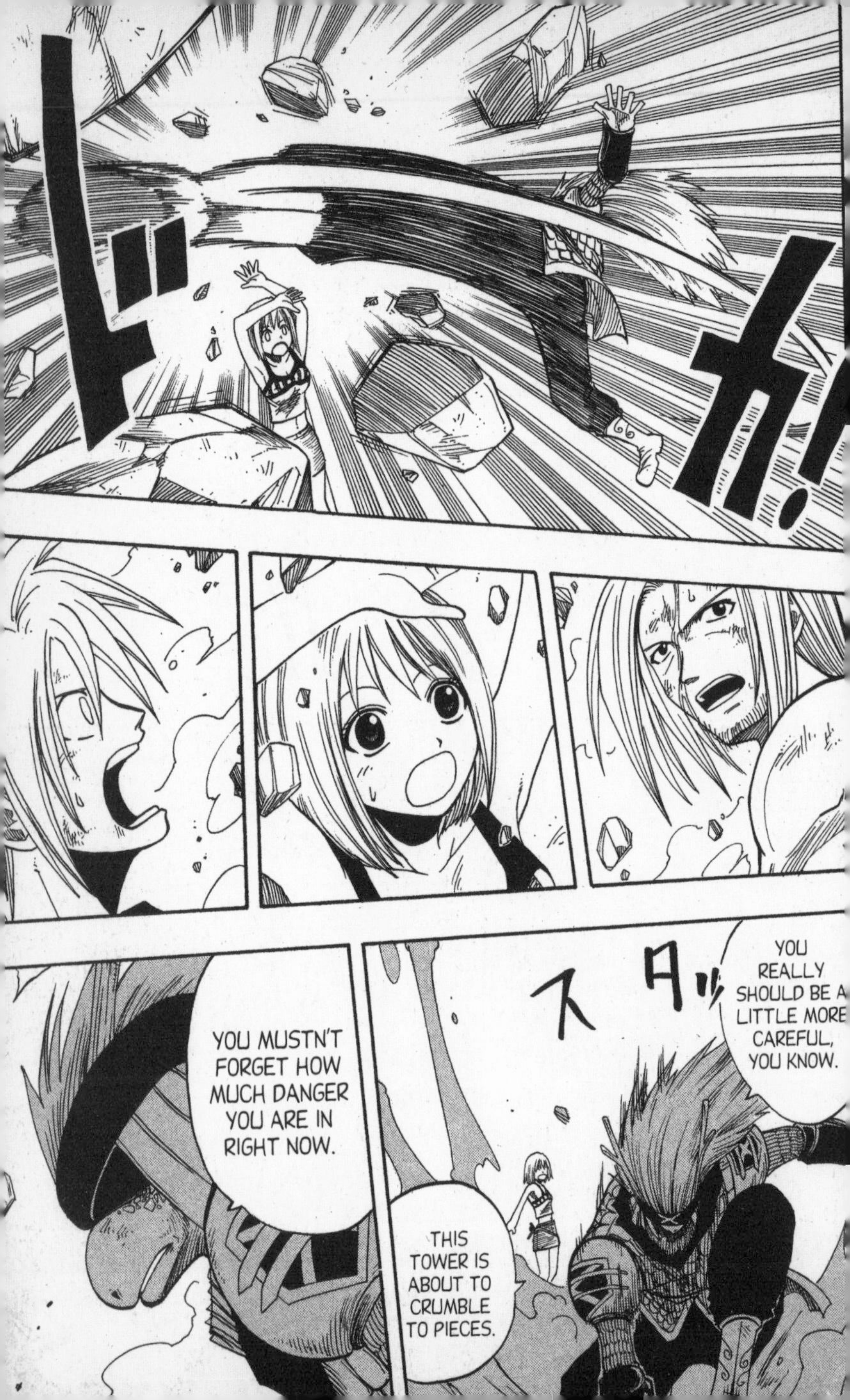
ドガ!!
スタッ
YOU REALLY SHOULD BE A LITTLE MORE CAREFUL, YOU KNOW.
THIS TOWER IS ABOUT TO CRUMBLE TO PIECES.
YOU MUSTN'T FORGET HOW MUCH DANGER YOU ARE IN RIGHT NOW.

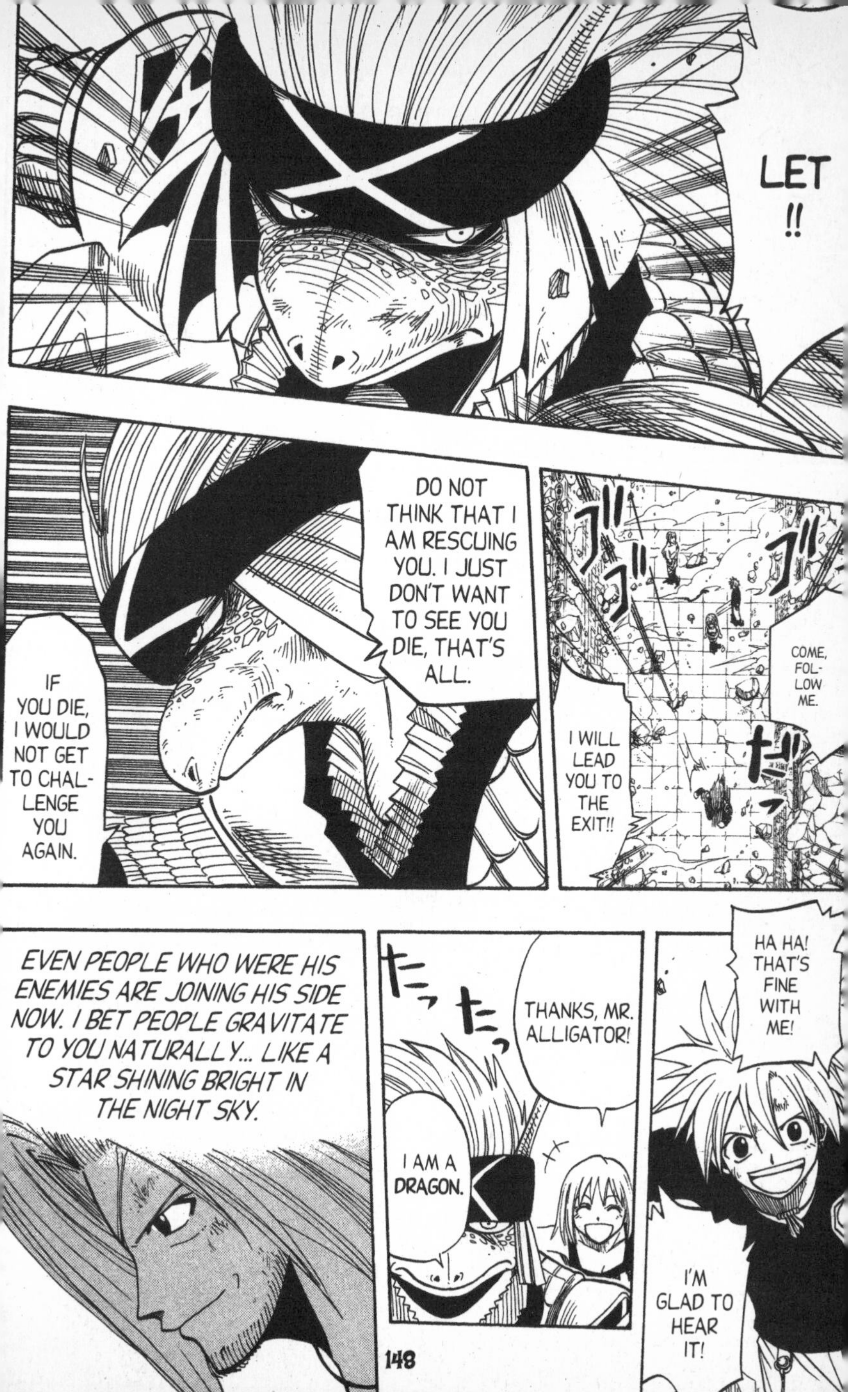
LET !!
COME, FOLLOW ME.
I WILL LEAD YOU TO THE EXIT!!
DO NOT THINK THAT I AM RESCUING YOU. I JUST DON'T WANT TO SEE YOU DIE, THAT'S ALL.
IF YOU DIE, I WOULD NOT GET TO CHALLENGE YOU AGAIN.
HA HA! THAT'S FINE WITH ME!
I'M GLAD TO HEAR IT!
THANKS, MR. ALLIGATOR!
たっ たっ
I AM A **DRAGON.**
EVEN PEOPLE WHO WERE HIS ENEMIES ARE JOINING HIS SIDE NOW. I BET PEOPLE GRAVITATE TO YOU NATURALLY... LIKE A STAR SHINING BRIGHT IN THE NIGHT SKY.

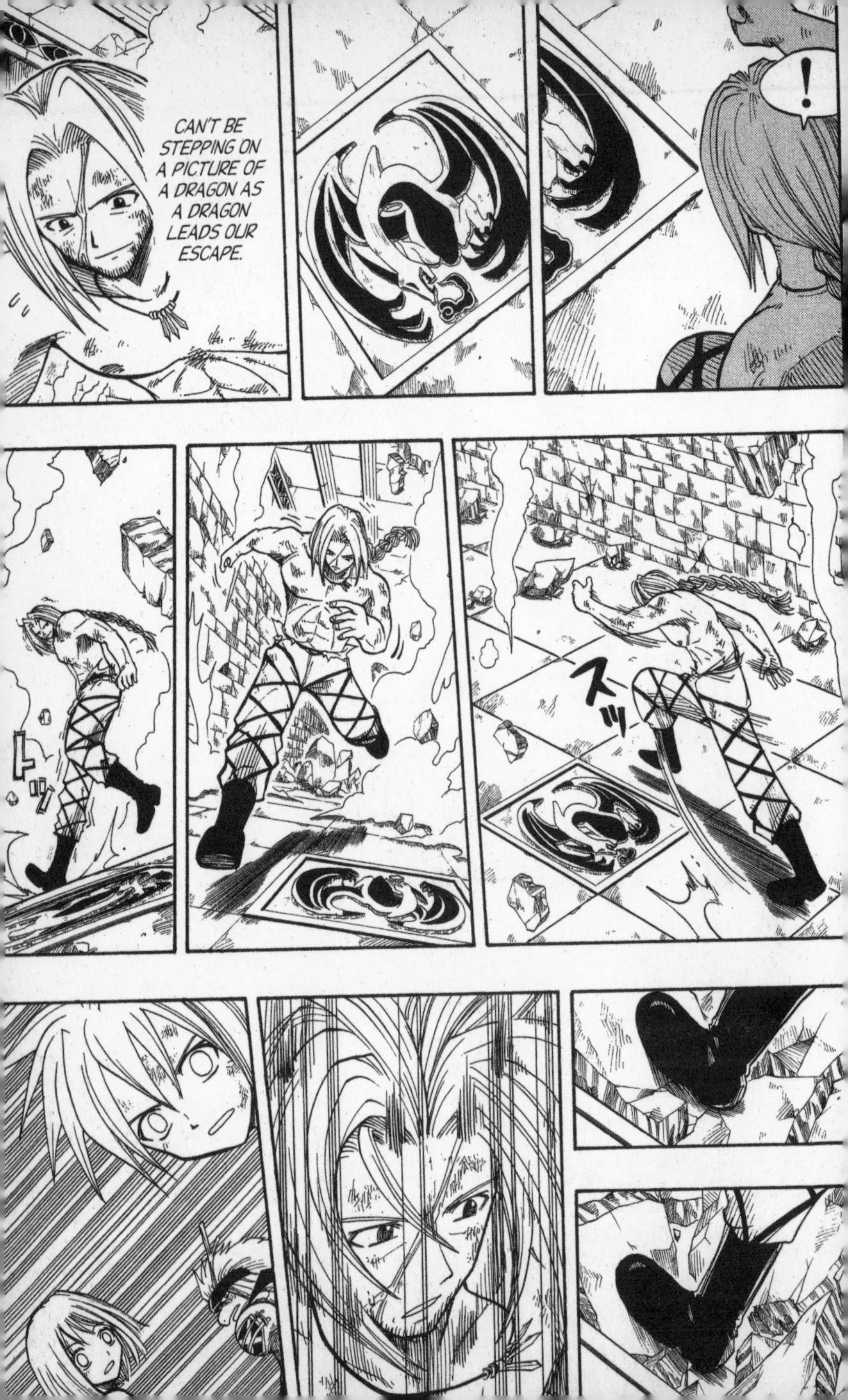
!
CAN'T BE STEPPING ON A PICTURE OF A DRAGON AS A DRAGON LEADS OUR ESCAPE.
スッ
トッ

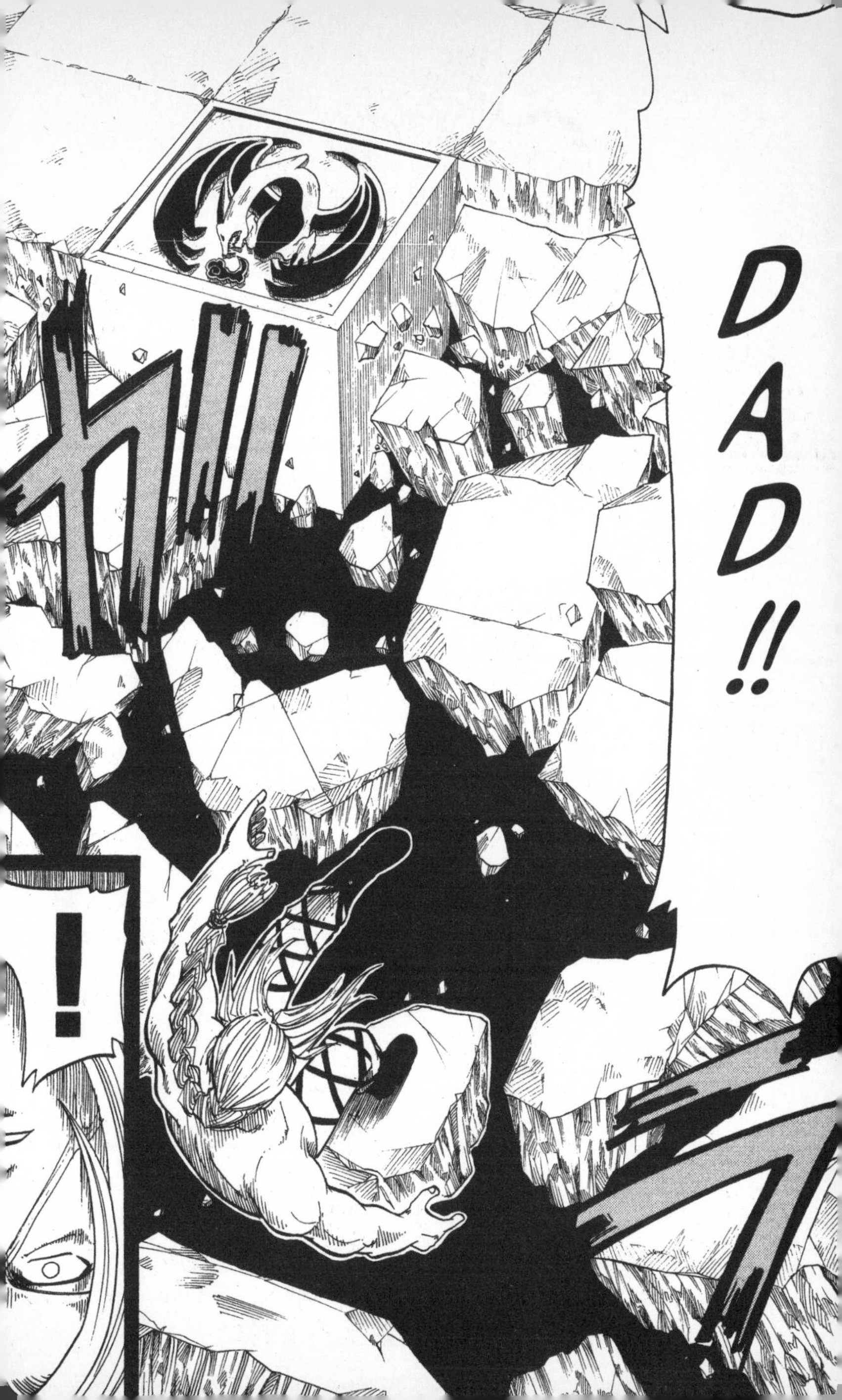
DAD!!
!

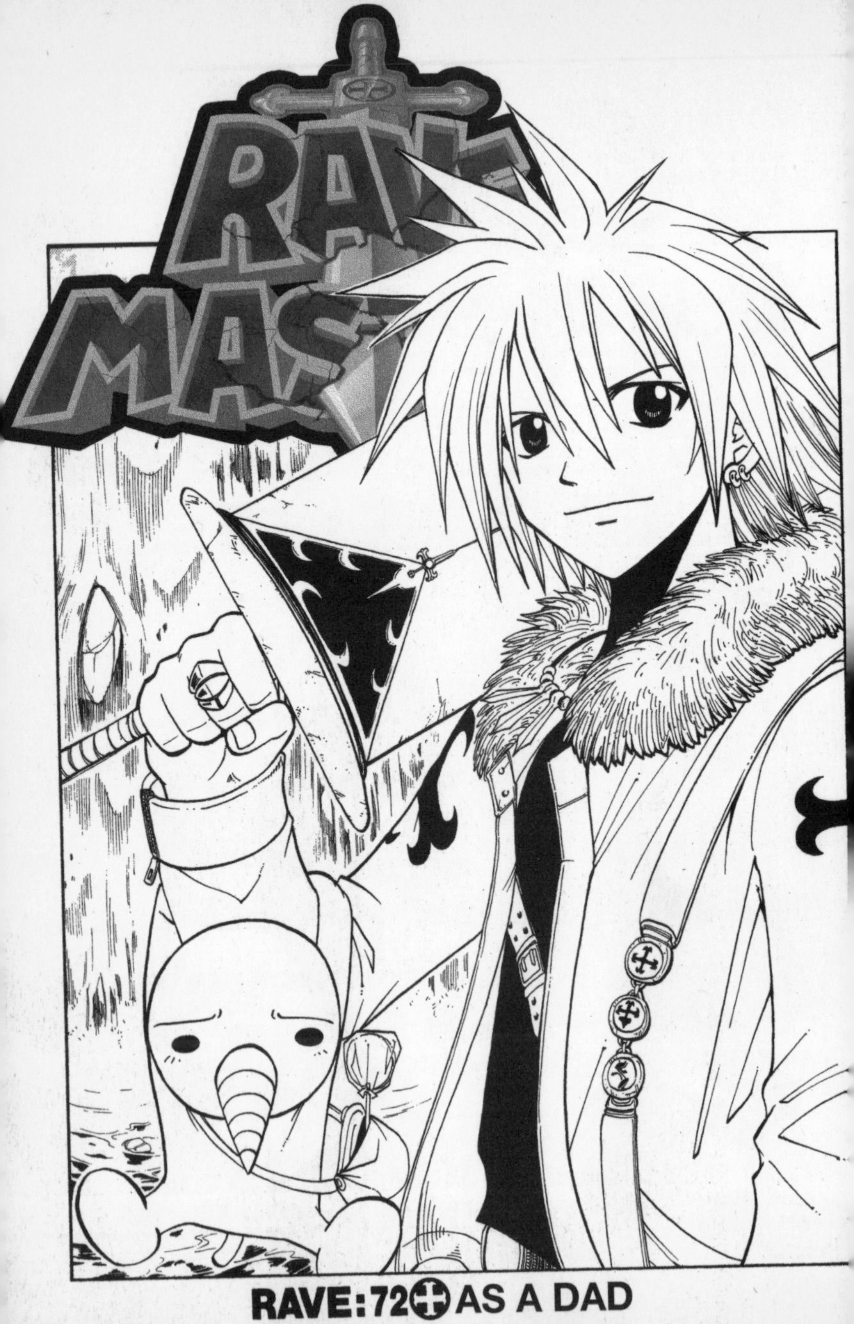

RAVE:72 AS A DAD

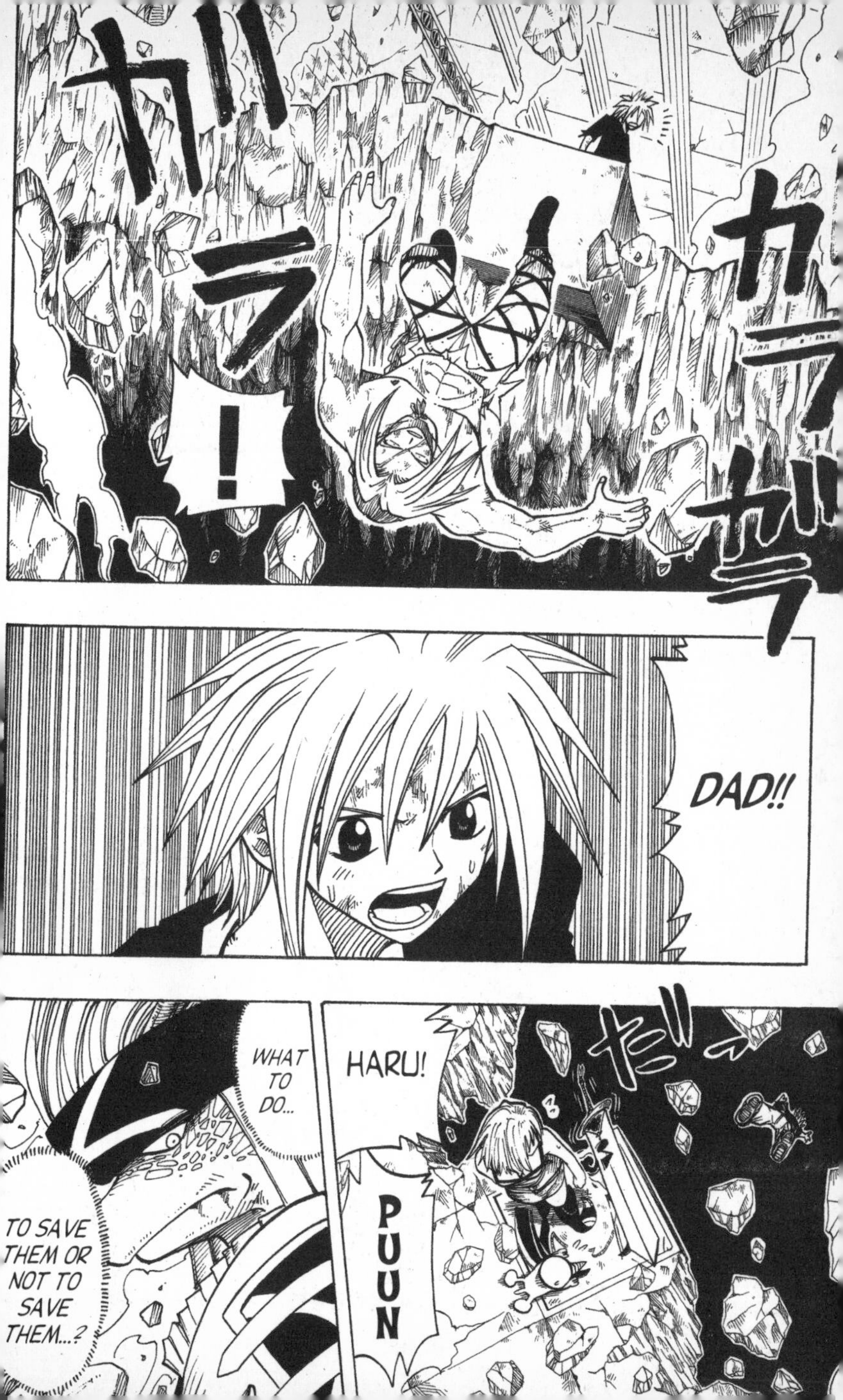

!
DAD!!
HARU!
PUUN
WHAT TO DO...
TO SAVE THEM OR NOT TO SAVE THEM...?

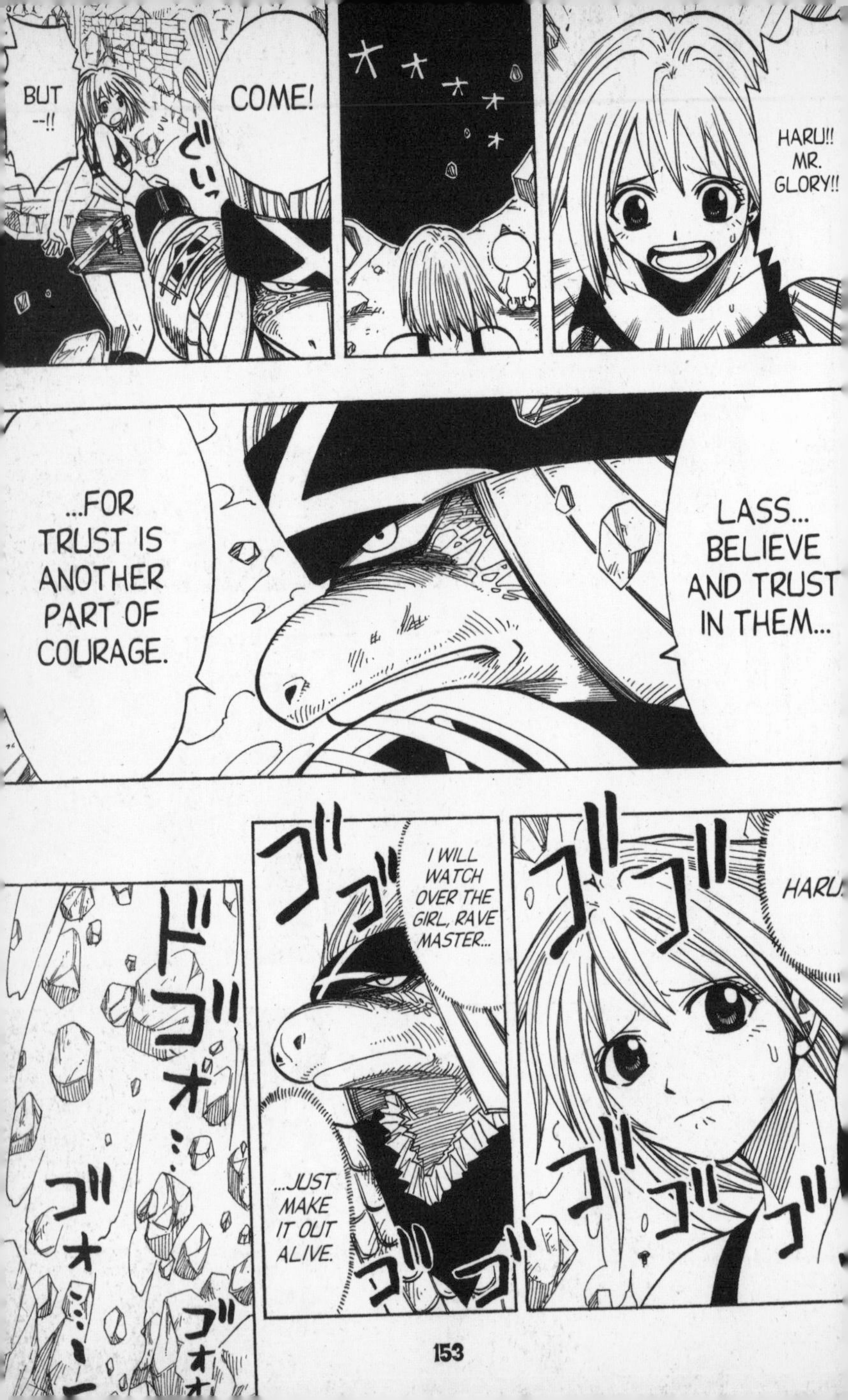
HARU!! MR. GLORY!!
COME!
BUT --!!
LASS... BELIEVE AND TRUST IN THEM...
...FOR TRUST IS ANOTHER PART OF COURAGE.
HARU.
I WILL WATCH OVER THE GIRL, RAVE MASTER...
...JUST MAKE IT OUT ALIVE.

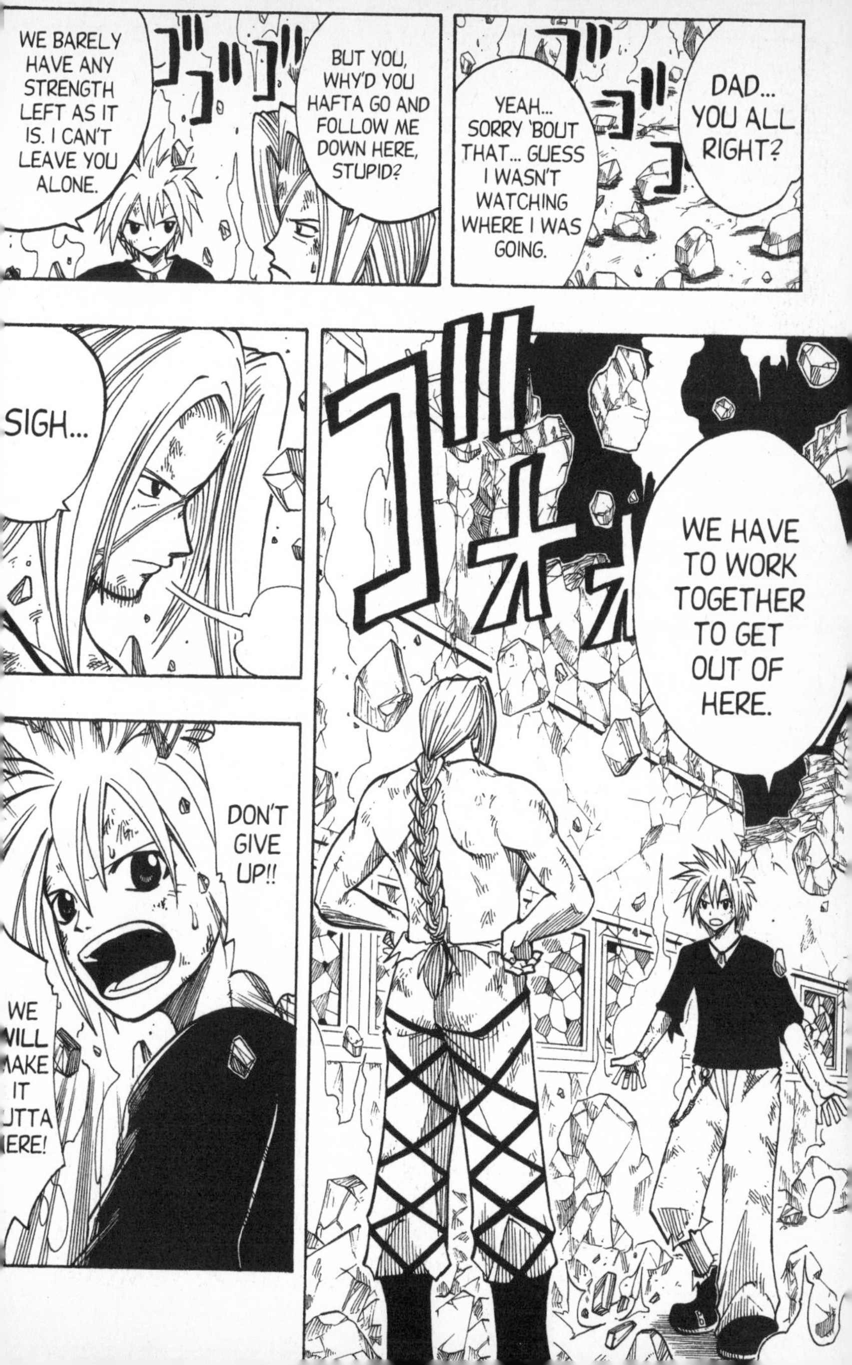
DAD... YOU ALL RIGHT?
YEAH... SORRY 'BOUT THAT... GUESS I WASN'T WATCHING WHERE I WAS GOING.
BUT YOU, WHY'D YOU HAFTA GO AND FOLLOW ME DOWN HERE, STUPID?
WE BARELY HAVE ANY STRENGTH LEFT AS IT IS. I CAN'T LEAVE YOU ALONE.
WE HAVE TO WORK TOGETHER TO GET OUT OF HERE.
SIGH...
DON'T GIVE UP!!
WE WILL MAKE IT UTTA ERE!

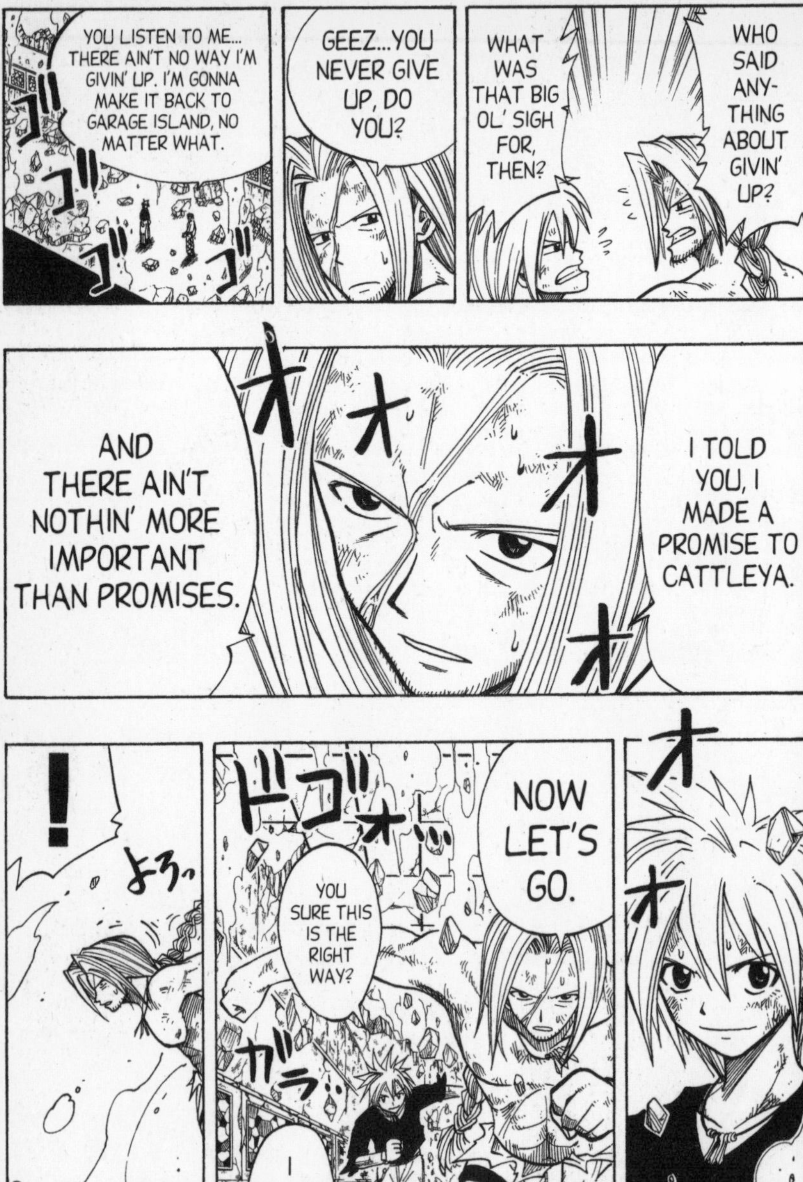
WHO SAID ANYTHING ABOUT GIVIN' UP?
WHAT WAS THAT BIG OL' SIGH FOR, THEN?
GEEZ...YOU NEVER GIVE UP, DO YOU?
YOU LISTEN TO ME... THERE AIN'T NO WAY I'M GIVIN' UP. I'M GONNA MAKE IT BACK TO GARAGE ISLAND, NO MATTER WHAT.
ゴゴゴゴ
I TOLD YOU, I MADE A PROMISE TO CATTLEYA.
AND THERE AIN'T NOTHIN' MORE IMPORTANT THAN PROMISES.
オオオオ
オオ
NOW LET'S GO.
ドゴォ
YOU SURE THIS IS THE RIGHT WAY?
ガラ
I THINK SO.
!
よろっ

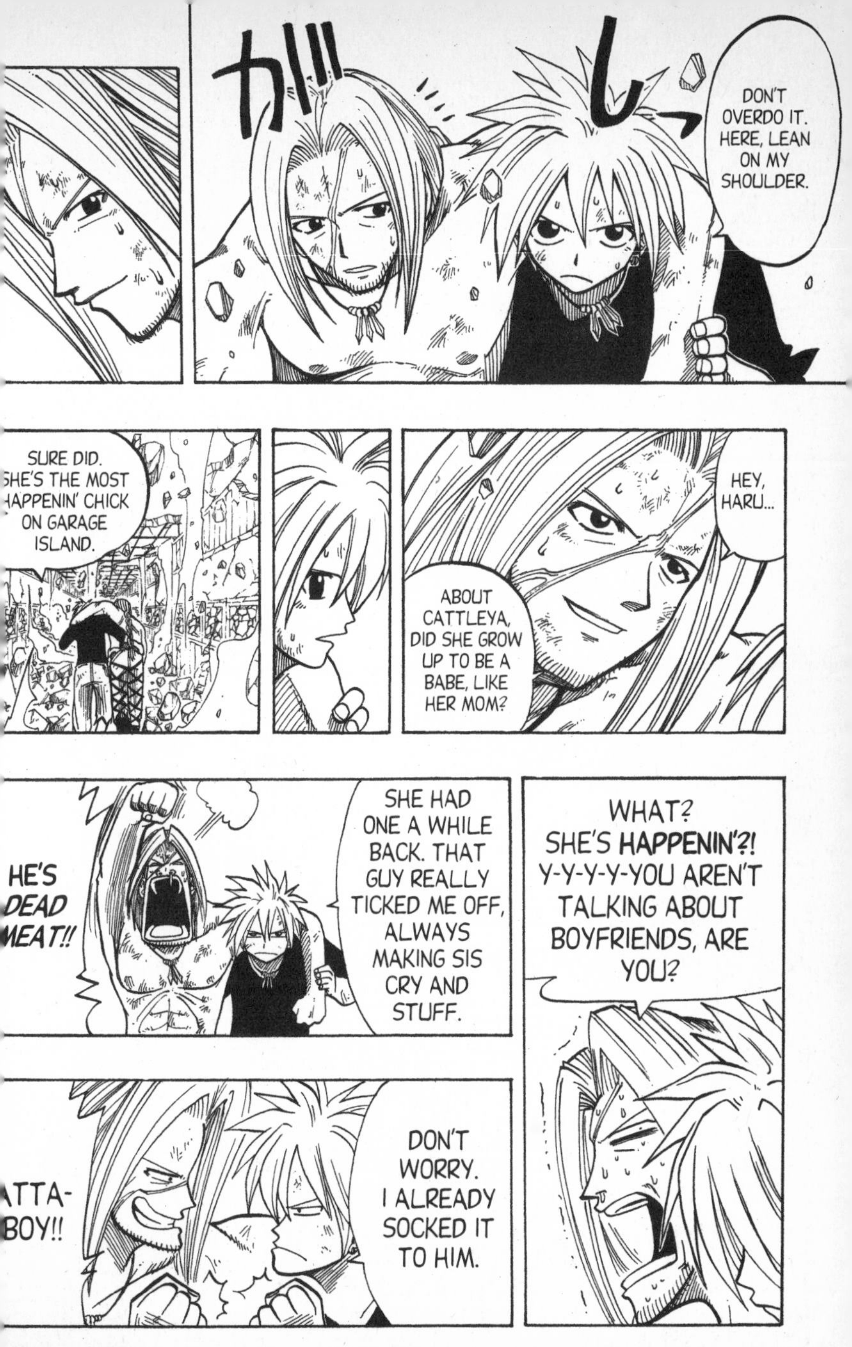
ガシッ
DON'T OVERDO IT. HERE, LEAN ON MY SHOULDER.
HEY, HARU...
ABOUT CATTLEYA, DID SHE GROW UP TO BE A BABE, LIKE HER MOM?
SURE DID. SHE'S THE MOST HAPPENIN' CHICK ON GARAGE ISLAND.
WHAT? SHE'S **HAPPENIN'**?! Y-Y-Y-Y-YOU AREN'T TALKING ABOUT BOYFRIENDS, ARE YOU?
SHE HAD ONE A WHILE BACK. THAT GUY REALLY TICKED ME OFF, ALWAYS MAKING SIS CRY AND STUFF.
HE'S *DEAD MEAT!!*
DON'T WORRY. I ALREADY SOCKED IT TO HIM.
ATTA-BOY!!

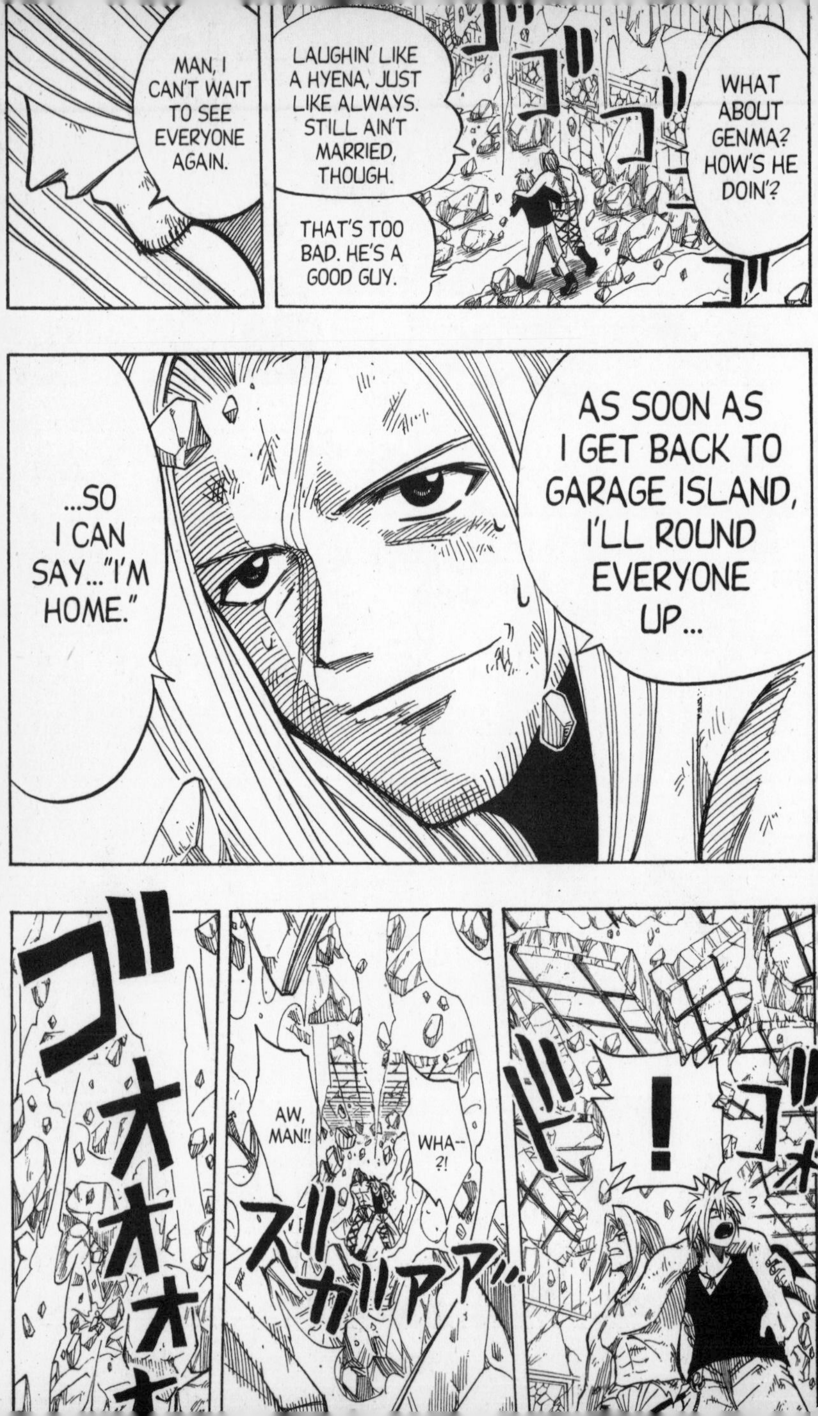

WHAT ABOUT GENMA? HOW'S HE DOIN'?
LAUGHIN' LIKE A HYENA, JUST LIKE ALWAYS. STILL AIN'T MARRIED, THOUGH.
THAT'S TOO BAD. HE'S A GOOD GUY.
MAN, I CAN'T WAIT TO SEE EVERYONE AGAIN.
AS SOON AS I GET BACK TO GARAGE ISLAND, I'LL ROUND EVERYONE UP...
...SO I CAN SAY..."I'M HOME."
!
WHA-- ?!
AW, MAN!!

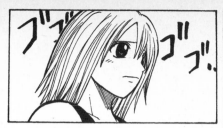

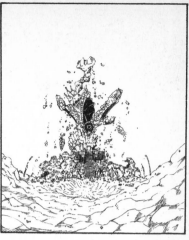

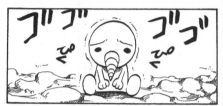

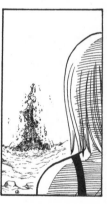

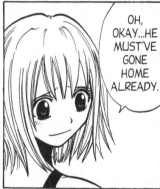

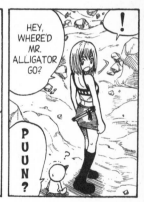

HEY, WHERE'D MR. ALLIGATOR GO?
!
PUUN?
OH, OKAY...HE MUST'VE GONE HOME ALREADY.
HARU... MR. GLORY...
PLEASE... HURRY UP AND COME OUT SAFELY.

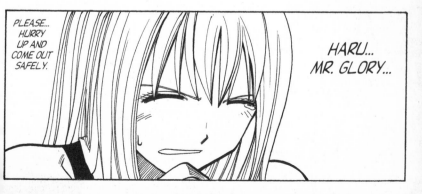

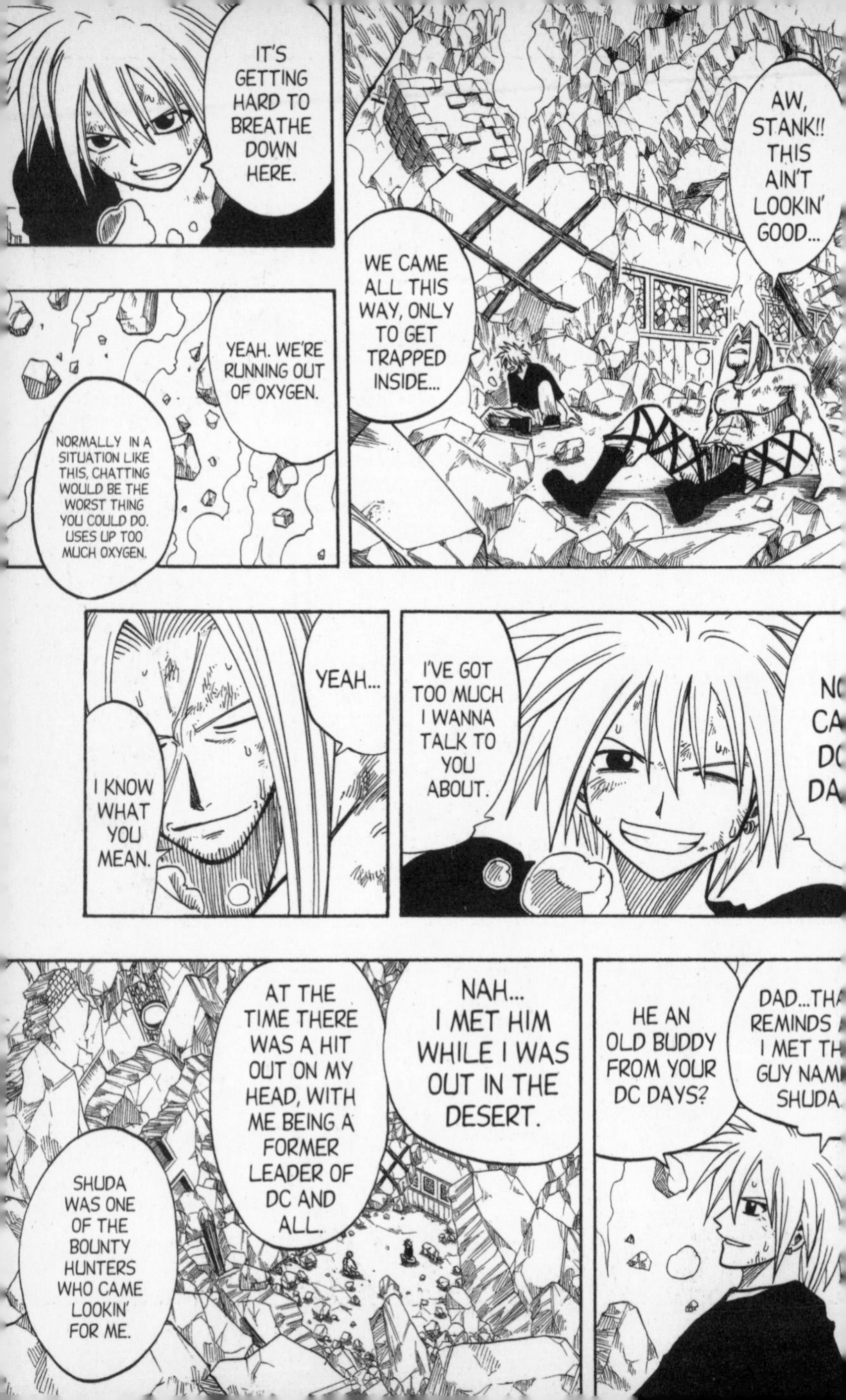
AW, STANK!! THIS AIN'T LOOKIN' GOOD...
WE CAME ALL THIS WAY, ONLY TO GET TRAPPED INSIDE...
IT'S GETTING HARD TO BREATHE DOWN HERE.
YEAH. WE'RE RUNNING OUT OF OXYGEN.
NORMALLY IN A SITUATION LIKE THIS, CHATTING WOULD BE THE WORST THING YOU COULD DO. USES UP TOO MUCH OXYGEN.
I'VE GOT TOO MUCH I WANNA TALK TO YOU ABOUT.
YEAH...
I KNOW WHAT YOU MEAN.
DAD...THA REMINDS I MET TH GUY NAM SHUDA.
HE AN OLD BUDDY FROM YOUR DC DAYS?
NAH... I MET HIM WHILE I WAS OUT IN THE DESERT.
AT THE TIME THERE WAS A HIT OUT ON MY HEAD, WITH ME BEING A FORMER LEADER OF DC AND ALL.
SHUDA WAS ONE OF THE BOUNTY HUNTERS WHO CAME LOOKIN' FOR ME.

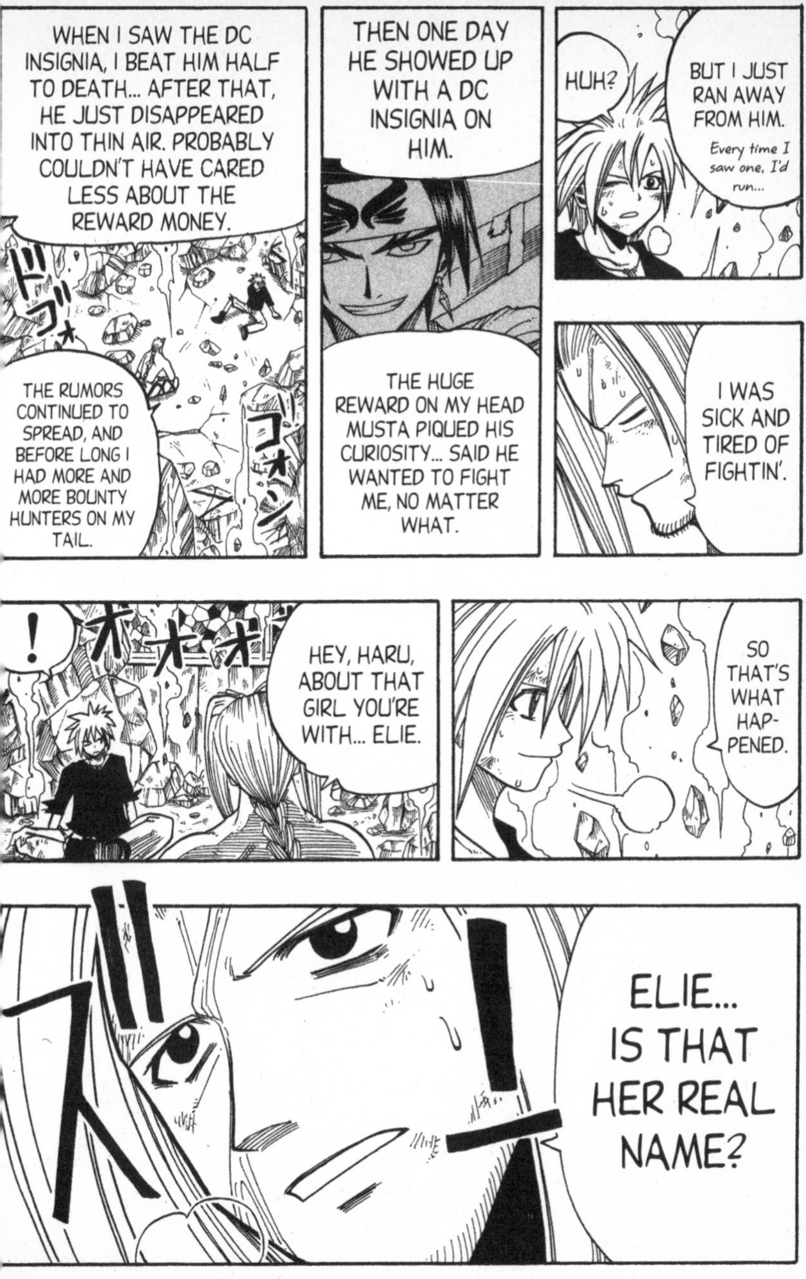
BUT I JUST RAN AWAY FROM HIM.
Every time I saw one, I'd run...
HUH?
I WAS SICK AND TIRED OF FIGHTIN'.
THEN ONE DAY HE SHOWED UP WITH A DC INSIGNIA ON HIM.
THE HUGE REWARD ON MY HEAD MUSTA PIQUED HIS CURIOSITY... SAID HE WANTED TO FIGHT ME, NO MATTER WHAT.
WHEN I SAW THE DC INSIGNIA, I BEAT HIM HALF TO DEATH... AFTER THAT, HE JUST DISAPPEARED INTO THIN AIR. PROBABLY COULDN'T HAVE CARED LESS ABOUT THE REWARD MONEY.
ドゴ
THE RUMORS CONTINUED TO SPREAD, AND BEFORE LONG I HAD MORE AND MORE BOUNTY HUNTERS ON MY TAIL.
ゴオン
SO THAT'S WHAT HAP- PENED.
HEY, HARU, ABOUT THAT GIRL YOU'RE WITH... ELIE.
オオオ
!
ELIE... IS THAT HER REAL NAME?

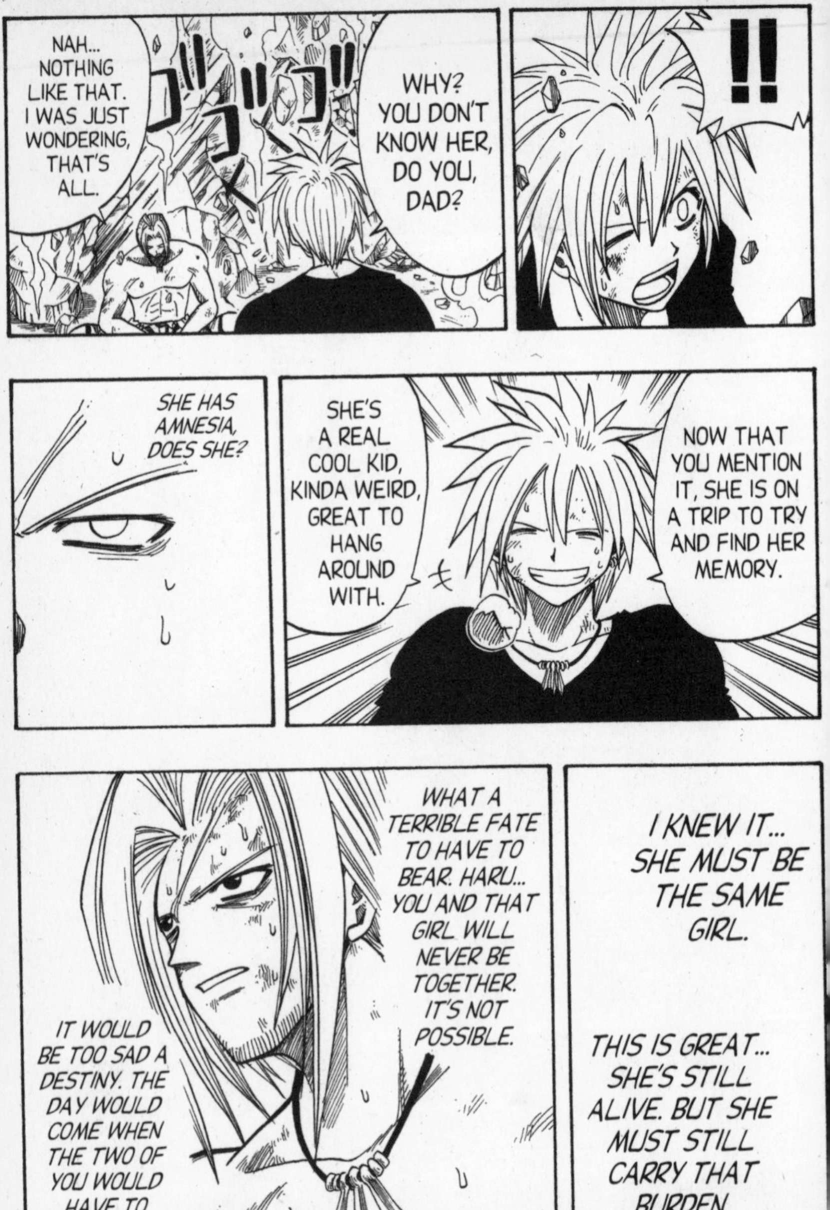
!!
WHY? YOU DON'T KNOW HER, DO YOU, DAD?
NAH... NOTHING LIKE THAT. I WAS JUST WONDERING, THAT'S ALL.
NOW THAT YOU MENTION IT, SHE IS ON A TRIP TO TRY AND FIND HER MEMORY.
SHE'S A REAL COOL KID, KINDA WEIRD, GREAT TO HANG AROUND WITH.
SHE HAS AMNESIA, DOES SHE?
I KNEW IT... SHE MUST BE THE SAME GIRL.
THIS IS GREAT... SHE'S STILL ALIVE. BUT SHE MUST STILL CARRY THAT BURDEN.
WHAT A TERRIBLE FATE TO HAVE TO BEAR. HARU... YOU AND THAT GIRL WILL NEVER BE TOGETHER. IT'S NOT POSSIBLE.
IT WOULD BE TOO SAD A DESTINY. THE DAY WOULD COME WHEN THE TWO OF YOU WOULD HAVE TO PART...

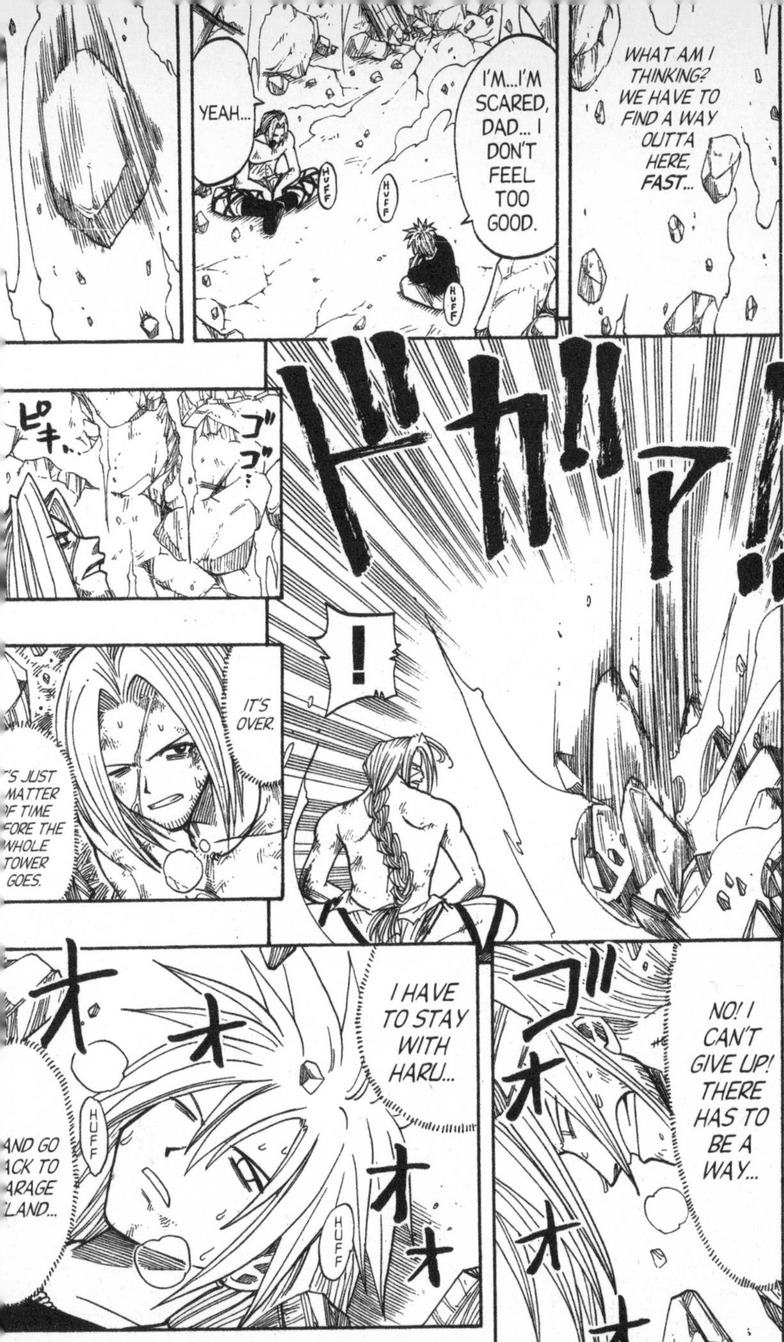
WHAT AM I THINKING? WE HAVE TO FIND A WAY OUTTA HERE, FAST...
I'M...I'M SCARED, DAD... I DON'T FEEL TOO GOOD.
HUFF
HUFF
YEAH...
HUFF
ドカ!!ア!!
!
ピキ‥
ゴゴ‥
IT'S OVER.
T'S JUST MATTER F TIME FORE THE WHOLE TOWER GOES.
NO! I CAN'T GIVE UP! THERE HAS TO BE A WAY...
ゴォォォ
I HAVE TO STAY WITH HARU...
AND GO ACK TO ARAGE LAND...
HUFF
HUFF
オォォォ

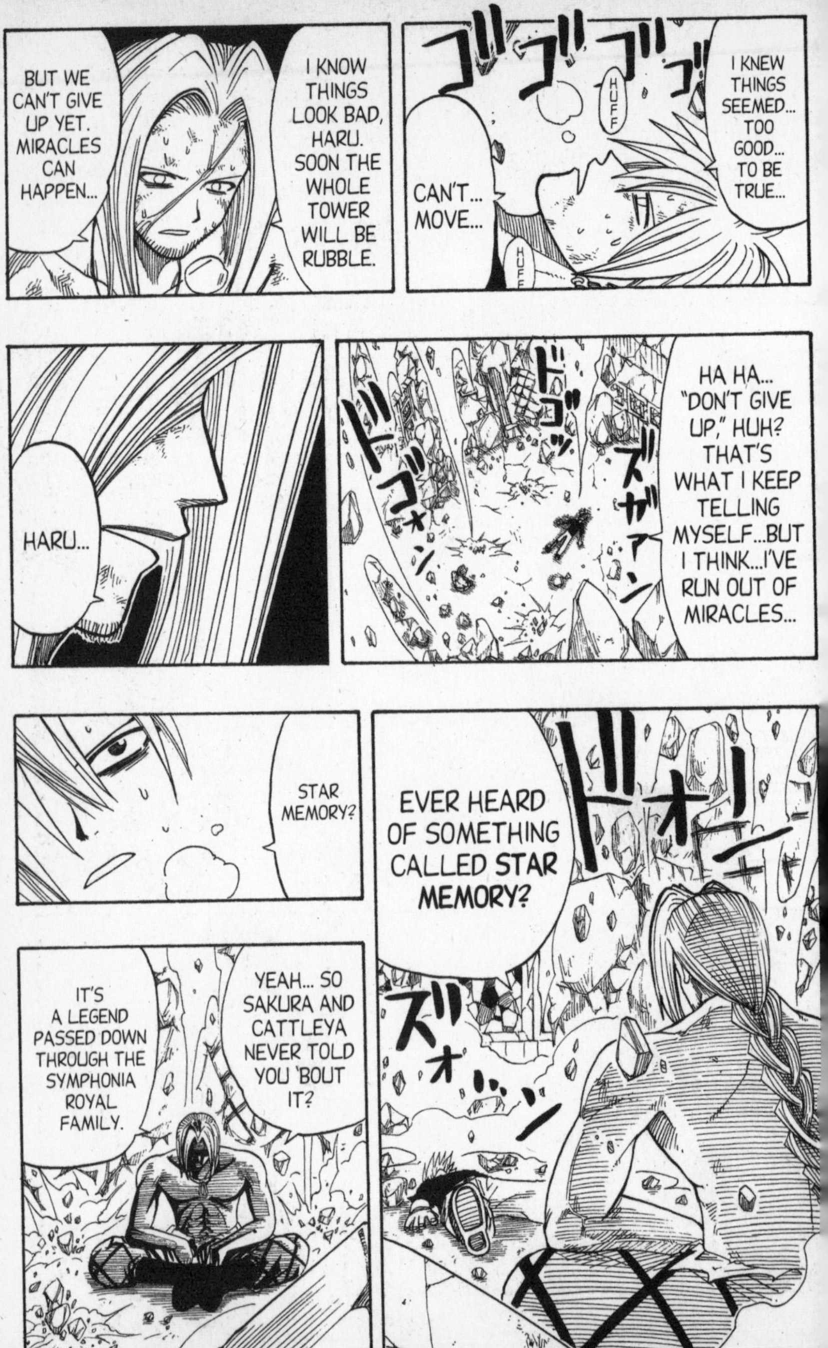
I KNEW THINGS SEEMED... TOO GOOD... TO BE TRUE...
HUFF
CAN'T... MOVE...
HUFF
I KNOW THINGS LOOK BAD, HARU. SOON THE WHOLE TOWER WILL BE RUBBLE.
BUT WE CAN'T GIVE UP YET. MIRACLES CAN HAPPEN...
HA HA... "DON'T GIVE UP," HUH? THAT'S WHAT I KEEP TELLING MYSELF...BUT I THINK...I'VE RUN OUT OF MIRACLES...
HARU...
EVER HEARD OF SOMETHING CALLED STAR MEMORY?
STAR MEMORY?
YEAH... SO SAKURA AND CATTLEYA NEVER TOLD YOU 'BOUT IT?
IT'S A LEGEND PASSED DOWN THROUGH THE SYMPHONIA ROYAL FAMILY.

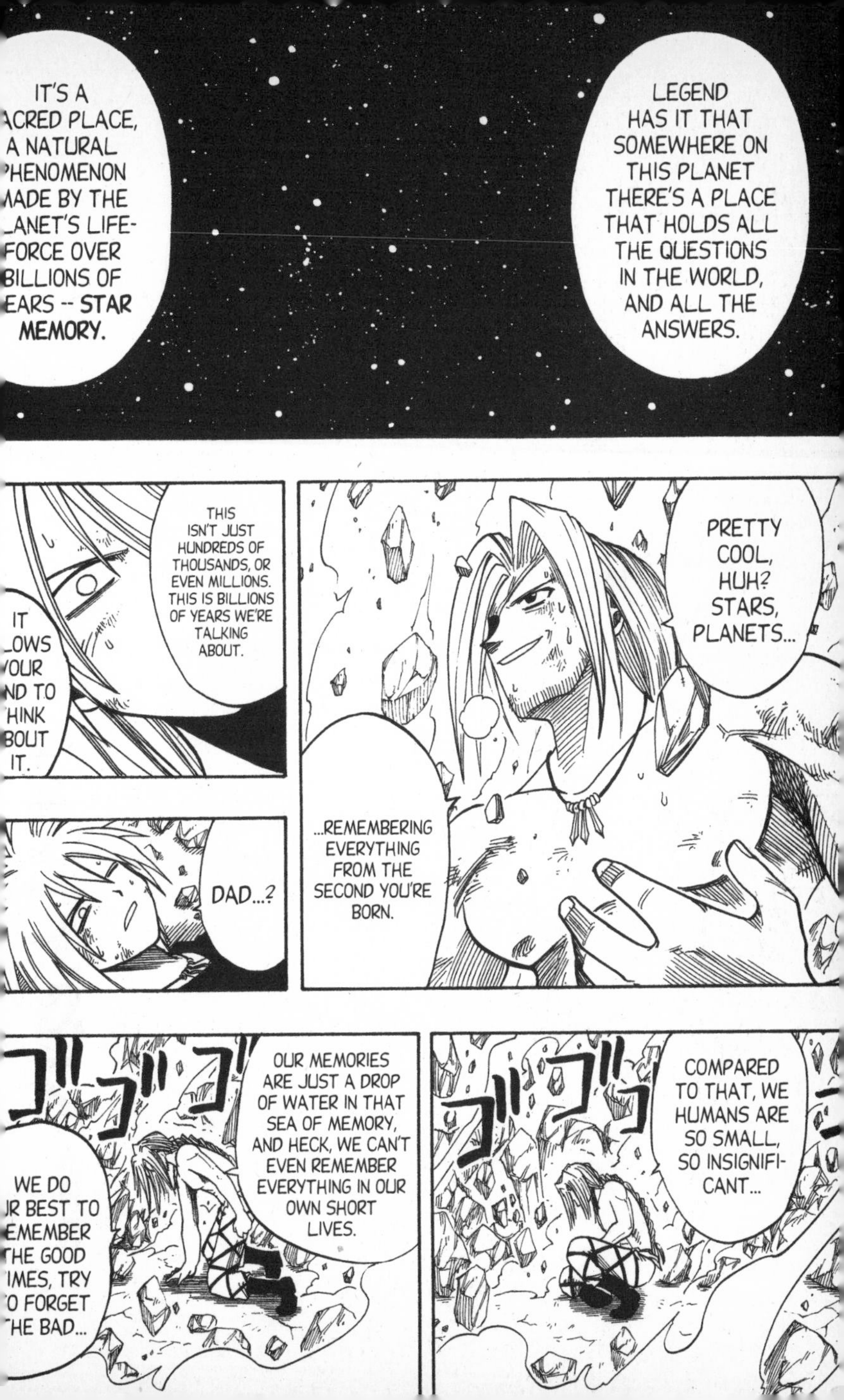
LEGEND HAS IT THAT SOMEWHERE ON THIS PLANET THERE'S A PLACE THAT HOLDS ALL THE QUESTIONS IN THE WORLD, AND ALL THE ANSWERS.
IT'S A ACRED PLACE, A NATURAL PHENOMENON MADE BY THE LANET'S LIFE-FORCE OVER BILLIONS OF EARS -- STAR MEMORY.
PRETTY COOL, HUH? STARS, PLANETS...
...REMEMBERING EVERYTHING FROM THE SECOND YOU'RE BORN.
THIS ISN'T JUST HUNDREDS OF THOUSANDS, OR EVEN MILLIONS. THIS IS BILLIONS OF YEARS WE'RE TALKING ABOUT.
IT LOWS OUR ND TO HINK BOUT IT.
DAD...?
ゴゴゴ
COMPARED TO THAT, WE HUMANS ARE SO SMALL, SO INSIGNIFI-CANT...
ゴゴゴ
OUR MEMORIES ARE JUST A DROP OF WATER IN THAT SEA OF MEMORY, AND HECK, WE CAN'T EVEN REMEMBER EVERYTHING IN OUR OWN SHORT LIVES.
WE DO R BEST TO EMEMBER THE GOOD IMES, TRY O FORGET HE BAD...

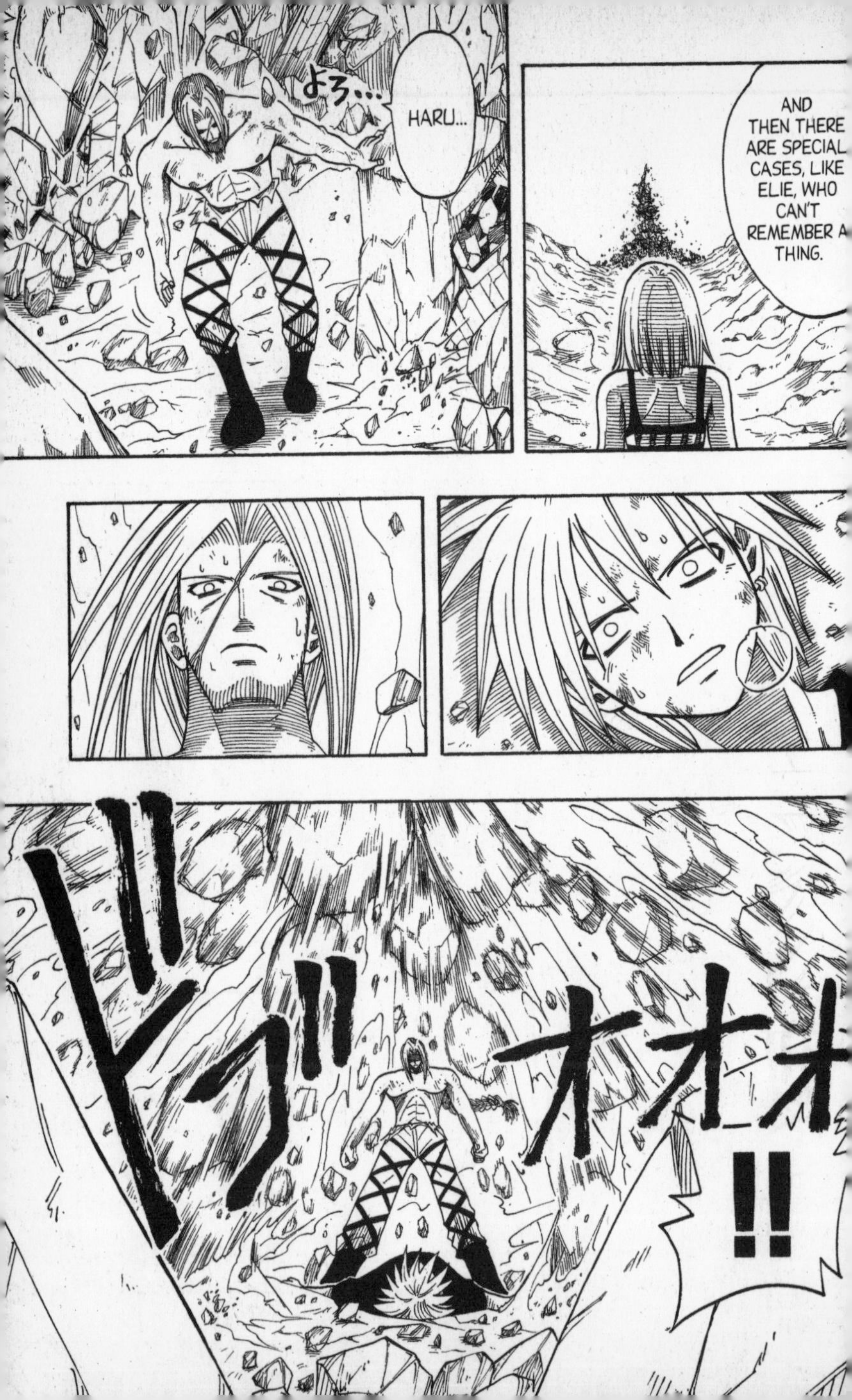
AND THEN THERE ARE SPECIAL CASES, LIKE ELIE, WHO CAN'T REMEMBER A THING.
よろ…
HARU...
ドゴオオオ
!!

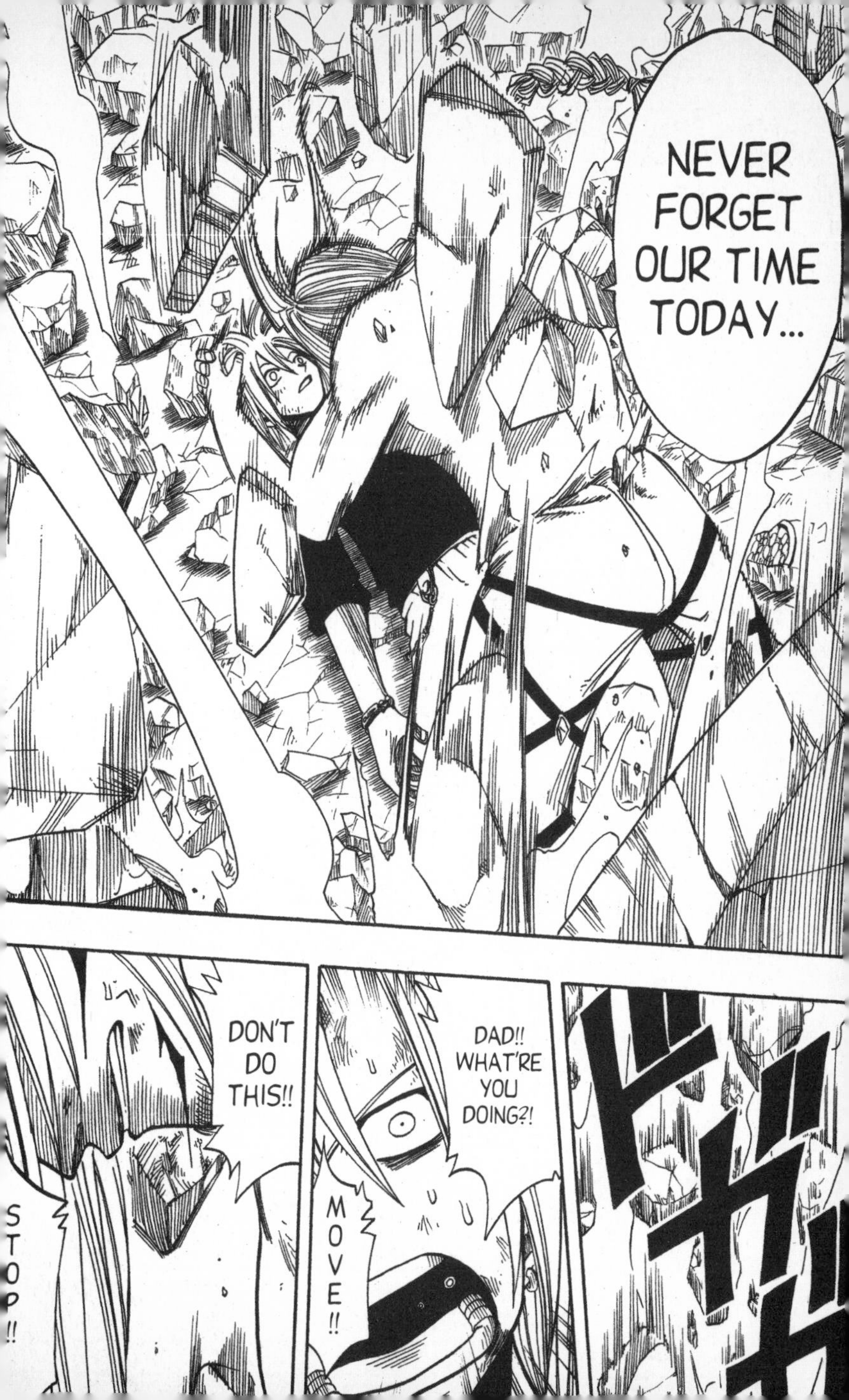
NEVER FORGET OUR TIME TODAY...
DAD!! WHAT'RE YOU DOING?!
MOVE!!
DON'T DO THIS!!
STOP!!

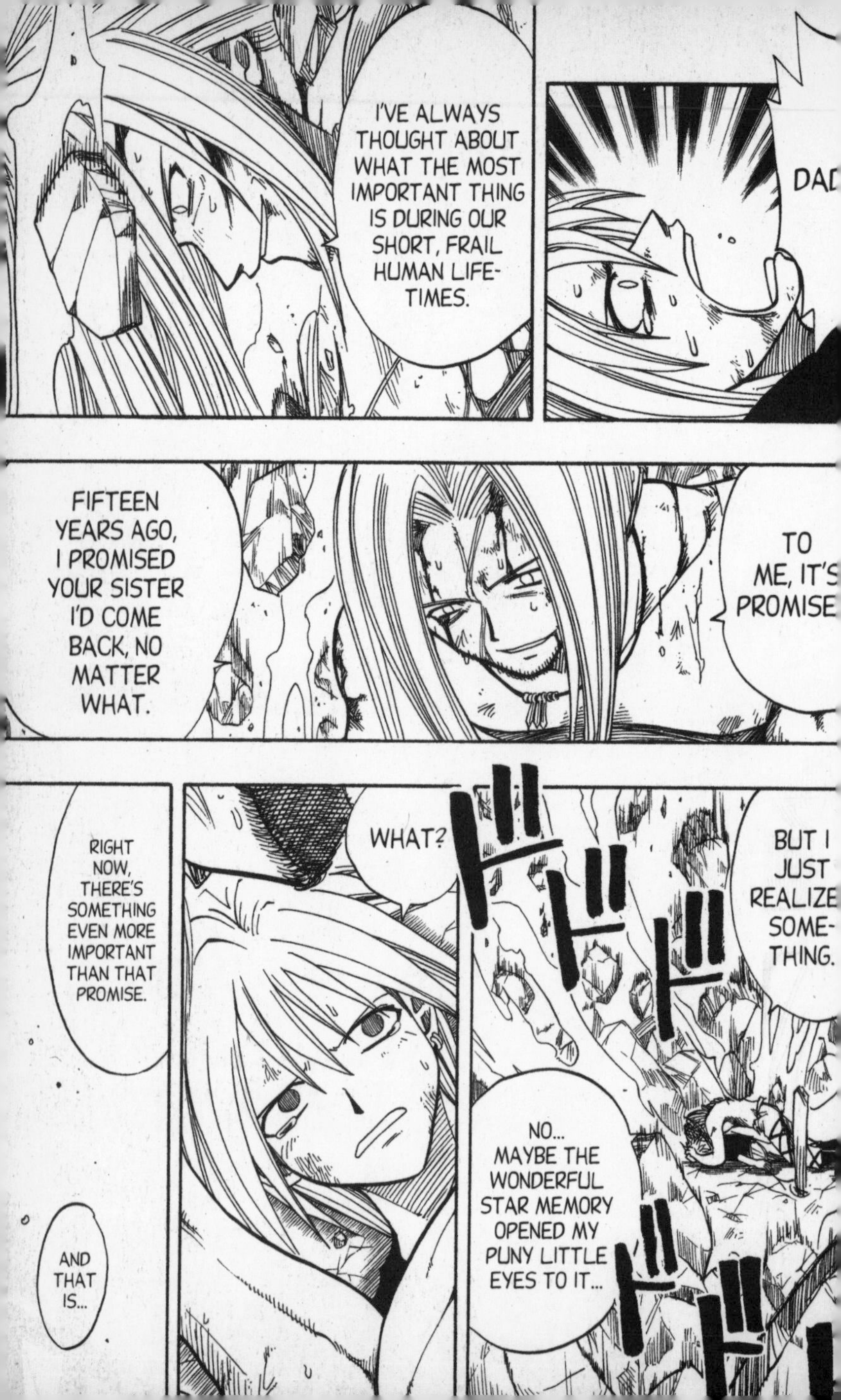
DAD
I'VE ALWAYS THOUGHT ABOUT WHAT THE MOST IMPORTANT THING IS DURING OUR SHORT, FRAIL HUMAN LIFETIMES.
TO ME, IT'S PROMISE
FIFTEEN YEARS AGO, I PROMISED YOUR SISTER I'D COME BACK, NO MATTER WHAT.
BUT I JUST REALIZE SOMETHING.
ドドドド
NO... MAYBE THE WONDERFUL STAR MEMORY OPENED MY PUNY LITTLE EYES TO IT...
ドド
WHAT?
RIGHT NOW, THERE'S SOMETHING EVEN MORE IMPORTANT THAN THAT PROMISE.
AND THAT IS...

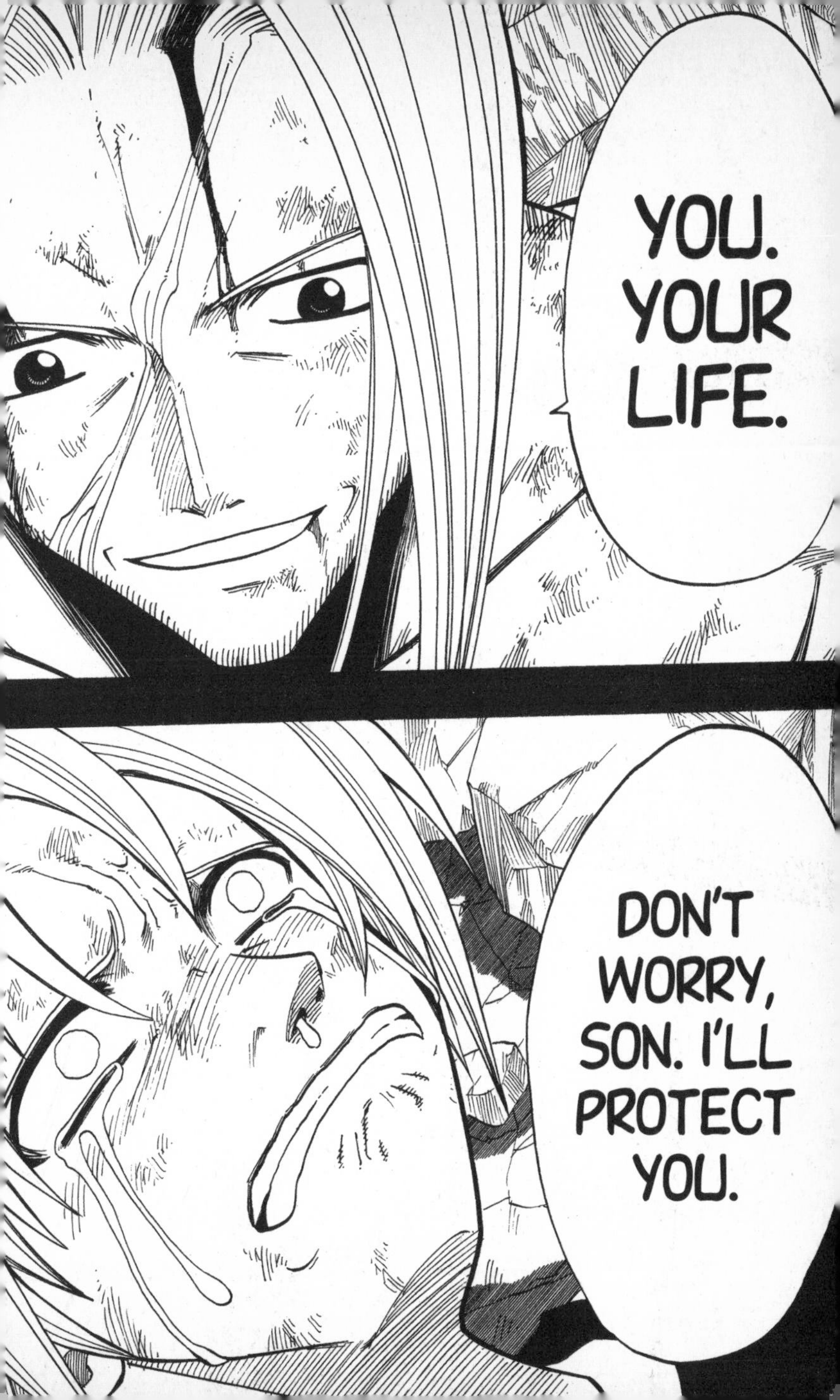
YOU. YOUR LIFE.
DON'T WORRY, SON. I'LL PROTECT YOU.

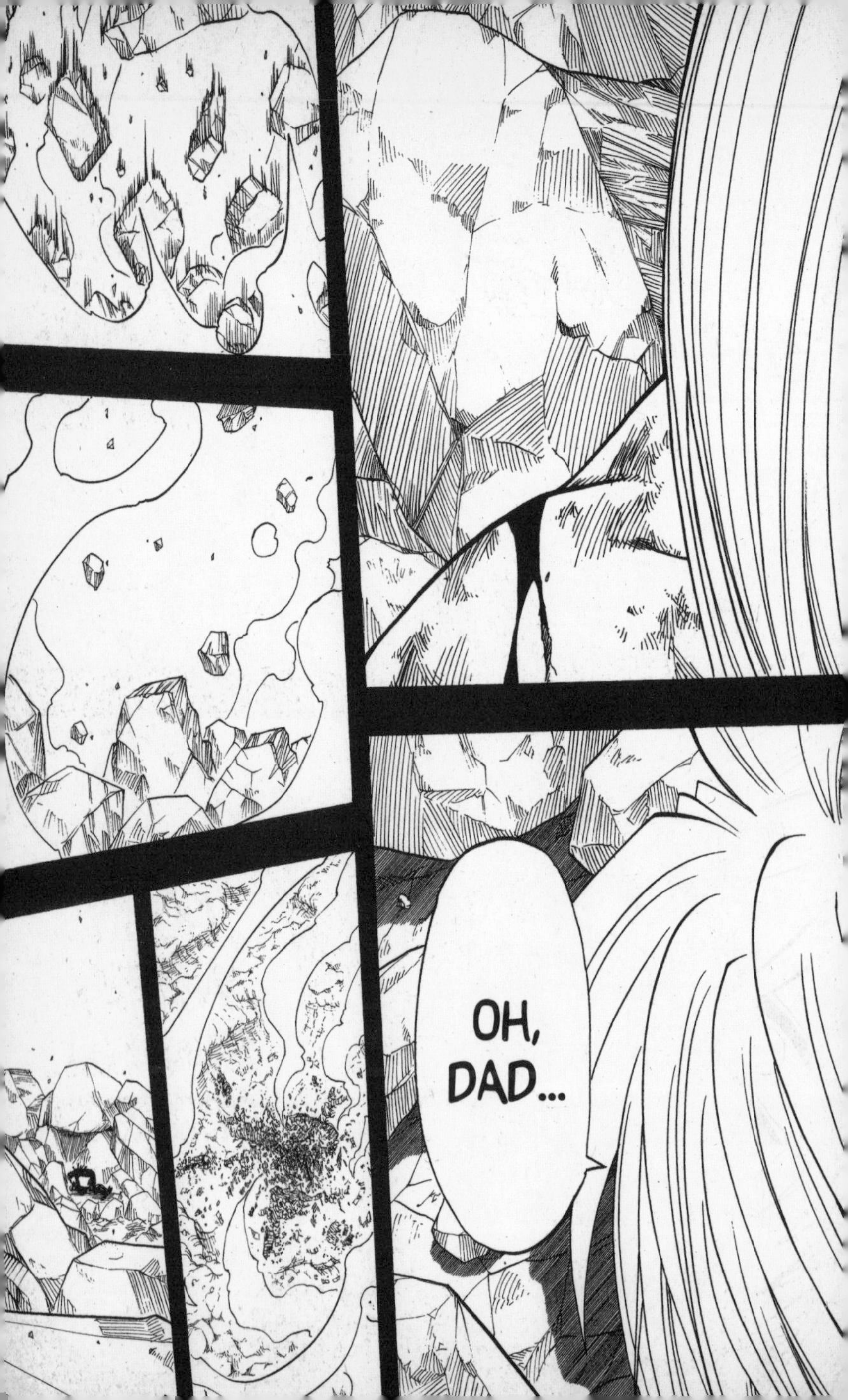
OH, DAD...

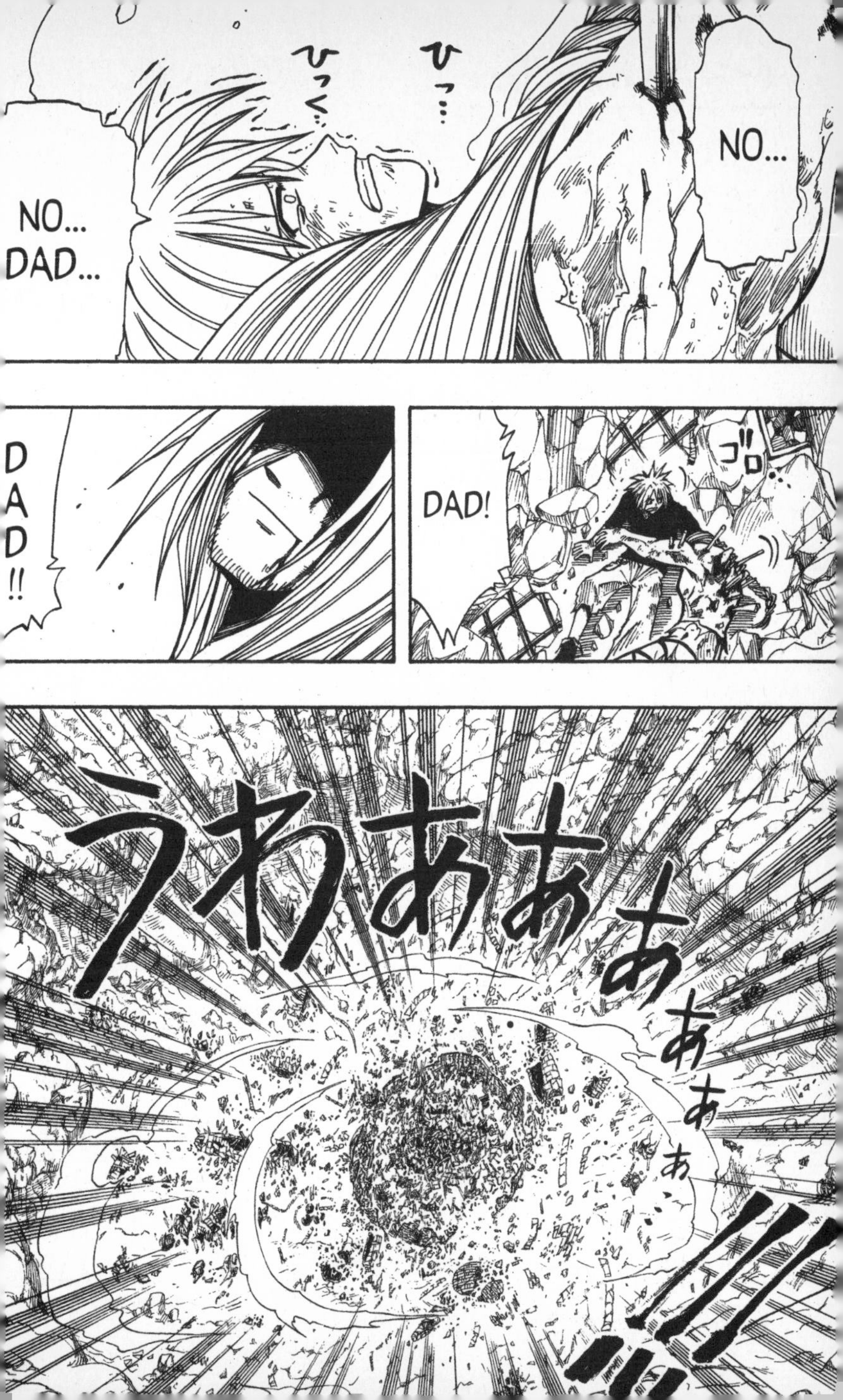

NO...
ひっ…
ひっく…
NO... DAD...
ゴロ
DAD!
DAD!!
うわああああああ…!!

Levin Minds the House

Number 8 - The Present

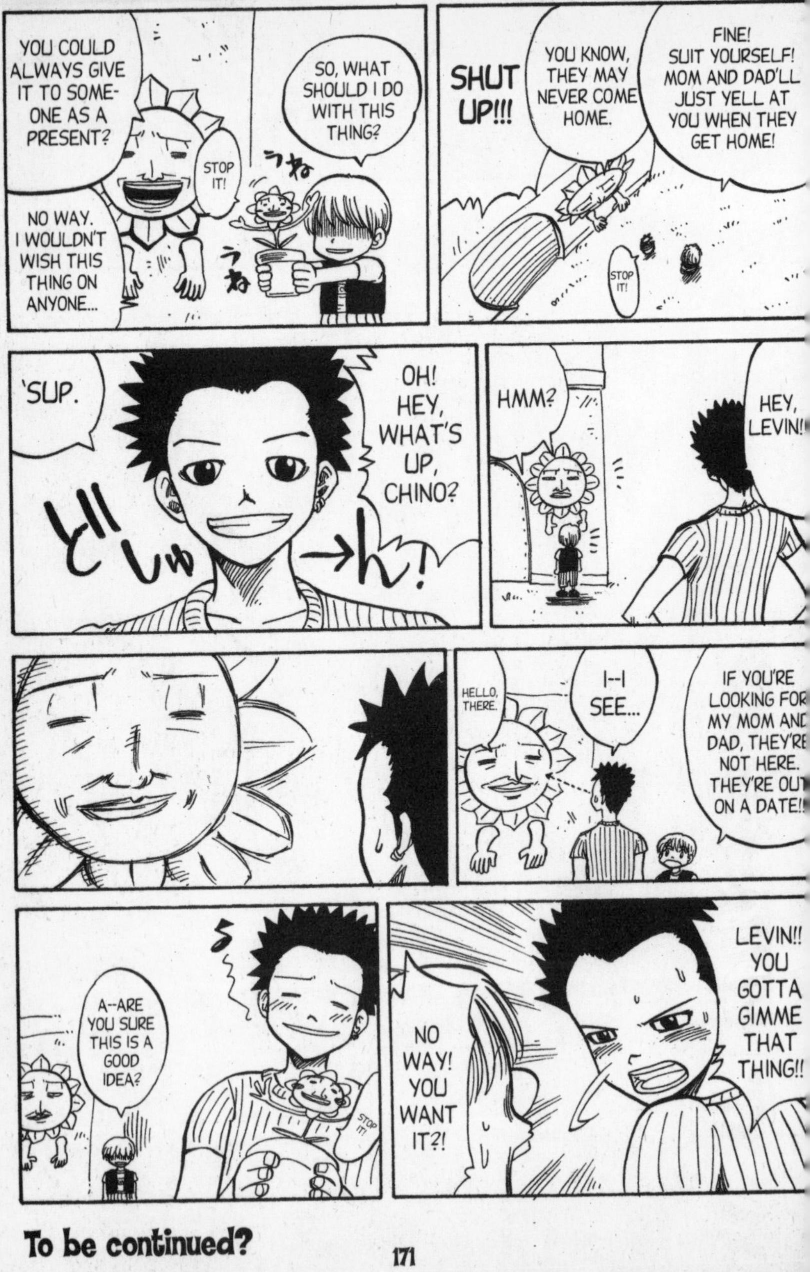
FINE! SUIT YOURSELF! MOM AND DAD'LL JUST YELL AT YOU WHEN THEY GET HOME!
YOU KNOW, THEY MAY NEVER COME HOME.
SHUT UP!!!
STOP IT!
SO, WHAT SHOULD I DO WITH THIS THING?
YOU COULD ALWAYS GIVE IT TO SOME-ONE AS A PRESENT?
STOP IT!
NO WAY. I WOULDN'T WISH THIS THING ON ANYONE...
HEY, LEVIN!
HMM?
OH! HEY, WHAT'S UP, CHINO?
'SUP.
IF YOU'RE LOOKING FOR MY MOM AND DAD, THEY'RE NOT HERE. THEY'RE OUT ON A DATE!!
I--I SEE...
HELLO, THERE.
LEVIN!! YOU GOTTA GIMME THAT THING!!
NO WAY! YOU WANT IT?!
STOP IT!
A--ARE YOU SURE THIS IS A GOOD IDEA?

To be continued?

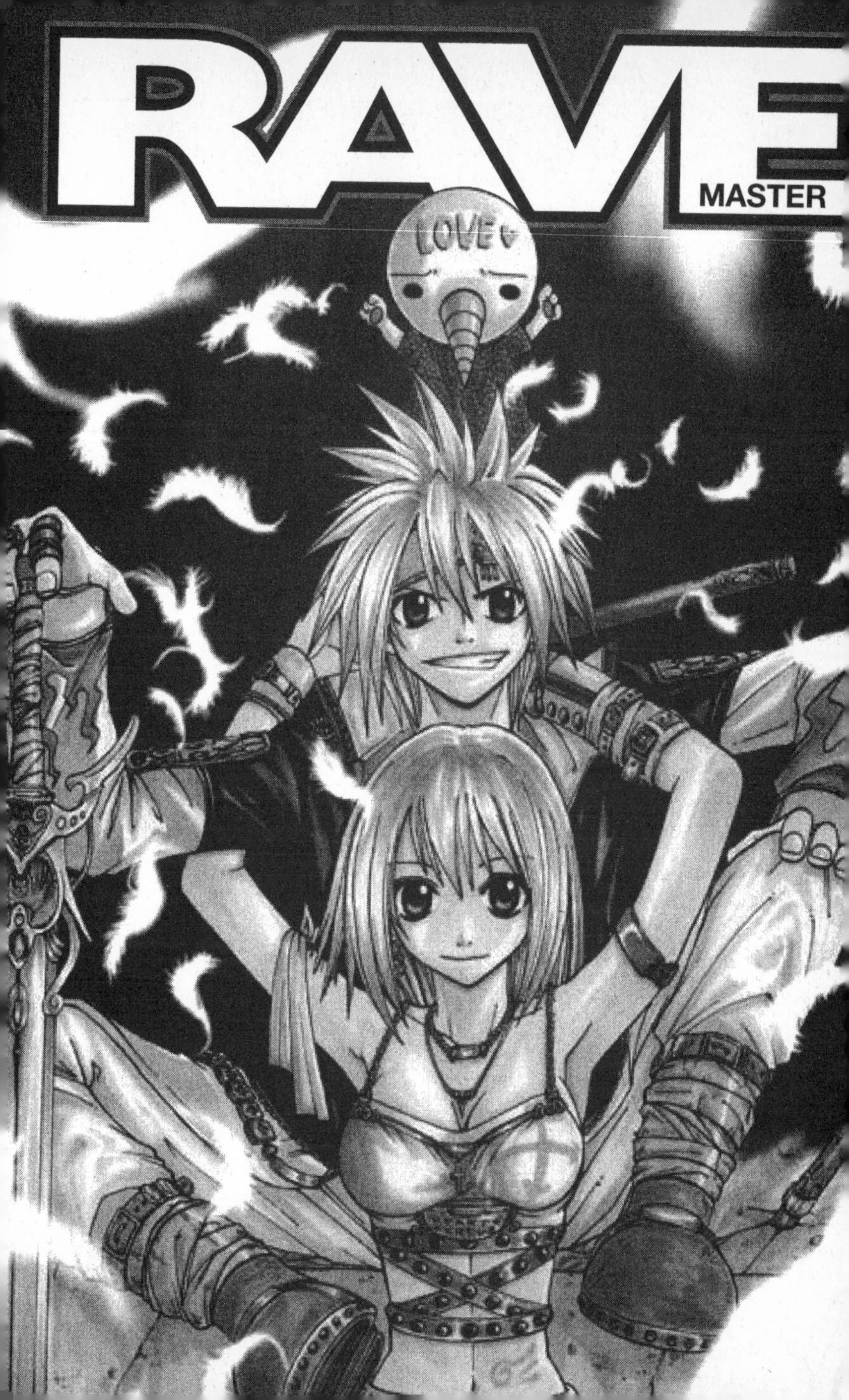
RAVE MASTER
LOVE

RAVE:73 ETERNAL BONDS

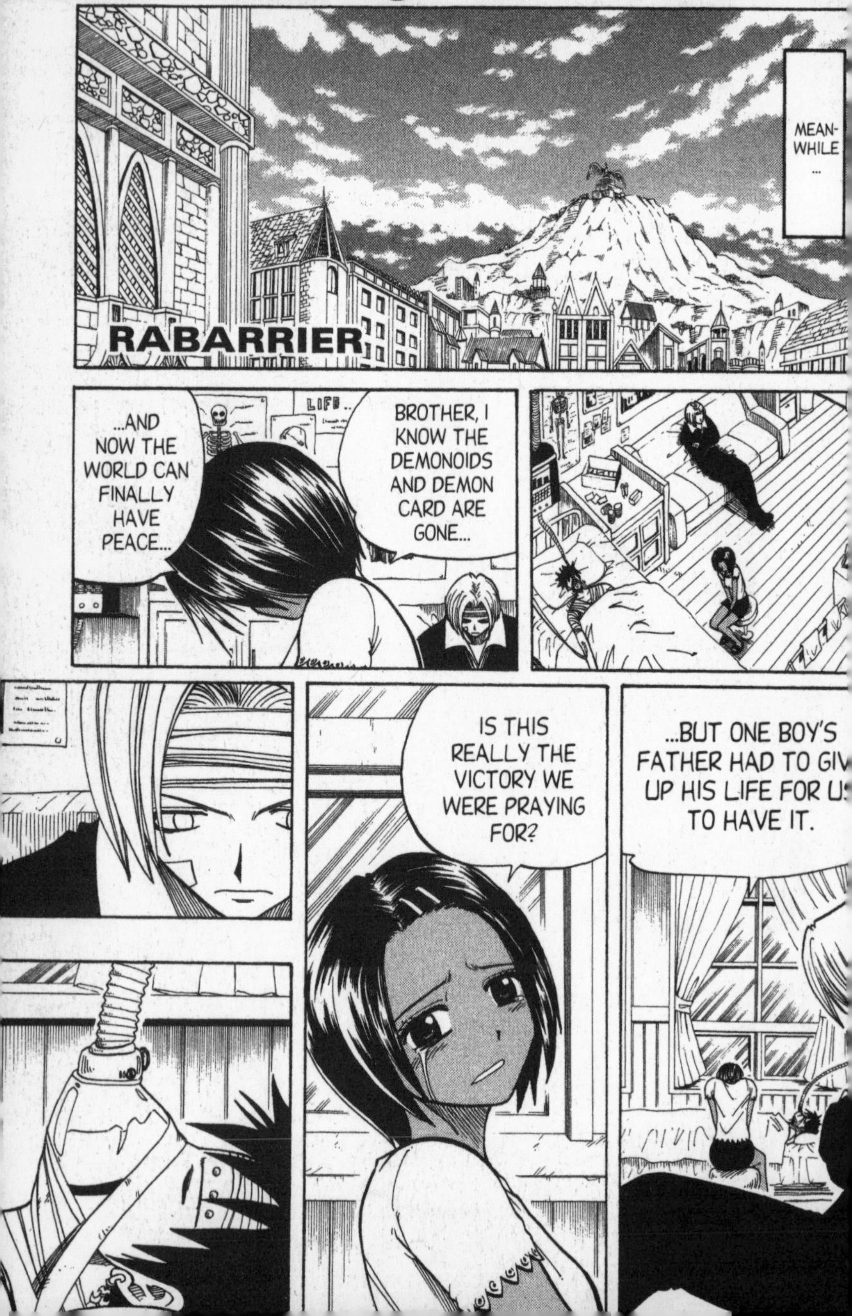

MEAN-WHILE...
RABARRIER
BROTHER, I KNOW THE DEMONOIDS AND DEMON CARD ARE GONE...
...AND NOW THE WORLD CAN FINALLY HAVE PEACE...
LIFE..
...BUT ONE BOY'S FATHER HAD TO GIV UP HIS LIFE FOR U TO HAVE IT.
IS THIS REALLY THE VICTORY WE WERE PRAYING FOR?

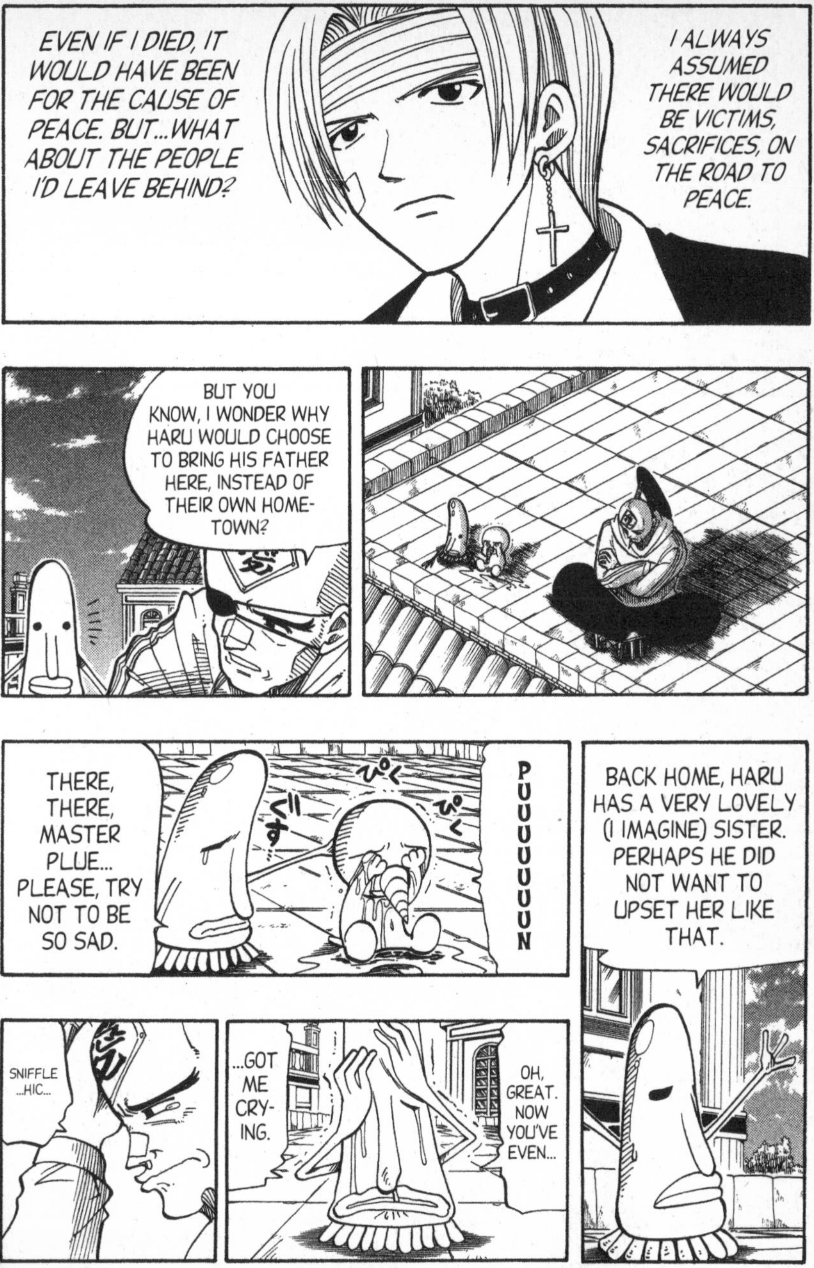
I ALWAYS ASSUMED THERE WOULD BE VICTIMS, SACRIFICES, ON THE ROAD TO PEACE.
EVEN IF I DIED, IT WOULD HAVE BEEN FOR THE CAUSE OF PEACE. BUT...WHAT ABOUT THE PEOPLE I'D LEAVE BEHIND?
BUT YOU KNOW, I WONDER WHY HARU WOULD CHOOSE TO BRING HIS FATHER HERE, INSTEAD OF THEIR OWN HOME-TOWN?
BACK HOME, HARU HAS A VERY LOVELY (I IMAGINE) SISTER. PERHAPS HE DID NOT WANT TO UPSET HER LIKE THAT.
PUUUUUUUN
ぴく
ぴく
ぐす
THERE, THERE, MASTER PLUE... PLEASE, TRY NOT TO BE SO SAD.
OH, GREAT. NOW YOU'VE EVEN...
...GOT ME CRY-ING.
SNIFFLE ...HIC...

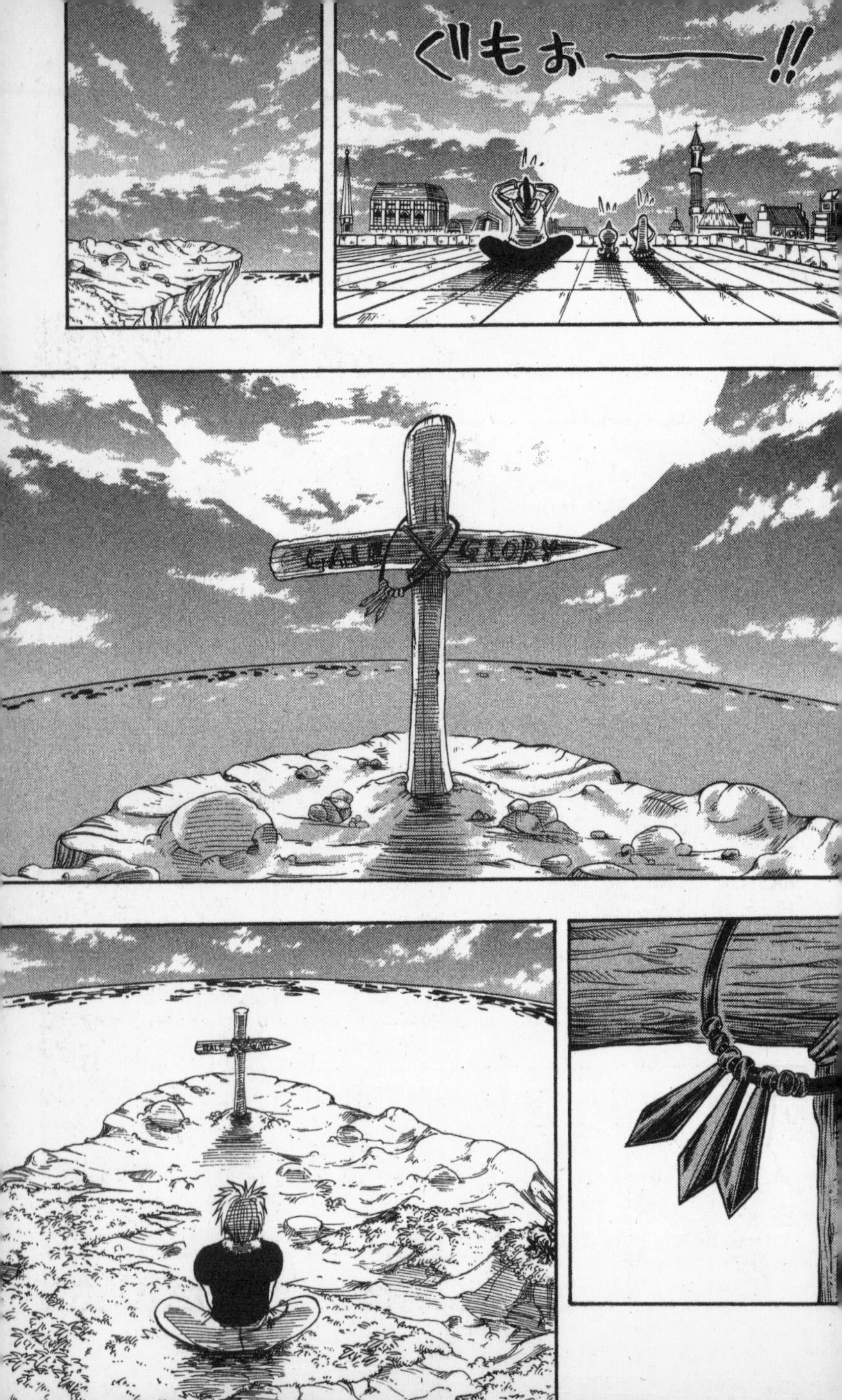
ぐもぉ――!!
GALE GLORY

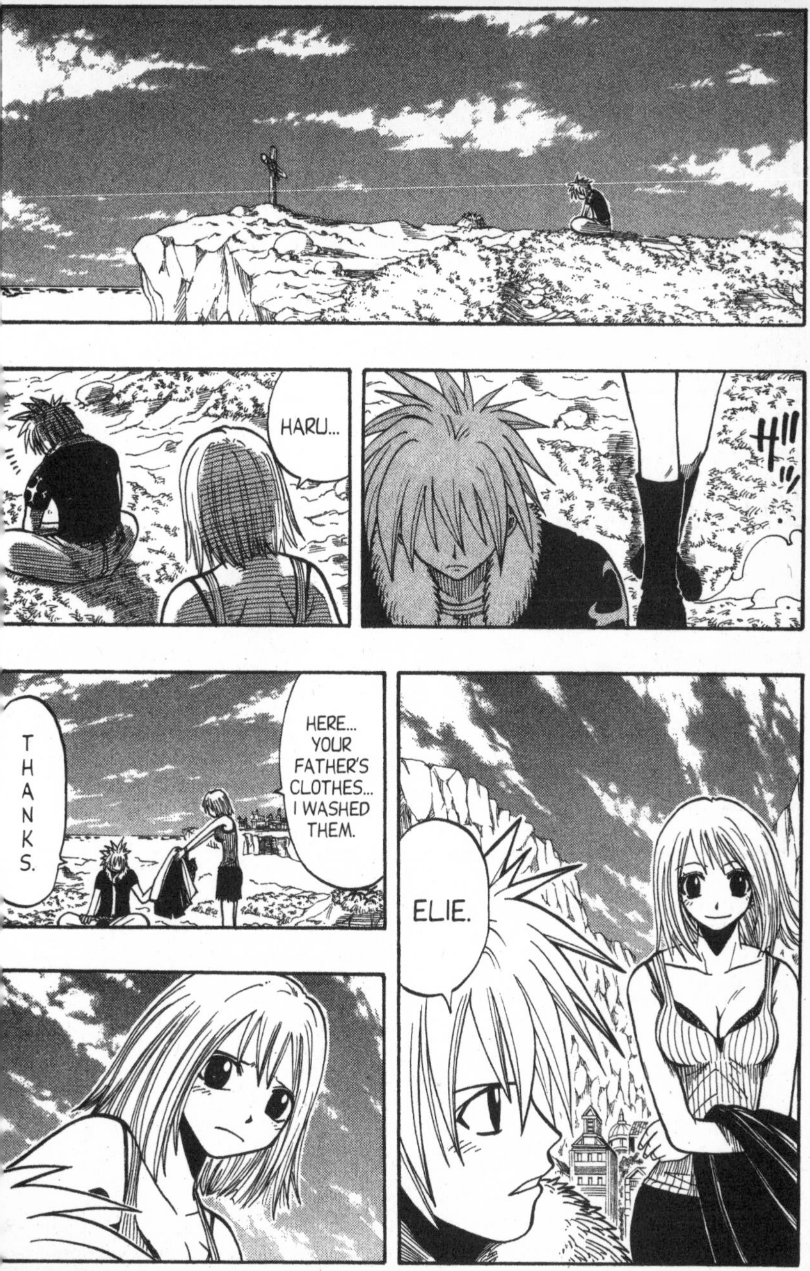
HARU...
ELIE.
HERE... YOUR FATHER'S CLOTHES... I WASHED THEM.
THANKS.

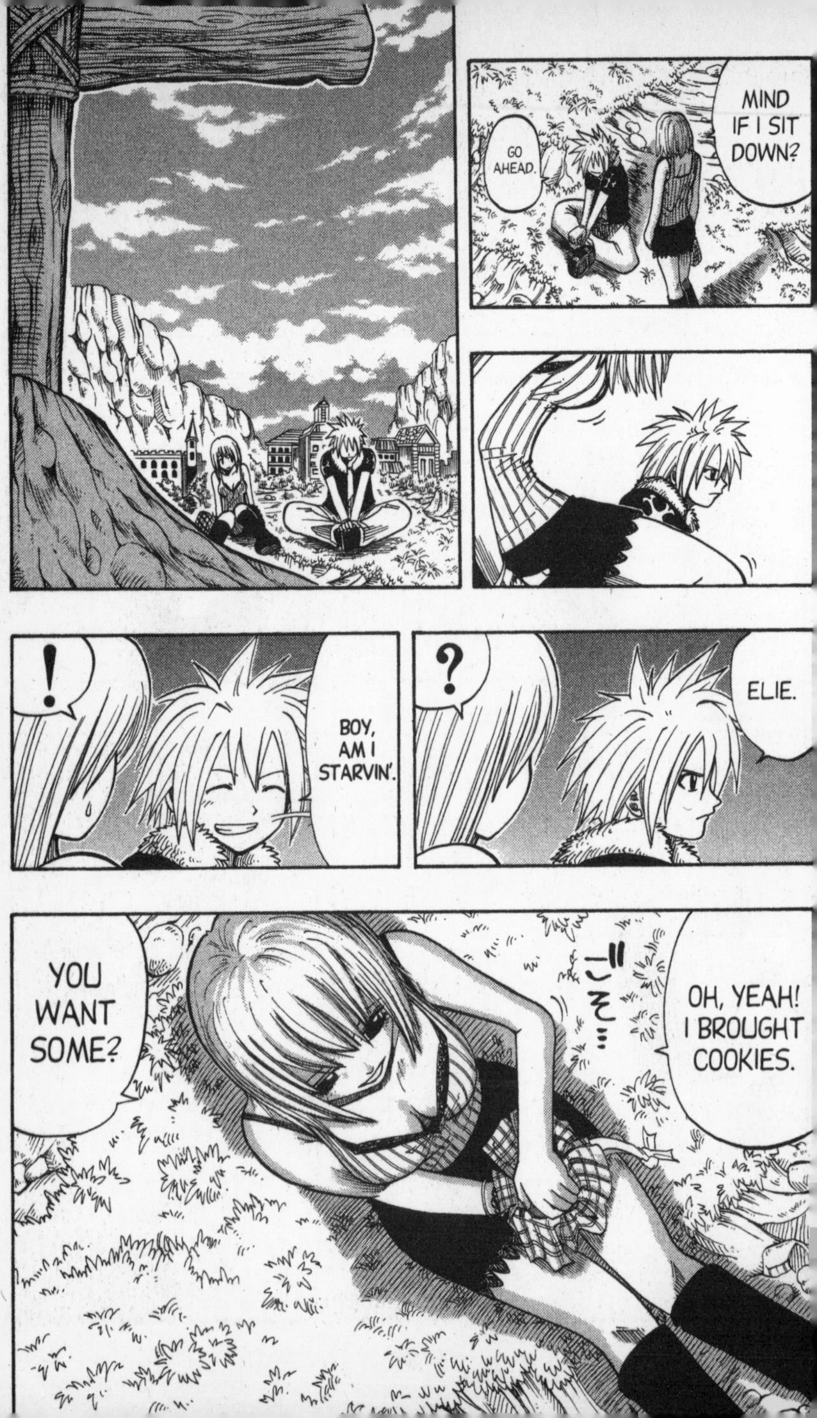
MIND IF I SIT DOWN?
GO AHEAD.
ELIE.
?
BOY, AM I STARVIN'.
!
OH, YEAH! I BROUGHT COOKIES.
ごそ…
YOU WANT SOME?

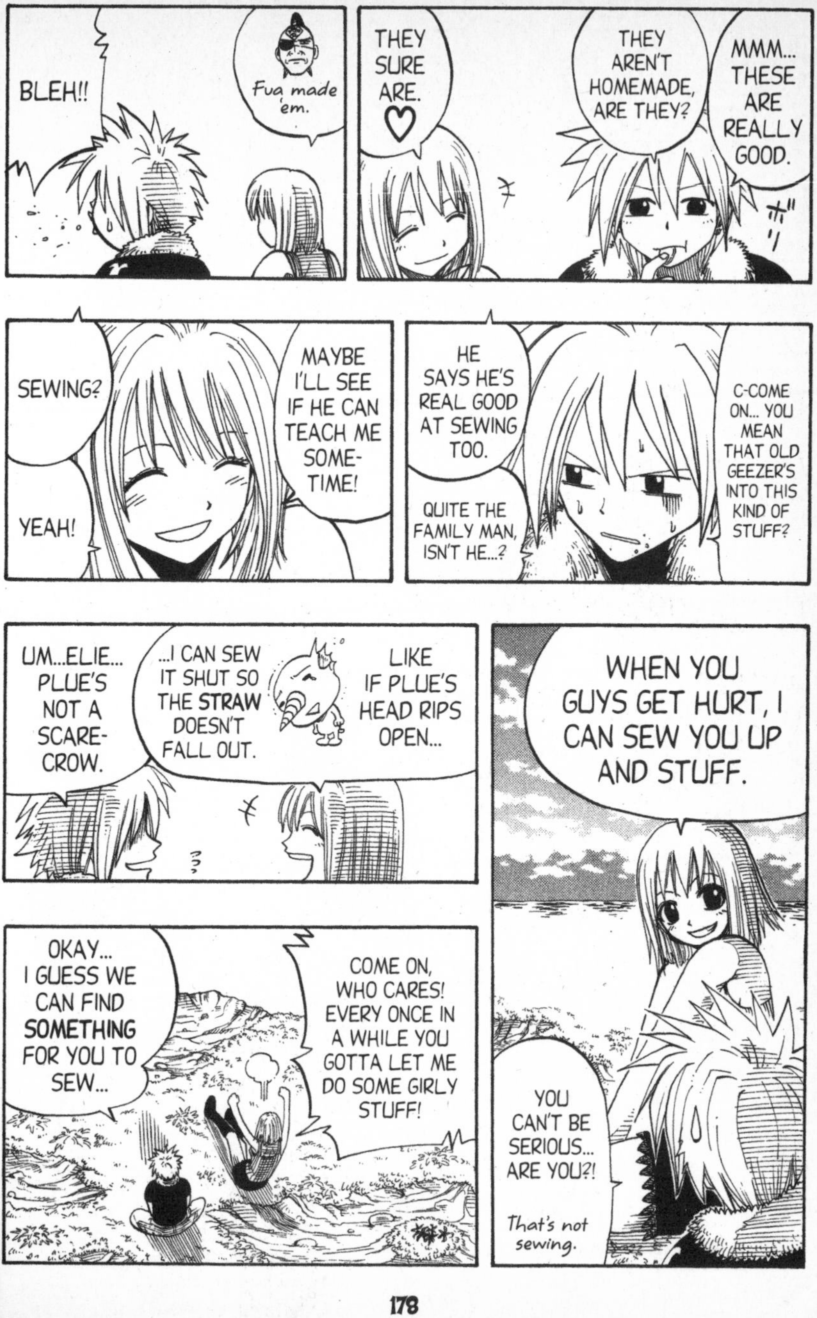
MMM... THESE ARE REALLY GOOD.
THEY AREN'T HOMEMADE, ARE THEY?
THEY SURE ARE. ♥
Fua made 'em.
BLEH!!
C-COME ON... YOU MEAN THAT OLD GEEZER'S INTO THIS KIND OF STUFF?
HE SAYS HE'S REAL GOOD AT SEWING TOO.
QUITE THE FAMILY MAN, ISN'T HE...?
MAYBE I'LL SEE IF HE CAN TEACH ME SOME-TIME!
SEWING?
YEAH!
WHEN YOU GUYS GET HURT, I CAN SEW YOU UP AND STUFF.
YOU CAN'T BE SERIOUS... ARE YOU?!
That's not sewing.
LIKE IF PLUE'S HEAD RIPS OPEN...
...I CAN SEW IT SHUT SO THE STRAW DOESN'T FALL OUT.
UM...ELIE... PLUE'S NOT A SCARE-CROW.
COME ON, WHO CARES! EVERY ONCE IN A WHILE YOU GOTTA LET ME DO SOME GIRLY STUFF!
OKAY... I GUESS WE CAN FIND SOMETHING FOR YOU TO SEW...

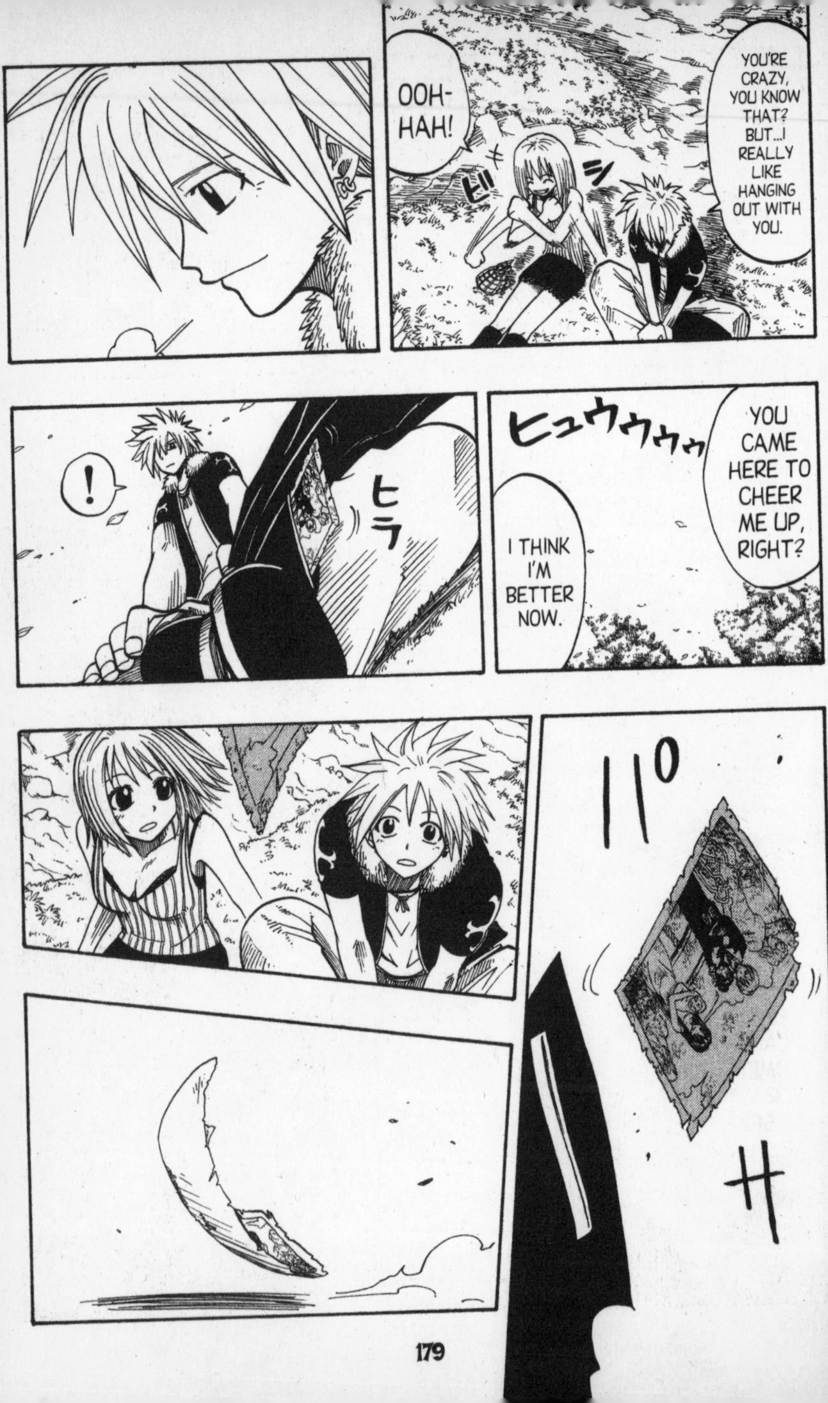
YOU'RE CRAZY, YOU KNOW THAT? BUT...I REALLY LIKE HANGING OUT WITH YOU.
OOH-HAH!
ヒュウウウゥ
YOU CAME HERE TO CHEER ME UP, RIGHT?
I THINK I'M BETTER NOW.
ヒラ
!
パ
サ

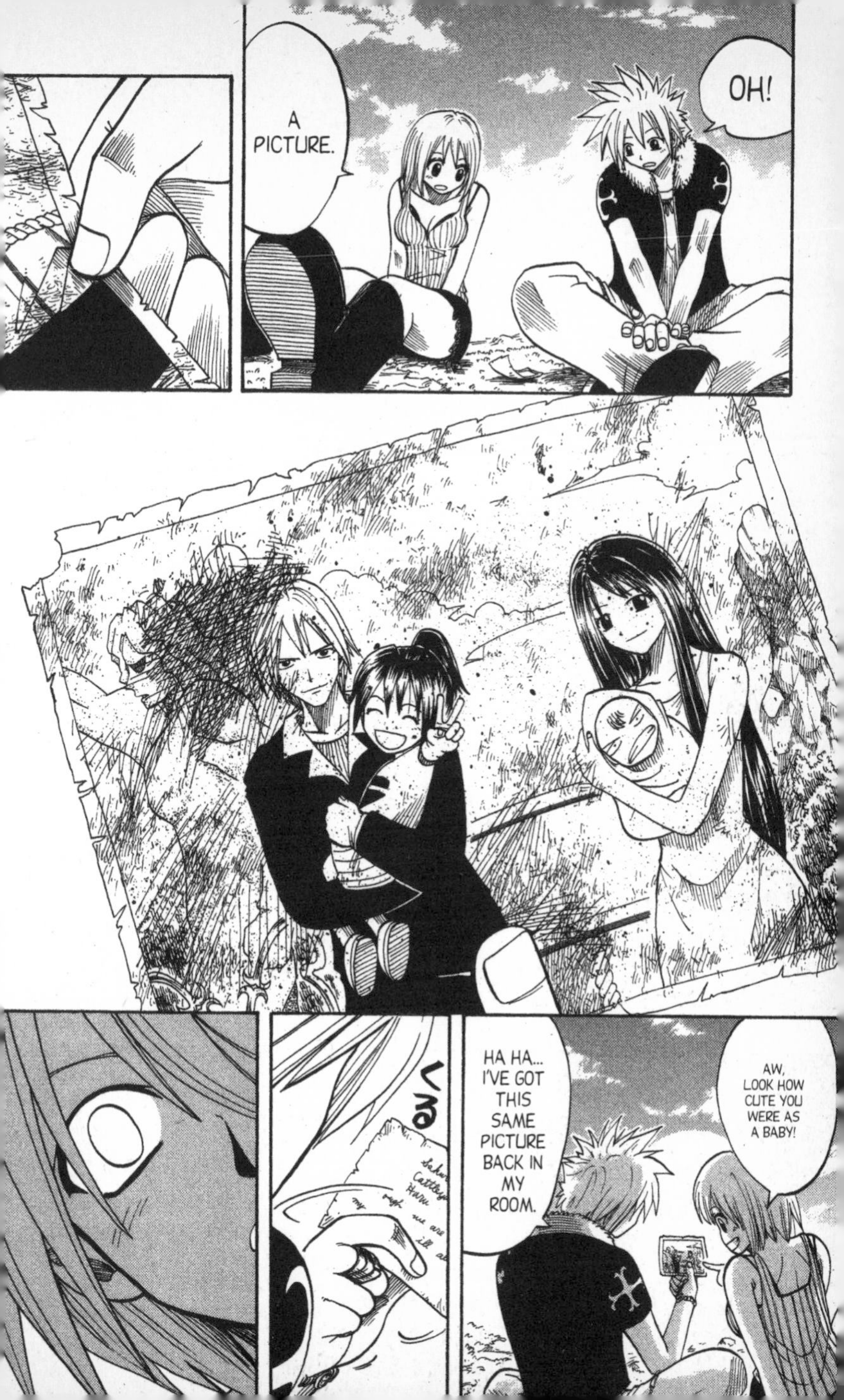

OH!
A PICTURE.
AW, LOOK HOW CUTE YOU WERE AS A BABY!
HA HA... I'VE GOT THIS SAME PICTURE BACK IN MY ROOM.
くる

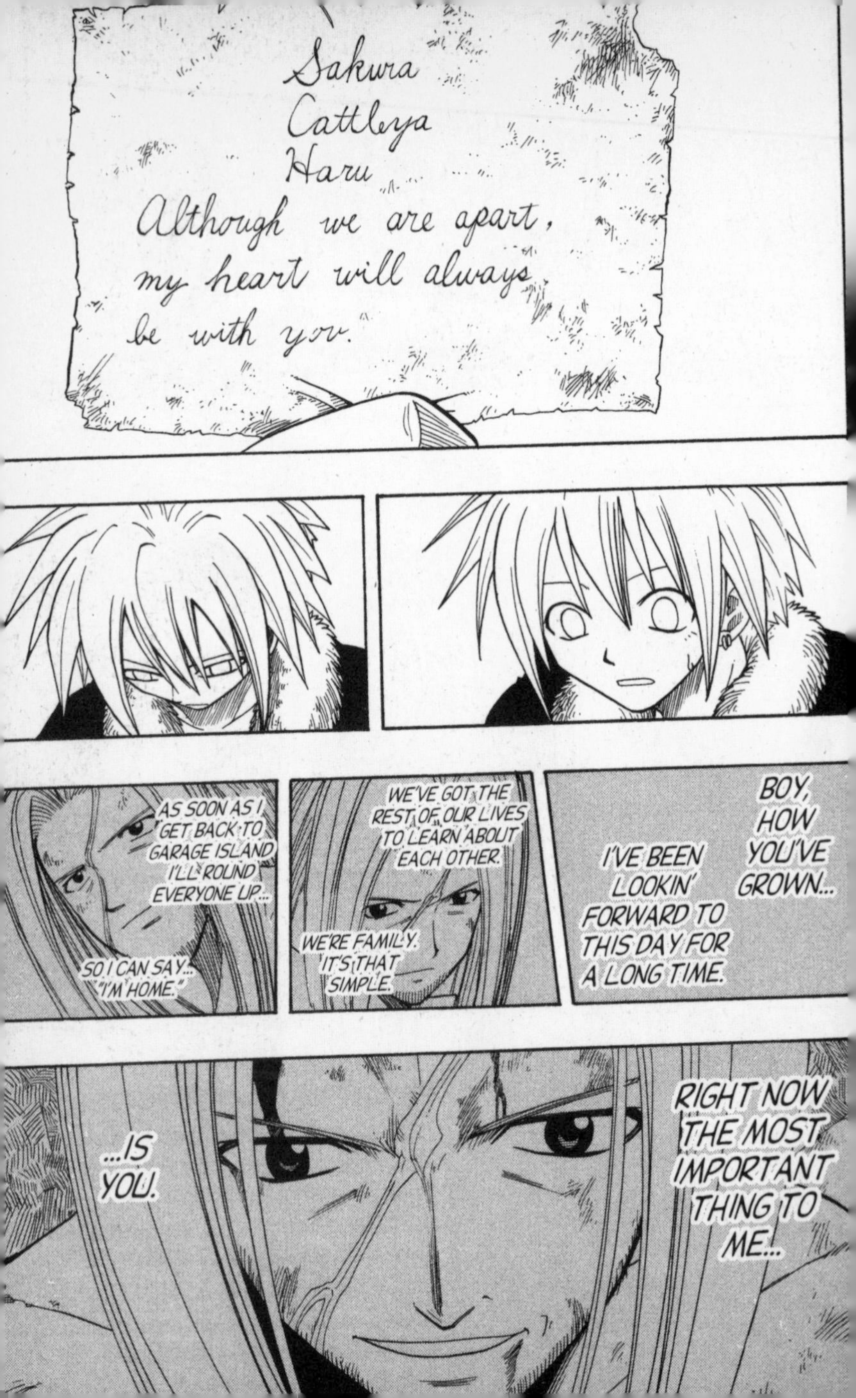
Sakura
Cattleya
Haru
Although we are apart, my heart will always be with you.
BOY, HOW YOU'VE GROWN...
I'VE BEEN LOOKIN' FORWARD TO THIS DAY FOR A LONG TIME.
WE'VE GOT THE REST OF OUR LIVES TO LEARN ABOUT EACH OTHER.
WE'RE FAMILY. IT'S THAT SIMPLE.
AS SOON AS I GET BACK TO GARAGE ISLAND I'LL ROUND EVERYONE UP...
SO I CAN SAY... "I'M HOME."
RIGHT NOW THE MOST IMPORTANT THING TO ME...
...IS YOU.

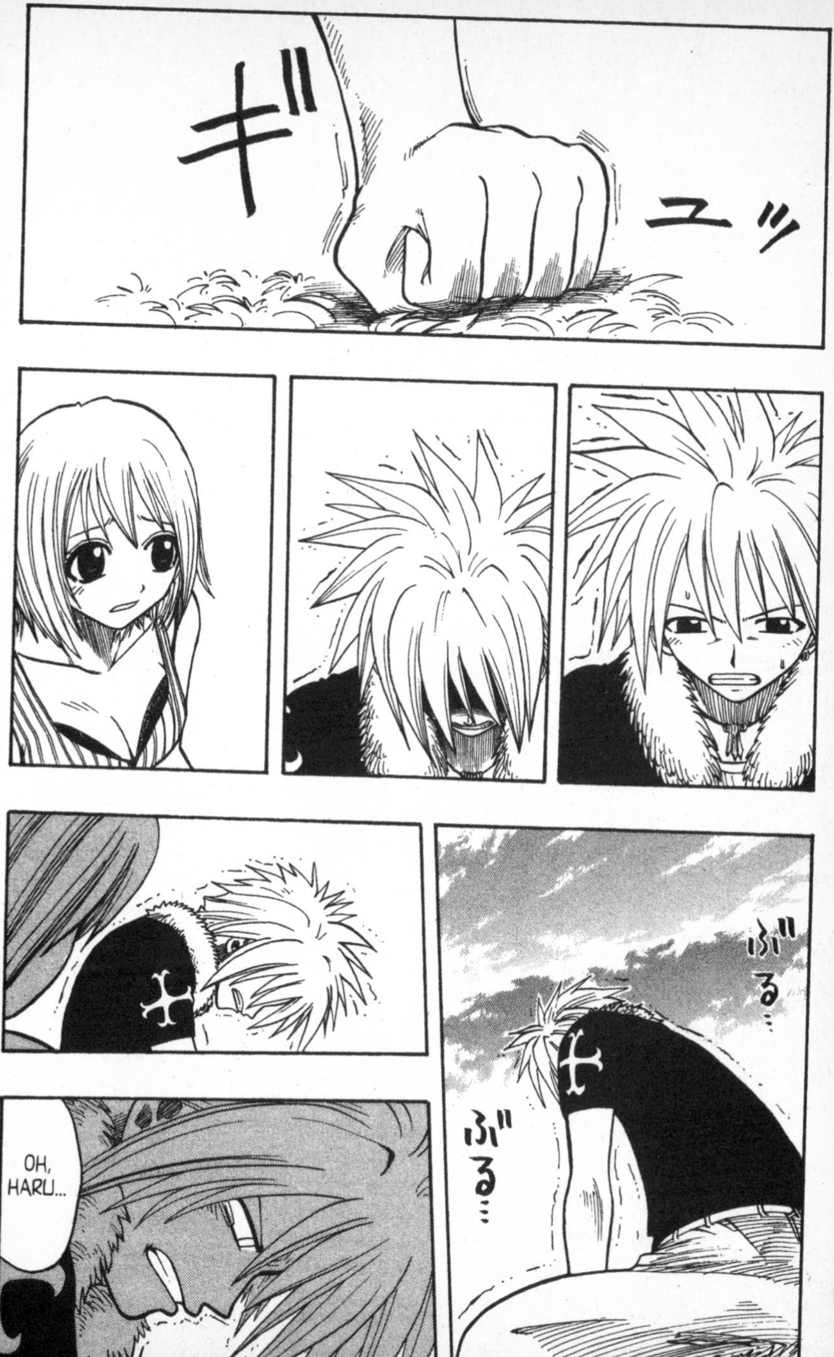

ギュッ
ぶる…
ぶる…
OH, HARU...

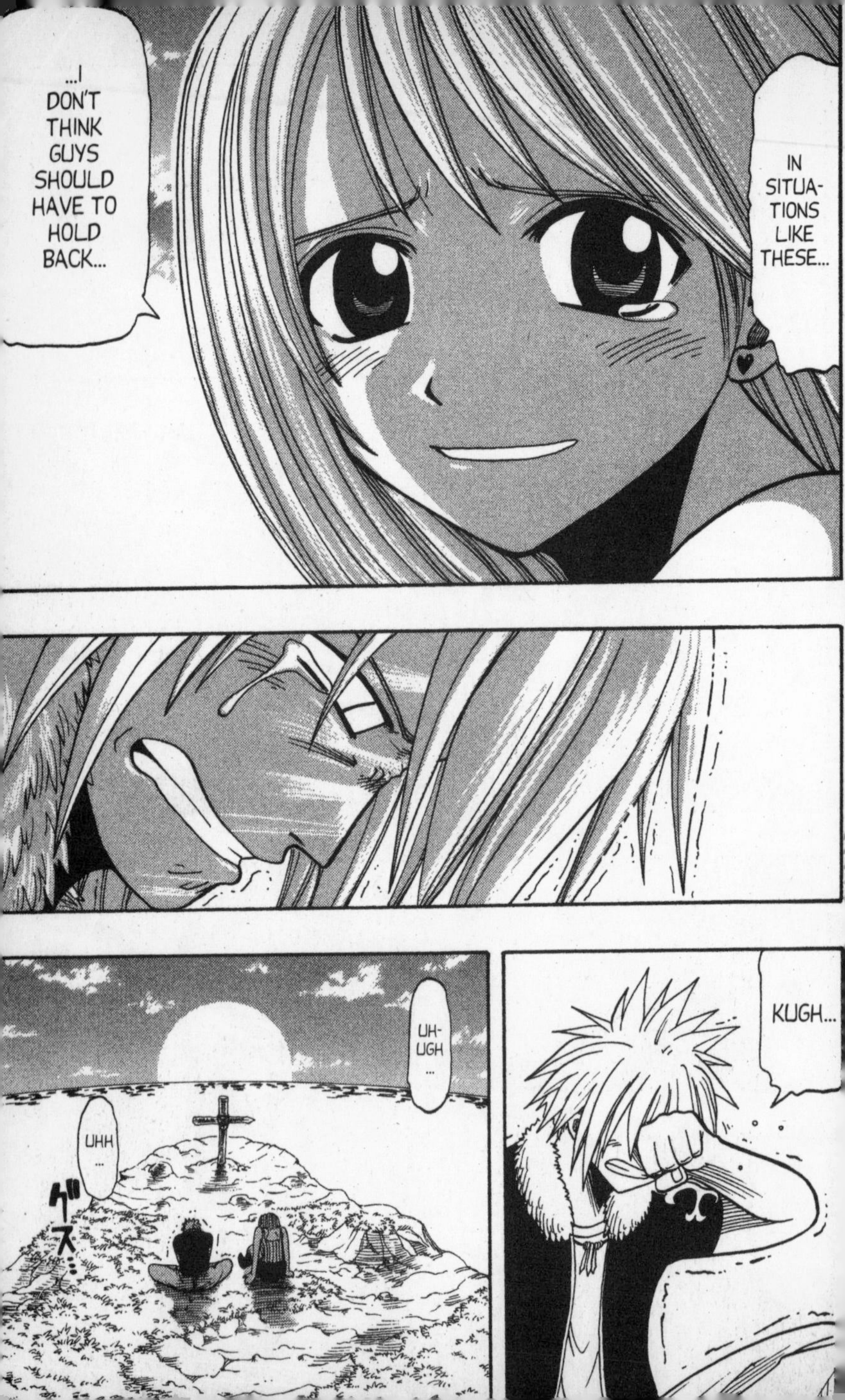
IN SITUA-TIONS LIKE THESE...
...I DON'T THINK GUYS SHOULD HAVE TO HOLD BACK...
KUGH...
UH-UGH ...
UHH ...
グス…

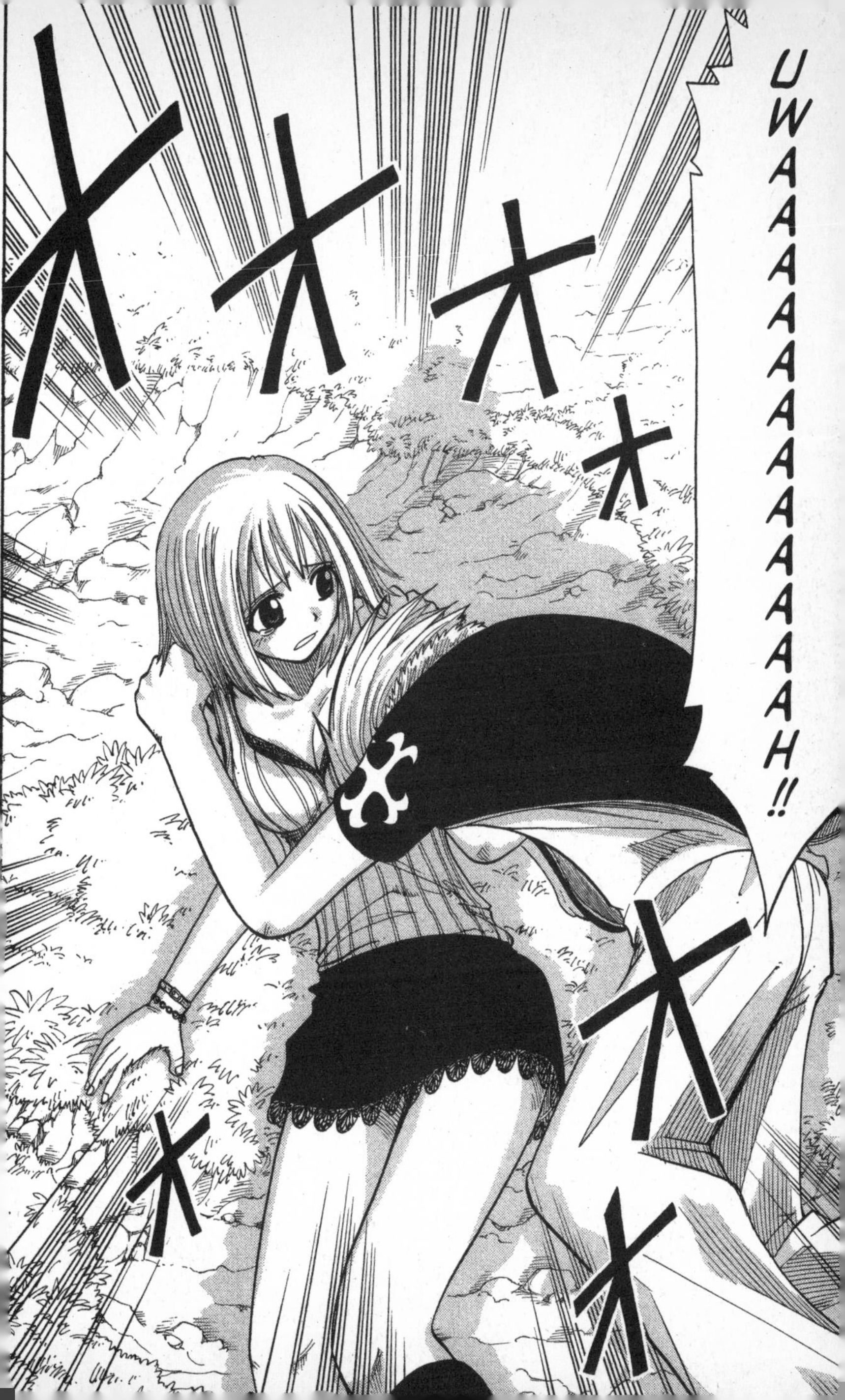
UWAAAAAAAAAAAAAAH!!
オオオォォォ

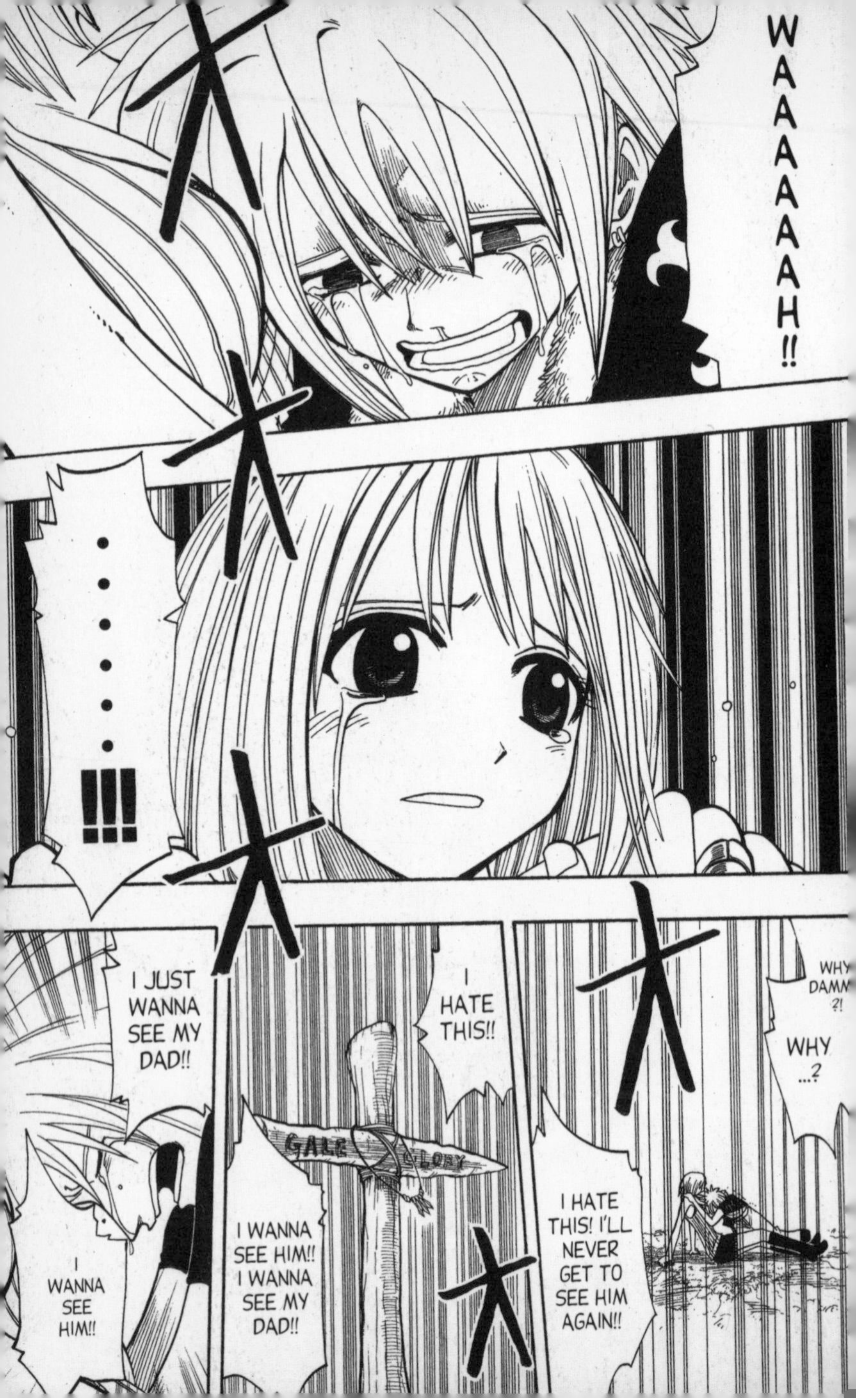
WAAAAAAAH!!
......!!!
WHY DAMM ?!
WHY ...?
I HATE THIS! I'LL NEVER GET TO SEE HIM AGAIN!!
I HATE THIS!!
GALE GLORY
I WANNA SEE HIM!! I WANNA SEE MY DAD!!
I JUST WANNA SEE MY DAD!!
I WANNA SEE HIM!!

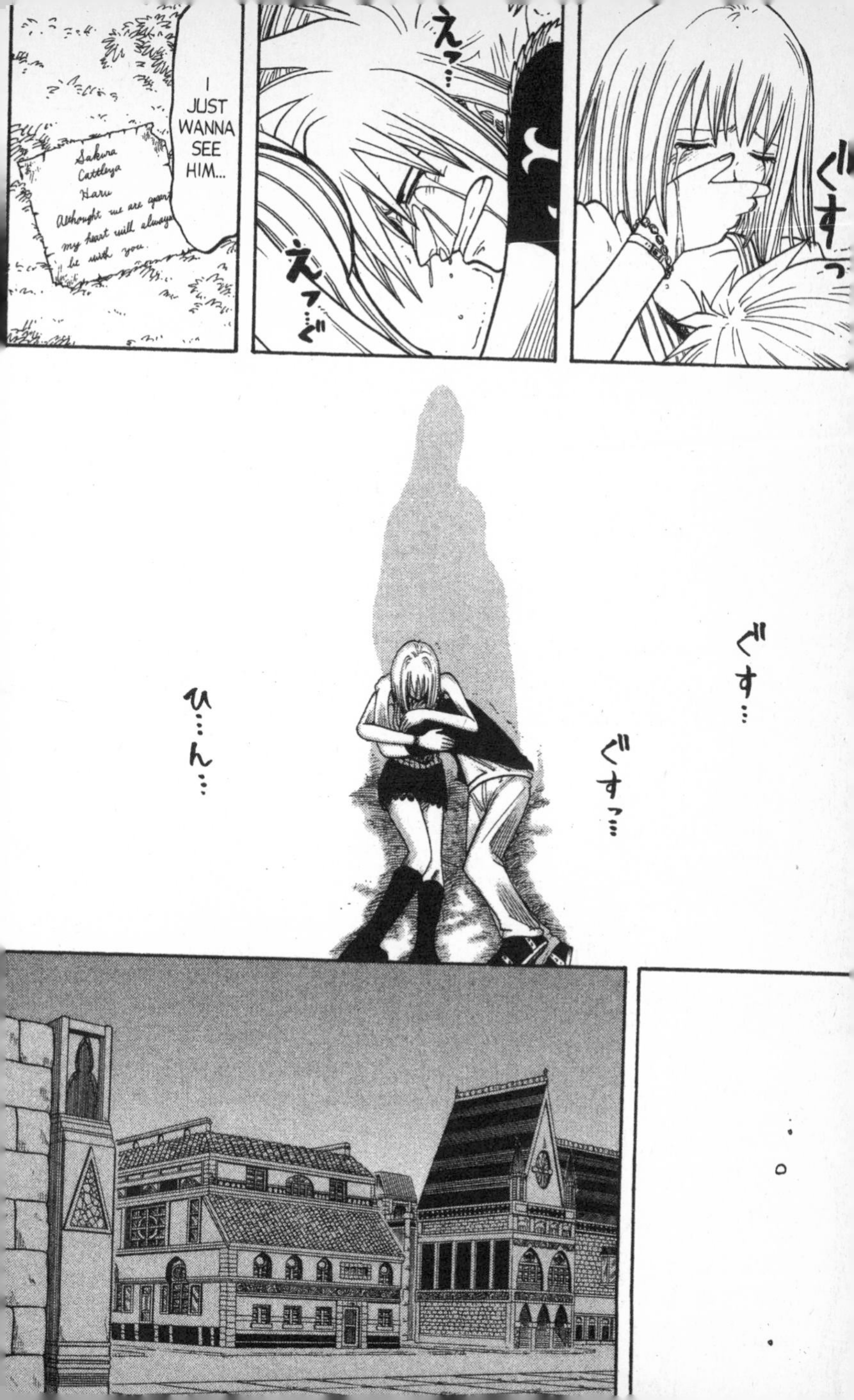
ぐすっ
えっ…
えっ…ぐ
I JUST WANNA SEE HIM...
Sakura Cattleya Haru
Althought we are apar
my heart will alway
be with you.
ぐす…
ぐすっ…
ひ…ん…
…

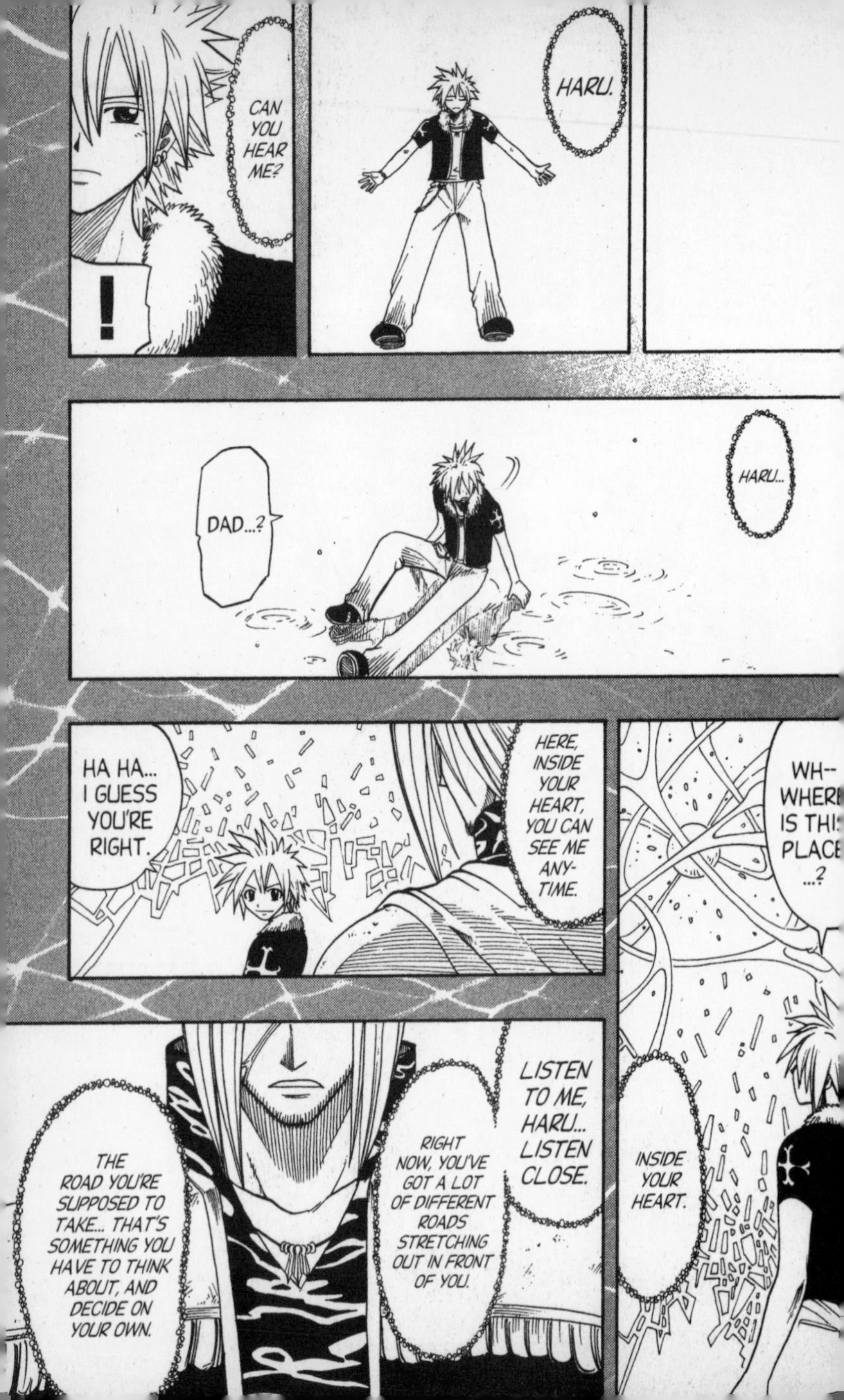
HARU.
CAN YOU HEAR ME?
!
HARU...
DAD...?
WH-- WHERE IS THIS PLACE ...?
INSIDE YOUR HEART.
HERE, INSIDE YOUR HEART, YOU CAN SEE ME ANY-TIME.
HA HA... I GUESS YOU'RE RIGHT.
LISTEN TO ME, HARU... LISTEN CLOSE.
RIGHT NOW, YOU'VE GOT A LOT OF DIFFERENT ROADS STRETCHING OUT IN FRONT OF YOU.
THE ROAD YOU'RE SUPPOSED TO TAKE... THAT'S SOMETHING YOU HAVE TO THINK ABOUT, AND DECIDE ON YOUR OWN.

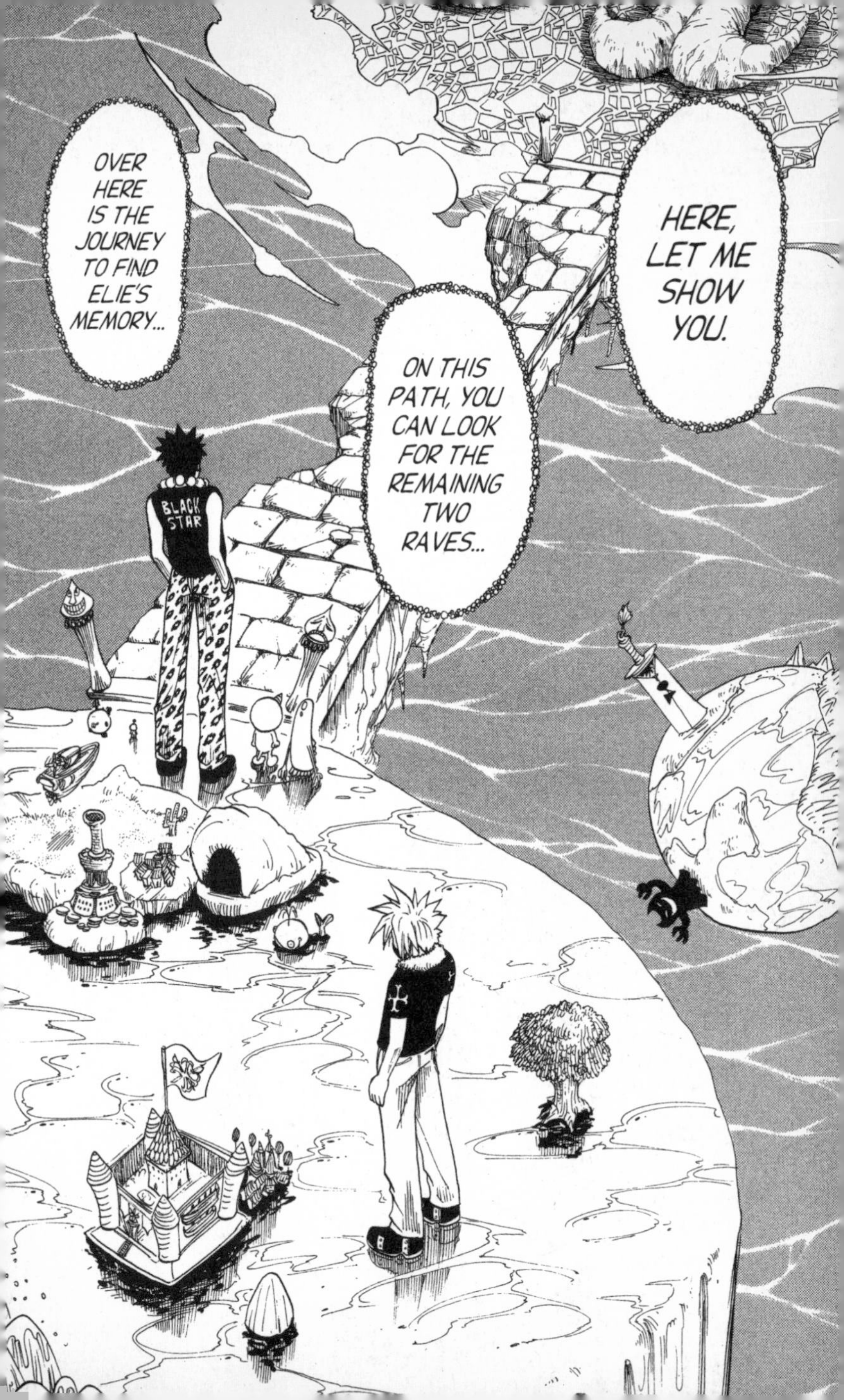

HERE, LET ME SHOW YOU.
ON THIS PATH, YOU CAN LOOK FOR THE REMAINING TWO RAVES...
OVER HERE IS THE JOURNEY TO FIND ELIE'S MEMORY...
BLACK STAR

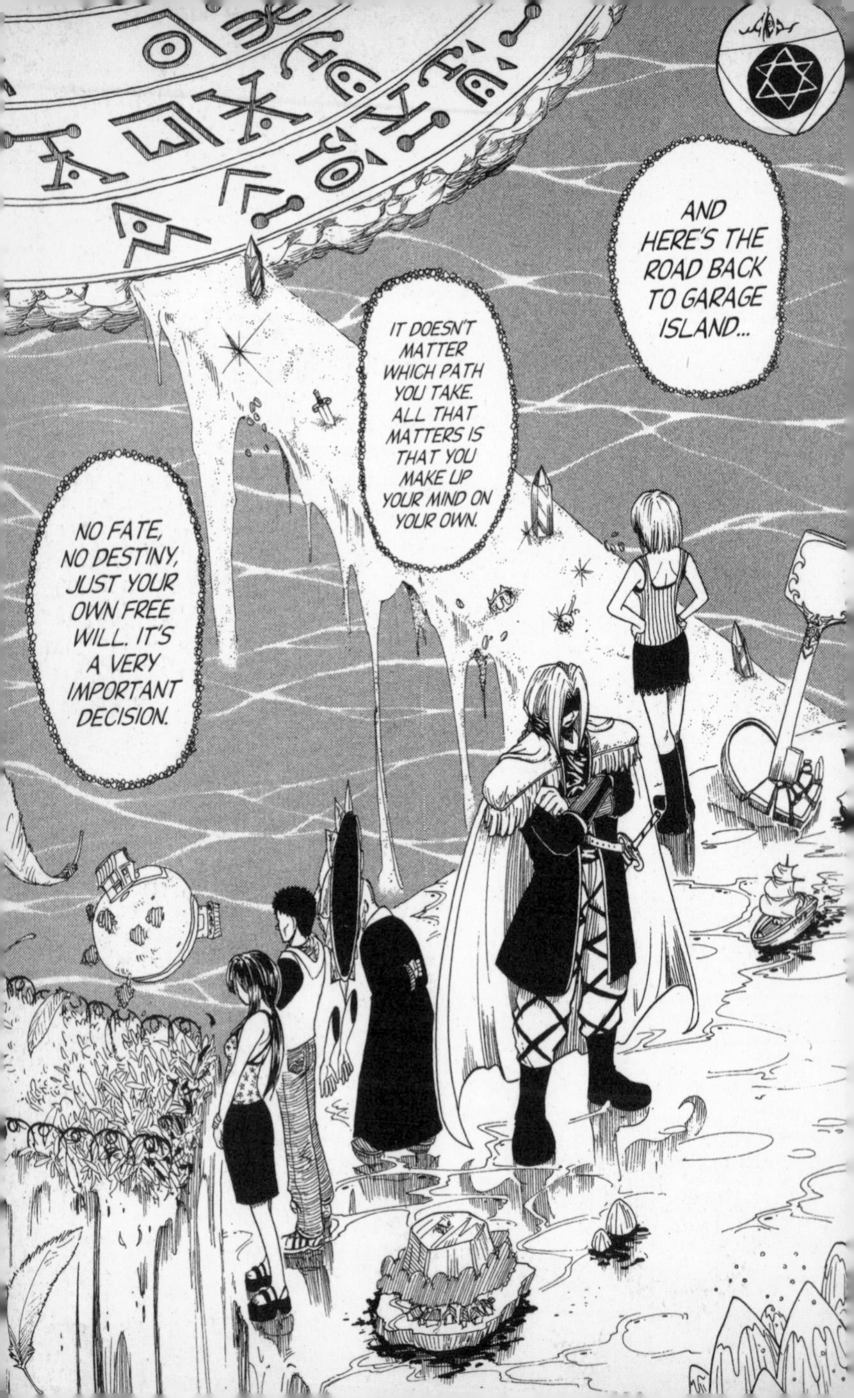
AND HERE'S THE ROAD BACK TO GARAGE ISLAND...
IT DOESN'T MATTER WHICH PATH YOU TAKE. ALL THAT MATTERS IS THAT YOU MAKE UP YOUR MIND ON YOUR OWN.
NO FATE, NO DESTINY, JUST YOUR OWN FREE WILL. IT'S A VERY IMPORTANT DECISION.

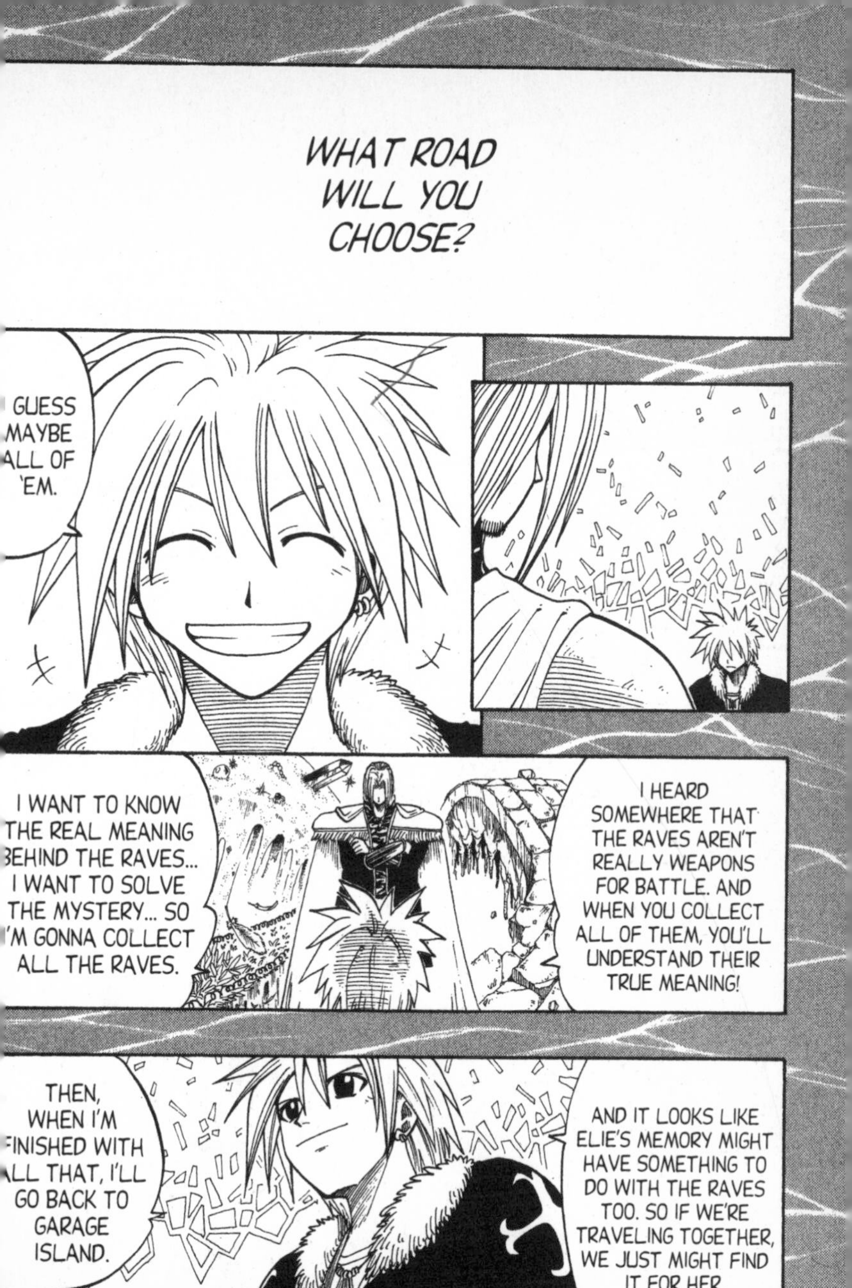
WHAT ROAD WILL YOU CHOOSE?
I GUESS MAYBE ALL OF 'EM.
I HEARD SOMEWHERE THAT THE RAVES AREN'T REALLY WEAPONS FOR BATTLE. AND WHEN YOU COLLECT ALL OF THEM, YOU'LL UNDERSTAND THEIR TRUE MEANING!
I WANT TO KNOW THE REAL MEANING BEHIND THE RAVES... I WANT TO SOLVE THE MYSTERY... SO I'M GONNA COLLECT ALL THE RAVES.
AND IT LOOKS LIKE ELIE'S MEMORY MIGHT HAVE SOMETHING TO DO WITH THE RAVES TOO. SO IF WE'RE TRAVELING TOGETHER, WE JUST MIGHT FIND IT FOR HER.
THEN, WHEN I'M FINISHED WITH ALL THAT, I'LL GO BACK TO GARAGE ISLAND.

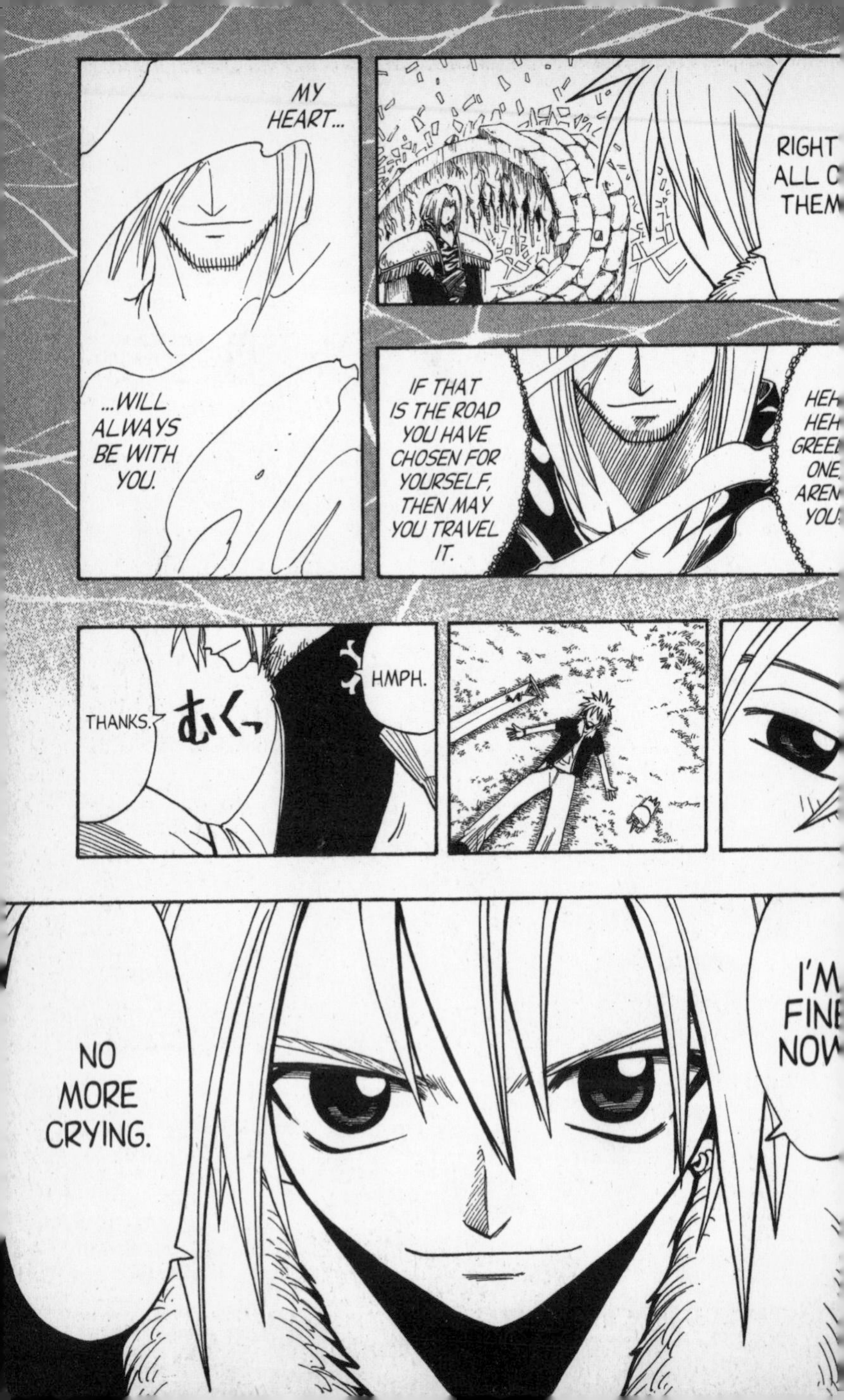
RIGHT
ALL C
THEM
HEH
HEH
GREE
ONE,
AREN
YOU
IF THAT IS THE ROAD YOU HAVE CHOSEN FOR YOURSELF, THEN MAY YOU TRAVEL IT.
MY HEART...
...WILL ALWAYS BE WITH YOU.
HMPH.
むくっ
THANKS.
I'M
FINE
NOW
NO MORE CRYING.

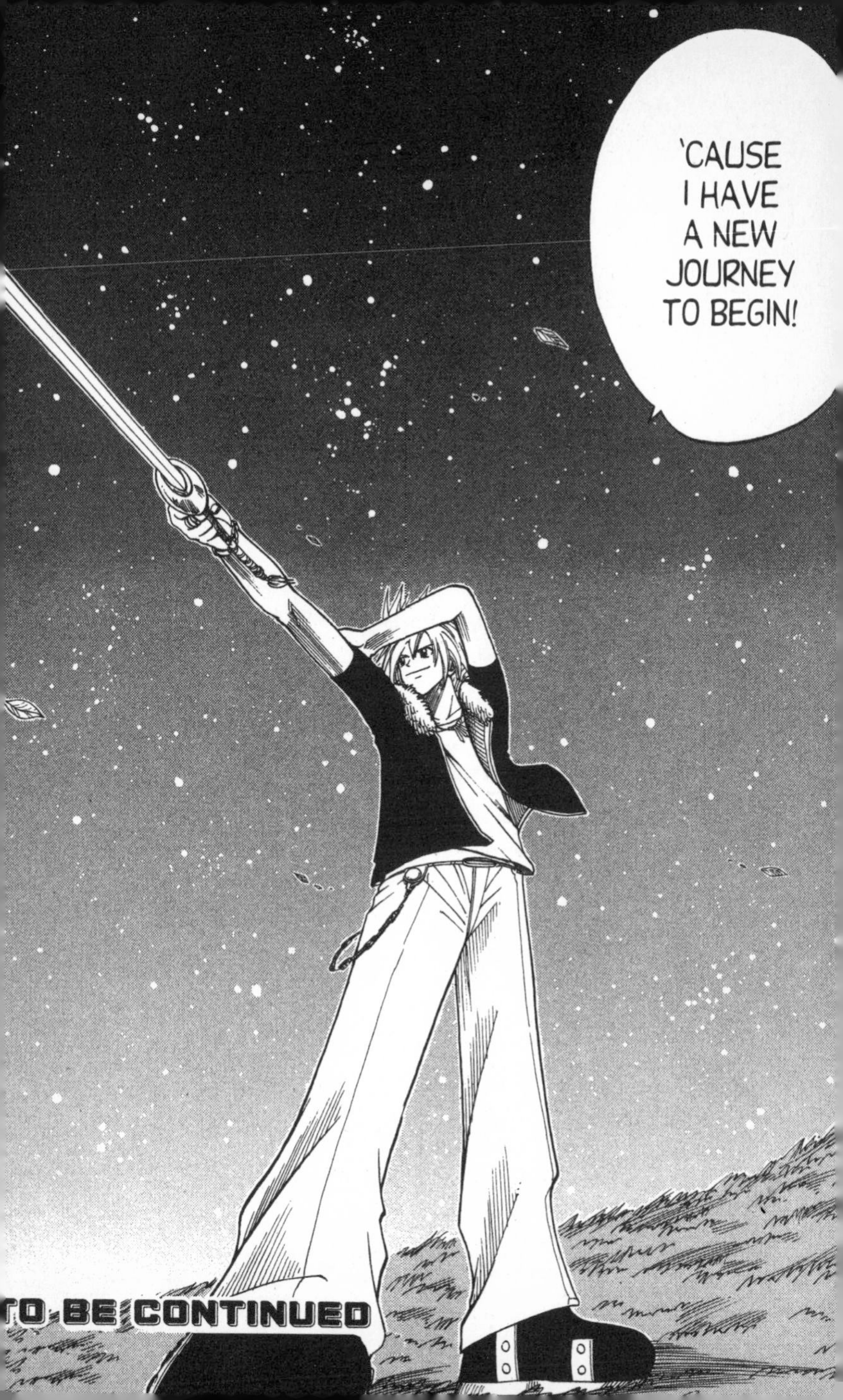
'CAUSE I HAVE A NEW JOURNEY TO BEGIN!
TO BE CONTINUED

Character Profiles

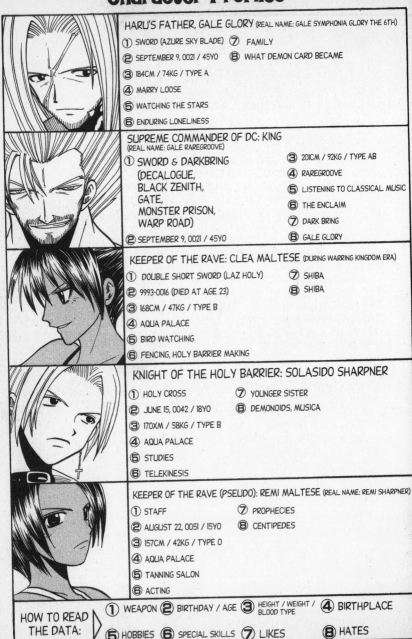

HARU'S FATHER, GALE GLORY (REAL NAME: GALE SYMPHONIA GLORY THE 6TH)

① SWORD (AZURE SKY BLADE)
② SEPTEMBER 9, 0021 / 45YO
③ 184CM / 74KG / TYPE A
④ MARRY LOOSE
⑤ WATCHING THE STARS
⑥ ENDURING LONELINESS
⑦ FAMILY
⑧ WHAT DEMON CARD BECAME

SUPREME COMMANDER OF DC: KING
(REAL NAME: GALE RAREGROOVE)

① SWORD & DARKBRING
(DECALOGUE,
BLACK ZENITH,
GATE,
MONSTER PRISON,
WARP ROAD)
② SEPTEMBER 9, 0021 / 45YO
③ 201CM / 92KG / TYPE AB
④ RAREGROOVE
⑤ LISTENING TO CLASSICAL MUSIC
⑥ THE ENCLAIM
⑦ DARK BRING
⑧ GALE GLORY

KEEPER OF THE RAVE: CLEA MALTESE (DURING WARRING KINGDOM ERA)

① DOUBLE SHORT SWORD (LAZ HOLY)
② 9993-0016 (DIED AT AGE 23)
③ 168CM / 47KG / TYPE B
④ AQUA PALACE
⑤ BIRD WATCHING
⑥ FENCING, HOLY BARRIER MAKING
⑦ SHIBA
⑧ SHIBA

KNIGHT OF THE HOLY BARRIER: SOLASIDO SHARPNER

① HOLY CROSS
② JUNE 15, 0042 / 18YO
③ 170XM / 58KG / TYPE B
④ AQUA PALACE
⑤ STUDIES
⑥ TELEKINESIS
⑦ YOUNGER SISTER
⑧ DEMONOIDS, MUSICA

KEEPER OF THE RAVE (PSEUDO): REMI MALTESE (REAL NAME: REMI SHARPNER)

① STAFF
② AUGUST 22, 0051 / 15YO
③ 157CM / 42KG / TYPE O
④ AQUA PALACE
⑤ TANNING SALON
⑥ ACTING
⑦ PROPHECIES
⑧ CENTIPEDES

HOW TO READ THE DATA: ▷

① WEAPON ② BIRTHDAY / AGE ③ HEIGHT / WEIGHT / BLOOD TYPE ④ BIRTHPLACE
⑤ HOBBIES ⑥ SPECIAL SKILLS ⑦ LIKES ⑧ HATES

About the characters

DUE TO CERTAIN CIRCUMSTANCES, THE CHARACTER PROFILE SECTION WAS CONDENSED FOR THIS ISSUE. INSTEAD I'LL TALK A LITTLE ABOUT THE CHARACTERS RIGHT HERE. FIRST OFF IS GALE. I CAME UP WITH THIS THINKING I WANTED TO HAVE IT PERTAIN SOMEHOW TO "HARU" (SPRING). "GALE" MEANS "A GUST OF WIND." ACTUALLY, WHEN THIS SERIES STARTED BEING SERIALIZED, I HADN'T DECIDED ANYTHING REGARDING GALE, AND I HELD OFF FIGURING IT OUT UNTIL THE KING STORYLINE. I WASN'T SURE IF THE GALE/KING BACKSTORY WAS REALLY THAT INTER- ESTING, BUT I WENT WITH IT ANYWAY, SO MAKING EVERYTHING MATCH UP AND BE CONSISTENT WAS PRETTY TOUGH (HA HA!). I HAD BEEN THINKING OF MAKING KING A DESCENDANT OF THE RAREGROOVES FOR A WHILE, BUT EVERY TIME HE APPEARS, HIS HAIR LOOKS DIFFERENT (HA HA!). I'M PRETTY PROUD OF THE WAY I HAD THEM BOTH DIE IN THE END.

I WAS A LITTLE DISAPPOINTED THAT I WAS ONLY ABLE TO WORK CLEA MALTESE INTO ONE CHAPTER. I REALLY WANTED TO WORK IN SOME OF HER BACKGROUND AND STUFF INTO THE STORY. THAT'S WHY IN THE UPCOMING *KOK* (KNIGHTS OF KINGDOM) SUPPLEMENT, WHICH DEALS WITH THE WARRING KINGDOM ERA, I MADE SURE SHE WAS TREATED IN A WAY THAT LEAVES A REAL IMPRESSION ON THE READER'S MIND. I WONDER IF THERE WILL BE A COLLECTION OF THE *KOK* STORIES? MAYBE, MAYBE NOT. ANYWAY, IF YOU GET A CHANCE TO READ IT, BE SURE TO LOOK FOR HER.

SOLASIDO AND REMI ENDED UP BEING PRETTY INCIDENTAL CHARACTERS THROUGH THE WHOLE THING. I HAD ORIGINALLY PLANNED ON HAVING THEM JOIN HARU'S PARTY, BUT THEY DIDN'T SEEM TOO MEMORABLE, SO I SCRATCHED THAT IDEA (HA HA!). BUT DON'T WORRY, THERE'S ALWAYS THE POSSIBILITY THAT THEY'LL SHOW UP IN THE STORY AT A LATER DATE. IF I CAN MAKE THEM MORE INTERESTING, THEY MIGHT JUST FIND THEMSELVES A PART OF HARU'S TEAM. (I SWEAR IT'S NOT JUST 'CUZ I DON'T WANT TO HAVE A CHARACTER WITH TAN SKIN--IT'S NOT THAT IT'S A BIG HASSLE PUTTING ON SCREEN TONE FOR HER SKIN COLOR.)

A LOT OF PEOPLE DON'T KNOW THIS, BUT WHEN I FIRST DREW SOLASIDO, HE HAD GREEN SKIN. TRUE STORY! HE WENT THROUGH SOME CHANGES TO END UP WHERE HE IS NOW, BUT I'M HAPPY WITH HIM.

"Afterwords"

THERE WEREN'T TOO MANY EXTRA PAGES THIS TIME, WERE THERE. IT MADE THINGS EASIER ON ME, BUT I WANT TO APOLOGIZE TO ALL YOU READERS OUT THERE WHO WERE LOOKING FORWARD TO SEEING MORE. I'M SORRY. BUT IT ISN'T ALL UP TO ME, SO THERE'S NOT MUCH I CAN DO ABOUT IT. THERE WASN'T ENOUGH ROOM FOR THE PAGES FOR ALL THE PROFILES I HAD PLANNED OUT, SO I HAD TO MAKE IT REAL COMPACT. BUT MAYBE IT'S BETTER THAT WAY? I THINK I'LL DO IT THIS WAY FROM NOW ON. BESIDES, IT'LL LEAVE ROOM FOR OTHER EXTRA STUFF TOO! OKEY-DOKEY, THAT'S SETTLED!

ALL RIGHT. WE'VE FINALLY COME TO A CLOSE FOR THE KING STORY ARC, AND THE NEXT VOLUME WILL TAKE US INTO A NEW DIRECTION. IF VOLUMES 1-9 OVERALL WERE ABOUT DEMON CARD, I PERSONALLY LIKE TO THINK ABOUT THIS AS THE "END OF PART I." JUST BETWEEN YOU AND ME, IN THE KING ARC ALL THE MYSTERIES ARE SOLVED, AND I WAS CONSIDERING MAKING IT THE END OF THE WHOLE SERIES. BUT THAT'S A LITTLE TOO CONTRIVED, AND THERE'S LOTS OF FUN STUFF I'LL BE ABLE TO DO WITH THE REST OF THE STORY, SO I DECIDED AGAINST THAT. OF COURSE I DIDN'T START OFF WITH THE INTENTION OF ENDING IT HERE, EITHER (HA HA!). I WAS THINKING THE END OF THE KING ARC WOULD BE RIGHT ABOUT THE MIDDLE OF THE WHOLE SERIES. BUT THEN ONE DAY, OUT OF THE BLUE, AS I WAS DRAWING, I WAS OVERCOME WITH THE SILLY DESIRE TO MAKE A BRAND-NEW SERIES, SO I WAS TRYING TO THINK OF HOW I COULD WRAP EVERYTHING UP AT THE END OF THE KING ARC. BUT I CAN'T JUST END ONE SERIES RIGHT IN THE MIDDLE OF THINGS TO START ANOTHER ONE. I'M STILL A NEWBIE IN THIS BUSINESS AND ALL! AND THAT WAS THE EXTENT OF MY DELIBERATIONS (APPROXIMATELY TWO HOURS). AFTER THAT, I DECIDED TO DEVOTE ALL MY ENERGY TO *RAVE MASTER*. DON'T GET ME WRONG, I'VE ALWAYS BEEN GIVING THIS MY ALL, OF COURSE. BUT I REALLY WANT TO MAKE *RAVE MASTER* BETTER AND BETTER! I'LL BE WORKING MY BUTT OFF TO DO IT!

ON THAT NOTE, *RAVE MASTER* WILL GO ON!! I GUESS!! THE NEXT VOLUME WILL BRING US INTO WHAT I PERSONALLY LIKE TO THINK OF AS THE "DESTINY" (TENTATIVE, ERR, IT DOESN'T REALLY MATTER ANYWAY) ARC OF THE STORY. SO I HOPE YOU ALL KEEP READING ALONG.

AND AFTER THAT WILL BE THE 3RD ARC, "SPACE," AND THE 4TH, "TOKYO," AND THE 5TH, "SOCCER," AND THE 6TH, "HORROR FLICK," AND THE 7TH, "PLUE'S RIGHT EYE," SO WATCH OUT FOR 'EM. I'M SORRY. I'M JUST KIDDING ABOUT THAT.

RAVE MASTER Fan Art!

HEY ASPIRING MANGA ARTISTS! WANT TO SEE YOUR PICTURES IN PRINT? WELL, IF YOU THINK YOU CAN DRAW A COOL-LOOKING HARU, A SEXY ELIE OR A FUNNY PLUE, SEND 'EM THIS WAY! WE'LL PICK ONE LUCKY WINNER FROM EACH ROUND AND SEND THEM A SPECIAL PRIZE! WHAT DO HAVE TO LOSE? NOTHING!

HOW TO SUBMIT:

1) SEND YOUR WORK VIA REGULAR MAIL (NOT E-MAIL) TO:

RAVE MASTER FAN ART
C/O TOKYOPOP
5900 WILSHIRE BLVD.
SUITE 2000
LOS ANGELES, CA 90036

2) ALL WORK SUBMITTED SHOULD BE IN BLACK-AND-WHITE AND NO LARGER THAN 8.5" X 11". (AND TRY NOT TO FOLD IT TOO MANY TIMES!)

3) ANYTHING YOU SEND WILL NOT BE RETURNED. IF YOU WANT TO KEEP YOUR ORIGINAL, IT'S FINE TO SEND US A COPY.

4) PLEASE INCLUDE YOUR FULL NAME, AGE, CITY AND STATE FOR US TO PRINT WITH YOUR WORK. IF YOU'D RATHER US USE A PEN NAME, PLEASE INCLUDE THAT TOO.

5) IMPORTANT: IF YOU'RE UNDER THE AGE OF 18, YOU MUST HAVE YOUR PARENT'S PERMISSION IN ORDER FOR US TO PRINT YOUR WORK. ANY SUBMISSIONS WITHOUT A SIGNED NOTE OF PARENTAL CONSENT CANNOT BE USED.

6) FOR FULL DETAILS, PLEASE CHECK OUT HTTP://WWW.TOKYOPOP.COM/ABOUTUS/FANART.PHP

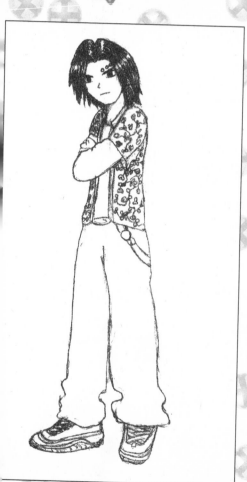

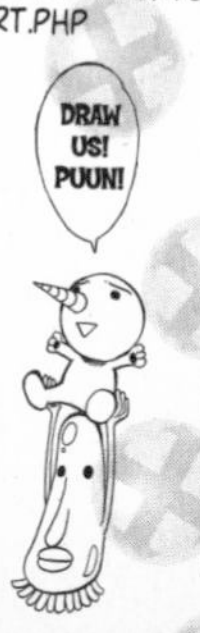

SARAH PREFERS MUSICA'S OLD HAIR CUT. WHAT DOES EVERYONE ELSE THING? LONG HAIR OR SHORT AND SPIKY? THE DEBATE THAT WILL NEVER DIE. THANKS FOR THE SWEET PIC!

ARAH S.
AN DIEGO, CA

DRAW US! PUUN!

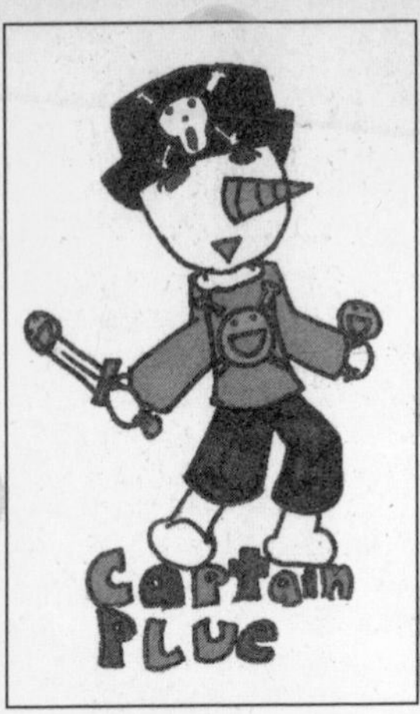
Captain Plue

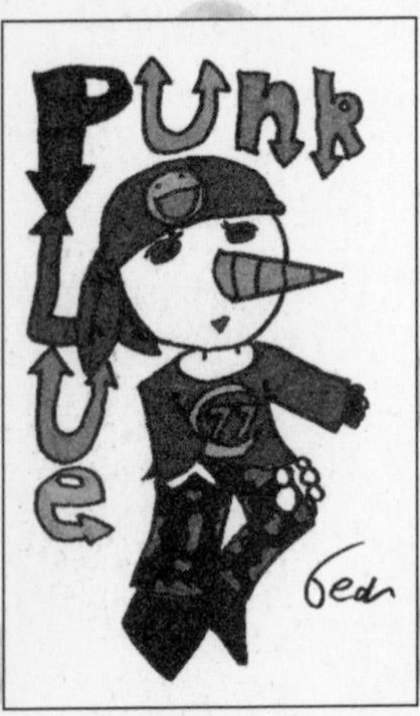
Punk
Plue
Jed

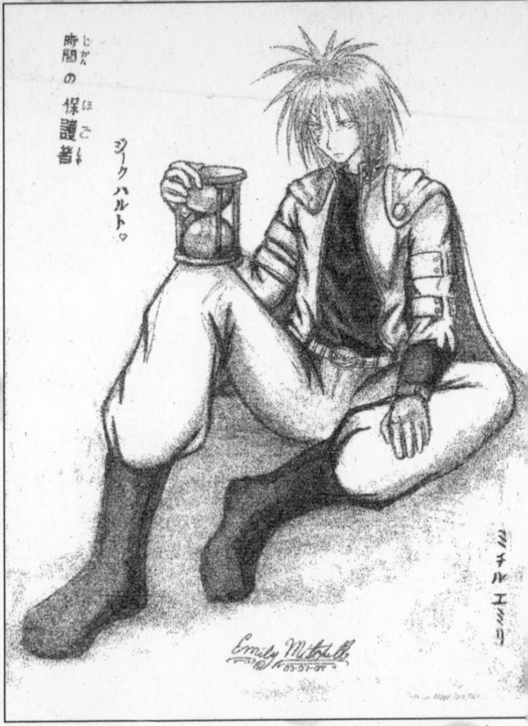
時間の保護者
ジークハルト♡
Emily Mitchell

PLUE AS A PIRATE—THAT'S AWESOME! LOOK FOR A PICTURE OF PLUE IN A BLUE DEVIL COSTUME ON THE COVER OF THE NEXT VOLUME. THANKS FOR YOUR GREAT DRAWINGS, JED!

JED H.
JACKSONVILLE, OR

AMAZING WORK, EMILY. SEIG HART REALLY IS THE HOTTEST GUY IN RAVE MASTER. DON'T WORRY—HE'LL BE BACK IN A BIG WAY IN THE NEXT VOLUME.

EMILY M.
SIGNAL MTN., TN

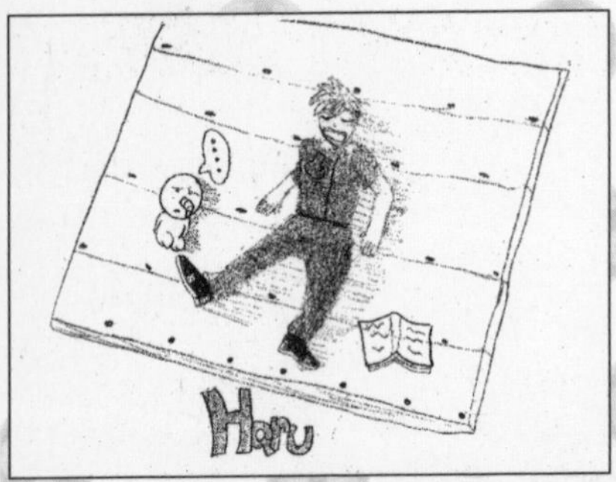
Haru

IS IT JUST ME, OR DOES PLUE LOOK BORED? (HA HA!) IT'S A LONG WAY FROM GARAGE ISLAND TO HIP HOP TOWN, ISN'T IT? COOL PIC, LINDSEY. KAWAII!

LINDSEY M.
AGE 12
WEATOUGE, CT

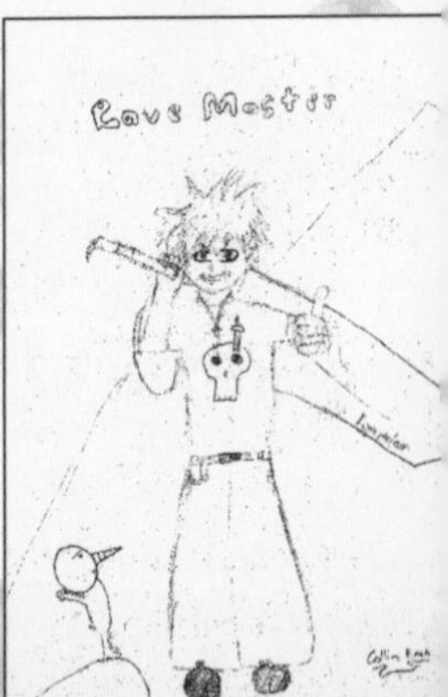
Rave Master

WITH THAT SHIRT AND THAT SWORD, I DON'T THINK ANY DEMON CARD PUNK WILL WANT TO MESS WITH HARU. NICE WORK, COLLIN!

COLLIN F.
SPRINGFIELD, VA

Accessory Rave-olution!

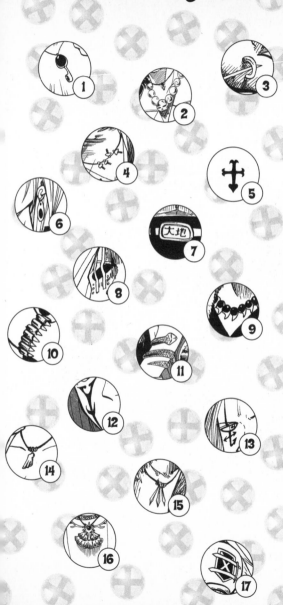

WELL, THE "KING ARC" IS OVER AND IT'S BEEN A WILD RIDE. HARU AND TEAM HAVE MET SO MAY PEOPLE ON THEIR QUEST, IT CAN BE DIFFICULT KEEPING TRACK OF WHO'S WHO. LET'S SEE IF YOU'VE BEEN PAYING ATTENTION TO THE LITTLE DETAILS. CAN YOU IDENTIFY WHICH PIECES OF JEWELRY AND TATTOOS GO WITH WHICH CHARACTERS? EACH CHARACTER IS USED ONLY ONCE. GOOD LUCK!

HARU GLORY
ELIE
MUSICA
GEORCO
SHUDA
RUGAR 70
POOSYA
BIS
LANCE
ROSA
GO
REINA
SEIG HART
JEGAN
MELODIA
LET
RIONETTE

Next time in Rave Master:

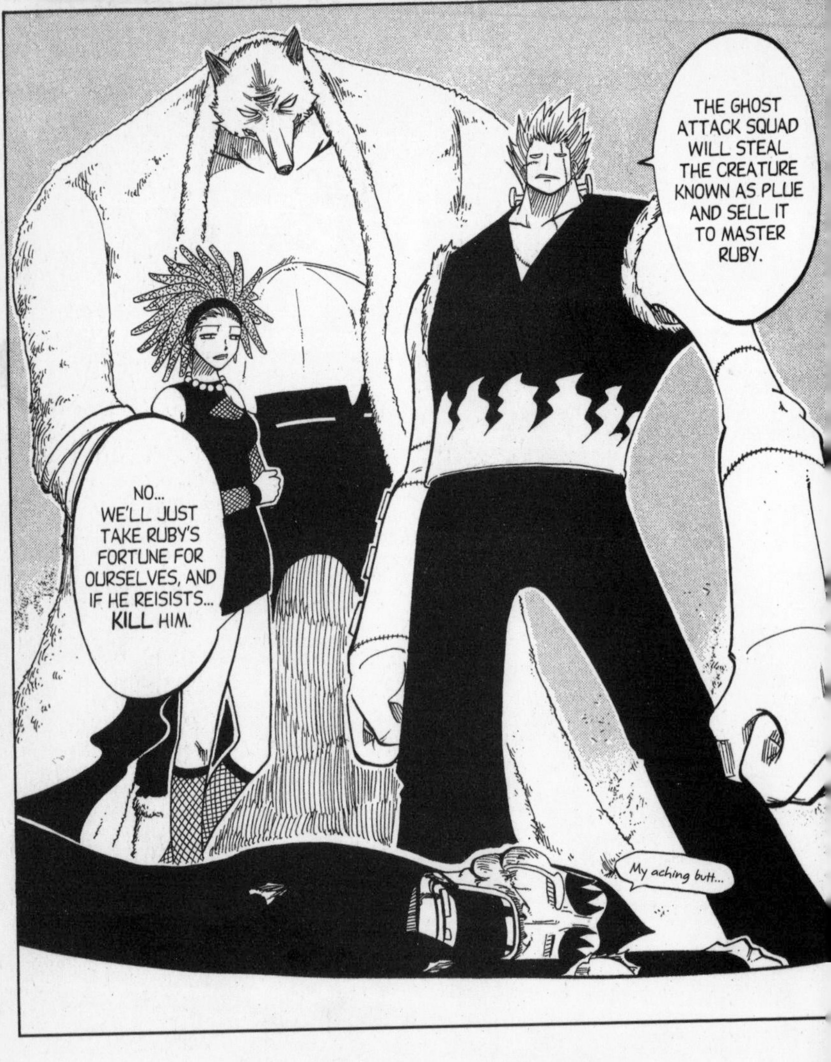
THE GHOST ATTACK SQUAD WILL STEAL THE CREATURE KNOWN AS PLUE AND SELL IT TO MASTER RUBY.
NO... WE'LL JUST TAKE RUBY'S FORTUNE FOR OURSELVES, AND IF HE REISISTS... KILL HIM.
My aching butt...

**New villains, new heroes, new quests–
the adventure continues in Rave Master Volume 10–
Available August, 2004!**

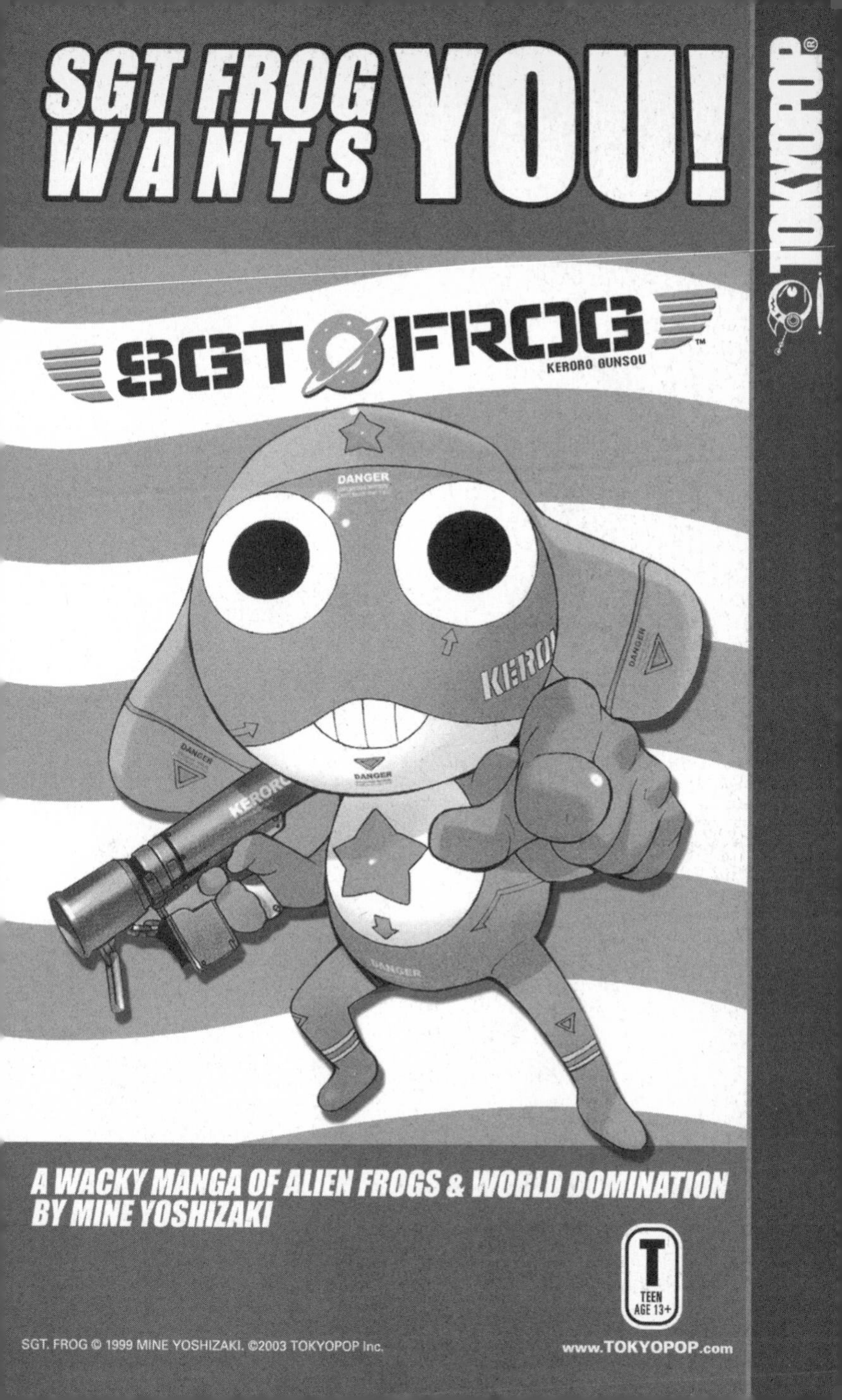

SGT FROG WANTS YOU!
TOKYOPOP
SGT FROG
KERORO GUNSOU
DANGER
KERORO
A WACKY MANGA OF ALIEN FROGS & WORLD DOMINATION
BY MINE YOSHIZAKI
T
TEEN AGE 13+
SGT. FROG © 1999 MINE YOSHIZAKI. ©2003 TOKYOPOP Inc.
www.TOKYOPOP.com

-WELCOME TO THE END OF THE WORLD

RAGNARÖK

www.TOKYOPOP.com

Available Now!

English version by New York Times bestselling fantasy writer, **Richard A. Knaak**

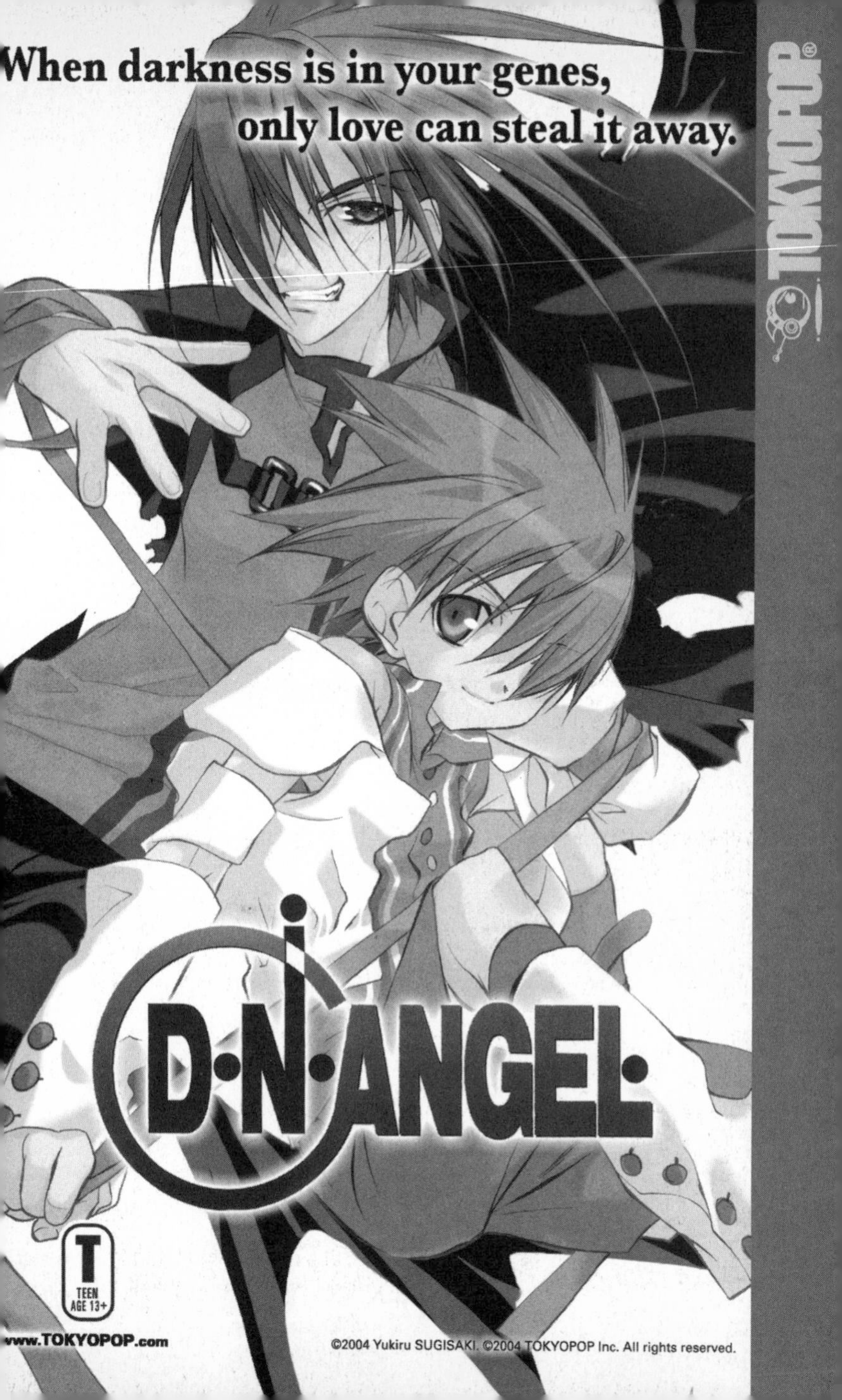
When darkness is in your genes,
only love can steal it away.
TOKYOPOP
D•N•ANGEL
T TEEN AGE 13+
www.TOKYOPOP.com
©2004 Yukiru SUGISAKI. ©2004 TOKYOPOP Inc. All rights reserved.

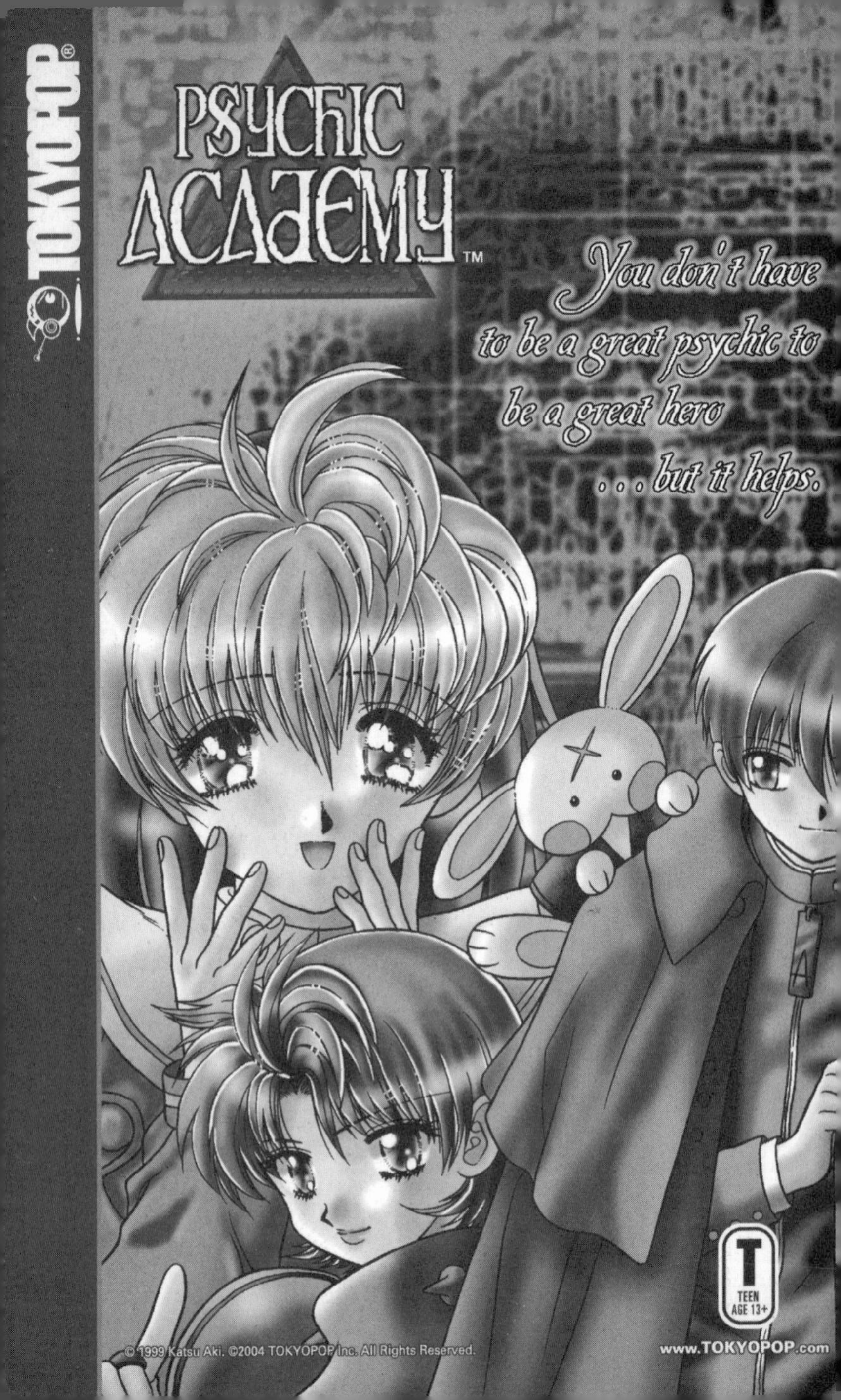
TOKYOPOP®
PSYCHIC ACADEMY™
You don't have to be a great psychic to be a great hero
. . . but it helps.
T TEEN AGE 13+
© 1999 Katsu Aki. ©2004 TOKYOPOP Inc. All Rights Reserved.
www.TOKYOPOP.com

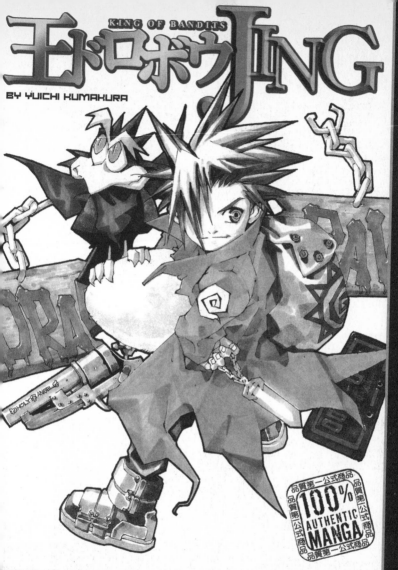

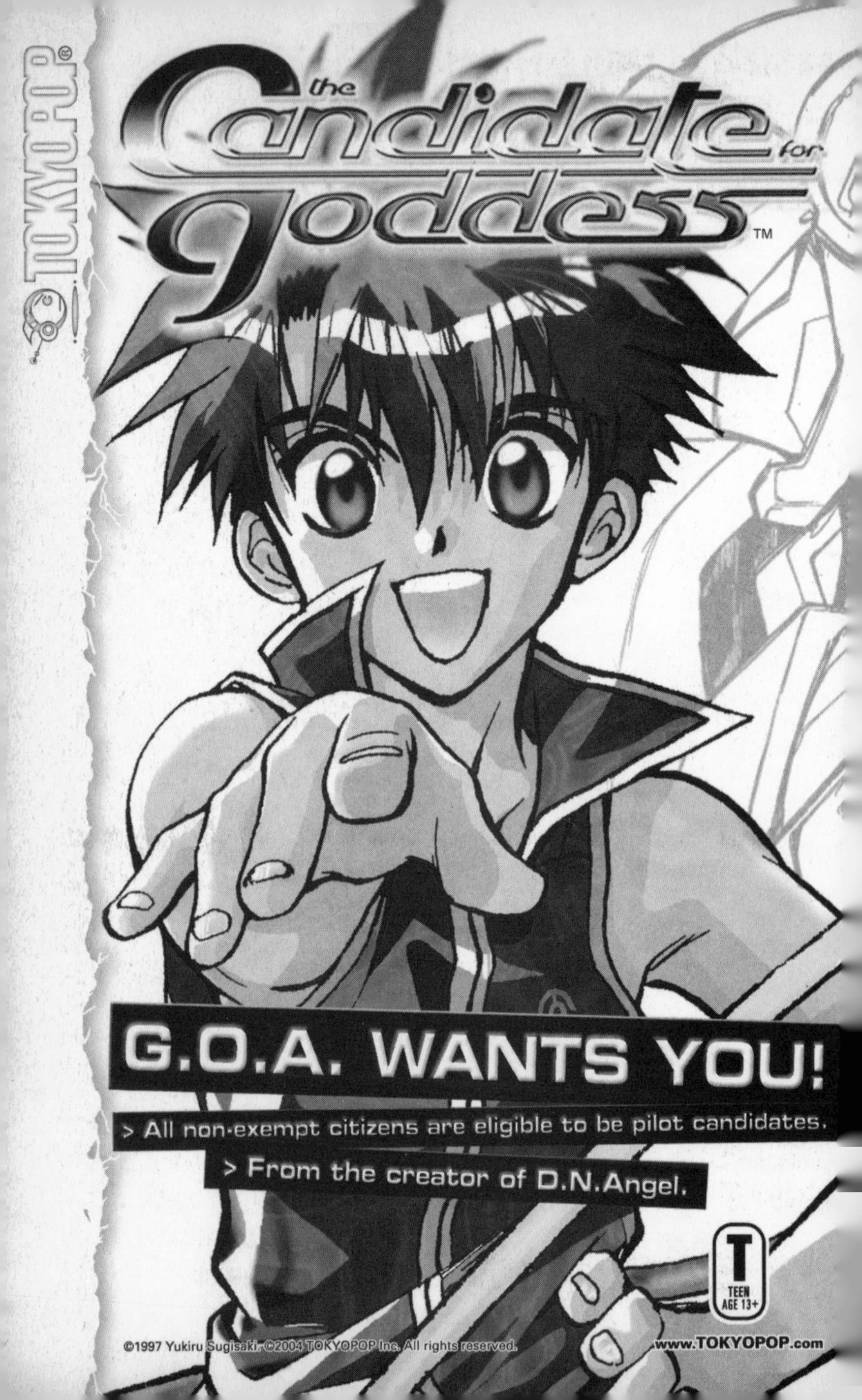
TOKYOPOP
the Candidate for Goddess™
G.O.A. WANTS YOU!
> All non-exempt citizens are eligible to be pilot candidates.
> From the creator of D.N.Angel.
T TEEN AGE 13+
©1997 Yukiru Sugisaki. ©2004 TOKYOPOP Inc. All rights reserved.
www.TOKYOPOP.com

ALSO AVAILABLE FROM 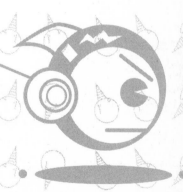TOKYOPOP®

For more
information visit
www.TOKYOPOP.com

03.30.04Y

ALSO AVAILABLE FROM 🐢 TOKYOPOP®

MANGA

.HACK//LEGEND OF THE TWILIGHT
ANGELIC LAYER
BABY BIRTH
BRAIN POWERED
BRIGADOON
B'TX
CANDIDATE FOR GODDESS, THE
CARDCAPTOR SAKURA
CARDCAPTOR SAKURA - MASTER OF THE CLOW
CHRONICLES OF THE CURSED SWORD
CLAMP SCHOOL DETECTIVES
CLOVER
COMIC PARTY
CORRECTOR YUI
COWBOY BEBOP
COWBOY BEBOP: SHOOTING STAR
CRAZY LOVE STORY
CRESCENT MOON
CROSS
CULDCEPT
CYBORG 009
D•N•ANGEL
DEMON DIARY
DEMON ORORON, THE
DIABOLO
DIGIMON
DIGIMON TAMERS
DIGIMON ZERO TWO
DRAGON HUNTER
DRAGON KNIGHTS
DRAGON VOICE
DREAM SAGA
DUKLYON: CLAMP SCHOOL DEFENDERS
ET CETERA
ETERNITY
FAERIES' LANDING
FLCL
FLOWER OF THE DEEP SLEEP
FORBIDDEN DANCE
FRUITS BASKET
G GUNDAM
GATEKEEPERS
GIRL GOT GAME
GIRLS' EDUCATIONAL CHARTER
GUNDAM BLUE DESTINY
GUNDAM SEED ASTRAY
GUNDAM WING
GUNDAM WING: BATTLEFIELD OF PACIFISTS
GUNDAM WING: ENDLESS WALTZ

GUNDAM WING: THE LAST OUTPOST (G-UNIT)
HANDS OFF!
HARLEM BEAT
HONEY MUSTARD
IMMORTAL RAIN
I.N.V.U.
INITIAL D
INSTANT TEEN: JUST ADD NUTS
JING: KING OF BANDITS
JING: KING OF BANDITS - TWILIGHT TALES
JULINE
KARE KANO
KILL ME, KISS ME
KINDAICHI CASE FILES, THE
KING OF HELL
KODOCHA: SANA'S STAGE
LEGEND OF CHUN HYANG, THE
MAGIC KNIGHT RAYEARTH I
MAGIC KNIGHT RAYEARTH II
MAN OF MANY FACES
MARMALADE BOY
MARS
MARS: HORSE WITH NO NAME
MINK
MIRACLE GIRLS
MODEL
MY LOVE
NECK AND NECK
ONE
ONE I LOVE, THE
PEACH GIRL
PEACH GIRL: CHANGE OF HEART
PITA-TEN
PLANET LADDER
PLANETES
PRINCESS AI
PSYCHIC ACADEMY
QUEEN'S KNIGHT, THE
RAGNAROK
RAVE MASTER
REALITY CHECK
REBIRTH
REBOUND
RISING STARS OF MANGA
SAILOR MOON
SAINT TAIL
SAMURAI GIRL REAL BOUT HIGH SCHOOL
SEIKAI TRILOGY, THE
SGT. FROG
SHAOLIN SISTERS

03.30.04Y

STOP!

This is the back of the book.
You wouldn't want to spoil a great ending!

This book is printed "manga-style," in the authentic Japanese right-to-left format. Since none of the artwork has been flipped or altered, readers get to experience the story just as the creator intended. You've been asking for it, so TOKYOPOP® delivered: authentic, hot-off-the-press, and far more fun!

DIRECTIONS

If this is your first time reading manga-style, here's a quick guide to help you understand how it works.

It's easy... just start in the top right panel and follow the numbers. Have fun, and look for more 100% authentic manga from TOKYOPOP®!

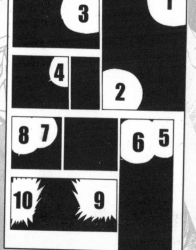

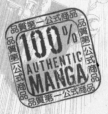